Introduction to Law in Canada

Second Edition

Richard A. Yates
Simon Fraser University

Ruth Whidden Yates
Simon Fraser University

Penny Bain
Simon Fraser University

Prentice Hall Allyn and Bacon Canada
Scarborough, Ontario

Canadian Cataloguing in Publication Data

Yates, Richard
 Introduction to law in Canada

2nd ed.
Previously published under title: Canada's legal environment.
Includes index.
ISBN 0-13-792862-9

1. Law – Canada. I. Yates, Ruth, 1944–   . II. Bain, Penny, 1948–   .
III. Title.   IV. Title: Canada's legal environment

KE394.Y38 2000   349.71   C99-930228-0
KF345.Y38 2000

ISBN 0-13-792862-9

Vice President, Editorial Director: Laura Pearson
Acquisitions Editor: Dawn Lee
Art Director: Mary Opper
Developmental Editor: Laura Paterson Forbes
Production Editor: Matthew Christian
Copy Editor: Karen Bennett
Production Coordinator: Peggy Brown
Marketing Manager: Christine Cozens
Cover Design: Lisa LaPointe
Cover Image: PhotoDisc

2 3 4 5   03 02

Printed and bound in Canada.

Contents

Chapter 2 Sources of Canadian Law   20

Chapter 3 Canadian Constitutional Law   42

Chapter 4 Protection of Human Rights   66

Chapter 7 Criminal Law   143

Chapter 8   Tort Law   168

Chapter 9   Family Law and Estates   201

Chapter 12   Property Rights   269

Table of Cases

Weblinks

Access to Justice Network
   <http://www.acjnet.org/>

ConflictNet
   <www.igc.apc.org/igc/issues/cr/>

Dispute Resolution Project, Department of Justice Canada
   <http://canada.justice.gc.ca/orientations/methodes/index_en.html>

Duhaime's Canadian Legal Information Centre. With links to legal dictionary, law societies, federal and provincial court decisions and legislation.
   <www.wwlia.org/ca-home.htm>

Federal statutes and regulations
   <http://canada.justice.gc.ca/Loireg/index_en.html>

Intellectual Property (US)
   <www.brint.com/IntellP.htm>

The Law Connection
   <www.educ.sfu.ca/lawconnection>

Roger Batchelor's Contract Law Page. A comprehensive site of contract cases, with links.
   <http://qsilver.queensu.ca/~law120/index.htm>

Supreme Court of Canada
   <www.scc-csc.gc.ca/services.htm>

Technical Arbitration and Conflict
   <www.batnet.com/oikoumene/tacr.html>

The UVic Institute for Dispute Resolution
   <http://dispute.resolution.uvic.ca>

Virtual Canadian Law Library
   <www.droit.umontreal.ca/doc/biblio/en/bv/bv.htm>

William R. Lederman Law Library Internet Links. Includes links to Canadian and international governments, court decisions and law schools.
   <http://qsilver.queensu.ca/law/lederman/sites.htm>

The World Wide Legal Information Association

Preface

The idea for a book that introduces Canadian law and legal institutions came as a result of our being involved in a number of law-related courses at Simon Fraser University for education, business and economics students. The courses were designed with the assumption that university students have a basic understanding of how our political and legal systems operate. Our experience is that many don't, and it is difficult to discuss principles and issues in the classroom without first providing students with information about the source and nature of our legal system, how laws developed and how they change. There was a clear need for a text that explained the history and institutions of the Canadian legal system and introduced the legal principles basic to the major areas of substantive law.

Canada's Legal Environment provides the essentials for courses introducing the political and legal systems, and can be an important resource for issues-oriented or advanced courses, as it gives students the fundamental information necessary to prepare them to deal with more complex principles and issues. We have made an effort to keep the content generic so that it will accommodate the needs of students in business, economics, criminology, political science and education courses that focus on Canada's constitution and government, the history and sources of Canadian law and the role of the courts. Sufficient information is provided about the major categories of law so that students can come to appreciate the impact that law has on all aspects of social life.

In this second edition of the text we have followed some of the suggestions of numerous students who have taken our courses. "Lighten up on the history and philosophy," they said, "and get more practical." As a result we've reduced the amount of space devoted to the history of the common and civil law systems and integrated theoretical ideas throughout with the intention of illustrating how legal theories are applied in Canada today. Canadian constitutional law and the protection of human rights are given considerable emphasis and prepare students to study the judicial system. We've added a new chapter on administrative law and alternative dispute resolution mechanisms, as these decision-making forums have become increasingly important. The second half of the text is comprised of six chapters, each concerned with a specific area of the substantive law in Canada, including criminal, tort, family, contract, commercial and property law. These chapters have been updated and new case law added to help illustrate and explain the legal principles in each of these areas. We have added study questions to each chapter and updated the lists of suggested readings to include new titles. Relevant Websites are on the Weblinks page.

We've been happy to welcome aboard the authoring team Penny Bain, who has had considerable experience in the practice of law and law-related educational endeavours. She has been the director of the Legal Information Department of the Legal Services Society of British Columbia and is now the executive-director for the BC Institute Against Family Violence. Her expertise in criminal and family law has been particularly helpful in this edition. We have also appreciated the assistance of Ron Rapin, recently retired from the Legal Services Society, who has patiently and meticulously reviewed the changes we have made to the text and offered many helpful suggestions. We would like to thank Bob Hayes of Conestoga College for his review of an earlier version of this manuscript. We are also grateful to Matthew Christian at Prentice Hall and to copyeditor Karen Bennett for their painstaking efforts to edit and format the text.

THE ROOTS OF THE LAW IN CANADA

INTRODUCTION

The law as we know it today has roots that are as ancient as language itself. While language determined and defined the character of a culture, the law mirrored or reflected its social, economic and political relationships and, as important, the relationships between people, their property and their country. Therefore, in order to understand social development and the history of a nation it is important to study its law, including the history and sources of that law as well as the way it is administered and enforced. To understand the role of law in Canada today, it is necessary to look at the roots of the civil law of France and the common law and parliamentary system of England, which were the sources for Canada's laws and legal institutions. Having reviewed the history of the legal system, it is important to look more carefully at the various sources of law and the way law has evolved. At that point we can begin to understand how French and English law has been modified and adapted to meet the needs of Canada as it grew toward social and political independence.

Over time the law has evolved to establish legal principles and rules that govern every citizen and institution. Citizens should be aware of their rights and obligations under the law as well as their responsibility to address and work toward changing the law. As we proceed in this text we will consider some of the major legal principles and issues that affect Canadians today, including such topics as the rule of law, parliamentary supremacy, the role of judges and the changing nature of the Supreme Court. We will consider the development of the law in relation to human rights, including some recent changes in the rights and freedoms of First Nations peoples. We will look at the reasons why there is an increasing reliance on alternative forms of dispute resolution and consider the impact they will have on traditional legal institutions. We will examine a number of specific areas of law, including criminal, tort, family and contract law, and review some of the important changes in the law that are essential to the changing nature of commercial and property interests.

Law not only provides a structure and order for society; it is an important procedure for resolving disputes. If there were no conflicts, there would be little need for law and no need for the enforcement mechanisms that go with it. But conflict is as constant as life itself, and thus the need to have some systematic and predictable way of dealing with it and of encouraging compliance. Laws acquire legitimacy when they emanate from some acknowledged authority, when they are made known to and apply to all and when they are fairly enforced. Shakespeare described what a world without law would be like in Act I of *Troilus and Cressida.*

> Take but degree [law] away, untune that string,
> And hark, what discord follows! Each thing meets
> In mere oppugnancy. The bounded waters
> Should lift their bosoms higher than the shores
> And make a sop of all this solid globe.
> Strength should be lord of imbecility,
> And the rude son should strike his father dead.
> Force should be right; or rather, right and wrong,
> Between whose endless jar justice resides,
> Should lose their names, and so should justice, too.
> Then everything includes itself in power,
> Power into will, will into appetite,
> And appetite, a universal wolf,
> So doubly seconded with will and power,
> Must make perforce a universal prey
> And last eat up himself.

So in fact a society needs to be governed by laws, not only people, and those laws must be consistent, known and capable of being obeyed. But laws are not to be carved in stone. As society changes, as people alter their values and views, so law must change. Bad laws can be made better; inequities can be redressed. The law is not a hallowed institution that should be beyond criticism or amendment. Nor should it be relegated to professionals specifically trained in its administration and enforcement. All citizens need to be aware of the laws and where they come from, not only to govern themselves but also to ensure that the laws are designed to fairly and properly govern others. Therefore, we begin by examining the roots of the law and the various perceptions of law that have influenced our legal environment.

A BRIEF HISTORY OF LAW

In most ancient cultures, law and religion were inseparable, with the law used to compel individuals to conform to the moral standards and rules of conduct demanded by the religion. Rules designed to maintain order have been identified in many cultures of the ancient world. They have been recorded on stone tablets, as in the Code of Lipit-Ishtar of Sumeria and the Code of Hammurabi, king of Babylon (ancient Iraq), the Mosaic Law of Israel, and, in ancient Rome, the Twelve Tables. (See Box 1.1 for examples from these ancient summaries of the law.) All affirmed the need to establish a set of rules of conduct, record them, communicate them to the people and enforce them in such a way that the members of the society recognized the need for compliance. The notion of authority was as important to ancient cultures as it is today. As long as the people acknowledged the legitimacy of the body authorizing the laws, social compliance was possible.

European Civil Law

The code-maker who had the most influence on modern laws was the Emperor Justinian, who ruled the eastern portion of the Roman Empire in the sixth century. He codified already existing laws as part of an unsuccessful campaign to retake Rome and reassert Roman influence after Rome had fallen into the hands of invading tribes. The Code was a collection of old laws, opinions from Roman jurists and new laws enacted by Justinian. Justinian's dream of reuniting the Roman Empire and restoring it to its former glory was not realized. The Germanic tribes were eventually successful in destroying the western portion of the empire and imposing their traditional laws on the areas they wrested from Roman power. But the centuries of Roman influence proved more durable and Roman law continued to provide a model from which the early Europeans, by adding their own customs, developed their own legal systems. Therefore, Germanic and Roman influences together shaped local law.

Box 1.1

Code of Lipit-Ishtar: "If adjacent to the house of a man the bare ground of [another] man has been neglected and the owner of the house has said to the owner of the bare ground, 'Because your ground has been neglected someone may break into my house: strengthen your house,' and this agreement has been confirmed by him, the owner of the bare ground shall restore to the owner of the house any of his property that is lost."

(Source: Robbins, Sarah, ed. *Law: A Treasury of Art and Literature.* New York: Hugh Lauter Levin Associates, 1990.)

Code of Hammurabi: "If a man who is a tenant have paid the full amount of money for his rent for the year to the owner of the house, and he (the owner) say to him before 'his days are full,' 'Vacate,' the owner of the house, because he made the tenant move out of his house before 'his days were full,' shall lose the money which the tenant paid him."

(Source: Robbins, Sarah, ed. *Law: A Treasury of Art and Literature.* New York: Hugh Lauter Levin Associates, 1990.)

The Mosaic Law: (a sampling) "He that smiteth a man, so that he die, shall be surely put to death" (Exodus 21:12). "If a man shall cause a field or vineyard to be eaten, and shall put in his beast, and shall feed in another man's field; of the best of his own field, and of the best of his own vineyard, shall he make restitution" (Exodus 22:5). "Thou shalt not raise a false report: put not thine hand with the wicked to be an unrighteous witness" (Exodus 23:1).

(Source: *The Holy Bible*, King James version.)

The early Christians, however, regarded secular law, whether German or Roman, to be inconsistent with the law of God, and so secular law fell into disfavour. Christians recognized God as the source of all law, and since God was by definition "good," then all of his laws were also good and should be applied universally. People involved in conflicts or injustices were encouraged to treat them as simply part of a dismal and harsh existence. They should put their temporal fates in the hands of God and look to their priests for leadership and direction. This spirit had a profound impact on the medieval world, as it demanded compliance with narrow, religious prescriptions that led to the period being characterized as the "Dark Ages." While the courts established after Roman or German models continued to exist, there was little respect given to the practitioners or to the "weak" individuals who resorted to them. The practice also developed where disputes were resolved with the help of the Church, which sanctioned trial by battle or ordeal. Trial by battle consisted of the disputing parties arming themselves and fighting with each other. The winner of the battle was declared the legal victor. The theory was that God strengthened the arm of the person in the right. Forms of trial by ordeal consisted of the accused taking a red-hot iron in his or her hand or thrusting his or her hand in boiling water to see if the resulting wound festered. If it healed cleanly he or she was in the right because God would protect the innocent.

The renewal of interest in intellectual and scientific pursuits in the thirteenth and fourteenth centuries also brought new attention to law. Some scholars repudiated Christianity's rejection of secular law and advanced ideas about law derived from the Greeks and Romans. It was possible for Justinian's Code to claim a position of influence once it became the basis for the legal curriculum at the University of Bologna, which was the primary institution in Europe to offer a degree in civil and canon law. Students were taught Roman law, but the goal of scholarly effort was not particularly directed toward establishing a practical system of law. Instead they worked to develop a philosophical and theoretical foundation for the law. From Bologna students went on to teach Roman law in universities throughout Europe. Clerics at Canterbury, England, who officiated in the church courts fell under its influence.

The theory about law advocated in universities originated with the Greeks and was refined by St. Thomas Aquinas. It was known as **natural law** theory because it was based on the idea that there was an essential connection between law and morality. If a law was good and just, it should be obeyed, but if a rule was inconsistent with moral principles, it was not law and there was no obligation to obey. Aquinas offered the following definition of law:

> Law is nothing else than an ordinance of reason for the common good, promulgated by him who has the care of the community. Human law has the nature of law insofar as it partakes of right reason… so far as it deviates from reason, it is called an unjust law and has the nature, not of law, but of violence… Such are acts of violence rather than laws because, as Augustine says, a law that is not just seems to be no law at all.

Roman law as taught in the universities was consistent with this philosophical approach to law being taught and studied as a product of pure reason. Since it was approached as an ideal, it was not this law that was actually applied at the practical level in the various towns and cities in Europe. They developed a variety of codes over the years that were an amalgamation of local traditions, Roman law and German influences. An important example of such a code was the Coutomes of Paris, used in that city and adopted in many other locations including Lower Canada (Quebec).

As time passed, the approach to the study of law began to change. Commentaries and glosses were written to accompany the Roman law taught in the universities, clarifying but also restricting the study of the code. The scholars became interested in bridging the gap between the ideal of law taught in the universities and what practically happened at the local level. This laid the foundation for subsequent codifications, which created practical universal laws designed to be applied in local courts, the most famous code being the Napoleonic Code. At the time of the French Revolution, the victors wanted to abandon anything royal and had Napoleon (before he was Emperor) supervise the creation of a legal code, free of royal influences or involvement. The result was the French Civil Code or Code Napoléon, which was a magnificent intellectual and practical achievement. It finally bridged the gap between the ideal of Roman law as taught at the universities and the need for a practical system of laws that could be applied at the local level. Further, it supplied one universal codification of law that at first was applied in all of France and eventually in many other countries as well.

English Common Law

In England the development of law took quite a different path. Britain had also been subject to Roman rule, but after the Romans' withdrawal the subsequent invaders felt the need to wipe away any vestiges of Roman influence. Judges declared the law as the need arose and followed each others' decisions, thus compiling a distinctive body of law that eventually became known as the common law of England. The English judges played a more significant role in the law-making process than their civil law counterparts. As in other parts of Europe, however, Roman law was taught in English universities and influenced the judges, especially the clerics, who played a very important role through English church courts until the decline of those courts in the thirteenth century. Thus, Roman law continued to have an influence on the development of the common law of England. The complex events in the historical development of Britain all left their mark on English law. We will only highlight a few of the most remarkable to illustrate their significance to modern common law principles. You may want to refer to the accompanying timeline to put other important events into chronological perspective.

The Norman Conquest

The Norman invasion that put William the Conqueror on the English throne in 1066 marked the transition to a unique feudal system. The landholding system began as a method of rewarding those who had sided with William in the war and as a means of punishing his opponents. He granted the use of the land to his supporters in return for their continued service. His enemies were dispossessed of their land, often becoming indentured servants to the new landholders, who assumed the titles of lords, barons and earls, each with varying rights to the land, all of which was owned by the king. An important factor of feudalism was the nature of the political power that it gave the king. Although the king appeared to be supreme, in fact he owed his power to the noblemen immediately below him and could only exercise it if they supported and sustained him in his position.

Early Courts

Noblemen were granted substantial tracts of land and assumed responsibility for maintaining order and dispensing justice in their jurisdictions. The laws applied were very primitive and usually based on the customs of the people. Sometimes laws were codified, but the system was neither complete nor sophisticated. Ecclesiastical courts also formed a sig-

nificant part of England's rudimentary legal system. Clergymen, sitting as judges in the •
church courts, were trained in Roman law and canon law and so decisions in these matters
reflected Roman legal principles. The remedies applied in the church courts were less severe
than in the other courts. This led to conflict and eventually to the monarch stepping in to cur- •
tail the jurisdiction of the church courts.

King's Peace

Another important development during William's reign was the concept of the *king's peace*.
It was recognized from Anglo-Saxon times that kings and lesser individuals had a special
right to punish those who disturbed the peace of their households. In German law the ideas
of law and peace were inseparable, a violation of a person's peace being a violation of law.
This was later extended to the king's highways and then to violent crimes committed anywhere.
William extended the concept of the king's peace to the entire kingdom, so that when any person harmed or acted wrongfully toward another, it was a breach of the king's peace. Later kings
would use the charge of breaching the king's peace to bring all manner of disputes into the
jurisdiction of their royal courts. In our legal system the procedure used in criminal matters,
where the state acts as the offended party, finds its origins in the concept of the king's peace.

Throughout this discussion of the development of common law, it is important to keep in
mind the ongoing struggle for control between monarchs and the nobility. One of the means
William used to preserve his hold on power was to centralize the tax-gathering arm of government. As long as the king was strong, as was William, he was able to maintain control, but
when a weak king was on the throne, the power of the nobles increased at the king's expense. A series of weak kings had eroded the king's power by the time the first Plantagenet,
Henry II, acceded to the throne in 1154. An important objective of Henry was to re-assert
monarchical power, and to that end he set out to create a more direct relationship between the
king and his subjects. He accomplished this by stripping the nobles of some of their administrative responsibilities, which he gave to his own representatives. He also gave people the
right to go to a king's court, rather than a court of a noble, to have their legal disputes settled.

The Royal Courts

By increasing the judicial jurisdiction of his courts, Henry managed to reduce the power
of the barons and began the process of centralizing the legal system. Some disputes such as
violations of the king's peace were taken to the king's courts by right and could not be dealt
with by the other courts. In many other matters, disputants had the choice of either going to
the other courts or to the royal courts, and the king made his method of disposing of the
matter a much more attractive proposition to the disputants. A number of royal court judges
were appointed to travel throughout the kingdom on different circuits, making royal justice much more available to the people.

The Writ System

Henry II also expanded the *writ* system. Originally, a writ was any letter written by the king
that ordered a person to do something, but it eventually became a document both authorizing
and defining legal action. The writ system that developed became one of the great determining factors in the development of the common law. In Henry's time the writ, which was issued

by the king's chancellor, gave people authority to appear before the royal judges. At first it served as a means of appealing decisions made in the courts operated by the nobles, but before long the chancellor was issuing writs directly, allowing people to bypass the manorial courts altogether. Soon a different style of writ was developed for each type of offence or dispute. If there was a new type of complaint, a new style of writ was created. This practice expanded so that, by the time of Edward I, there were as many as 70 different kinds of writs available. The writ system became very important. Choosing the right writ was a procedural requirement, and an action would be defeated if it were not done correctly. The writ system played a role in the creation of a permanent central court that came to be known as the Court of Common Pleas. English common law was dominated by the writ system for some 700 years.

Juries

Another important innovation that took place in the time of Henry II was the increased use of juries in royal courts. The *grand jury* consisted of 12 prominent knights brought together to ensure that wrongdoers were brought to justice. When travelling judges came to town, it was the responsibility of these men to produce offenders and lay complaints. The *petite jury* participated in the trial of the action itself, not as deciders of fact (as is the practice today) but as witnesses to the action. Since the judge was a stranger to the community, local people familiar with the facts were brought together. People facing trial by battle or ordeal could opt instead to be tried before a royal court and jury. Although the number and influence of the royal courts increased significantly, the local and manorial courts were still vitally important. It was only the important matters that were brought before the royal courts. The lesser courts still dealt with the bulk of disputes between the parties, much as our provincial courts do today.

The *Magna Carta*

Two relatively weak kings succeeded Henry II. Richard I spent most of his time on the Continent on crusades, and King John was unpopular. John was probably neither as inept nor as evil as legend would have him, but he did put heavy pressure on the nobles to support his campaigns to preserve continental possessions. They revolted because of the tax burdens he imposed, and the rebellion culminated in John signing the *Magna Carta* at Runnymede in 1215. Nowadays the *Magna Carta* is considered a great document in the establishment of liberty and freedom. In fact, it fell far short of this. In reality, the *Magna Carta* entrenched feudal inequities. It gave rights to the barons at the expense of the king, but it left the vast majority of the people – the peasants and serfs – unprotected by its provisions.

The *Magna Carta* was just another step in the ongoing struggle for power between the barons and the king. Most clauses restricted the king's arbitrary power to extract financial payment from the nobility in the form of taxes. In the process, the position and power of the Great Council of nobles became entrenched. Sections of the *Magna Carta* dealing with legal processes would also have a lasting impact. Because the nobles found it inconvenient to follow the king and his justices as they travelled around the country, one provision in the *Magna Carta* stated that ordinary lawsuits had to be heard at a specified place. This resulted in the Court of Common Pleas sitting permanently at Westminster. Provisions for permanent travelling courts or assizes, having regular and specified circuits, were also built into the agreement. Another important provision gave freemen the right to be tried before their peers, according to principles of justice to be applied equally to all people, and this important principle was eventually extended to all of the king's subjects.

Stare Decisis

The royal judges did not impose a body of rules created by one person or group of people. The judges avoided creating law; rather they merely applied the laws that already existed in the customs and traditions of the people as they found them. The royal courts were one unified body under the jurisdiction of the king, and they eventually developed one system of rules common to the whole kingdom. This may have started when the judges met together to discuss their cases, and the practice developed that the judges followed and eventually became bound to follow the decisions of other judges in similar cases. In the continental system of law, it was rules embodied in codes that were binding on judges. Because of the absence of a written code of law in England, it became a practice that is still in effect today that a judge in the common law system is bound to follow prior decisions made by judges in equal or higher courts. This is the practice of following precedent; it is otherwise known as *stare decisis* — to stand by decided cases. This practice also gave the law the elements of constancy and predictability that are the hallmarks of a viable legal system — that is, a person could determine whether his or her actions contravened an existing law and could even predict what consequences would be likely if that law were broken. It should be noted that when judges were faced with problems where there were no customs, traditions or precedents that applied, they would make law, borrowing from a variety of sources, including Roman or canon law. But the idea that they were merely giving voice to a principle of law that was already in existence and was already common to the people was retained.

In 1772, the great writer and lexicographer Samuel Johnson said:

> It is sufficient for our purpose that every just law is dictated by reason; and that the practice of every legal Court is regulated by equity. It is the quality of reason to be invariable and constant; and of equity, to give to one man what, in the same case, is given to another. The advantage which humanity derives from law is this: that the law gives every man a rule of action, and prescribes a mode of conduct which shall entitle him to the support and protection of society. That the law may be a rule of action, it is necessary that it be known; it is necessary that it be permanent and stable. The law is the measure of civil right; but if the measure be changeable, the extent of the thing measured never can be settled.

(Chapman, R.W., ed. *Boswell: Life of Johnson*, 3rd ed. Oxford: Oxford University Press, 1970, p. 496.)

Edward I and Parliament

The next personality to dominate English legal history was Edward I, who came to the throne in 1272. He is often referred to as the "English Justinian" because of the great proliferation of legislation passed during his reign. Edward's reaffirmation of *Magna Carta* ensured the growth and strengthening of parliament. Although he considered himself an absolute monarch, Edward turned to the group of nobles who had been referred to as the "Great Council" and were now called "parliament" to obtain approval for his policies, especially in the area of taxation. Edward's use of Parliament culminated in the Model Parliament, summoned in 1295. It was made up of representatives from various classes of people. In addition to the nobility and clergy normally there, two knights from each county or shire and two burgesses from each town were present. Although there were times in subsequent periods when Parliament was disbanded, the foundation for what Parliament eventually became was firmly established during the reign of Edward I, laying the foundations for a modern parliamentary democracy.

Over a century before, Henry II had strengthened his own position and weakened the barons by encouraging people to use the royal courts. This was facilitated by the provision of writs, and where there was not a writ already in existence, new ones were created. But Henry's grandson, Henry III, was forced by the barons to agree that no new writs could be created. This agreement was subsequently modified by Edward I in 1285 in the *Statute of Westminster II*, when the chancellor was again given power to modify existing writs as the need arose. But new causes of action could not be created. This decision is extremely important since, from that time, common law judges took the position that their function was merely to apply the law already in existence rather than make new law. The job of making new law now fell upon Parliament (or, more correctly, king and council). Thus the concept of **supremacy of parliament** began to develop.

The legal profession began to assert itself during the reign of Edward I. Although there were some lawyers before this time, the great proliferation of legislation and the numerous cases being heard in the courts made it necessary to have trained people to deal with all the information. Students and apprentices developed the practice of gathering together, living in common lodgings and spending time teaching each other the law. From this practice developed the *Inns of Court*, which have been of such importance in modern times. Aspiring lawyers learned law by discussing it with their fellows and superiors at the Inns of Court, by attending court and listening to arguments, and by seeing the courts in action. They also developed the practice of writing down what happened in the courts to assist in the learning process. This laid the foundation for that great body of recorded cases available to lawyers today.

During the next century Parliament endeavoured to secure for itself three distinct powers: control of national revenue and expenditure, the exclusive right to pass laws, and the right to determine general policies for the nation. These rights were neither easily nor finally won until after the English Civil War. But the foundation for them was laid during the period between Edward I and Richard II, including the separation of the House of Commons and House of Lords as well as the practice of elections for representatives to the Commons.

Common Law Courts and Court of Chancery

Common law courts had established their jurisdiction and developed in procedure and stature, but by the fourteenth century they were becoming stagnant. They were very structured and restricted in their approaches toward resolving problems, largely because of the writ system and its extremely technical requirements. Emphasis was on procedure rather than fairness or the merits of the case. Also, the process of following precedent contributed to an inflexible system.

The king was the acknowledged fountainhead of justice. It was this principle that had allowed him to create the common law courts in the first place. But because of the problems associated with common law courts, it soon became common practice for individuals dissatisfied with limitations of common law courts to petition the king directly for relief. Eventually the king gave the responsibility of hearing these matters to his chancellor. This practice led to the development of a separate court that eventually became known as the Court of Chancery.

This court was not simply another common law court. It was designed to provide relief from the inadequacies of common law and common law courts, and so it must be viewed as a completely different court system. More importantly, the Court of Chancery developed a separate body of law known as **equity**. The development of the Court of Chancery, then, is very significant because it resulted in a new system of law occupying a place alongside the English common law system. While the chancery and common law courts found themselves in competition, the idea behind the creation of the Court of Chancery was to provide a method for dealing with the inadequacies of common law. Equity was never meant to stand as a complete body of law by itself. It was said that *equity* was a gloss on common law or, in other words, was meant to smooth out the roughness of common law. Equity was designed to complement common law and to solve problems associated with it, not to replace it.

Equity

The key to understanding equity is that, initially at least, there were no specified rules. Remedies were applied at the discretion of the decision-maker. As the use of the Chancery Court grew, there was increasing dissatisfaction with its decisions, especially among common law judges and lawyers. This led to confrontation with the common law courts. Their main criticism was based on the fact that the Court of Chancery did not follow precedent and could reach a decision unhampered by the legal rules and technicalities that had been so laboriously developed in common law courts. At one stage it was suggested that equity was so arbitrary that it varied with the length of the chancellor's foot, meaning that every time there was a new decision-maker in the Chancery Courts, parties appearing before him could expect a different decision from that reached in previous, similar cases. Chancery judges felt the sting of these criticisms and they gradually introduced the practice of following prior decisions. Eventually, the Court of Chancery became as rule-bound, inflexible and tied to the past as common law courts. It would be wrong to assume that the law of equity today means fairness and justice. More correctly, the law of equity is simply that body of law that was developed in the early Courts of Chancery. Eventually the Court of Chancery and the common law courts were merged into one court system. But the two bodies of law developed by those courts, equity and the common law, continue to be a unique and important aspect of our legal system today.

Henry VIII and the Attempt to Balance Power

Another significant event in the development of the legal system was Henry VIII's break with the Roman Church in 1534, thus further distancing England from the influence of continental Europe and Roman law. Throughout the time of the Tudors, the monarchs became stronger. Their power was based on popularity, and while parliament still played an important role, it was becoming clear that a confrontation between monarch and parliament was inevitable. The main point of conflict revolved around the question of what was the supreme authority, the king or parliament. Was the king subject to the law created by parliament, or was the king the source of law, and parliament subject to his will?

Parliament's main function and source of power during this period was to grant the crown money and supplies. In addition, its power to pass statutes made it the highest court in the land. Among the important statutes passed during the time of the Tudors were those designed to reform English land law, the laws of bankruptcy and the poor laws that went along with them. With the development of a principle that enabled the courts to enforce agreements, the body of rules that eventually became the law of contract grew tremendously, including the concept of consideration. Many important advances, especially in the field of tort law, took place at this time. They resulted from the development of the concept "action on the case," which allowed the court to deal with many different kinds of disputes. As mentioned above, common law was driven by the writ system and by forms of action. In tort law the writ of trespass was very important, forming the basis for actions such as assault and battery and false imprisonment which involved the direct application of force. Trespass to land, trespass to chattels, and conversion also developed from this writ. But in many instances the action didn't fit trespass or other writs, and so a special writ was drawn up based on the new case or circumstances. This "action on the case" became very important. Many areas of our modern law trace their origins to this unique form of action, originally meant to cover indirect or unintended consequences of the offending conduct. The modern law of negligence developed from "action on the case."

Merchant Law

Prior to this time, merchant traders were governed by their own rules and customs developed within their merchant guilds. These guilds controlled trade between continental Europe and England and functioned independently of the various court jurisdictions, resolving disputes between themselves and developing their own system of law to deal with them. This system of law was known as **Law Merchant**. As the guilds declined and eventually dissolved, the merchants turned to local courts to enforce their rights and claims and to settle their disputes. In England the responsibility for hearing such disputes fell upon the Court of Admiralty. In the brief period in which it handled these matters, the Admiralty Court adopted and applied the Law Merchant. When the Court of Admiralty's role in these matters was taken over by common law courts, judges simply adopted the law that had been used in the admiralty court. In this way, an essentially foreign body of law was taken into the English legal system and became part of common law. A great portion of the Law Merchant was based on Roman civil law. Because of this, there are many concepts that apply to mercantile transactions that are different from the principles of the common law.

The English Civil War (1642–1648)

It was during one of the confrontations between Charles I and Parliament that the *Petition of Right* was drawn up by the Commons and imposed on the king in 1628. This statute set out many fundamental liberties that were said to be the right of all subjects rather than the result of a royal grant or privilege. These liberties included the abolition of arbitrary taxation, arbitrary imprisonment and martial law, and discontinuance of the practice of billeting troops with the populace. When Charles was forced to call Parliament in order to obtain funds to support his hostile intervention in Scotland and found Parliament unsympathetic to his cause, he soon dissolved it. Shortly thereafter, because of reverses in Scotland, Charles was forced to recall Parliament. This was the famous "Long Parliament," which required the king to sign the *Bills of Attainder*, resulting in the execution of some of his most loyal advisers. These advisers had been a symbol of royal power, and their fall was a victory for Parliament. Charles also was forced to sign the *Triennial Act*, which provided that he could not dissolve Parliament without consent of the House of Lords and the House of Commons.

Many radical reforms were introduced by the Long Parliament. Charles responded by charging a number of members of the House of Commons with treason. When he and his armed forces came to arrest them, Parliament was so enraged that the split was irreparable. The ensuing Civil War pitted the forces of Parliament (the Roundheads) against the forces of the King (the Cavaliers). The parliamentary forces, under Oliver Cromwell, defeated the royalists and executed Charles in 1649.

The Impact of the English Civil War on the Courts

The significance of the revolution was that the authority of Parliament was firmly established, and for a period of time under Cromwell, there was no monarch on the throne. Even though the monarchy was restored in 1660 it was clear that there had been a considerable reduction in the monarch's prerogative, or the unfettered exercise of royal power. During the Civil War the judges had aligned themselves with the parliamentary forces. The common law itself formed a bastion of limitation on the power of the king. Common law was thought to have always existed, and it was clear that an important premise on which it rested was that the king was subject to its provisions. One eminent author has suggested that "In the hands of Coke [the Chief Justice], the common law forged the axe that beheaded Charles I."[1] The principles of common law as well as the judges provided support for Parliament's position.

An important result of the revolution was that it freed judges from royal interference. Previously, judges sat at the pleasure of the monarch and could be dismissed if they took a position or made a decision the monarch didn't like. After the revolution, judges could only be removed for cause or for bad behaviour, thus freeing them to make decisions without fear of political reprisal. Judges were enabled to interpret parliamentary statutes and apply the common law as they deemed appropriate, in an impartial environment. Respect for and the influence of judicial decisions were thereby enhanced.

During the reign of James II, the House of Lords attempted to reassert its power as a court, and developed the practice of hearing original first instance actions. The Commons objected to this power, and the issue was eventually resolved when the House of Lords gave up its right to hear such cases, while steadfastly holding onto its power to hear appeals. Today, the House of Lords is the highest court of appeal in England.

In the battle for supremacy between Parliament and the king, Parliament emerged victorious, but it was not clear what this supremacy meant for the courts. Common law courts supported Parliament but felt that common law was above both king and Parliament. Except in rare circumstances, common law was considered to be immutable, constant and unchangeable. It eventually became apparent that Parliament had the power to modify common law and equity, and this power has been more and more frequently exercised until today, when the practice of Parliament modifying, changing or overriding the common law and equity by statutory enactment is commonplace. The primary role of the courts in such circumstances was affirmed as interpreters and decision-makers, with the duty to apply the law rather than create it.

Legal Theory in England

Natural law theory no longer seemed appropriate for or consistent with the way the legal system had developed. It could no longer be said that laws emanated from religious dictums; nor were they all based on morals or even on sound reason. By the nineteenth century it was clear to philosopher Jeremy Bentham and jurist John Austin that in order for a law to have validity it must be given by an authorized person or body and that laws should not be defined in terms of morality. Positive law, as Austin termed it, did not have to be justified on either moral or rational grounds. If a law were passed by a person or group that had the authority to do so, then it was the law and should be enforced. With the affirmation of parliamentary supremacy and with it the exclusive right to create new law, this new philosophical approach to law, called **legal positivism**, presented a more reasonable ground for defining and describing what law is. Thus, what was law depended on who created it rather than personal moral values or reasoned beliefs.

Legal positivism became the dominant legal theory to develop, in tandem with the concepts of representative democracy and parliamentary supremacy that had evolved in the English legal system. The theory helped to clarify and justify the role of Parliament as primary law-maker and the courts' role as interpreters and enforcers of the law. The effect of aligning with such a theory is that judges see their role as applying the law, no matter what effect the decision has on the parties. If the decision results in an injustice to the parties before them, that is the concern of the legislators, whose job it is to amend or change the law to make it more just or fair. In a positivist legal system, the judge must determine whether there is any parliamentary legislation or case law that applies to the case at hand, and if there is, apply that law no matter how distasteful the outcome. And when the statute is inconsistent with pre-existing case law, the statute must prevail. A judge in a positivist jurisdiction must function within a fairly rigid structure, but the advantage of the system is that it is possible to predict what a judgment will be in a given case. When the parties know the likely outcome beforehand, they are encouraged to settle their dispute, which reduces the pressure on the court to resolve conflicts.

NINETEENTH-CENTURY REFORMS

The nineteenth century was a time of great political reform, with subsequent pressure on the legal system. Socialism became a new factor in the political environment. The right to vote was extended in a series of steps through the *Reform Acts*. The original was passed in 1832, and further extensions of the franchise were made in 1867 and 1884, finally allowing all male adults to vote. Queen Victoria was responsible for creating the modern relationship between the British Crown and the government. This relationship is embodied in the concept of the constitutional monarch. Monarchs became advisers to prime ministers, rather than the other way around. But even a constitutional monarchy, as it exists in England today, does not mean that the monarch is without power or without a role to play in government. As advisers, they are kept informed of what is going on and have the right to be consulted when decisions are taken. This role must not be taken lightly, since prime ministers and legislators come and go but the monarch often reigns for decades.

Many important reforms and changes took place in the court process, the common law and equity during the nineteenth century. In 1832, the *Uniformity of Process Act* abolished many of the technicalities that had plagued common law, by simplifying and rationalizing procedures. Other reform legislation followed. In 1832 and 1833, the vast majority of writs or forms of action were abolished. In 1860, the modern method of initiating an action through a writ of summons took the place of most other methods of commencing an action. Standardized rules of procedure were also introduced at this time. Common law courts began using equitable remedies, and judges in the Courts of Chancery were permitted to decide matters of law that otherwise would have been left to the common law courts. Thus, the line between the common law courts and chancery, at least regarding the law they applied, began to blur.

The *Judicature Acts*

All these reforms and changes were eclipsed by the *Judicature Acts* of 1873–75. These acts amalgamated the common law courts, the Court of Chancery and several other specialized courts into one single, Supreme Court of Judicature. That court consisted of the High Court and the Court of Appeal. The High Court was the highest trial court in England, and the Court of Appeal heard appeals from it. The House of Lords was still available to hear appeals from the Court of Appeal.

The main result of this amalgamation was that in each level of court a judge would have the right to apply statute law, the common law or equity, as the situation dictated. And so, although one amalgamated court structure was created, the two bodies of judge-made law — common law and equity — remained separate and complementary to each other. In more recent times there have been other modifications and refinements to the court structure of England. However, Parliament, in the form of the House of Lords, remains the ultimate court of appeal. Initially, all lords had the right to sit on an appeal case brought to the House of Lords. Later the practice grew of having only the Law Lords sitting to hear appeals. They were legally trained judges, elevated to the House of Lords to fulfill this judicial function. When appeals were brought to the House of Lords from the colonies and dominions, the Privy Council of the House of Lords, which consisted of the same judges, heard them.

The *Judicature Acts* of 1873–75 also had a great impact on court procedures. Amalgamation of the courts resulted in the use of one common procedure for all divisions of the High Court. The writ system had already been abolished, but with the amalgamation of the courts, the procedures were further simplified and rationalized. Also, the technical complexity associated with equity was simplified. Prior to this time, the procedures used in the Chancery had become so cumbersome and technical that great delays were involved, so much so that some litigants could not expect their matter to be dealt with during their lifetime. The *Judicature Acts* of 1873–75 also provided that, where there was conflict between common law and equity, the rules of equity would prevail.

Great reforms also took place in the substantive law during the nineteenth century. Industrialization created a series of problems and colliding interests that had to be dealt with. The *Factories Act*, workers' compensation legislation and labour law all developed out of these pressures. Economic concepts such as *laissez-faire* dictated the course of the development of contract law. Many areas of substantive law were created or significantly modified during this century. The development of family law, labour law, contract law, tort law, changes in real property law and the beginnings of consumer law were among some of the areas of law affected by social changes in the nineteenth century. Changes also took place in the law of wills and estates, and there was a new concern for basic human rights and civil liberties. As well there were new developments in company law and partnership.

Another significant development in the nineteenth century was the practice of codifying common law provisions in many areas of substantive law. This was in response to moves on the Continent, where several countries passed their own versions of a civil code. The *Partnership Act*, the *Bills of Exchange Act*, the *Sale of Goods Act* and even the Canadian *Criminal Code* are examples of attempts to codify already existing principles as set out in the precedents of common law. These acts, as a rule, do not contain new or unique rules; rather they summarize the principles of common law. Although there are several examples of codifying common law principles, no overall, cohesive codification system was ever introduced in England. The common law system, as a result, retained its unique character, primarily being based on judge-made law and being governed by the rules of precedent and *stare decisis*.

THE CANADIAN LEGAL SYSTEM

Canadian legal history cannot be understood without knowing something of its beginnings in England and France or without appreciating that developments in those two countries continued to influence the law in Canada even after Confederation. New France began as a French colony and thus was governed by the political and legal systems of France. Despite the French defeat on the Plains of Abraham, the people of Quebec resisted the imposition of English law, and when the *Quebec Act* was passed in 1774 it affirmed that French civil law would continue to determine the legal system in place there. Changes in Quebec law have paralleled changes in France, primarily involving the introduction of various civil law codes, culminating in the Code Napoléon, which was the model for the Civil Code of Quebec, enacted in 1866.

In British North America, each distinct jurisdiction inherited its legal system from England while it was a colony. Thus each province assumed English law at a different time, some prior to 1867 and some after. As the law changed in England, each colony and later each province had to pass its own legislation to accommodate those changes, including the amalgamation of the courts under the *Judicature Acts* and various other acts and particularly the criminal law, which had undergone major reforms in the 1820s. In 1931 the *Statute of Westminster* provided that no enactment of the Canadian Parliament could be rejected by the English Parliament, nor would any English statute automatically extend to Canada.

With Canada's gradual move toward independence, our path has diverged from France and England's. Cases decided in the Supreme Court of Canada created new precedents binding on all inferior courts. Statute law has been modified and amended to meet the needs of this country and its people. There have been many reforms and changes to our laws and legal system that we have initiated as a nation. It is important to remember that it is the common law and historical structure that we have discussed in these pages that now provide the basis for Canada's system of government and substantive law in all provinces, except Quebec.

> More than two hundred years have passed since English law and English legal institutions were rooted in a yet unborn Canada. Sustained at first by remote control from Westminster and by domestic control of colonial governors, the English tradition has survived Canadian legislative and judicial independence, and remains a vital and omnipresent force in Canadian law.
>
> Chief Justice Bora Laskin: *Hamlyn Lectures*

There are a number of legal principles and conventions adopted by Canada from Britain which should be mentioned now because they have done much to shape our legal institutions. The first is the concept of the **rule of law**. This principle reflects the idea introduced by the Greek philosopher Aristotle, who distinguished between "the government of laws" and the "government of men." The rule of law means that no person (including monarchs and government officials) are above the law and that there should be no arbitrary exercise of state power. All members of society are subject to the law. A person acting on behalf of the government must be able to point to some law to justify his or her actions. In Canada, as in Britain, the courts continue to hold even government officials accountable if they fail to obey the law.

We also stand by the principle that everyone is entitled to "equal justice under law" – that is, no one can be punished except for a distinct breach of an established law. The process for determining guilt or liability for an illegal act must be fairly and evenly applied. The rules of natural justice are applied to ensure that people get a fair hearing when there has been a charge or complaint made against them. There is some assurance that "we will be governed not necessarily by decisions that we would like, but by decisions made by impartial persons applying settled, consistent and rationally defensible general principles."[2] Basic human rights are also protected because of the traditions inherited from Britain. Most of these rights have now been entrenched in the *Charter of Rights and Freedoms*, but that does not suggest that they were not safeguarded prior to the Charter. We will deal with individual rights in a chapter devoted to human rights and the Charter.

The Application of Legal Theory

It is useful to contrast the impact of British traditions on the Canadian legal system and the impact they have had on the United States. Canadian legal institutions tended to adopt the philosophical position set out by John Austin called legal positivism. The effect of that was to acknowledge the supremacy of law whether it be judge-made law or statute, no matter what the consequences. It was not up to the courts to adjust it to suit the case.

The US was founded on revolution and thus Americans needed to set up a system that was markedly different than Britain's but still based on the same democratic principles. In establishing a three-cornered system where each seat of power had the right to check and balance the power of the other, the Americans created a system in which three distinct bodies, the office of the President, the Congress and the courts, had the right to make law. The roles of each of these bodies were not as clearly defined as they would be in a system where parliament is recognized as supreme. It became necessary for the Americans to look at law differently than the positivists had. Americans were not comfortable with equating laws with morals either, but they recognized that most laws had a moral component or at least would be enforced by judges who had some moral grounding upon which they would inevitably base their decisions. It was therefore inappropriate to use that criterion to determine whether a law was valid. Late in the nineteenth century the great jurist Oliver Wendell Holmes posited an approach toward law that became the root for the legal theory now known as **American legal realism**.

The realists asserted that what is law is determined by what the courts will enforce. A law may be on the books and may have been enacted through legitimate channels, but if no court would enforce it, then it is not a law. Holmes saw the danger in treating the law as a system of rules. He felt that any model or system artificially simplifying or imposing structure on the law distorted the role of the courts. Legal realists are not concerned with developing legal theories, rules or a structure within which the law operates; they are concerned with predicting what will happen in a courtroom. Legal realism is a method of attacking legal problems and processes without reference to theory, and it acknowledges the role of judges who make the decisions that affect the people who appear before them. While Americans follow precedent and the principles of common law, judges adopting a legal realist approach are likely to feel less bound by prior decisions than are their positivist counterparts. They look to past similar decisions, but they are more inclined to take into consideration the individual circumstances and social realities of the case; they are more inclined to apply their personal moral values. Thus their decisions may be affected by their own circumstances.

When all these factors play a role in the decision-making process, the problem is predicting what the decision will be. As in any other jurisdiction, prediction is an important part of the way the law is applied. Lawyers in the United States, therefore, put a good deal of effort into predicting what a given judge will do based on what he or she has decided in the past. Common law and *stare decisis* still play an important role in decision-making in the US, and in the vast majority of cases that come before the courts, a system of rules is applied in making a decision. But when the case before a judge would create an injustice if the normal rules are applied, the judge is more likely to be persuaded by considerations of justice and fairness or social, economic or even cultural factors within his or her jurisdiction. The effect of such freedom of action is that judges in American courts are often in the position of law-makers, and this is particularly true at the Supreme Court level. For this reason Supreme Court justices are nominated by the President and must be approved by Congress before they are appointed. Their political leanings, their philosophical stance and their beliefs and attitudes are carefully examined before their appointment can take place. Because some judges are elected to the bench, their political views are important factors. They may not be neutral and may not be recommended for their objectivity. Their personal motives and beliefs are expected to play a role in their decision-making activities.

Judges in Canada are appointed by the appropriate governing body but they are not subjected to the same kind of political scrutiny that attends a judicial appointment in the States. The primary reason for that is that in the Canadian system, which follows a positivist legal theory, a judge is expected to interpret and apply the law and generally does not have the range of discretion allowed a US judge. A more detailed discussion of the role of judges in Canadian courts can be found in the chapter of the text devoted to the judicial system.

CONCLUSION

Canada's legal environment has a long and rich tradition despite the relative youth of the country. Although this brief overview of legal history and theory is cursory at best, it should be clear that some understanding of legal history is necessary to know how the law and the legal institutions operate today. Oliver Wendell Holmes suggested that, "History must be a part of the study (of law), because without it we cannot know the precise scopes of rules....It is a part of the rational study, because it is the first step towards an enlightened skepticism, that is, towards a deliberate reconsideration of the worth of those rules."[3] In order to understand how judges apply the rules when they are faced with parties in conflict, we need to understand all the factors that contribute to decisions. Those judges must interpret and apply the laws in place — laws founded on statutes, common law and the principles of equity — and they must follow the procedural rules that ensure the process is fair and justice is served.

The next chapter examines those elements that together constitute the law that is applied in court decisions. Knowing the law makes us better clients if we are involved in a legal dispute and more critical observers of those who make, enforce and report on the law.

LEGAL TIMELINE – BRITAIN

Early sixth century	Anglo-Saxon Kings – hereditary monarchs
1066	Norman Conquest – feudal landholdings
1106	Henry I – reorganized English judicial system (King's Court)
1154	Henry II – First Plantagenet King – travelling courts – jury system
1215	King John – *Magna Carta* – established rights of the Church and landholders
1295	Edward I — Model Parliament – representative government. Courts of King's Bench and Common Pleas supplemented by Court of Chancery
1352	Edward III – Division of Parliament into two houses
1485	Henry VII – First Tudor King – restored strong monarchy and central government
1534	Henry VIII – Broke with Roman Church
1625	Charles I – Second Stuart King – civil war between King and Parliament, 1642–1648
1650	Cromwell – Lord Protector of England – head of Rump Parliament
1660	Charles II – Emergence of two-party system
1689	William III – Constitutional Monarchy – parliamentary supremacy. *English Bill of Rights*; Parliament began to modify common law
1727	George II – Second Hanoverian King – Cabinet responsible to Parliament
1776	American *Declaration of Independence*
1793–1815	French Revolutionary and Napoleonic Wars
1873–75	*Judicature Acts* – amalgamated common law courts and Court of Chancery

LEGAL TIMELINE – CANADA

1608	Colony of New France established
1664	French civil law established in New France
1759	New France conquered by British on Plains of Abraham
1766	*Royal Proclamation* – implemented English common law and constitutional practices
1774	*Quebec Act* – Quebec to use French civil law; criminal law to be based on common law
1791	*Constitution Act* – Quebec divided into Upper and Lower Canada; colonies granted representative assemblies and British-style parliament
1820–40	Dissension between Upper and Lower Canada
1840	*Act of Union* – established first Parliament of the United Province of Canada
1848	Canada adopts principles of responsible and cabinet government
1867	*British North America Act* – division of power between federal government and provincial governments of Ontario, Quebec, Nova Scotia and New Brunswick
1870	Manitoba, Alberta and Saskatchewan join Confederation
1871	British Columbia joins Confederation
1873	Prince Edward Island joins Confederation
1875	Supreme Court established

1931	*Statute of Westminster* – Canadian Parliament gains independence from British Parliament
1949	Newfoundland joins Confederation
1982	*Constitution Act* – Federal Parliament final legislative body for Canada; enactment of the *Charter of Rights and Freedoms*

QUESTIONS FOR DISCUSSION AND REVIEW

1. Why does a society need laws?

2. Compare the evolution of law in a civil law and a common law jurisdiction.

3. Trace the influence of Roman law on the common law.

4. Were early common law judges abandoning their responsibility when they merely declared laws already in place?

5. Consider the importance of an authorized law-making body in the development of a viable legal system.

6. What is the relationship between common law and statutory law?

7. How do the three legal theories described in this chapter affect a person's definition of law?

8. Are the common law and statutory law adequate vehicles for protecting individual rights?

9. List the institutions and primary legal principles that Canada inherited from Britain.

NOTES

1. Potter, Harold and Albert K.R. Kiralfy. *Potter's Historical Introduction to English Law*, 4th ed. London: Sweet & Maxwell, 1958, p. 43.

2. Waddams, S.M. *Introduction to the Study of Law*, 2nd ed. Toronto: Carswell, 1983, p. 10.

3. Holmes, O. W. *Collected Legal Papers*. New York: Harcourt, Brace, 1920, p. 180.

FURTHER READING

Banfield, Jane, ed. *Readings in Law and Society*, 5th ed. Toronto: Captus Press, 1993.

Case, Roland and Daniel J. Baum. *Thinking About Law: An Issues Approach*. Toronto: IPI Publishing, 1995.

Kent, Edward Allen, ed. *Law and Philosophy*. New York: Appleton-Century-Crofts, 1970.

Martin, Franklin. *Introduction to Quebec Law*. Toronto: Copp Clark Pitman, 1984.

Milton, S.F.C. *Historical Foundation of the Common Law*. Toronto: Butterworths, 1981.

Smith, J.C. and David N. Weisstub. *The Western Idea of Law*. Toronto: Butterworths, 1983.

Waddams, S.M. *Introduction to the Study of Law*. Toronto: Carswell, 1983.

SOURCES OF CANADIAN LAW

Law is experience developed by reason and applied continually to further experience.

Roscoe Pound

The previous chapter explored the historical setting of the English common law system. Common law is the product of a thousand years of experience in conflict resolution. It is not possible to understand today's system of laws without understanding how it got that way. This chapter builds on that historical foundation to discover the sources of modern law in Canada. While people in civil law jurisdictions like Quebec can look to a set code and specific statutes to determine the law on a given matter, common law jurisdictions must turn to a number of different sources in order to gain a full understanding of a legal issue. Three distinct kinds of law, each with a different root, form the basis of modern law in English Canada: common law, equity and statutes.

The term *common law* is often used to describe the whole system of law in place in those countries that have adopted it. The entire system, however, is named after that unique portion: the law created by common law courts and embodied in case law, which comprises the decisions handed down and recorded by judges in those courts. Equity, on the other hand, is that body of law developed by the Courts of Chancery and intended to supplement common law. Together, common law and equity make up that portion of our law referred to as judge-made law. The other major portion is the body of law created by legislation, the statutes and regulations passed under parliamentary or legislative authority.

LAWS SET A MINIMUM STANDARD

Now that we know something about where law has come from, it would be interesting to play a little with the idea of what law is. We suggested earlier that law is a procedure for resolving conflict, but it is much more than that since it also serves to order personal, social, and commercial relationships and even control private behaviours. Law has an impact on most aspects of human life. It provides a predictable guide and limit to our actions. As long as we conform to the demands of the law, we avoid bumping against it or have it bring down upon our heads its heavy weight. It is the threat of that possibility that keeps many from acting in unacceptable ways, in serving their own interests at the expense of their neighbours or business associates. Most of us act on personal moral principles and most of those principles are consistent with or greatly surpass legal requirements. But we all need to remember that the law sets out the minimum standard of behaviour that society is willing to tolerate, and regardless of our own moral values we are required to at least live by that standard or suffer the legal consequences of our acts. Legal consequences are then a deterrent since the possible punishment must be weighed in the balance of whatever personal satisfaction might be derived from breaking a law or offending the rights of others.

Judicial Procedure

The courts, which are the ultimate enforcement branch of the law, only intervene when there has been a suspected violation of a law or in order to determine the nature of rights and obligations between parties. A judge, who is appointed to his or her position by the recognized governing body, has a duty to follow proper procedural rules (another form of law). Judges hear and weigh evidence, determine which laws apply to the case, and then make decisions that favour one of the sides in an action. The decision must not be arbitrary, and in very few instances can a judge exercise discretion. Determining the appropriate sentence to be imposed is one area where judges have such discretion, but even then there are rules and guidelines. "There is no better guarantee of impartiality and rationality in decision-making than the requirement of reasons open to the scrutiny of the public and of an appellate tribunal."[1] The judge must point to the law and justify both his or her interpretation of it and the final decision. The reasoning he or she uses must be based on sound legal principles and follow the accepted traditions of society. In order to understand that decision-making process, one must look at that process, and we begin here with a consideration of the laws that judges consult, where those laws come from, and the rules that determine how judges choose between them.

Because of the principle of supremacy of parliament, every court in Canada is first required to determine if there is a statute in place that affects the case. If there is and the statute has been appropriately passed and applies in the court's jurisdiction, then the judge interprets the terms and applies the statute. If no statute applies, then the judge looks to the common law and the principles of equity to find a case precedent, and where the facts in the precedent case are sufficiently similar to the one at hand, the judge applies a similar decision. One of the tasks of a judge is to choose between the precedent cases that the lawyers for each side present to support the position of their client. Selecting the most appropriate case is called "distinguishing the case." A judge compares the relevant facts of the cases presented to the court, and by choosing not to recognize a case where the facts are materially different and choosing to follow the decision in the case that most closely approximates the matter at hand, the cases are distinguished. Since following precedent is an accepted principle in common law jurisdictions, once the judge distinguishes the case, he or she is bound to follow the decision made in the prior case. While statute law takes priority over case law, it is important to remember that when the judge applies a statute in a specific case, that decision becomes a precedent to be referred to in future cases, and so the courts become preoccupied with prior cases even where statutes do apply. It is also important to point out that statutes are sometimes merely summaries of the case law, and so we will look first at how the common law system works.

THE COMMON LAW

> Reason is the life of the law, nay the common law itself is nothing else but reason.
>
> Sir Edward Coke

In creating common law, judges borrowed from many different sources, each source having a distinctive influence on the nature of the law. Common law is best understood as a product of its history rather than as a reflection of any kind of rational or logically cohesive process. Common law was developed by common law courts, specifically the Court of Common Pleas, the Court of King's Bench and the Court of the Exchequer. Justiciers in these ancient courts operated under the assumption that the law they expounded had always been there; that they merely discovered and gave voice to it. In theory at least, this law was not created by judges or any other body; rather, it was common to all the people. Thus, a major component of common law in England is based on the customs and traditions found in place at the time common law was being developed. Judges merely borrowed and adopted these rules, giving them formal recognition by their judgments. Sir William Blackstone, a famous eighteenth-century judge, once said that the decisions of courts of justice are merely the evidence of what the common law is.

Customs

The customs we refer to here are of two types: general and specific. The *general customs* of ancient England became part of common law through judges' decisions. Those decisions became precedents that were binding whenever a situation with similar facts came before the court. Before William the Conqueror, there were three main bodies of customary law in the territories that were to become known as England. William unified England administratively, but until the time of Henry II, the laws varied with geographical location. Henry started the process whereby one cohesive system of laws common to all England was developed. He did this by appointing judges and making their courts available to all the people. The role of the judges was not to impose an arbitrary or preconceived system of rules and laws, but to give people access to the royal courts, to discover the laws by which the people had traditionally governed themselves, and to apply those locally developed laws in a more consistent and predictable way.

General customs are no longer a source of law because they have long since been embodied in precedent cases or otherwise overridden by statute law or equity. *Specific customs* are usually limited to a particular geographical location or to a particular profession or trade. Examples are the customary use of an old dock, the use of water from a particular source, or even the fee that may be charged for a special service. To be valid, the custom cannot be in conflict with either common law or a statute (although it may be an exception to it). As well, the custom must have been in place from time immemorial. This requirement generally means that it goes back as long as people can remember, or to the year 1189 AD, the date fixed by statute in 1275 as the limit of legal memory. Any such customary right enjoyed at that date was unchallengeable.[2] As well, the custom must have been in continual existence, practised and openly accepted by the population. Additionally, the custom must be reasonable, be consistent with other such customs, and have been treated over the years by all parties as compulsory. Only when all these requirements are met will specific customs qualify as law. Specific customs are rarely important today because most have been overridden by local bylaws, statutes, regulations or other legal principles.

Some of the customs of Native peoples in Canadian history are now finding their way into common law. Natives have a different concept of property rights; they do not view land as belonging to anyone. Rather, it is a sacred trust for their use and enjoyment as long as it is preserved for others and for future generations. Canadian courts have acknowledged this right to some degree, and it has, in turn, been confirmed constitutionally. That is not to say that the courts have recognized all Native land claims. Issues related to such claims are frequently before the courts, and the decisions often demonstrate the courts' inability to address Native justice issues adequately or fairly, because the judges are bound by a law that is not common to the Native peoples. Most recent court decisions relating to Native rights have done little more than to encourage provincial legislatures and Parliament to address these issues by amending or creating appropriate legislation or negotiating treaties.

Roman Influence

As judges looked for local customs upon which to base their decisions, they recognized that they could not rely solely on them to form the basis of a sophisticated system of law. As a result, common law judges borrowed from other sources, including Roman civil law, canon, or church, law, and the Law Merchant developed by the merchant guilds in Europe. In fact, it is quite surprising that Roman civil law did not become the law of England in the same way that it, or derivations of it, eventually supplanted the customary legal systems that had been in place in continental Europe. When common law was in its formative stages of development, intellectuals and academics believed that Roman civil law was the only law worth studying. Certainly during the Middle Ages, at both Oxford and Cambridge, Roman law was taught. English common law, which was developing at the time, was not. Lawyers such as Henry de Bracton in the thirteenth century received their grounding and education in Roman civil law. Bracton incorporated some of this civil law into his writings, which were highly influential. Thus, Bracton's Roman law education, as well as that of his contemporaries, had a substantial influence in shaping common law.

Most of the impact of Roman law on common law has been indirect. However, its influence on other areas, from which common law derived many legal principles, has been significant. For example, the courts of the Admiralty, through which the Law Merchant and maritime law were adopted into common law, were presided over by judges trained in the Roman civil law system. The Law Merchant was based on Roman civil law, and developed along with the merchant guilds that regulated the activities of the business class of the day. The procedure used in the Admiralty Court was taken directly from the civil law tradition. Canon law, used in the ecclesiastical courts, was essentially based on Roman civil law, and the priests who presided over the church courts and for many years the Courts of Chancery were trained in the Roman law. Some areas of common law that have been influenced significantly by Roman civil law are the law of bailment and the separation of ownership and possession of property, the concept of an easement in real property, and commercial relations and obligations in general. The law of wills and estates, especially as it relates to the testamentary bequests of personal property, and even torts and contracts have also been influenced by Roman civil law.

Canon or Church Law

Since the earliest stages in the development of common law, the church had its own courts, with special jurisdiction over disputes involving the general populace as well as the clergy. As a result, canon law, as developed by the Roman Catholic Church and applied in the English church courts, also exerted a great influence on the development of common law. Religion was a dominant feature of life in the Middle Ages, so it is not surprising that there existed in England and continental Europe numerous ecclesiastical courts with extensive power and jurisdiction. The centre of this religious authority was embodied in the Pope. His representatives, the priests and clerics, claimed supreme authority in any matter that could remotely be classed as spiritual.

In England their claims led to great conflict between the church and the monarchy. For centuries church courts dominated the contest, playing an important role in the legal structure. In addition the fact that the church claimed up to one third of the income of its feudal devotees created some resentment with the king, who helplessly watched much-needed funds leaving England. Eventually, the power of the church was reduced and the special areas of jurisdiction that had been given to ecclesiastical courts were taken over by common law courts. The bodies of law developed by these church courts, however, were retained and incorporated into the common law of England. Because there was such a close connection between the church courts and the Roman civil law system, church courts were another important vehicle by which Roman civil law influenced the common law of England. Matrimonial and family matters were handled by the church courts. The principles they developed, although greatly modified by statute, are still in effect today. Similarly, the law of wills and estates fell within the jurisdiction of the ecclesiastical courts; modern rules in these areas, as well as the whole subject of testamentary gifts, come from the law developed by them and later incorporated into common law.

Mercantile and Maritime Law

Another important source that common law judges turned to in creating common law was the body of rules created by merchants. Traders banded together in professional organizations called merchant guilds. Because merchants regularly travelled to trading fairs throughout Europe, a common system of rules to govern their activities was important. As a result, they created an internationally enforceable body of rules called the Law Merchant. Many of these rules can be traced as far back as the Babylonians and Phoenicians, before they were incorporated into Roman law. As trade grew, new codes of conduct as well as other rules and customs were added, until a unique and distinctive body of law emerged.

Early English courts recognized the existence of the law of the merchants and were willing to enforce it. The Court of Chancery, recognizing the need for speed, was particularly willing to circumvent the slow, stolid pace of the English system. It allowed merchants from the Continent to enforce claims against English merchants, thus bypassing the lengthy procedural process. As the merchant guilds declined, disputes between merchants were increasingly handled by the regular courts of England. Eventually, the Admiralty Court assumed the primary responsibility for hearing such disputes. The Admiralty Court's jurisdiction to deal with these matters was later taken over by the common law courts.

It is often said that common law courts simply applied the customs and traditions of the land as they found them. It is, perhaps, easier to understand why common law courts so readily adopted the Law Merchant if we recognize that common law judges treated the Law Merchant as the customs of merchant traders involved in disputes, and applied those customs as the law. But the Law Merchant should not be viewed as simply a set body of rules imported into common law. The practice of the merchants continually changed and developed. The customs of the merchants were adopted by common law, but as these customs developed, common law was also able to adapt. An example of such flexibility is found in the merchants' practice of developing new forms of negotiable instruments, which common law judges readily accepted.

The rules governing the sale of goods, the law of negotiable instruments (bills of exchange), insurance law, trademarks, and even partnership and agency are all important areas of common law that originated in the Law Merchant. Several of these areas have since been codified by statute. The *Marine Insurance Act*, the *Bills of Exchange Act* and the *Sale of Goods Act* are three important examples of such codification.

Related to the law of the merchants was maritime law, which dealt with the carriage of goods at sea and the responsibilities of the mariners transporting them. The Admiralty Court was originally created to deal with these matters, and its jurisdiction was eventually extended to mercantile law as well. Although the Admiralty Court eventually lost jurisdiction over mercantile law to the common law courts, it retained the right to hear matters dealing with maritime law until the merger of the courts in the nineteenth century. The personnel of the Admiralty Court were all trained in civil law and, thus, educated in the Roman civil law system. Therefore, Roman law had considerable influence not only on maritime law, as adopted by English common law, but also on mercantile law. As well, maritime law, like mercantile law, had to be somewhat cohesive between nations, which explains the predominant influence of Roman law in the field of maritime law.

THE DOCTRINE OF FOLLOWING PRECEDENT

Predictability is one of the main requirements of a legal system. Those involved in disputes must be able to look at the dispute, test it against well-established, accepted legal principles, and predict what will happen if the matter goes to court. This process encourages parties to settle the dispute between themselves. In the continental system, legal certainty is ensured because there is a body of rules, set out in codes that are binding on the courts. In common law jurisdictions, however, judges require a different guide to keep their decisions from being arbitrary. The heart of the English common law system, its unique feature and, as a result, the most important source of law is the body of case decisions or precedents set by judges.

Following precedent ensures that the law remains certain and predictable. What makes the law predictable is the principle that prior judges' decisions are binding on subsequent judges. This process is called *stare decisis*, which means to stand by the decided case. It is not difficult to understand where the idea comes from. In the common law system, judges originally believed that they were not making new law when they decided the cases before them, but rather were discovering and giving voice to legal principles that had existed from time immemorial.

In fact, the judges often did make new law; but, in theory at least, they merely stated legal principles that had always existed. Once a judge has discovered such a legal principle, it is not appropriate for another judge to come along later and decide a similar case in a different way. Once the decision is made and the law declared, the decision itself has a stature much greater than the judge who declared it. A subsequent court, faced with the same problem, cannot change the decision without declaring that the original court was wrong in its understanding of the law. Thus, once one court has made a decision dealing with a particular subject matter, no later court is likely to alter it. The first decision then becomes a precedent, binding on subsequent courts facing similar cases. This process became institutionalized, and except in very rare circumstances, courts were required to follow the decisions of prior courts in similar matters. Although the doctrine of precedent was developed in common law courts, it was eventually adopted in Chancery and Admiralty courts. The Courts of Chancery adopted the process of following precedent as a result of their rivalry with common law courts. When they adopted this principle, their status and prestige went up in the eyes of the judges and lawyers of common law courts, greatly reducing the friction between them.

> *Stare decisis* is usually the wise policy, because in most matters it is more important that the applicable rule of law be settled than it be settled right. The Court bows to the lessons of experience and the force of better reasoning, recognising that the process of trial and error, so fruitful in the physical sciences, is appropriate also in the judicial function.
>
> Judge Brandeis, *Lawyer's Quotation Book*, p. 87

Ratio Decidendi

Even if the decision being presented to the court as a binding precedent is clearly sound law, the judge has some tools to avoid applying it when he or she does not wish to. Only the **ratio decidendi** of the case (literally, the root of the decision) is binding as precedent. A judgment consists of several important features. It usually involves a summary of the facts necessary to reach the decision, the reasoning process of the judge leading to the decision, the decision itself, and the actual judgment or order. The *ratio decidendi,* or binding part of the judgment on subsequent courts, is the opinion of the judge or the legal principle upon which the decision is based. If more than one judge is involved, which is usually the case at the appeal level, and if the judges reach their decisions for different reasons, it can sometimes be difficult to determine exactly what the *ratio decidendi* of a particular case is. It may not be the actual words the judge uses, but rather the principle the case stands for that determines the precedent. Hence, it is common to see lawyers arguing about what the ratio of a particular case is or how its application must be limited. The judges in their turn might avoid applying a particular precedent by construing the *ratio* in a way that suits them or by heeding the lawyers' request to limit its application.

Several other features are built into the process of *stare decisis* that allow a judge some room to manoeuvre. Under certain circumstances, any level of court is free to ignore a precedent. For example, when a parliamentary enactment or regulation overrides the law set out by precedent, the precedent must be ignored. If some higher court overrules it, the prior decision can be ignored. Finally, when the *ratio* is clearly in error (either because a statute or an important case was not properly considered by the judge), then obviously a mistake has been made and the decision can be ignored.

Obiter Dicta

In many judgments there are comments or asides made by the judge that are not directly associated with the actual decision or that are unnecessary to the reasoning process leading to the decision. Such comments are referred to as **obiter dicta** ("words in passing"), and they are not binding. For example, while explaining the reasons for a decision, a judge will often suggest what might have happened had the facts been different. Such a statement is clearly an ***obiter dictum*** because it is a gratuitous statement. Such a speculative comment would not form part of the binding decision. While it is only the *ratio decidendi* that is binding on a judge, the comments made gratuitously (*obiter dicta*) may be valuable or persuasive. A judge may be persuaded that another judge's comments, made as an aside, are a correct summary of the law, and he may choose to follow them. In this way such judicial asides can become more influential on future courts than the *ratio* of the original case. If there are no binding precedents that a judge must follow, it is common practice for the lawyers presenting arguments to present cases from other jurisdictions, which do not have binding force in any case. These are presented to persuade the judge to adopt that line of reasoning in reaching his or her decision. How persuasive a non-binding precedent is to the court will depend on its source. A decision of the House of Lords in England is no longer binding on Canadian courts. That court has great prestige in Canada, however, and so its decisions are very persuasive. Generally, Canadian judges feel more persuaded by British and Commonwealth cases than by decisions made in the United States, but in special situations an American decision can have great influence. For example, in the area of insurance, our law is closer to that of the United States. In such cases, therefore, American decisions are very important.

Distinguishing the Case

Often the lawyers on each side of a case will present the judge with several different precedents that seem to require that he or she decide in their favour. The judge must then rationalize the apparently conflicting precedents, determining the legal principles to be applied to the case while taking into consideration any appropriate qualifications and exceptions. In the process, the judge may set aside a precedent that does not closely fit the situation before the court, giving reasons for rejecting it. This is called *distinguishing* one case from another. In effect, the judge will say that a precedent is good law but does not apply to the case at hand because the facts are different.

For example, a person is in a fight and, in the process of defending himself, causes injury to the attacker. If he were subsequently sued for battery, the plaintiff might present the judge with a precedent showing that when a person strikes another causing injury, a battery has been committed.[2] The judge in this situation, however, would distinguish the case. He would say that, although that precedent is good law, it does not apply to the case before the court because the injury took place in the process of the defendant defending himself. The judge would choose to follow another precedent presented by the defendant, showing that a victim of an assault can use as much force as is necessary to defend himself, and so long as he does not use excessive force, he is not responsible for any injury the attacker might suffer.[3] Judges not only use this process of distinguishing cases to dispose of precedents obviously not intended to cover the situation being dealt with, but also to avoid applying certain precedents they may not like. This process of distinguishing cases has been developed into a fine art. One of the major criticisms of the common law system is that it has become too detailed and hairsplitting in its application. The practice of distinguishing cases has contributed greatly to the validity of that criticism.

What Decisions are Binding on Whom?

Although practised for centuries, *stare decisis* did not become the dominant feature of the legal system until as late as the nineteenth century. It required not only that decisions of higher courts would be binding on lower courts, but also that decisions of courts at the same level would be binding on subsequent judges in the same court. In more recent times the highest courts have tended toward the American approach. The Supreme Court of the United States considers itself free to go against its own prior decisions when it believes it is appropriate to do so. The British House of Lords announced in a practice statement that they now consider themselves free to depart from prior decisions of the House of Lords when they believe it right to do so. In Canada, judges of the Supreme Court have made it clear that in the right circumstances they, too, will depart from prior decisions of the court.

The question of which cases are binding on a particular court and which are not is a complicated one in Canada, with its 10 provinces, three territories and federal government. Each province has its own court system, with a court of appeal (or its equivalent) at the top of the provincial court hierarchy. Above that is the Supreme Court of Canada. A decision of the Supreme Court of Canada is binding on all courts within Canada at any level. Note, however, that when the Supreme Court of Canada hears a case requiring its interpretation of a provincial statute, its decision will only be applicable to those provinces having similar statutory provisions in place. Also, a decision of the Supreme Court of Canada that involves the application of the civil law in Quebec will not apply to the rest of Canada.

The decision of a provincial court of appeal is binding on all other courts within that province, but it has only persuasive authority on the courts in other provinces. Similarly, a decision of the highest trial-level court in a province is binding on judges lower in the hierarchy. Decisions of lower courts may or may not be binding, depending on their status and location. Thus, a decision of the Court of Appeal in British Columbia is not binding on a Provincial Court in Nova Scotia because it is not part of the same provincial hierarchy. Such a decision would be persuasive only. A decision of the Appeal Division of the Supreme Court of Nova Scotia, however, would be binding on the Provincial Courts of Nova Scotia.

Advantages and Disadvantages of Following Precedent

There are some advantages to the case law approach. Case law's certainty and predictability, as well as its air of practicality (because the cases deal with day-to-day problems), allow for incremental changes and prohibit grandiose theories and pronouncements. There are, however, some considerable disadvantages. The main disadvantage is the rigidity of common law. As the system became more complex and a great body of case law was developed, the process of a court being bound to follow prior decisions in similar situations became a considerable restriction. Today, there is little room for the courts to manoeuvre and create new law. As a result, common law has become inflexible and very slow to adapt either to new situations or to social change. For this reason, most new laws and modifications to existing law are accomplished by statute. Parliament (or the legislative assemblies in the provinces) have thus taken over from common law courts as the pre-eminent source of new law.

One of the significant differences between the continental system of following a prescribed code and the English system of following precedent is the degree of generalization. The codes, by their nature, set out broad general principles. The function of continental judges is to take that broad generalization and apply it to the specific case before them, going from the general to the particular. In common law, however, the precedent-making cases are particular in their nature and well detailed. The function of common law judges is to look at the precedent cases and to develop a consistent principle from the whole group — that is, to choose one of the detailed, specific precedents and follow it. The judicial decision-making process, as a result, is quite different. One advantage of the civil law system is that, within the parameters of the general rule to be applied, the judge has considerable flexibility, whereas the flexibility of the common law judge is quite limited once a binding precedent or line of precedents is found. Another problem with the common law system is that the law has sometimes developed in an illogical way, with anomalies getting built into the structure, leading to other compensating anomalies.

As a general rule, these disadvantages can be worked around. It is interesting to observe, however, that most emerging nations choose to adopt continental civil law as their system of law. Only those nations colonized or conquered by England have adopted the English common law system.

Law Reports

The practice of recording judges' decisions made the tradition of following precedent both persuasive and binding. As paper became more common and the printing press was developed, the capacity to publish those decisions gave students and practitioners access to the law. In the early stages, this was largely an informal and sporadic process, mainly performed by private people for their own and their friends' edification. Trial notes were usually taken by students or kept by counsel for their own information. Early records of English cases are contained in publications called *The Year Books*, which cover the early period up to the year 1535. Because of their age, brevity and questionable accuracy, however, they are seldom used today.

In the mid-sixteenth century, the process of compiling reports of judges' decisions became more formalized, although it was still a private occupation. Many eminent lawyers participated in the process, with even the great jurist Sir Edmund Coke taking a turn. This series of law reports is referred to as *The Reports*. They are listed under the name of the person compiling them, and they cover the period from 1537 to 1865. In 1865, the formal process of law reporting was established. This modern series of law reports, known as *The Law Reports*, continues to this day. *The Law Reports* are now supplemented by a more frequent publication, the *Weekly Law Reports*. In addition to these authorized reports, a number of commercial publishers have continued over the years to issue their own summaries of legal cases. The *All England Reports* are an important example. Similar law reports exist in all common law countries. They are also important in countries that use a civil law system, but in those jurisdictions the reported cases have a different role to play.

In Canada, there are several important law reports available in the various jurisdictions. Federally, the commercially produced *Dominion Law Reports,* now in their fourth series, provide for all of Canada a general reporting of the most important cases decided by both the provincial and federal level courts since 1912. The semi-official *Supreme Court Reports* record decisions made by the Supreme Court of Canada. In addition to these reports, there are various important regional reports. The *Western Weekly Reports* cover important decisions from British Columbia, Alberta, Saskatchewan and Manitoba. The *Atlantic Provinces Reports* provide the same coverage for the Maritime Provinces. Each province has its own volumes of reported cases. In addition to the provincial and regional reports, there are several series of reports dedicated to specialized areas of law, such as the *Canadian Bankruptcy Reports*, the *Business Law Reports*, *Canadian Criminal Cases* and the *Motor Vehicle Reports*.

Computer technology has also had an impact on the reporting process. It is now possible to research case law on CD-ROMs, which are indexed and annotated to facilitate easy access, and we expect this service to be available soon on the Internet. At the time of the writing of the 2nd edition of this text, the first moves have been made to make available judges' decisions as well as statutes and other government publications on the Web. Judicial decisions of the British Columbia and Federal courts are now available.

There are a number of publications, such as the *Canadian Encyclopedic Digest* and the *Canadian Abridgement*, designed to provide assistance to lawyers and students of the law. These are more like encyclopedias or, in the case of the *Canadian Abridgement*, very brief summaries of cases, listed by topic to allow for easy research. These are not authoritative, because they do not contain the actual judges' decisions; rather, they are a summary of what the writer or editor thinks is important in the case. For purposes of study they are invaluable, because they help the researcher find the appropriate cases. For the purposes of binding the court, however, the original judge's decision must be presented. In most law reports, the editors begin the report of an actual judgment with a headnote, usually consisting of a one- or two-page summary of the facts of the case and the important conclusions and legal principles embodied in the judgment. These summaries can be helpful, but they are not part of the judgment and are not binding on the court. In fact, they are sometimes inaccurate and misleading.

Other writings are available to assist law students and judges to understand the law. Newspapers and magazines directed to lawyers are available, as are textbooks and articles published in legal journals that provide useful information about cases, but they do not have any binding authority on the court. The status given to the writings of legal scholars is different in common law jurisdictions than it is in civil law countries. As a general rule, in the common law system the writings of such authors are of little persuasive authority and infrequently used by the courts.

Because careful case records were not kept during the formative stages of the common law system, we only have the work of learned authors to rely on. As a result, authors such as Glanville, Bracton, Coke, Littleton and Blackstone have a special status. Their writings are viewed not only as authoritative sources, but also as the embodiment of the common law of England in their time. Their writings are referred to as "books of authority," as opposed to merely persuasive writings, as is the case with modern texts. The works of these early writers are, in effect, among the original sources of law.

EQUITY

All the sentences of precedent judges that have ever been cannot altogether make a law contrary to natural equity.

Thomas Hobbes: *Leviathan*

The body of law referred to as equity is another major source of law, and the only other source for judge-made law in our legal system. The term *equity*, as it is used in our law, has several distinct meanings. The first is a general meaning equated with justice or fairness. Thus, saying that the results in a particular case were equitable is the same as saying that the results were just or fair. More particularly, however, equity refers to that body of rules developed by the Court of Chancery before the passage of the British *Judicature Acts* in 1873-75 amalgamated the courts. This special body of rules, referred to as equity, may or may not be fair in the modern sense. Although it is hoped that the rules are fair and just, it is important not to confuse the use of the term *equity* with fairness and justice when it is being used in this more restrictive sense.

The main feature of the body of rules and principles developed by the Courts of Chancery is their remedial nature. They were designed to overcome deficiencies that then existed in the common law system. For example, where the common law might recognize a right but not be able to provide an adequate remedy because it was limited to an award of damages, the Court of Chancery would step in and provide a more appropriate remedy, such as an injunction. To further complicate matters, a few equitable principles, meant to be remedial, were developed by other courts to overcome some deficiencies of common law. The Admiralty Court, and even the common law courts themselves, developed remedial principles that must be included in the body of law called equity. For example, the common law courts developed the principle of quasi contract, which is clearly accepted as part of the body of law referred to as equity. In addition, as has been readily acknowledged, there have been developments in the law of equity since the amalgamation of the courts in 1873–75. In the following discussion, we will use the term *equity* to refer to the body of law developed by the Court of Chancery. It is important to remember, however, that the actual body of law referred to as equity is, in fact, a little broader than that definition would suggest.

Court of Chancery

The role of the Court of Chancery cannot be properly understood without an appreciation of the procedural restrictions in place in the common law courts. The writ system was, in effect, a straightjacket on the development of common law. It restricted the development of new areas that could be dealt with in common law courts and created a structural rigidity within which there was little room for compromise or change. The writs, in fact, shaped not only the actions that could be brought, but also the way in which they could be dealt with in court. Other severe procedural restrictions contributed to the frustration experienced by litigants before common law courts. For example, no one with an interest in the matter before the courts could give evidence in relation to it. Thus, the people with the best knowledge of what had happened could not testify. The Chancery Court, however, suffered no such restriction. The person seeking redress would petition the court for a remedy, the other party would be summonsed before the court, and the judge, in an effort to establish the truth of the matter, would ask probing questions of both parties. In the early stages of their development, the Chancery Courts were both extremely flexible and free to proceed and decide as they saw fit. In fact, one major criticism of the judges of the Chancery Courts was that their decisions were arbitrary and that there were no rules consistently applied to all cases coming before the Chancery.

> Equity is a roguish thing. For Law we have a measure, know what to trust to; Equity is according to the conscience of him that is Chancellor, and as that is larger or narrower, so is Equity. 'Tis all one as if they should make the standard for the measure we call a 'foot' a Chancellor's foot; what an uncertain measure! One Chancellor has a long foot, another a short foot, a third an indifferent foot. 'Tis the same thing in the Chancellor's conscience.
>
> John Seldon, *The Lawyer's Quotation Book*, p. 31

While common law was very strict, structured, and predictable, equity was considered chaotic and arbitrary. Only as the practice developed of writing down the decisions of the

Chancery Court and making them publicly available did the Court of Chancery accept the doctrine of *stare decisis* and adopt the practice of following prior decisions. Equity, in its early stage of development, can almost be viewed as the conscience of the common law system. In fact, the Court of Chancery has been referred to as a court of conscience. The writ system and *stare decisis* gave predictability and structure to common law courts, but some method was needed for dealing with the inequities that such restrictions created. As the king's chancellor was already responsible for issuing the writs that formed the basis of the common law system, it is not surprising to find that the chancellor was given the burden of hearing petitions for relief from that system. The chancellor eventually appointed others to help (first a series of clerks, then the masters, and eventually the vice-chancellors), which resulted in a completely separate court structure with a different body of rules. Those rules are sometimes referred to as an appendix to the common law, indicating their relation to, but separateness from, the body of law developed by common law courts.

The people who presided over and shaped the development of the original Courts of Chancery were all clerics trained in civil and canon law. Thus, the law of equity has not escaped the influence of Roman law in its development, particularly in relation to the procedures used. Common law judges and lawyers were very critical of the seeming arbitrariness of the decisions made in these courtrooms. By the time a compromise was worked out between them, the Court of Chancery had begun to change. Lawyers, rather than clerics, were appointed as chancellors. As the decisions of Chancery Courts were reported and published, its lawyers also introduced the practice of following precedent, thus overcoming one of the major areas of contention.

In the process of gaining predictability and respectability, however, the law of equity also lost one of its most valuable features: the flexibility that had allowed chancellors to make decisions based entirely on how they perceived fairness or justice would be best served. While this characteristic was seen as arbitrary and chaotic from the point of view of common law lawyers, it was the very reason the Chancery Court and the law of equity had been created. The change not only preserved the Court of Chancery, but also ensured that the law of equity would remain a major institution in the English common law system. However, it also brought an end to one of the primary reasons for the existence of the Court of Chancery. It could no longer be described as a court of conscience.

Amalgamation of Courts

By the eighteenth and nineteenth centuries, the Court of Chancery had become more cumbersome, restrictive, and generally worse in its procedural delays than the common law courts. Many who started an action in the Chancery Court could not expect to see the outcome of the case in their lifetime. Charles Dickens was driven to attack the court in his powerful novel *Bleak House*.

> The lawyers twisted it into such a state of bedevilment that the original merits of the case have long disappeared from the face of the earth. It's about a Will, and the trusts under a Will — or it was once. It's about nothing but Costs now.

> from *The Lawyer's Quotation Book*, p. 15

Reform of the Court of Chancery became necessary and Parliament undertook the challenge, culminating in the *Judicature Acts* passed between 1873 and 1875, by which the

Court of Chancery and the common law courts were amalgamated into one court system. The two bodies of rules, however, remain separate. Today, many argue that the distinctions between the two bodies of rules are breaking down and that they ought to be considered as one great body of rules. In any event, the rules of equity must be considered, at best, a second body of rules complementary to the common law. Equity is often referred to as a gloss on common law, meaning that it puts a finish on it or completes it. Common law, without equity, could function as a complete legal system although with some deficiencies; but equity, without common law, would be incomplete and wholly inadequate.

Impact on Canadian Courts

Variations of Chancery courts were set up in the British colonies, but they were not well accepted as chancellors were most often appointments from Britain who applied the complex and unsatisfactory procedures of the British courts and were unfamiliar with colonial needs and practices. The Legislative Assembly of the United Province of Canada passed three *Judicature Acts* in 1849. The *Chancery Act* remodelled the Court of Chancery so that it was headed by a Chancellor, who ranked next to the Chief Justice of the Court of Queen's Bench. The *Judicature Act* of 1881, modelled on the English *Judicature Acts*, consolidated common law and equity. While the effect of the *Judicature Acts* was to eliminate the jurisdiction of the Chancery Court and make all of the equitable rights concurrent with common law principles, it is still possible to distinguish contemporary laws and procedures that have their basis in equity.

Equitable Principles

A few of the areas in which important contributions were made by the Chancery Court are the law of trusts, equitable rights in mortgage transactions, special remedies such as the injunction, and specific performance. The development of the declaratory order or judgment, rescission of contracts where fraud or mistake are involved, the order to make an accounting, and the appointment of a receiver all find their roots in equity. Many of the legal procedures involved in modern litigation, such as the discovery of documents, interrogatories, and the use of the summons and subpoena also came from the procedures developed in the Court of Chancery.

The law of equity features a number of generalized rules, called *maxims of equity*, that provide a framework for applying the law to specific problems. They are the overriding rules upon which equitable principles are administered. To illustrate how they are used, a few of the maxims follow.

- *A person who seeks equity must have clean hands.* This means that a person seeking an equitable remedy must not be tainted by fraudulent conduct or other wrongful behaviour. If a person has entered into a contract as a result of another person's misrepresentation and comes to the court seeking a remedy of rescission (returning the parties to their original position), he or she had better not be shown to have committed any misrepresentation or other wrongful conduct as well.
- *Equity will not suffer a wrong to be without a remedy.* If a person agrees to sell a unique piece of property, signs a contract to that effect, but then refuses to give up possession of the item, the only remedy under common law available to the purchaser is damages.

This would be a completely inadequate remedy if the purchaser could not find another item exactly like it. A Court of Chancery, in these circumstances, would have ordered specific performance, requiring the contract to be fulfilled and the item given to the person entitled to it.

- *Delay defeats equity.* There is a concept in equity called *laches*, which means that a person who has unaccountably delayed seeking a remedy will not be permitted to obtain it, because the court will assume it is not really important to him. This is not the same thing as a limitation period, which sets a specific time period within which an action must be brought.
- *Equity looks to the intent rather than the form.* Even though the documents in a mortgage appear to give the creditor undisputed title in the event of a default, equity looks to the intention of the parties, which was to provide security for a loan, and will, as a result, allow the debtor to redeem the property.
- *Equity follows the law* and *Equality is equity* are two other maxims that describe equitable principles.

The law of equity made a major contribution in the field of trusts. Other legal systems contain nothing quite like it. The legal title to property might be given to one person, making him the legal owner of that property according to common law. However, the transfer may have been made with a condition, imposing a duty to use the property in a certain way in order to provide some benefit to a third person. People quite commonly create such trust arrangements to ensure that their families are taken care of after their deaths. In such cases, the person creating the trust transfers his property to a trustee, who becomes the legal owner of the property. That trustee is charged with the duty of managing the property, obtaining rents, incomes, profits, and so on. After taking a fee for his service, he is required to pay over those profits to the family members who are to receive the benefit of the trust. Under common law, the trustee has no obligation to do all this; the property is now his, and he can do with it as he wishes. The law of equity, however, recognizes the trustee's obligation to make use of the property to the benefit of the family, and it will enforce this duty.

The Court of Chancery also developed some specialized remedies that assisted victims to obtain a remedy in contract law, as well as in other fields. Sometimes the victim of a wrong has no way of showing just how much he has lost. For example, the means of making a profit from a transaction, as well as all the records, may be in the hands of the wrongdoer. In these circumstances, the accused is required to appear before a judge and account for his activities. He must give a detailed accounting of any monies earned and pay over any profits to the victim. Sometimes the only way to preserve the value of property that is in the hands of a wrongdoer is to have someone else take over that property and manage it. The Court of Chancery developed the practice of appointing a receiver to manage property in such circumstances. Finally, the discovery of documents, now an important part of our litigation procedure in all forms of actions, was developed in the Court of Chancery. The discovery of documents involves one party to a lawsuit requiring the other party to produce for inspection any document that may have an effect on the outcome of the case. Allowing both parties to inspect such documents puts them on an equal footing; they both know what is going on, and have the same chance to prove their claims. It also goes a long way toward persuading the parties to settle a matter before it ever gets to court. It should be remembered that judges will follow the common law unless it creates a serious inequity; the determination of the inequity is at the discretion of the courts.

STATUTE LAW

Without a notion of a lawmaker, it is impossible to have a notion of law, and an obligation to observe it.

John Locke: *An Essay Concerning Human Understanding*

Legislation is the third and today the most important source of law. Following the seventeenth-century English Civil War, the principle of the *supremacy of parliament* was firmly established. From that time on, an act of parliament overrode any principle of common law or equity that was inconsistent with it. Even though the common law rule or equitable principle had been in place for centuries, the supremacy of parliament effectively changed the law. There are, of course, many statutes predating the English Civil War that have the force of law today. However, the Civil War and the victory of the parliamentary forces effectively established parliament as the ultimate law-making power in England and ensured that its statutes were the supreme and ultimate authority in the land.

The concept of parliamentary supremacy was one of the major disputes that triggered the American Revolution. When the United States successfully broke with England, they adopted a system of government involving checks and balances. Congress, which consists of the House of Representatives and the Senate, is the body that corresponds to parliament, but in the United States it is not supreme. The Supreme Court, Congress and the Executive branch, in the form of the Presidency, are considered equal; there is a balance of powers between the three bodies.

Canada, however, followed the English example and recognized the supremacy of parliament, allowing for the important distinction that in Canada there would be two levels of government — the federal and provincial — with each having supreme authority within their constitutionally-defined jurisdictions. The ultimate source and maker of law in this country is the legislative body having jurisdiction in the area. Because Canada is a confederation with 11 legislative bodies, each must be considered supreme in its own right, and therefore they are the ultimate makers of law. The heart of our constitutional law, as found in the *Constitution Act, 1867,* is the division of powers between the federal Parliament and the provincial legislative assemblies.

The introduction of the *Charter of Rights and Freedoms* into the Constitution of Canada in 1982 is a second major distinction between the British and Canadian approaches to parliamentary government. In England, Parliament is supreme and unfettered in the enactment of its powers. Theoretically, it can make law dealing with any topic, no matter how extreme, unfair, or unjust. In Canada, an intentional limitation on the power of the federal Parliament, provincial legislative assemblies or any government agency or representative has now been built into the constitutional structure. Any parliamentary enactment inconsistent with the basic human rights and freedoms of Canadians set out in the Charter may be declared invalid (***ultra vires***, or beyond the power of the body making it) and be struck down by the courts. Thus Canada has moved a little toward the American constitutional model by adopting a limited judicial check on the supremacy of parliament.

Governments' Legislative Power

During the formative period of English history, it was rare to have a statute change the law. It was generally believed that the law was embodied in common law. Neither the king nor his council should meddle with it. Not until 1649, after the Civil War, did the passage of statutes modifying or changing the law become more common. Even then the use of this process, although recognized as authoritative, was the exception rather than the rule. With the great reforms of the nineteenth century, however, the passage of legislation to change laws became the rule. In the last half of the twentieth century, the focus changed from legal reformation to a proliferation of legislation designed to adapt to a rapidly changing world.

When the British colonies in Canada adopted English law, they assumed not only the law as embodied in common law and equity, but also any statutes of general application that had been passed in England before the time of adoption. As a general rule, modern legislation has overridden these prior English statutes. Either directly or by implication, they have been repealed or replaced. It is still possible on rare occasions, however, to hear a lawyer in a Canadian court arguing that some obscure English statute in place in prior centuries is still applicable, even though it has long since been repealed in England. These statutes are usually of no more than historical interest. For our purposes, when we speak of legislation, we are speaking of a modern body of statutes, passed by either a provincial legislative assembly or the federal Parliament.

The Canadian system supports three levels of government: federal, provincial and municipal. Municipal councils are not legislative bodies, and their by-laws are not a separate source of law. Local by-laws have the force of law only because the city council or municipality has been given authority to create such by-laws by provincial legislation. When legislation is considered as a source of law, it must include municipal by-laws as well as any other statutes passed under the authority of the provincial legislative assemblies or the federal Parliament.

The governments of the Northwest Territories, Nunavut and the Yukon have a similar position. They are not yet provinces, and their territorial assemblies do not have constitutional standing as supreme parliamentary bodies. They do not have constitutionally-based power to pass valid legislation. The laws of these territories are valid and have the force of law because these bodies have been authorized by federal parliamentary power. They are creatures of the federal Parliament, in much the same way as cities and municipalities are creatures of provincial legislatures. The significance of this relationship is that these bodies are entirely at the mercy of the body to which they owe their power. The federal government could freely disband or make any other changes to the territorial assemblies. The provinces can and do make changes with respect to their cities.

Delegated Powers

Another example of delegated legislative power is found in the myriad government agencies that have been given authority by the provincial or federal governments that created them to make rules dealing with the operation of particular areas. The rules created by government administrators under the authority of statutes are called regulations; they have the same force of law as the legislation authorizing their creation. For example, a workers' compensation board is created by provincial legislation called the *Workers' Compensation Act*, and the chairman of its board (or the minister responsible) is given the power under that act to make the regulations necessary to fulfill the goals of the legislation. The board's authority would include the power to specify under what circumstances a person will receive compensation, and how much. As long as the regulations are within the limits of the authority granted by the legislation, they have the force of law.

There are many examples of both federal and provincial bodies authorized to create such regulations. In fact, the rules and regulations passed in this way are more voluminous than the provincial and federal legislation authorizing them. In Canada, therefore, when we consider legislation as a third source of law, we must look at the legislation passed by Parliament and the legislatures as well as the regulations passed under their powers of delegation in the form of municipal by-laws, territorial statutes and government agency regulations. All these together constitute the legislative source of our law.

Legislative Publications

Statutes and regulations are published on a regular basis. Each level of government publishes its enactments and regulations in a newspaper format called the *Gazette*. Each province publishes its legislation annually in volumes, which are added to the body of provincial statutes. Ontario's *Arbitration Act* is cited as S.O. 1991, c. 17, and can be found in the volume of Ontario statutes published in 1991 at chapter 17. The federal government publishes its statutes in a similar way. Occasionally these volumes of statutes contain new laws, but usually they are modifications or changes to already existing statutes or law. To find any current enactment governing a particular problem, it is necessary to find all of the amendments as well. This would be an extremely difficult task, in some cases requiring a researcher to trace changes back many decades, were it not for the fact that every few years the federal and provincial governments summarize any changes to their legislation. These summaries are referred to as the revised statutes of the particular province, or, federally, as the *Revised Statutes of Canada*. The most recent revision of federal legislation occurred in 1985 (R.S.C. 1985); when looking for current federal law, it is usually not necessary to look any further back than the *Revised Statutes of Canada, 1985*. The Yukon and the Northwest Territories also provide a summary of their legislative enactments, even though these enactments are passed under the umbrella of federal authority. Similar publications are made of the regulations enacted by various governmental agencies. Municipal and city by-laws are made available to the citizens residing in the particular areas affected by them.

Not all published legislation is of interest as a source of law. Many enactments are simply part of the process of carrying on the business of government. Although they have the force of law, they have little to do with the ongoing legal system. Budgetary bills or statutes creating crown corporations or other administrative bodies are examples. As well, many private bills are passed that are important only to a limited number of people or to a particular geographical area, such as statutes controlling zoning or naming landmarks. They have no impact on the general law of the country. Most legislation passed by the provincial legislatures and the federal Parliament falls into this category. As statutes are applied in court, errors in draftsmanship or unintended results become apparent. Sometimes the policies of government change. The government must then amend the statutes so they more closely reflect its policies. In the process, many provisions of existing statutes are amended, repealed or replaced.

Legislative Process

Only a small portion of the effort of legislative bodies is devoted to the creation of new law. New statutes are important, however, because they can make radical revisions to the law, creating an entirely new direction. Historically, changes to the law, which were made by judges in the common law system, occurred slowly and minutely, almost imperceptibly. A new statute, however, can make drastic changes with the stroke of a pen. Most major statutory enactments are not unique to any one jurisdiction. They are often borrowed from other areas. For example, the *Sale of Goods Act*, the *Statute of Frauds* and the *Partnership Act* show only minor variations from province to province in Canada. Many statutes, such as the federal *Bills of Exchange Act*, are borrowed from other countries. Some are just consolidations or summaries of previous case law. Some types of legislation, however, such as human rights codes, labour relations codes and consumer protection legislation, may strike out in new directions. The personal property security acts recently introduced in most common law provinces are examples of a new direction in legislation that significantly changes the law in an attempt to create a standardized approach to the problem.

A statute starts out as a bill presented either to Parliament or a legislative assembly by an elected representative. Whether they are representatives of the government or the opposition, each member has the right to propose a bill. Only rarely, however, will a bill introduced by an opposition member receive the support required to become law. The initial process of putting a bill before the House of Commons or Legislative Assembly is referred to as the first reading. It is done without debate or discussion. Once a bill is before the House or Legislature, it can be presented for second reading, to be approved in principle after discussion of its general content and purpose. At this stage most bills presented by the opposition are defeated. Once a bill has received second reading and been approved by simple majority vote, it goes to the committee stage. In committee, a bill is examined provision by provision and, in some instances, with public hearings. When the committee stage is completed, a bill is presented back to the House for third reading. At this stage amendments may be recommended and further debate may take place. Finally, a bill is given third reading (approval by vote) and is thus passed by the House or Legislature. At the federal level, this process must be repeated in the Senate, where the bill is subjected to "sober second thought" and usually given the Senate's stamp of approval. Even then, a bill does not become law until it has received royal assent. For a bill to receive royal assent, the Queen's representative in Canada (the Governor General at the federal level or the Lieutenant Governor at the provincial level) must approve it by signing the bill on behalf of the Queen. The bill may not become law immediately if it has provisions that set out how and when it will be implemented, such as a requirement that it be proclaimed in force by a cabinet order-in-council.

INTERPRETATION

A major task faced by the courts is determining what the statutes, regulations, and by-laws mean in terms of the law. Unlike the civil codes, which are usually worded in broad terms, statutory enactments in common law countries are carefully worded and very specific. There can still be problems, however, in determining exactly what was intended by their provisions. When a judge interprets a prior judge's decision, he or she must find the *ratio decidendi*, or legal principle, embodied in the case. This likely involves a process of reasoning and expanding upon the judge's words, because the general principle being applied is not always clearly and simply stated. Statutes, however, are different. In a statute, the legal principle is supposed to be clearly set out. The judge is not generally permitted to make inferences or to reason about what was meant by the provision. He or she must apply the statute as it is written. To make statutes even clearer, the practice today is for legislators to set out the aims and objectives in the act, leaving much less room for judicial interpretation. There can still be problems determining just what the statutory provision means. The legislative body makes the law, but the judge must apply that law to the situation before him or her. Once a ruling has been made on a statutory provision, the rules of precedent come into play and other judges in the jurisdiction must follow the rule in similar cases.

Rules of Statutory Interpretation

In order to minimize the possibility of a judge misinterpreting the statute, legislators can impose some very involved and strict rules for statutory interpretation. Usually, the statute itself will begin with a definition section, which lists several of the terms used in the statute, along with a statement specifying how they are used. The judge must follow this terminology. In addition, there are both federal and provincial interpretation statutes that set out certain rules of interpretation applicable to all statutes. For example, the *Interpretation Act* will set out what happens when a time limit specified in legislation falls on a weekend or holiday. Interpretation acts also set out specific definitions to be applied to words generally used in statutes.

In addition to these legislated interpretation rules, the courts have developed their own rules to guide them in the process of interpreting statutes and applying them to specific situations. Over the years, the courts have developed three main rules of statutory interpretation. These are the *literal rule*, the *golden rule* and the *mischief rule*. The *literal rule* means that when the words and phrases embodied in the legislation are clear and unambiguous, their meaning must be given effect according to their ordinary meaning. The words used must be accepted as embodying the dictionary meaning, and simple rules of grammatical construction must be applied to the sentences. When the words set out in a statute are clear and unambiguous, they must be applied as written, even if the judge does not like the result. This is the foremost principle of interpretation and is, indeed, the one most commonly applied.

The *golden rule* is really just a qualification of the literal rule. That is, the words in the statute must be given their literal interpretation and the sentences their normal grammatical structure, unless the result leads to a logical absurdity, an inconsistency or a repugnancy. Should this happen, the golden rule allows the court to move from the literal interpretation of the words and grammatical structure only so far as is necessary to remove the conflicting construction. Usually this involves looking more generally at the context of the ambiguous words. This is, in effect, a common-sense solution to such an interpretation problem.

The *mischief rule* is somewhat different. If there is an ambiguity in the statute, the court may look at the reason why it was originally passed in order to determine how the ambiguity should be resolved. What is the purpose of the legislation? What mischief is the statute designed to suppress, or what remedy is being advanced by it? The judge, when applying the mischief rule, looks to this remedy or mischief, and then interprets the ambiguous provision of the statute in a way that gives effect to the remedy or suppresses the mischief. Another often-heard way of expressing this rule is to say that the judge seeks the intention of parliament — a convenient myth, since the scope of a judge's search is limited to the statute. Generally, no extrinsic evidence or legislative history is allowed. The golden rule and the mischief rule must be viewed as optional paths to statutory interpretation, which a judge can choose when an ambiguity is present. The literal rule, then, says the statute must be applied literally, as written, unless there is an ambiguity. The golden rule says that when there is such an ambiguity, common sense can be applied to determine the meaning. The mischief rule, on the other hand, says that when there is such an ambiguity, attention should be given to the problem the statute was created to solve, and it should be interpreted in a way that solves the problem.

In fact, there may be other precedents or prior cases in which similar expressions have been interpreted in other statutes. If so, they will be persuasive to the judge. If the particular problem of interpreting the statute has been dealt with by a higher court in a previous case, it forms a binding precedent on subsequent cases and must be followed.

Statutory Preambles and Presumptions

The preamble, in those jurisdictions where such preambles are included in legislation, may also be helpful in the process of interpreting the meaning of a provision of a statute. The preamble summarizes the purpose of the legislation and its objectives and thus can be very helpful in resolving interpretation problems. As well, many jurisdictions give two titles to an act, a long one and a short one. The short title is usually a convenient name by which the act is commonly called. The long title, however, typically embodies the purpose of the act. It can be very helpful in determining the objectives of the legislators when they passed the statute, and thus aid in the court's interpretation of it. For example, the first statute found in the *Revised Statutes of Canada, 1985* has a short title, *Access To Information Act* (R.S.C. 1985, c. A-1), but the actual name of the act is "An act to extend the present laws of Canada that provide access to information under the control of the government of Canada."

A number of judicial presumptions have been established over the years which guide the court in this process of statutory interpretation. For example, there is a presumption that legislation will not deprive a person of property or liberty; a presumption that *mens rea*, or guilty mind, must be present for criminal liability; a presumption against the alteration of the common law; a presumption that the Crown is not bound by an act of parliament; and a presumption against the retroactive effect of any statute. These presumptions are operative and will determine the effect of a statute, unless another intention is clearly stated within the body of that statute. Once a statute has been interpreted and applied to a given case by the judge, the decision sets a binding precedent. Subsequent judges, then, if they are lower in the court hierarchy, are bound to interpret a particular provision of a statute in the same way.

CONCLUSION

We have now laid the framework upon which legal decision-making rests in Canada. The traditions and principles essentially originate in England with common law and equity and in the parliamentary system that developed there. Now we must look at the unique ways that these principles and procedures have been adopted, modified and applied in Canada. Beginning with the *British North America Act* of 1867, Canada undertook the long process of becoming independent from England. The process has been marked with a number of events and constitutional documents that have contributed to the distinctive nature of the Confederation of Canada.

QUESTIONS FOR DISCUSSION AND REVIEW

1. Consider the advantages and disadvantages of a new country inheriting a legal system.

2. Oliver Wendell Holmes stated that, "It is revolting to have no better reason for a rule of law than that it was laid down in the time of Henry IV." Defend or refute this statement.

3. What is the justification for adopting the customs of another jurisdiction?

4. Should the rules set out by any body, for example a church or the merchant guilds, have any influence on our laws?

5. Discuss whether the most significant characteristic of a legal system should be predictability or flexibility.

6. List and explain some of the measures judges use to avoid applying a precedent.

7. How has the *Charter of Rights and Freedoms* affected the role of judges in Canadian courts?

8. Why are law reports such an important part of a common law system?

9. Explain the role of equity in our legal system.

10. Given that statute law plays the pre-eminent role in our legal system, discuss the statement made by a contemporary jurist that the common law is dead.

11. Consider the distinctive roles of legislators and judges and discuss the contribution each makes to the law-making process.

12. Do you think judges should have the right to impose their interpretations on acts of parliament?

NOTES

1. Waddams, S.M. *Introduction to the Study of Law*, 2nd ed. Toronto: Carswell, 1983, p. 12.

2. For example, *Karpow v. Shave*, [1975] 2 W.W.R. 159 (Alta.).

3. For example, *Cockcroft v. Smith* (1705), 88 E.R. 872.

FURTHER READING

Altschuler, Bruce E. and Celia A. Sgroi. *Understanding Law in a Changing Society*, 2nd ed. New Jersey: Prentice Hall, 1996 (for a US perspective).

Banfield, Jane, ed. *Readings in Law and Society*, 6th ed. Toronto: Captus Press, 1995. See particularly Section Two.

Gall, Gerald L. *The Canadian Legal System*. Toronto: Carswell, 1995

Milson, S.F.C. *Historical Foundation of the Common Law*. Toronto: Butterworths, 1981.

Ogilvie, M.H. *Historical Introduction to Legal Studies*. Toronto: Carswell, 1982.

Smith, J.C. and David N. Weisstub. *The Western Idea of Law*. Toronto: Butterworths, 1983.

CANADIAN CONSTITUTIONAL LAW

*A constitution is more than a mechanical set of ground
rules. It is a mirror reflecting the national soul. It reflects
those values the country regards as important, and also
shows how these values will be protected.*

Cheffins, R.I. and R.N. Tucker. *Constitutional Process in Canada*,
2nd ed. Toronto: McGraw-Hill Ryerson, 1976, p. 4.

The constitution is the source of a government's right to exercise authority over a nation's peoples and institutions. A national constitution is based on the traditions and customs of its citizens, whether they are embodied in a written document or understood through long and accepted practice. Our review of English history and the development of its laws and government demonstrates that it is not necessary to produce a single document giving official recognition to authority and law in order to have a viable constitution. On the heels of a revolution, the Americans were anxious to reduce British influence when they constructed a constitutional document that has supported the growth of that powerful democracy. The authors of the American constitution had the foresight to include an amending formula that has enabled legislators and jurists to respond to social change. The original document that brought the Dominion of Canada into existence was an act of the British Parliament that, among other things, gave Canada a constitution based on traditions and customs and legislative enactments developed in England. Since that significant beginning, Canadians have gradually developed a constitutional framework that is uniquely their own. This chapter will review the process of Canada's development, from an act of the British Parliament through the patriation process to the modern Canadian Constitution now in place.

CANADIAN CONSTITUTION

Confederation

Initiated by the Fathers of Confederation and passed by the British Parliament, the *British North America Act*, now referred to as the *Constitution Act, 1867*, united the three Canadian colonies, creating Canada with four provinces, and provided for the inclusion of other colonies and territories in the Dominion. Its terms shaped the Canadian governmental and legal system by incorporating into the Canadian Constitution all of the constitutional traditions of Great Britain. The Act recognized the power of the Crown and Parliament of Great Britain over the Canadian Dominion. In retrospect, the Act's most important function was to divide powers between the two levels of government created by Confederation. This accommodated the most significant difference between the new Dominion and its parent: while Great Britain had only one governing body, Canada, before its first century was past, would have a federal Parliament, 10 legislative assemblies and two territorial governments. Many of the provisions in the *Constitution Act, 1867* that granted provincial power recognized the cultural, ethnic, and language differences that were in place in Canada, especially with respect to Quebec. The most accommodating manifestation of this recognition was the granting of education rights and responsibilities to the provinces. However, in the areas of interprovincial trade and commerce, banking, currency, and so on, the *Constitution Act, 1867* created a unified system that made it easier for the original colonies, now joined in Confederation, to trade with each other and to survive and prosper.

Box 3.1

I look to the future of my adopted country with hope, though not without anxiety; I see in the not remote distance, one great nationality bound, like the shield of Achilles, by the blue rim of ocean — I see it quartered into many communities — each disposing of its internal affairs — but all bound together by free institutions, free intercourse, and free commerce; I see within the ground of that shield, the peaks of the Western mountains and the crest of the Eastern waves — the winding Assiniboine, the five-fold lakes, the St. Lawrence, the Ottawa, the Saguenay, the St. John and the Basin of Minas — by all these flowing waters, in all the valleys they fertilise in all the cities they visit in their courses, I see a generation of industrious, contented moral men, free in name and in fact, men capable of maintaining in peace and in war, a Constitution worthy of such a country.

Thomas D'Arcy McGee
"Constitutional Difficulties between
Upper and Lower Canada,"
House of Assembly, Québec,
May 2, 1860.

No common system of law was imposed on the provinces as they entered Confederation. Section 129 of the *Constitution Act, 1867* makes it clear that the law in place in the respective colonies at the time they entered Confederation would continue to be the law of that province, with the exception of those areas assigned to the federal government. Thus, the law of British Columbia when it became a colony was the law of England as of 1858. The prairie provinces received the law of England as of 1870. As we explained in Chapter 1, Quebec used French civil law prior to Confederation, but in 1874 it adopted a civil code based on the Code Napoléon. Ontario adopted English law as of 1792; in the Maritimes, the year for the reception of English law is generally considered to be 1758, and 1832 for Newfoundland. Under the *Constitution Act, 1867,* the British Parliament retained ultimate control of Canada's destiny. It could pass legislation binding on Canada and it controlled Canada's foreign policy. As well, the Canadian Parliament could not make significant changes to Canada's Constitution without the approval of the British Parliament. The Judicial Committee of the Privy Council of the House of Lords was the highest court of appeal for Canadian legal cases.

Statute of Westminster

Canada's maturation as a nation has involved the difficult process of adapting what was inherited from Britain, accommodating French Quebec's special interests, taking control of its own destiny, and incorporating laws that adequately express the values and protect the rights Canadians have come to cherish. As Canada grew into nationhood, especially after its contributions in World War I, it began to want to play a greater role in its own foreign policy. In 1930, an imperial conference was held, at which Great Britain and the Dominions adopted a convention ensuring that no future enactments of the Parliament of the United Kingdom would affect the Dominions unless they requested the enactment. This was embodied in the *Statute of Westminster*, passed in 1931. From that time to the present, Canada has been free from unwanted legislative interference from the Parliament of Great Britain.[1] However, a number of enactments of the British Parliament passed since 1867 continue to form part of the Constitution of Canada. The only other remaining ties with England were the British monarch, who exercised his or her power through the Governor General in Canada, the Judicial Committee of the Privy Council, which was the final court of appeal in legal matters and disputes, and the requirement that any constitutional changes had to go through the British Parliament. Appeals to the Privy Council were abolished in 1949.

The Canada Act

Before 1982, the statutes controlling the federation of Canada were enacted by the Parliament of Great Britain and could not be changed or amended by the Canadian government without its approval. By convention, such a request would always be granted, but Canada had no power to make the amendment on its own. In 1982, the *Canada Act* of the United Kingdom was simultaneously passed in Canada and Great Britain, giving Canada the *Charter of Rights and Freedoms* as well as full control over the amending process of its Constitution. Thus, the last legal ties, whereby the Parliament of Great Britain could pass legislation affecting Canada, were cut. The reigning British monarch remains the king or queen of Canada, although the power wielded by the Crown's appointees, the governor general and lieutenant governors of each province, has been severely limited by convention.

Common Law Conventions

Another part of the Constitution of Canada is embodied in the common law rules developed over the centuries in British courts and, more recently, in Canadian courts. Among other constitutional conventions acknowledged in the *Statute of Westminster* are the "principles and rules of responsible government...which regulate the relations between the Crown, the Prime Minister, the Cabinet and the two Houses of Parliament."[2] Their main purpose is to ensure that the government operates according to the values and principles of the electorate. While the conventions are not legally enforceable in court, political expedience demands that they be adhered to.[3] Until 1982, the primary area of concern in Canadian constitutional law was the division of powers between the federal and the provincial governments. When the *Canada Act*, which included the *Charter of Rights and Freedoms,* was passed, a new and important concern was added to Canadian constitutional law.

Canadian constitutional law is now embodied in the *Constitution Act, 1867*, the *Constitution Act, 1982*, other statutory enactments, common law, and constitutional conventions. The *Constitution Act, 1867* regulates relationships between different levels of government by the division of powers, and the *Charter of Rights and Freedoms* guarantees individual liberties against oppression by government and its agencies. The term "constitutional law," in this sense, covers any rules relating to the exercise of governmental power. Many use the term in a much more restricted sense, however, referring only to those rules controlling government that are entrenched. Normally, if the federal Parliament or a provincial legislature wishes to change a statute that has been passed by them, it is a relatively simple matter. Changing an entrenched provision, however, involves a much more difficult process and requires constitutional amendment.

CONSTITUTIONAL CHANGE

Meech Lake Accord

Because of the diverse nature and interests of the regions making up the Canadian federation, constitutional law in this century has been primarily concerned with the smooth relations between federal and provincial governments, as well as the preservation of French culture in Quebec. The constitutional changes of 1982 attempted to resolve the differences between cultural communities in Canada. Unfortunately, they only served to further alienate French interests, and Quebec did not consent to the passage of the *Canada Act* and the patriation of the Constitution. In 1986, federal and provincial leaders attempted to work out a compromise at a conference held at Meech Lake. An accommodation that significantly changed the process of constitutional amendment was finally agreed to by the prime minister and the first ministers. The Meech Lake Accord had to be ratified by provincial legislatures by June 1990. Newfoundland's legislature objected primarily to the amending formula, and rejected the Accord by a narrow margin. The Manitoba legislature was prevented from approving the Accord by a single member, who refused to provide the necessary unanimous approval necessary before the ratification deadline. Elijah Harper felt that Native peoples of Canada had not been included in the Accord, nor had provision been given for the rights of aboriginal self-government.

Charlottetown Accord

In 1992, another Accord was reached, at the Charlottetown Constitutional Conference. In this agreement, the prime minister and the 10 provincial premiers, along with the leaders of territories and the Chief of the Assembly of First Nations, developed a Consensus Report on the Constitution. The Charlottetown Conference was the culmination of a long series of meetings on constitutional reform which included political representatives from federal, provincial and territorial governments, as well as numerous royal commissions that held public meetings throughout the country over a two-year period. In this document the political leaders reached an agreement to amend the Canadian Constitution in a number of fundamental areas. The Senate would be reformed to become an elected body with six members from each province, one from each territory and provision for representation from the First Nations. The power of the Senate would increase to reflect its being an elected and representative body. The House of Commons would be modified to respond to the reduction of Senate members from the most populous provinces, Ontario and Quebec, and Quebec would be guaranteed 25% of the seats in the House of Commons. The Supreme Court would be recognized and entrenched in this constitutional amendment, and attention was given to the division of federal and provincial powers. Perhaps the most significant clause in the Charlottetown Accord was the recognition of the inherent right of aboriginal Canadians to self-government. Although not specific about what shape self-government might take, the Accord would have opened the way for Native peoples to begin the transition process with the cooperation of both federal and provincial governments.

In order to ensure national support for the Consensus Report, Prime Minister Brian Mulroney decided to hold a referendum in which the people of Canada could decide whether or not the constitutional amendments should be pursued. The referendum was held in late October of 1992 and attracted a large voter turnout. The result was that 54% of Canada's voters rejected the Accord. Only Newfoundland, Prince Edward Island, New Brunswick and the Northwest Territories gave significant margins to the *Yes* side of the question. The largest negative vote was in British Columbia, where almost 68% of the voters turned it down. It was interesting to observe that in Quebec, where the largest negative response was expected, the *No* side won by only a 10% margin.

Quebec Referendum

In the federal election of 1994 Quebec elected enough separatist members to Parliament to form the official opposition. The Bloc Québécois, under the charismatic leadership of Lucien Bouchard, and the separatist Premier of Quebec, Jacques Parizeau, called for a referendum that asked Quebecers if they wanted Quebec to become a separate nation with special ties to Canada characterized by the term "sovereignty association." The lead-up to the referendum caused great dissension and dismay among Canadians that was not relieved by the very narrow margin of victory for the *No* side. Just under 51% of Quebec voters elected to remain a part of Canada. Since then there has been some decrease in the attention given to the question of separation, but it remains an ongoing threat to the unity of the nation.

First Nations Treaties

Aside from the question of whether Quebec will remain a part of the Canadian federation, a second major concern now is how the Native people of Canada will pursue their treaty and land claims and their perceived right to govern themselves. New treaties in British Columbia, along with initial rights to self-government granted to some BC bands, may set precedents that can have profound implication for other Native bands across the nation. British Columbia was in the unique position of having few treaties in place when it joined Confederation, unlike other regions where most of the bands had entered into treaties. After a number of failed attempts in which the courts tried to deal with land claim questions, the government of British Columbia has negotiated a treaty with the Nisga'a of northern BC. The British Columbia Premier described the treaty as follows: "The land, resources and money in the Nisga'a Final Agreement resolves their land claim and enables the Nisga'a to move from dependency to greater self-reliance."[4] (At the time of writing, this treaty had not yet become law.) Although the BC situation is unique because few treaties were signed there and valid treaties are in place in much of the rest of the country, it is possible that the precedents set in BC will prompt other bands to ask for similar considerations and perhaps even make future constitutional amendments necessary.

Individual Rights

Another significant area of interest prompting constitutional change has been the need to protect individual rights and freedoms. The first tentative steps on the part of the federal government to ensure civil rights were contained in a 1960 act of Parliament. This bill, introduced by Prime Minister John Diefenbaker and passed by his Conservative government, was designed to ameliorate the fears of minority groups in Canada, whose rights not only had been threatened but also were sometimes revoked by majority political action. The problem with the *Canadian Bill of Rights* was twofold: it had no constitutional status, and it could easily be modified or overturned by new legislation. Courts were reluctant to implement its terms because their decisions could be overruled by other statutory law and the standard rules of statutory interpretation required that it be interpreted narrowly, the opposite of what was intended and necessary to accomplish its purpose. One of the main features of the constitutional reforms passed in 1982 was the *Canadian Charter of Rights and Freedoms*, which entrenched the fundamental rights and freedoms of individuals in their dealings with government. (The Charter will be the major focus of the following chapter.)

Constitutional Documents and Principles

Although the division of powers and individual rights and freedoms have been the major focuses of constitutional law in Canada, several other important aspects of the Canadian constitutional structure must be given consideration. Canada inherited very important constitutional documents and traditions from Britain, including *Magna Carta*, the *Petition of Right* and the *Bill of Rights*. Canada has also assumed the principles of responsible government, parliamentary supremacy, the rule of law, the cabinet system of government, and constitutional monarchy. Many of these institutions were not immediately introduced into the Canadian system with the *Constitution Act, 1867*. Rather, they have been incorporated over time, as justified by the needs and requirements of the Canadian structure.

RESPONSIBLE GOVERNMENT

"Responsible government" is the phrase used to describe a parliamentary system where the majority of elected representatives authorize a cabinet of ministers to oversee the functions of government. The idea of responsible government is entirely based on conventions developed in England and was recommended by Lord Durham in 1838 when he was Governor General of British North America. Conducting the complex business of government through the elected assembly had proven unworkable and it was suggested by Lord Durham that the governor appoint an executive council from among the representatives to administer the affairs of state. Hence, in the modern parliamentary system in Canada, the Prime Minister appoints individuals to carry the responsibility of the various ministries of the government from among the elected members of the ruling party. This system has been adopted in each of the provinces as they entered Confederation.

Supremacy of Parliament

Essential to responsible government is the concept of the supremacy of parliament. We indicated in previous chapters how this concept evolved. Parliament has the power to make any law it deems fit, and all citizens are subject to its will. The federal Parliament and the legislative assemblies are considered supreme in their respective areas of jurisdiction. Although Confederation took place in 1867, it was not until 1931, in the *Statute of Westminster*, that the federal Parliament was truly recognized as supreme in its own right. Today, the federal Parliament is supreme, in that it is not answerable to any other level of government.

Because Canada is a federation, it is often claimed that it has two levels of government. While this claim is accurate in that Canada has federal and provincial governments, each with its own legislative power, the statement is misleading insofar as it indicates that one level is higher than the other. The federal government has broader powers, in the sense that the laws it makes apply to a broader geographical area, while the laws made in a province apply only within its boundaries. The federal Parliament, however, is not considered to have a higher power or more authority to make laws than do the provinces. An important effect of the *Constitution Act, 1867* is that it assigned the power to make laws to each of these autonomous, legislative bodies. Some powers were given to the federal government to override provincial governments. One that may still be in effect is the right to declare certain works or undertakings for the benefit of Canada, allowing the federal government to transfer them from provincial to federal jurisdiction.

If either the federal or the provincial governments pass legislation beyond their power or competence under the *Constitution Act, 1867*, or if they violate the *Charter of Rights and Freedoms*, or act in some other illegal way, it is fully appropriate for that legislation to be challenged in the courts. Indeed, one of the primary roles of the courts when a statutory law is to be applied in a case is to determine if the statute was properly passed by the appropriate level of government and to determine if it conforms to the terms of the Charter. If the court finds that the legislation fails either of these tests, it will be declared *ultra vires* or beyond the power of the assembly that passed it, and thus be found invalid.

The Governor General

> The Canadian Governor General long ago ceased to determine policy, but he is by no means, or need not be, the mere figure-head the public imagine. He has the privilege of advising his advisers, and if he is a man of sense and experience, his advice is often taken.
>
> Sir Wilfrid Laurier, quoted in O.D. Skelton, *Life and Letters of Sir Wilfrid Laurier* (Toronto, 1921), p. 86n.

The preamble of the *Constitution Act, 1867* clearly states that Canada is to have a constitution similar in kind to Great Britain. Thus the *Constitution Act, 1867* recognizes that executive power rests in the monarchy. In Canada that power is vested in the British monarch's representatives, the governor general and the lieutenant governor of each province. Although a monarch in Great Britain, or his or her representatives in Canada, appear to have great power, especially in terms of the *Constitution Act, 1867*, there is an accepted convention in both countries that that power will be exercised only on the advice of the prime minister and cabinet. The power to summon parliament and to assent to legislation are now mere formalities evidenced in the speech from the throne that traditionally begins new sessions of parliament or the final signing-off of a new statute.

The Prime Minister

In theory, the choice of the prime minister or premier is made by the governor general or lieutenant governor. In fact, because of the principle of the supremacy of parliament, the prime minister and premiers are chosen from the body of representatives forming the Parliament or legislative assembly. This choice is always based on the prime minister or premier being the leader of the party having the greatest number of elected members in the House of Commons or legislative assembly. Where there are more than two parties involved, there is the possibility of a minority government. This means that none of the parties has a clear majority without the support of one of the other parties. When this happens, the leader of the party that can show it has the support of one of the other parties will become the prime minister or premier, who is responsible and will remain in power only so long as he or she has the confidence of the majority of the House of Commons or the legislative assembly.

The Cabinet

The *Constitution Act, 1867* does not even mention the positions of prime minister or cabinet. Nevertheless, because of the principle of the supremacy of parliament and the concept of responsible government, the prime minister and cabinet are part of the Canadian parliamentary tradition. In the cabinet system of government, the prime minister chooses his or her cabinet ministers from among the elected representatives sitting in the House of Commons. In theory at least, the prime minister of Canada stands supreme, holding all power. He or she, as the spokesperson for Parliament, is unchecked by any other level of government, save only the governor general. This concept has been modified somewhat. Under the provisions set out in the Charter, the Supreme Court has undertaken to provide a check on the activities of the prime minister and all aspects of government. In general, however, as long as the prime minister retains the confidence and support of the members of Parliament, he or she has the power to govern the nation without restriction.

The House of Commons

The House of Commons is made up of locally elected representatives, usually belonging to a recognized political party. A requirement of the *Constitution Act, 1867* is that a federal election be held at least once every five years. The federal government divides the country into constituencies by population density and geographical area. Political parties nominate and select candidates, usually through a party electoral process, to run in the federal election and to represent constituencies. Eligible residents in each constituency vote for a candidate to represent them in the House of Commons. The party having the most representatives forms the governing party and its leader becomes the prime minister. The party with the next greatest number of representatives in the House forms the official opposition.

Members of the House of Commons are responsible to their constituents. They present, debate and vote on bills put before the House. From their ranks, the party leader chooses cabinet ministers or, if they are an opposition party, shadow cabinets. Cabinet ministers are given portfolios in the areas in which the government has power under the *Constitution Act, 1867*; these ministers head the departments related to their portfolios. Their duties include the responsibility to deal with matters in their areas of jurisdiction and to introduce bills or proposals to be heard during parliamentary sittings. Government departments have become large bureaucratic institutions; their appointed officials wield great power and influence as they organize and administer their departments and perform the functions of government.

The parliamentary system is dependent on party solidarity, which means that the party can count on its members to support bills it places before parliament. In rare circumstances, members are given leave to vote according to their own consciences, as was the case with the capital punishment and abortion bills brought before the House in the last half of the twentieth century. In general, however, a member who votes against his or her party is subjected to disciplinary measures, such as being removed from cabinet and being forced to join the backbenchers (members who have not been appointed to a cabinet post). If the problem persists, they can be forced to leave the caucus and sit as independents. The procedure for electing members to provincial legislative assemblies and their function as members in these assemblies is essentially the same as for the House of Commons.

Box 3.2

Be skeptical about law, and about the institutions of society. They can all be improved. Citizens should know that the persons in power: The Prime Minister, the Premiers, the MPs, are ordinary people like themselves. To suggest that they have any special insight or wisdom is mistaken. I think that there should be no undue reverence paid to the people who hold these offices. This is essentially a free society. We enjoy freedom of speech. We can criticize the Prime Minister or the Premier. ...Far from weakening society, it serves to strengthen it. ...We have the opportunity here to argue about the way we are governed, to say that our leaders don't know what they are doing and should be replaced. That's why we have the largest measure of freedom of any country in the world.

Tom Berger, former Justice of the Supreme Court of British Columbia, Special Joint Committee on Senate Reform, 1983.

The Senate

The Senate is a parliamentary body with many of the responsibilities of the House of Commons, but it is composed of people appointed by the federal government. Like the House of Commons and the governor general, the Senate is an institution recognized in the *Constitution Act, 1867*. It is, however, a matter of much concern and debate that an unelected body has the power to amend or veto bills passed by the House of Commons. Convention has restricted the power of this body, but it can still exercise its power to interfere with and forestall the passage of legislation. The lengthy debate the Senate gave to the Goods and Services Tax legislation, delaying its passage until well after the date the prime minister and cabinet had planned to put it into effect, is an example of that body's attempt to voice what it believes to be the popular will. Senate reform, while especially sought after by the western provinces, is a concern at all levels of government. Some suggest that the Senate be made up of elected members, who can then effectively exercise representative power. Others suggest that the regional representation be altered to give a greater voice to the smaller provinces, and still others advocate that the Senate be abolished altogether. Today, Senate effectiveness has been drastically curtailed because its members are not elected.

LEGISLATIVE PROCESS

The Rule of Law

Because the government of Canada has adopted the policy of choosing the prime minister and members of cabinet from among elected representatives, it has institutionalized the principle of parliamentary supremacy. Parliament is supreme, but it must be emphasized that it is Parliament as a body that is supreme, not any single member of that body. The prime minister and the cabinet members are subject to the will of Parliament and cannot act arbitrarily. This principle is referred to the as the **rule of law**, and requires that any government official be able to point to some law that gives him or her the authority to act. Such action is justified only so long as the law is valid and properly passed under the rules associated with parliamentary democracy. The rule of law is a basic constitutional principle, applicable in Canada, Britain and many other democratic countries. In essence, the rule states that although Parliament is supreme, it and the officials associated with it cannot act arbitrarily. Government officials cannot rely on their status to interfere with the rights of a person; rather, they must rely on some empowering legislation to authorize their actions. Citizens are thus protected from any arbitrary actions of government.

Perhaps no incident better illustrates this protection against arbitrary government action than the case of *Roncarelli* v. *Duplessis*.[5] Roncarelli, a restaurateur in the city of Montreal, had a liquor licence associated with his business. He was also a friend of a rather zealous Christian religious sect known as the Witnesses of Jehovah, an organization that had experienced some conflict with Roman Catholicism, the predominant religion in Quebec. A number of Jehovah's Witnesses were arrested for the distribution of religious tracts. Roncarelli, who was quite wealthy, made it his practice to provide bail for Witnesses arrested in the Montreal area. He had put up bail for some 380 members when provincial officials changed the rules, requiring that cash be put up in the amounts of $100 to $300. Roncarelli at no time participated in the activities that precipitated the arrests; his only involvement was to put up security to obtain the Witnesses' release. After deliberations between the liquor commission and Maurice Duplessis, then premier of the province, Mr. Duplessis directed that the liquor licence held by Mr. Roncarelli be revoked. In the words of the court,

> The step was taken as a means of bringing to a halt the activities of the Witnesses — to punish the appellant for the part he had played not only by revoking the existing license but by declaring him barred "forever" and to warn others that they would similarly be stripped of provincial "privileges" if they participated in any activity directly or indirectly related to the Witnesses and to their objectionable campaign.

As a consequence of being denied a liquor licence, Mr. Roncarelli's 33-year-old business failed. He then sued Mr. Duplessis for damages, claiming Mr. Duplessis had abused the position of his office. The Supreme Court of Canada agreed with Mr. Roncarelli, awarding him damages and stating that Mr. Duplessis could neither rely on his office nor on what he considered to be the public interest to support his actions. He had to point to some statute that authorized him to cancel the licence. While there was a statute authorizing the cancellation of a licence, the power to do so was given to another official, not to the premier of the province. Therefore, Premier Duplessis had abused the power of his office. This case illustrates the principle of the rule of law. No matter what the motives of the government official are, and no matter how sincere, if his or her acts are without authority, they are illegal.

THE CONSTITUTION ACT, 1867

Peace, Order and Good Government

Section 91 of the *Constitution Act, 1867* begins by declaring that the federal government has the power to

> make laws for the peace, order and good government of Canada in relation to all matters not coming within classes of subjects by this Act assigned exclusively to the legislatures of the provinces.

In addition to giving the federal government power to deal with matters left out of the division of powers, the peace, order and good government clause gives it power to deal with matters having a national dimension. These include emergency situations, such as war or catastrophe. In wartime, the power to wage war and pass legislation with respect to munitions production, wages, and conscription falls to the federal government. The *War Measures Act* has been invoked on a number of occasions to give the government such powers. While war may be the emergency that gives rise to the exercise of that power, it may continue even after peace has resumed. The federal government, under the *War Measures Act*, had rent controls in place during World War II that were continued and held to be valid for five years after the war ended.

Even the threat of insurrection is enough to justify the use of these powers. In October 1970, when the British trade commissioner to Canada was kidnapped and a Quebec cabinet minister was murdered by the Front de Libération du Québec, the federal government invoked the *War Measures Act*. This allowed for the arrest and detention, without trial, of about 500 people. The arrests were concentrated in Quebec but some people were even arrested in British Columbia. Although only a handful of these people were ever convicted of any wrongdoing, the validity of the exercise of this power was not successfully challenged. Another example of the use of the "peace, order and good government" power unrelated to war or insurrection was during the economic emergency following a period of inflation in the 1970s. The federal government used this general power to bring in wage and price controls; its power to do so was upheld in the inflation case.[6]

The *War Measures Act* has been replaced by the *Emergencies Act*,[7] providing similar but more controlled powers. This Act also provides for internal emergencies and incorporates several safeguards, making the abuse of these extensive federal powers much less likely. Clearly, if a matter becomes a concern to the whole country, even though it seems local or private in its nature, the federal government may have power to deal with it through this clause. For instance, if an epidemic were to become a national health crisis, the federal government would have the power to deal with it as a matter of national concern.

The Division of Powers

The division of legislative power and authority between the federal and provincial governments is an important aspect of Canadian constitutional law. The designation of jurisdiction is set out primarily in sections 91 and 92 of the Act. Section 91 lists a number of areas that are assigned exclusively to the federal government. The "peace, order and good government" clause ensures there is no gap in which either the federal or the provincial government has the power to enact law. The framers of the *Constitution Act, 1867* did not anticipate such developments as air transportation, broadcasting and telecommunications; therefore, no power was assigned to create legislation in relation to these areas. As a result, they fall exclusively to the federal government. Section 92 lists the areas assigned to the provinces. The distribution of powers does not create distinct categories; rather, it gives each government the authority to pass certain types of legislation. A certain amount of overlap between provincial and federal powers exists which may lead to a conflict. If the validity of some statute is challenged on the basis of this division of powers or such a conflict arises, the courts may be required to interpret the matter.

Adjudicating a Statute

Since Confederation, the overwhelming subject matter for litigation in the area of constitutional law, at least until 1982 and the passage of the *Charter of Rights and Freedoms*, dealt with the distribution of powers between the federal and provincial governments, as set out in the *Constitution Act, 1867*. When the validity of a statute is being challenged, the courts must first determine "the true nature" of the statute. In order to do so, the court must characterize the law, such as being primarily concerned with consumer credit, or tort liability, or the regulation of insurance, or real estate, or transportation or broadcasting. The court then determines the true nature of the legislation in terms of the heads of power as set out in sections 91 and 92. For example, banking is an area assigned to the federal government, while the building code or zoning legislation that affects the building of a bank is a matter falling within the competency of the municipality. The municipality has been given its authority by the provincial government, and this matter comes under the provincial jurisdiction of property and civil rights. If, however, the provincial government used its zoning power to prohibit the building of banks in any area except a particular zone in a city's downtown core, then this legislation would primarily regulate where banks could do business. Such a statute, although appearing to be zoning legislation, would, in its true nature, be banking legislation.

Determining the true nature of the legislation also determines its validity. If the level of government that was assigned that particular head of power passed the statute, then it is valid. The court will declare any statute that oversteps its assigned authority as invalid, or *ultra vires*, which simply means that it is beyond the power of the particular body. Such legislation would then be void.

Concurrent Jurisdiction

Some types of legislation overlap between the two levels of government and can be passed by either or both. For example, some driving offences fall within the provincial property and civil rights jurisdictions as well as the federal *Criminal Code*. There are also some areas in which concurrent jurisdiction is given to both the federal Parliament and the provincial legislatures. Subsection 92a(3), for example, gives the provinces power to deal with the export of natural resources, but also makes it clear that that power is to be concurrent with the federal Parliament's right to pass legislation in relation to trade and commerce. Old-age pensions, agriculture and immigration matters also involve some concurrent jurisdiction.

Federal Powers (Section 91)

The powers listed in section 91 of the *Constitution Act, 1867* that are given exclusively to the federal government are found in the Appendix at the end of the text, where the *Constitution Act, 1867* is set out in full. Our discussion will not deal with each of the specified areas; instead, we will look at a few areas of interest.

The Courts

The federal Parliament plays an important role in relation to the courts. It created the Federal Court, which hears cases directly related to the federal government, and the Supreme Court of Canada. It has also established specialized federal courts, such as the Tax Appeal Court.

Under section 91 of the *Constitution Act, 1867*, the governor general, who responds to the direction of the prime minister, has the responsibility of appointing judges to the superior courts of the provinces, including the courts of appeal, and the trial level superior court. The appointment power of the federal government clearly delineates between what can be classified as a superior or inferior court within the province. Provincial courts and magistrates' courts, as well as various administrative tribunals such as the Labour Relations Board, all have personnel appointed by the provincial government. Therefore, they do not qualify as, nor do they have the authority of, a superior court. Any attempt to give these provincial courts and tribunals the same power usually found in a superior court is invalid, unless that court has a federally-appointed judge. For example, attempts have been made in several provinces to establish a family court to deal not only with divorce, but also with maintenance and juvenile matters. When this attempt was made in British Columbia, it was declared invalid because the court was to be presided over by a provincially-appointed judge, which did not satisfy the requirement of section 96 of the *Constitution Act, 1867*. This court's powers subsequently had to be substantially curtailed and it could not deal with such matters as divorce.

With the exception of criminal cases, the court structure as well as the procedures followed in the courtroom are determined by each province. In fact, most provinces have adopted their court structures from the British example, with a provincial court of appeal and a trial level court having *superior* jurisdiction. Until recent times, most provinces had intermediate courts, such as county or district courts, as well as *inferior* courts, such as the magistrates' or provincial courts. These county and district courts have now been abolished in all provinces, and in most provinces the inferior courts have been amalgamated into one provincial court structure.

Criminal Law Enforcement

The federal Parliament has the power, as set out in subsection 91(27) of the *Constitution Act, 1867*, to determine criminal law matters in Canada. While the provinces are responsible for the structure of the provincial criminal courts under subsection 92(14), the procedure to be followed in these courts and the criminal law itself are federal matters. The police and the criminal prosecution resources fall within the provincial capacity as part of the administration of justice power under subsection 92(14). Although each province has the right to set up its own provincial police force, and each city and town can provide for its own policing, few provinces have gone that route. Most provinces, with the exception of Ontario and Quebec, have contracted with the Royal Canadian Mounted Police (RCMP), a national police force created by the federal government, to form their provincial police forces. In these cases, the RCMP comes under the control of the provincial governments contracting its services. As well, many municipalities have contracted with the RCMP for police services. The function of the RCMP, when contracted out to small jurisdictions, is to enforce not only the *Criminal Code* but also provincial statutes and municipal by-laws. The RCMP also has the responsibility for enforcing some federal statutes in all the provinces and municipalities, even where another police force is present.

The resources used to prosecute in criminal cases normally fall under the jurisdiction of the provincial attorney general. In addition to a formal organization, a number of local lawyers in some jurisdictions are given the contract to prosecute provincial and criminal offences. In the field of corrections, the federal government has jurisdiction over penitentiaries, in which sentences of two years or more are served, while the provincial government has jurisdiction over prisons, in which sentences of less than two years are served.

Trade and Commerce

Subsection 91(2) gives the federal government the power to make legislation with respect to "the regulation of trade and commerce." This is a broad-reaching power, but it does not give the federal Parliament the power to make all laws in relationship to trade and commerce. The provincial governments have the right to pass legislation in relationship to provincial trade and commerce matters under the subsection 92(13) property and civil rights provisions. The federal government's power in relation to trade and commerce is restricted to interprovincial and international trade. Only when a business carries on commercial activities beyond its provincial borders does the power of the federal government come into play. Grain and oil, however, are two areas in which the federal government's power to regulate has been extended to even local aspects of trade. The Supreme Court of Canada upheld the decision of a Manitoba Court of Appeal that declared the validity of a federal statute that not only regulated the interprovincial sale of wheat, but also regulated the sale of wheat grown in Manitoba to a local feed mill. The court found that control of the local trade was a necessary part of controlling the interprovincial and international trade. Thus, in these instances at least, the power of the federal government to regulate interprovincial trade and commerce has eclipsed any power a province has to regulate industry at the local level.

Transportation

Transportation is another area in which both the federal and the provincial governments have jurisdiction. Under subsection 92(10) of the *Constitution Act, 1867*, provincial governments have jurisdiction to make law in relation to "local works and undertakings." However, a series of exceptions are listed. These include shipping, railways, telegraphs, other works and undertakings that either connect the provinces or extend beyond their borders, as well as similar undertakings that connect a province with a British or other foreign country. A provision is also included in 92(10)(c) that allows the federal government to assume jurisdiction by declaring that a work is classified as one "for the general advantage of Canada or for the advantage of two or more provinces," even though such a work may be completely incorporated within one provincial boundary. Thus, railway lines, with the exception of those that operate exclusively within a province, are covered by federal legislation. Shipping, canals, and even bus lines and trucking companies are covered by federal legislation because they fall within this definition of a work or undertaking that is interconnective. There are also other provisions in the federal portion of the Act that affect interprovincial shipping and railway lines: Subsection 91(9) controls beacons, buoys and lighthouses; subsection 91(10) covers navigation and shipping; and subsection 91(13) covers ferries between provinces or between a province and another country.

Communications

Broadcasted communication, in the form of radio, television and telecommunications, also falls exclusively within federal jurisdiction because it is a matter of national concern. It has been suggested that, because radio waves do not respect provincial boundaries, the power to exercise control over radio and television is derived from 92(10). There is an important question left, however, as to whether the provincial government has authority to regulate cablevision and other forms of cable communications. In the *Capital Cities Communications v. CRTC* case,[8] the Supreme Court of Canada decided that cable television was an extension of normal broadcast and television communications and, therefore, fell under the complete control of the federal government. As the nature of cable-broadcasted television changes, however, this position may yet be challenged by the provinces. Even where federal control of television and other forms of broadcasted communication is certain, there are still some provincial laws of general scope that apply to the television medium. Quebec had a statute prohibiting the use of animated cartoon characters in advertising directed at children. In the *Attorney-General of Quebec v. Kellogg's of Canada* [9] case, the Supreme Court of Canada held that the Quebec legislation was valid and applied to all forms of advertising, not just to television. In other words, the statute was a law of general application.

Large telephone companies, such as Bell, and their operations are clearly within federal jurisdiction because they are interprovincial. It is likely that most telephone companies, even local ones, fall under federal jurisdiction because of their interconnectivity. However, the federal government has allowed the provinces to regulate local companies. Newspapers and other forms of publication, theatre, and the film industry all clearly fall within provincial jurisdiction, unless their activities can be identified as criminal. For example, if seditious libel, counselling for a criminal offence, or obscenity are involved, the *Criminal Code* applies.

International Treaties

The federal government has exclusive jurisdiction in the area of creating international treaties. Treaties between Canada and another country involve agreements between appropriate levels of government. When the *Constitution Act, 1867* was first passed, it was believed that Britain would be responsible for Canada's foreign affairs and so it was assumed that treaty-making power was vested in the British government. The *Constitution Act, 1867* does not specifically give any level of government authority to make treaties, although section 132 clearly gave the Canadian government the responsibility for ensuring that any treaty obligations Canada or the provinces have undertaken by reason of formerly being part of the British

Empire are adhered to. The only body now having international status sufficient to enter into treaties is the federal government, although some provinces, notably Quebec, have challenged this position. The implementation of such treaties, however, is another matter.

The Privy Council decided that the power to implement British Empire treaties, bestowed on Canada in section 132, does not by analogy extend to treaties entered into by the federal government. In the *Labour Conventions* case in 1937,[10] the Privy Council held that once the treaty was created, its domestic implementation required legislation. Which level of government had the authority to make laws in relation to the subject matter covered by the treaty depended on the provisions of sections 91 and 92. Because the Labour Convention treaties dealt with hours of work, minimum wages and so on, these were matters of a local nature and clearly fell within provincial jurisdiction. As a result, while only the federal government has the power to enter into treaties with foreign countries, if such treaties deal with matters that would normally fall under provincial jurisdiction, the federal government must seek the cooperation of the provinces in order to implement and enforce the treaty provisions. Of course, if a treaty were to fall in an area entirely within federal jurisdiction, as was the case with the *Radio Reference* case,[11] the cooperation of the provinces is not required.

Finally, although the federal government has exclusive jurisdiction to make treaties with foreign countries, it does not exclude the provincial governments from entering into arrangements with other countries or states, as long as those agreements are not intended to be binding under international law. Although not all provinces agree, it is generally accepted that when such arrangements are intended to be legally binding, they will constitute treaties, and thus must involve a cooperative exercise between the province and the federal government in reaching the agreement with the foreign country.

Native Indians

Another important power given to the federal government under section 91 was the power to pass legislation with respect to Native Indians and the lands reserved for them. This provision was included without the involvement or consent of the Native peoples, who heretofore had made all their treaty arrangements with England. This fact has become an important issue as Natives try to enforce the terms of original treaties. As it had the power to make laws for Natives, in 1868 the federal Parliament passed an "Act for the gradual civilization of Indian peoples," designed to assimilate Native people. Three tools of assimilation were advocated under the *Indian Act*. The first was the creation of reservations, which in most cases did not correspond to the traditional territories the tribes had occupied. Secondly, band councils with limited powers were appointed to replace tribal governments. The Act also defined who could be classified as Indian and to which band they belonged. Such paternalistic legislation has been the source of much anger and resentment among the First Nations people.

Another point of controversy in First Nations affairs is the fact that the *Constitution Act, 1867* did not give this power exclusively to the federal government. Native reserves did not become federal land simply because they were included in a treaty. Because ownership of land comes under provincial jurisdiction, provinces also can determine what land may be included in a reserve or which lands Native people can have access to. This has caused much conflict where treaty rights are in dispute. The *Indian Act* gives Natives certain rights and status, but because they are also subject to provincial law, those rights may not be enforceable in the province. Exceptions are listed that stipulate what kind of provincial laws would be inconsistent or in conflict with federal regulations relating to Natives or reserve lands. As well, any provincial law that specifically singles out Native Indians or reserve lands, or one that interferes with the federal government's power to pass laws in relation to Natives and reserve lands, would be invalid. Also, provincial laws that affect a Native's right to fish or hunt, or laws that interfere with the aboriginal and treaty rights contained in section 35 of the *Charter of Rights and Freedoms*, are also invalid. Subsection 35(1) recognizes and affirms the "existing aboriginal and treaty rights of the aboriginal peoples of Canada." Considerable court time has been expended trying to determine the meaning of the word *existing*. It has been established that existing rights are those that had not been extinguished when the *Constitution Act, 1982* was passed. But this changed with the Supreme Court decision in *Delgamuukw v. British Columbia* in December of 1997 since it affirmed subsection 35(1) of the *Constitution Act* and recognized aboriginal title to land as an aboriginal right and along with it an entitlement to the exclusive use and occupation of the land and its resources. It also affirmed that aboriginal title could be established through evidence of historical use of the land and not exclusively by existing treaties. The decision also affirmed that evidence of such historical use could be provided by oral histories.[12]

Taxation

Taxation is one of the most important powers associated with any level of government. Under subsection 91(3) of the *Constitution Act, 1867*, the federal government has the power to make laws in relation to "the raising of money by any mode of taxation." The federal government, therefore, is empowered to impose any taxation that can be borne within the society, whether the method be direct or indirect. The provincial governments' power of taxation, however, is somewhat limited. Under subsection 92(2), the provincial power to tax is limited to making laws in relationship to "direct taxation within the province in order to the raising of a Revenue for Provincial Purposes." Provincial sales taxes, which are imposed on the purchase of goods, are examples of such direct taxation. The manufacturer's sales tax that existed before 1991, however, is an example of an indirect or hidden tax. The *Constitution Act, 1982* broadened the powers of the provincial governments by conferring on them the right to levy an indirect, or excise, tax on the production of natural resources. This provision, which was included as an amendment to the *Constitution Act, 1867*, became section 92a. As a result of this power, provincial governments now have the right to impose excise taxes on forest resources, oil and gas, minerals, and even the exportation of electricity. Personal income tax, collected from individuals and corporations, is an example of a direct tax and, therefore, both the provincial and federal governments have the power to levy such taxes. Most provinces have entered into a cooperative scheme whereby the federal government collects both the federal and the provincial income taxes and then distributes the provinces' share back to them. Quebec, however, has retained a separate means of collecting provincial income taxes.

Natural Resources

Another important area in which both the federal and the provincial governments have jurisdiction is the field of natural resources. As a general rule, natural resources in the form of mineral deposits, oil and gas, wildlife, and even hydro-electric power fall within provincial jurisdiction. Note, however, that ownership of resources and the power to make laws in relation to them are two distinct questions. The provincial and the federal governments may each have designated crown lands and have proprietary rights in relationship to them. However, even federally-owned crown land located within provincial boundaries is subject to provincial laws designed to regulate those resources. Such resources located in the territories fall under the jurisdiction of the federal government, although it has delegated many of its powers relating to those natural resources to the territorial governments. Subsection 92a(3) gives the provinces the power to deal with the export of natural resources. However, it makes it specifically clear that that power is to be concurrent with the federal Parliament's right to pass legislation in relationship to trade and commerce.

In those areas of provincial jurisdiction in which natural resources are exploited, the federal government may have an impact on development and production. As a general rule, if the natural resource is produced and sold within the province, it falls under provincial control. However, because products of the mining, forestry, and fishing industries are sold both internationally and interprovincially, the sale of those items is clearly under federal control. The federal government not only can make regulations in relationship to the sale of those commodities, including applying quotas or restricting where they can be sold, but also has the right to levy excise taxes and other forms of fees when the items are sold. This federal control was a particularly contentious issue between Alberta and the federal government in relation to the federal energy policy on oil and natural gas produced by that province. The power of the provincial governments in relation to non-renewable, natural resources and hydro-electric power has been firmly established by the 1982 amendments to the *Constitution Act, 1867.*

Who owns resources found on the seabed off coastal provinces and who has the authority to regulate them is another important question debated in the courts. The *B.C. Offshore Reference* case,[13] which took place in 1967, firmly established that in the case of British Columbia such offshore rights are vested in the federal government, and that provincial boundaries end at the low-water mark of its shores. The undersea bed and any minerals located there were in federal territory and subject to federal regulations. In the Newfoundland offshore case,[14] that province attempted to establish that its status upon entering Confederation was different from British Columbia. This argument was rejected by the Supreme Court of Canada, which declared the territory and resources off Newfoundland's shores also subject to federal jurisdiction.

Paramountcy

The areas assigned in the *Constitution Act, 1867* are considered to be sources of power rather than lists of things. As a result there can be an overlap of powers between the federal and provincial governments. The same law could be passed validly by both the federal and the provincial governments, taken from different points of view and relying on different sources of powers. When this happens, there may be conflict. The doctrine of **paramountcy** simply states that when a valid provincial enactment and a valid federal enactment are in conflict, the federal legislation will prevail. The doctrine of paramountcy requires that federal law must be obeyed when an inconsistency exists between federal law and provincial law. This does not affect the validity of any other portion of the provincial law, however, other than that portion conflicting with the federal statute. As well, paramountcy does not make the provincial law invalid or illegal; rather, the federal statute simply overrides the provincial law. The topic of paramountcy only comes into play when valid provincial and federal legislation is in conflict. Because of the distribution of powers under the *Constitution Act,*

1867, such overlapping jurisdiction and conflict are rare occurrences. The operation of the rule of paramountcy, although important, is unusual.

Delegation Of Powers

There may be times when either the provincial or the federal governments wish to give up their power voluntarily to the other level of government. This is called delegation, and there are some severe limitations on its availability in Canadian constitutional law. In order to understand the restrictions on the power of the legislative bodies to delegate, one must first start with the proposition that, within the particular fields that have been assigned to them and with certain minor limitations, the powers of the federal government and of the provincial legislative assemblies are supreme. Any attempt by one level of government to give up its power to another level of government would change the distribution of power set down in the *Constitution Act, 1867*, and thus accomplish a constitutional amendment without going through the proper constitutional process. It is basic constitutional law in Canada, therefore, that the federal Parliament and the provincial legislative assemblies cannot give up their power by delegating it to the other level of government. This is not to say, however, that delegation does not take place.

In fact, a great deal of law, mainly in the form of regulations, is created through the use of delegated power. In such cases, however, power must be delegated to an inferior body. If a provincial legislature enacts a statute that delegates its power to create rules and regulations under an act to a minister or a lieutenant governor in council (the cabinet), then that provincial legislative assembly has given up no power. They have, rather, assigned the exercise of their power to an inferior body. Because the legislative assembly is supreme, the power still resides in it. Only if an abdication or surrender of parliamentary power takes place is delegation invalid. For example, the provincial and the federal governments believed it would be best to have an old-age pension scheme introduced at the federal level. Because old-age pensions fell under provincial jurisdiction, however, the provinces' attempts to give to the federal government their power to make law in relationship to old-age pensions were declared invalid. In the *Nova Scotia Inter-delegation* case,[15] the Supreme Court of Canada held that such an attempt at interdelegation of powers between the provincial and federal governments was invalid because, in effect, it altered the distribution of powers under the Constitution. Finally the provincial governments and the federal government had to turn to the Parliament of Great Britain to have the Constitution amended, in order to give the federal government the power to pass law in relation to old-age pensions.[16]

Delegating the exercise of power to an inferior body, such as a government agency or board, presents no such difficulty. The great body of regulations passed under various statutes are accomplished by incorporating a provision into the statute giving power to the minister or the cabinet to make the rules and regulations necessary to accomplish the purposes of the statute. The regulations created under this delegated power are usually greater in volume and in number than the actual statutes themselves. It is also common for the legislative body, through the statute, to delegate power to a board or an administrative tribunal charged with implementing the policies and provisions set out in the enabling statute. Thus, the employment insurance commissions, workers' compensation boards and labour relations boards in the various provinces all have been given a considerable amount of delegated power to carry out their mandates.

Federal and provincial governments found it possible to accomplish indirectly that which they could not do directly; that is, they could delegate their power to another level of government by using this principle of delegation to an inferior body. For instance, in the *Prince Edward Island Potato Marketing Board* case,[17] a marketing board had been created to govern and control the sale of potatoes in eastern Canada. Since Prince Edward Island was the most important producer of such potatoes, that province created the Prince Edward Island Potato Marketing Board and delegated to the board its regulatory powers relating to the sale of potatoes. The market for the sale of its potatoes, however, was primarily in Ontario and, to a lesser extent, in the other provinces of eastern Canada. The federal government wanted to give Prince Edward Island the power to regulate the sale of its potatoes outside the province, but it could not do so directly. To get around the prohibition in this instance, the federal government delegated to the Prince Edward Island Potato Marketing Board, just as the province of Prince Edward Island had done, its power to make regulations relating to the sale of potatoes. The Board then had delegated power delegated from both the federal and the provincial governments and was able to carry out its responsibilities without any difficulty. The federal government had not given up its power to another autonomous and sovereign legislative body; rather, it had delegated its authority to an inferior body, albeit a provincial one, and in the process did not give up any actual power.

Adoptive Legislation

Adoptive legislation is another way in which governments can get around the prohibition on the surrender of their legislative authority to another level of government. The government, federal or provincial, can accomplish adoptive legislation if it incorporates a provision in its legislation adopting a given provincial or federal statute, or portion thereof, as its own. For example, the federal government may include a section in the *Indian Act* declaring that provincial motor vehicle acts in the various provinces, as they then exist or are modified in the future, are adopted as federal legislation and apply to the Indian reserves located in those provinces. A similar type of delegation takes place when federal legislation is passed that gives the provinces the right to opt in or opt out. The *Lord's Day Act*, which was criminal law under federal jurisdiction (but no longer in force because of the Charter), prohibited certain types of activities on Sunday. This legislation applied throughout Canada. However, the legislation contained a clause that allowed the provinces to opt out of its operation. The result was that the *Lord's Day Act*, with its prohibition against Sunday activities, only applied in the few areas that had chosen not to opt out of its provisions.

Federal Intrusion into Provincial Areas

Historically, the federal government has not hesitated to declare a work to be "for the general advantage of Canada," thus bringing it under federal jurisdiction. For example, all grain elevators, flour mills, feed mills, feed warehouses and seed cleaning mills have been so designated. However, because the use of this declaratory power, contained in 92(10)(c), can be viewed as an unwarranted intrusion into the area of provincial powers, it has rarely been used in the last 40 years. Although the federal government does not make it a practice to use these legal powers or to take over these areas of jurisdiction, this is not to say that it does not use other extra-legal methods of interfering with and controlling provincial legislation.

One of the most effective methods employed by the federal government to involve itself in areas of provincial jurisdiction is that of exercising its taxation authority. By exerting its great spending power, it can put indirect pressure on the provinces to initiate policies in a particular area of provincial jurisdiction.

The power to make law in relation to education matters is one of the areas that has been assigned exclusively to provincial governments, with the exception of some assurances in section 93 of the *Constitution Act, 1867*, to ensure that the position of denominational schools is protected. Over the years, however, the federal government has developed great influence in the field of education within the provinces. This is especially true in the field of post-secondary education, as a result of a conditional grant program that the federal government developed with the provinces. In the 1950s, the federal government developed the practice of paying half the costs associated with post-secondary education. It also has direct control of education on Native reserves, military bases and in the territories, although in the latter case this authority has been delegated to the territorial governments of the Yukon, Nunavut and the Northwest Territories. As well, departments such as Canada Manpower, because of their specialized training programs, have become such significant customers of various provincial training schools that they can dictate the content of programs. The federal government exercises great influence in the provincial areas of health and welfare in the same way.

Provincial Powers (Section 92)

The most significant source of provincial power in the *Constitution Act, 1867* is subsection 92(13), which gives the provinces authority to pass laws in relation to "property and civil rights within the province."[18] The law in relation to commercial activities such as contracts of sale (provincial *Sale of Goods* statutes) is an example of this authority. Not all matters of private rights have been assigned to the provinces. Specific provisions in section 91 assign to the federal government certain private matters, such as banking, negotiable instruments, interest rates, bankruptcy, patents and copyrights. However, the property and civil rights clause is, in effect, a general catch-all provision that bestows tremendous powers upon the provinces.

Another catch-all provision of the *Constitution Act, 1867* is subsection 92(16), often referred to as a residuary power. It gives the provinces authority to make laws in relation to "all matters of merely local or private nature of the province." Under this section, the provincial governments clearly have the power to make laws in relation to such matters as labour relations, business activities, local trade and commerce and the regulation of professions, as well as various other commercial activities within the province. However, if any of these activities become extra-provincial in nature or are declared a work for the general advantage of Canada, they then come under federal jurisdiction.

There are many other areas, such as municipal institutions, shops, taverns, auctioneers and other licensed business establishments, that have been exclusively assigned to the provincial government. The maintenance of hospitals and long-term-care institutions are also provincial responsibilities. While the provinces have the power to regulate the incorporation of companies for provincial purposes, the federal government can regulate the incorporation of companies that carry on business in more than one province. Alternatively, companies can incorporate in one province and then register to do business in other provinces, thus avoiding federal involvement.

Constitutional Amendment

Autonomy appears to be the essence and the principal consequence of the patriation of the Canadian Constitution. In other words, Canada is exclusively responsible for amending its Constitution. Besides severing all British legislative ties, the *Constitution Act, 1982*, sections 38 to 45, sets out a formula for amending the Constitution. Some parts of the Act can be amended by federal Parliament alone; some can be amended by provincial legislatures through a simple legislative enactment. The federal government can do the same in relation to matters that concern the executive government of Canada, the Senate, or the House of Commons. In some other matters two thirds of the provinces, with 50% of the population, as well as the federal Parliament, must be in agreement. In some matters such as language rights, the role of the Queen or the Supreme Court there must be unanimity among all 11 governments.

This amending formula, as critics have pointed out, is flawed in at least two ways. The first criticism points to the difficulty in securing the consensus required for amendments. With this built-in impediment, few will have the tenacity to propose amendments that are likely to be objected to by one or more of the provinces. The second criticism relates to the practice of having only the prime minister or one of the premiers propose amendments, which means that constitutional reform will remain the preserve of a small group of party leaders. As constitutional expert Peter Hogg succinctly puts it, "When constitutional change must be initiated and agreed to by those who already wield the bulk of the political power, there is powerful reinforcement of the status quo."[19]

CONCLUSION

Constitution-building in Canada has been a process of assimilating the democratic and parliamentary traditions inherited from Britain, appropriating its laws and judicial systems and then working to achieve independence from the country that gave it birth. The *British North America Act* set out the structure and separation of powers in the new Dominion. Canada fared well under the British model of governance, which gave supreme power to Parliament and the legislatures in their respective jurisdictions. But there was no legal limitation on the power of the legislators. Canadians had to rely on convention and the political power vested in the election process to curtail the abuse of power by legislators and to ensure certain basic rights and freedoms. With the passing of the *Constitution Act, 1982*, however, Canada placed restrictions on the sovereignty of its Parliament and provincial legislatures, and thus created a slight but important shift in direction away from parliamentary supremacy. The next chapter examines the reasons why it was considered necessary to protect basic human rights and freedoms in a constitutional document and identifies the other legislation that Canadians can turn to when their rights have been infringed.

QUESTIONS FOR DISCUSSION AND REVIEW

1. What are the advantages and disadvantages of a "ready-made" constitution for a new nation?

2. The *British North America Act* was amended many times to accommodate the growth of Canada through acts of the British Parliament. Describe the nature of this constitutional constraint and the impact it had on Canada's development as a nation.

3. Quebec has not signed the *Constitution Act* of 1982. What have been some of the reasons and consequences of their not being party to the Act?

4. State some of the problems that are associated with majority rule and suggest how they might be overcome.

5. Should the British monarch still have representatives in Canada? Consider the benefits and drawbacks of such representation.

6. Discuss whether the effects of party discipline inhibit members of Parliament from representing their constituencies.

7. Consider instances when an elected official has acted beyond his powers and the response of the media and citizens in those circumstances.

8. Describe the role of the courts when applying statute law to a case.

9. The BNA Act divided the powers of the two levels of government. Discuss whether this division of powers is adequate to the demands of modern economic and political realities.

10. The amending formula for the Constitution is problematic. Suggest ways that constitutional amendments might be more efficiently and effectively accomplished.

NOTES

1. "No Act of Parliament of the United Kingdom passed after the commencement of the Act shall extend or be deemed to extend, to a Dominion as part of the law of the Dominion, unless it is expressly declared in that Act that that Dominion has requested, and consented to, the enactment thereof." *Statute of Westminster.*

2. *Statute of Westminster*, 1931 (U.K.), 22 Geo. V, c. 4.

3. Hogg, Peter. *Constitutional Law of Canada.* Toronto: Carswell, 1985, p. 13.

4. Clark, Premier Glen. "Your Guide to the Nisga'a Treaty." Victoria, BC: Government of British Columbia, 1998.

5. *Roncarelli v. Duplessis*, [1959] S.C.R. 121.

6. Re *Anti-Inflation Act*, [1976] 2 S.C.R. 373.

7. *Emergencies Act*, R.S.C. 1985 (4th Supp.), c. C-22.

8. *Capital Cities Communications v. CRTC*, [1978] 2 S.C.R. 141, 36 C.P.R. (2d).

9. *Attorney-General of Quebec v. Kellogg's of Canada*, [1978] 2 S.C.R. 211, 19 N.R. 271, 83 D.L.R. (3d) 314.

10. *Attorney-General of Canada v. Attorney-General of Ontario*, [1937] A.C. 326, 1 D.L.R. 673 (P.C.).

11. *Re Rankin v. R.*, [1940] Ex. C.R. 105.

12. *Delgamuukw v. British Columbia*, [1991] 3 S.C.R. 1010.

13. *Reference Re Offshore Mineral Rights (B.C.)*, [1967] S.C.R. 792.

14. *Re Nfld. Continental Shelf*, [1984] 1 S.C.R. 86.

15. *Attorney-General of Nova Scotia v. Attorney-General of Canada*, [1951] S.C.R. 31.

16. Section 94a, *Constitution Act, 1867.*

17. *Prince Edward Island Marketing Board v. Willis*, [1952] 2 S.C.R. 392.

18. The term "civil rights," as it is used here, does not refer to the human and civil liberties that are generally considered the subject matter of human rights codes and the *Charter of Rights and Freedoms*. Rather, the term refers to what we normally refer to as private law matters, as opposed to public law matters such as criminal law.

19. Hogg, p. 76.

FURTHER READING

Dawson, R.M. *Democratic Government in Canada.* Toronto: University of Toronto Press, 1971.

Fournier, Pierre A. *Meech Lake Post-Mortem.* Montreal: McGill-Queen's University Press, 1991.

Hawkes, David C. *Aboriginal People and Government Responsibility.* Ottawa: Carleton University Press, 1989.

Hogg, Peter W. *Constitutional Law of Canada.* Toronto: Carswell, 1977.

Lyon, N. and R.G. Atkey, eds. *Canadian Constitutional Law in Modern Perspective.* Toronto: University of Toronto Press, 1970.

Magnet, Joseph E. *Constitutional Law of Canada*, 2nd ed. Toronto: Carswell, 1985.

Scott, F.R. *Essays on the Canadian Constitution.* Toronto: University of Toronto Press, 1977.

4

PROTECTION OF
HUMAN RIGHTS

*If human rights and harmonious relations
between cultures are forms of the beautiful, then
the state is a work of art that is never finished.*

F. R. Scott

HUMAN RIGHTS LEGISLATION

The path of constitutional development in Canada has been one of adoption and adaptation. Canada adopted the British system, which honoured individual rights on the basis of tradition and long practice. These rights were understood and presumed; it was not, in most cases, found necessary to reduce them to writing. What safeguarded these rights was a democratic system of electoral representation and accountability and an independent judiciary that considered the rights of individuals and minority groups. As well, the nature of common law itself, which "tends to favour individual rights and freedoms when they come into conflict with state interests,"[1] provided a backstop when officials of the government acted beyond the bounds of the law. In the view of most Canadians, these protections worked well enough. However, when a number of blatant violations of basic human rights occurred and the traditional safety nets failed to function, legislators and jurists began to look at the system they had inherited and began to ask how it could be adapted to guarantee civil liberties and human rights.

The Americans had taken a different route in their journey toward independence. At an early stage of its national development, the United States enshrined constitutional provisions that were intended to ensure the racial, ethnic and religious equality of its citizens. The US Supreme Court was designated as the body with the responsibility for safeguarding those rights. For Canadians, however, the fundamental question was whether they should rely on an elected political body for the protection of rights and freedoms or on a non-elected, appointed court. While the history of Canada has generally been a peaceful, non-confrontational one, there have been significant examples of racial and religious intolerance, which in today's light seem to have been supported by discriminatory legislation and not appropriately redressed in a conservative court. There are some Canadians who can attest to the harmful effects of discriminatory legislation. Native people of Canada have been subjected to much paternalistic and destructive legislation; immigrant Chinese were charged a discriminatory head tax before they could enter Canada; and Japanese-Canadians were forced into internment camps and had their lands and property confiscated during World War II. The courts were no help in these situations. Statute law overrides common law, and because there was appropriately-passed legislation in place sanctioning such actions, these individuals found there was no law that could protect them. Could Canadians, then, rely on the political process to provide adequate protection to minority groups against the intolerance of the majority?

Rights Awareness

Before we can respond to that question, there are two aspects to the problem that must be considered. Individuals and groups can experience discrimination and intolerance from either their fellow citizens or their government. Although the harm caused is similar in both instances, the different sources of discrimination pose distinct problems from the point of view of constitutional and statutory law. It is not difficult for a government, with the political will to do so, to pass legislation designed to protect individuals against having their rights interfered with by others. Such person-to-person discrimination can be controlled simply by passing appropriate legislation within the federal and provincial legislatures, and by affording victims the opportunity to take their claims before a court, which can apply appropriate remedies. In our discussion concerning the human rights codes passed by government, it will become evident that ensuring basic human rights also depends on an aware and conscientious citizenry who have agreed to comply with the spirit of the law.

Providing protection for individuals against inappropriate or prejudicial conduct on the part of government is quite another question. It is small reassurance when a federal or provincial government passes legislation stating that no member of government can discriminate against individuals or groups if, because of the principle of parliamentary supremacy, that legislation can be changed or overruled by that government at any time. What is needed is some sort of constitutional guarantee that a government or its representatives cannot exercise such power without the possibility of having it challenged in the courts.

Rights v. Privileges

Before we proceed with a discussion of human rights legislation, it is important to clarify what we mean by rights and to distinguish them from the privileges we enjoy in a free and democratic society. People think of a **right** as something basic and protected, so that if another interferes with that right, some recourse is available. A **privilege**, on the other hand, is something that the state or other individuals have granted, which may be withdrawn at will. As a general rule, when a privilege is involved, such as a person granting another the privilege of walking across his property, the state will not interfere when such a privilege is withdrawn. When a right is involved, however, as would be the case when a person has an easement across another person's property, such a right can be enforced in the courts. When rights and privileges are dispensed by the state, things become a little more complex. There is little dispute that an established right ought to be enforceable in a court, even when that right is in relationship to the state, such as the right to vote or the right to live wherever one wants. However, when the state grants a privilege, should the state be free to withdraw that privilege at will? One of the effects of modern human rights legislation, as well as of the *Charter of Rights and Freedoms*, is that it restricts the conditions under which the state can withdraw such a privilege. For example, the state issues business licences, and that is generally considered a privilege. If a licence is refused or withdrawn because the person applying for it is of a particular ethnic origin, however, then that act, under the *Charter of Rights and Freedoms*, would be discriminatory and prohibited.

There are many different kinds of human rights. Those usually protected by legislation include political rights, which involve the obligation to hold elections and to allow freedom of speech and association in connection with those elections, as well as the right to vote. Freedom of the press is a political right as well. Economic rights include the right to hold private property and to earn a living. Equality rights preclude discrimination on the basis of a variety of factors. Legal rights ensure that people charged with an offence are accorded due process. Basically, provincial human rights acts protect rights to equal treatment, as well as economic rights in relation to property, employment, and wages. Political, legal and equality rights are protected by the *Charter of Rights and Freedoms*. A further distinction in the assignment of this responsibility can be made: provincial human rights acts protect against interference by individuals; the Charter protects people from interference by government.

Human Rights Under Common Law

Until the middle of the twentieth century, individuals whose personal rights had been violated had to rely on the courts for a remedy. The basis for the courts' decisions rested on common law, which had few provisions specifically designed to protect human rights. "The common law's position is that a person is free to do anything that is not positively prohibited."[2] And government was free to override what few common law protections were protecting human rights simply by passing appropriate legislation. Only the passage of legislation specifically designed to protect human rights and the adoption of a bill of rights that was immune from ordinary legislative change could guarantee civil liberties.

Jurisdiction

Under the Canadian system of parliamentary supremacy, Parliament and the legislative assemblies were free to pass any sort of legislation appropriate to their fields of jurisdiction. The sole question of concern to the courts was whether or not a particular provincial or federal enactment fell within the power of that level of government. The courts made it clear that whether or not legislation made a good use of power was not within their jurisdiction. They ruled only on the question of whether the power to pass the law fell to the province or to the federal government. The function of the court was not to limit this power in any way, nor to determine whether the law was good, bad or discriminatory; the court's job was to determine whether the legislature or Parliament had jurisdiction in that field under the *Constitution Act, 1867* and whether it had exceeded that power.

PROVINCIAL HUMAN RIGHTS ACTS

A number of steps were taken by provincial governments to legislate against racial discrimination, beginning with Ontario's *Racial Discrimination Act* in 1944. British Columbia and Saskatchewan followed within the next few years with limited legislation prohibiting racial and religious discrimination. Subsequently, all provinces passed some form of legislation guaranteeing basic human rights and freedoms, initially in specific areas such as social assistance and fair employment practices as well as in the field of accommodation and services, such as restaurants and hotels. Typically, such legislation was found in various statutes, but finally it became the practice to consolidate the statutes into one provincial human rights act or code. Private matters between individuals is a provincial concern. What legislation is in place varies from province to province. By the end of the 1960s, most provinces had in place basic human rights legislation prohibiting discrimination on the basis of race, religion and ethnic origin. Most provincial acts prohibit discrimination in the granting of publicly available accommodations and services, such as restaurants, hotels and apartment buildings.

A major area in all provincial human rights legislation prohibits discrimination in the field of employment and wages, but where the qualification is a bona fide requirement for the job, such as size or physical strength for firefighters or construction workers, it may be permissible. There is, however, a duty to accommodate the needs of workers when it places no great hardship on the business. Thus, the religious tenet of Seventh-Day Adventists not to work on Saturday, their Sabbath, may have to be accommodated by a rearrangement of shifts. When disabled workers are involved it may be necessary to widen the aisles and install lifts so that they can do their jobs. Another important provision passed by all jurisdictions and contained variously in employment standards legislation or the labour codes of the provinces is the requirement of equal pay for equal work, with no discrimination allowed on the ground of gender.

Another important area in which human rights legislation prohibits discrimination is the field of property occupancy, including sales and rental. All jurisdictions in Canada prohibit discrimination in this area, although there are exceptions where bathroom, sleeping or cooking facilities are shared. Most provinces also prohibit discrimination in the sale of property. Another important provision of human rights legislation protects complainants from retaliation, such as employment termination or eviction.

Who Is Protected by the Legislation?

There are significant limitations on this protection, however, because the statutes usually do not affect private relations between individuals. For example, someone renting a room in his or her house could not be prevented from discriminating against people of other racial, religious or ethnic groups. In all provinces, discrimination is prohibited not only in employment opportunities and wages but also in determining membership in professional organizations, such as law societies and medical associations. Some provinces have not included any protection against discrimination on the basis of sexual orientation. Until the Supreme Court made it clear that they would impose this protection even when it wasn't mentioned in the provincial act,[3] homosexuals could not be assured of obtaining many of the benefits afforded a spouse. Just how far these rights for same-sex couples extend, however, is still not clear. Today, a particular concern is the area of privacy, especially with regard to invasive methods of gathering and storing information. Several provinces have now adopted legislation designed to protect individual privacy. Currently, access and distribution of consumer credit information, as well as information held by governments and their agencies, is controlled under provincial human rights legislation. One of the most significant advancements of modern human rights legislation is the protection now provided individuals against sexual harassment and retaliation for spurned attentions not only by superiors in the employment organization but also from fellow workers.

In *Vriend v. Alberta* the Supreme Court of Canada found that the failure to include sexual orientation in the Alberta human rights legislation infringed the section 15 Charter right to equality and that sexual orientation can be read into the legislation. Vriend was employed as a laboratory coordinator by a college in Alberta. He revealed that he was a homosexual and the college terminated his employment. The sole reason given was his non-compliance with the college's policy on homosexual practice. The court determined that the omission of sexual orientation as a protected ground in the provincial human rights legislation creates a distinction between homosexuals and heterosexuals. The exclusion of the ground of sexual orientation, considered in the context of the social reality of discrimination against gays and lesbians, clearly has a disproportionate impact on them as opposed to heterosexuals. It denies substantive equality to the former group. The court decided that sexual orientation would be read into the impugned provisions of the Act as the most appropriate way of remedying this under inclusive legislation.[3]

The British Columbia Act

Differences do exist in the legislation of the various provinces with respect to discrimination, although those differences are small because of the requirement that they comply with the *Charter of Rights and Freedoms*. We will refer to the BC statute to illustrate the contents of most acts and point out differences in the Ontario Act. In British Columbia, the *Human Rights Code* applies to publications, the provision of accommodation services and facilities, employment, advertising for employment, wages, belonging to unions and professional associations, tenancy arrangements and the purchase of property. Ontario expands this to include harassment in employment and accommodation as well as discrimination in contracts generally, not just for the purchase of property. Discrimination is prohibited on the basis of race, colour, ancestry, place of origin, religion, marital status, physical or mental disability, sex and sexual orientation. Ontario includes citizenship and family status as well. This prohibition also extends in specified areas to discrimination on the basis of age, political belief (in BC) and a conviction unrelated to the area of employment. Ontario also prohibits discrimination on the basis of receiving public assistance where accommodation is concerned. In British Columbia the age for the purposes of discrimination is between 19 and 65 whereas in Ontario it is 18 and 65. There is no prohibition against age discrimination in British Columbia with respect to accommodation and service or with respect to the sale of property whereas in Ontario there is. In the field of employment and membership in unions and associations, the list is further extended to preclude discrimination because of a conviction on a criminal or summary charge that is unrelated to the intended employment. It should be noted that there are exceptions to this prohibition against discrimination. In BC and Ontario it is permissible to discriminate with respect to employment if the discrimination is based on a bona fide occupational requirement with respect to sex, a requirement of public decency, with respect to age, seniority or retirement or with respect to tenancy arrangements, where the facilities are shared or the rental unit is designated for a particular group.

The British Columbia legislation provides for the creation of a Human Rights Commission, consisting of a chief commissioner, a deputy chief commissioner and a commissioner of investigation and mediation. The corresponding body in Ontario is also called the Human Rights Commission. A person can file a complaint with the Commissioner of Investigation and Mediation, or the Commissioners can file complaints on their own. The Commissioner of Investigation has extensive power to investigate and also has the power to dismiss matters where appropriate or encourage a mediated settlement. If not dismissed or settled, the disputed matter goes before a Human Rights Tribunal for a hearing and adjudication. In Ontario the Human Rights Commission receives or initiates a complaint which, if not settled or dismissed, goes to the Board of Inquiry for a hearing. The Human Rights Tribunal (and Ontario's Board of Inquiry) have a considerable amount of discretionary power including the right to dismiss the complaint, order a person to comply with the provisions of the Act, require offenders to take steps to correct the problem, or order the payment of compensation for any wages lost or other damage done. In Ontario the Board of Inquiry also has the power to assess up to $10 000 compensation for mental anguish, and in that province the attorney general can opt to treat the matter as an offence, with a fine up to $25 000. In BC the decision of the tribunal is final, whereas in Ontario the decision of the board can be appealed to the divisional court. It is interesting to note that while the statutes are striking in their similarity, the provinces manage to maintain considerable uniqueness in their approach to human rights.

While the nature of discrimination has undergone breathtaking change, Canada's system of human-rights enforcement has scarcely changed in the 35 years since Ontario opened the doors of the country's first commission...

The commissions were required to investigate every complaint, but were granted wide latitude to reject cases where there seemed little evidence of discrimination...

Years later, the legal grounds for discrimination have tripled to include less blatant, more pervasive human-rights abuses. A barrage of new and bewildering complaints — none more tortuous than sexual-harassment allegations — has been unleashed. And as increasing numbers of people with credible stories of discrimination have been turned away by a besieged commission, the power to toss out cases at will has come under scrutiny.

"It seems to me we as Canadians have to begin to rethink our whole approach to human-rights enforcement," says Catherine Frazee, former chief commission of the Ontario Human Rights commission, now a human-rights consultant.

"The whole infrastructure we've set up for human-rights enforcement is far too cumbersome for the handling of individual complaints, and is not appropriately being focused on the identification and removal of barriers and the addressing of systemic issues."

Philp, Margaret. "Drowning in Grievances."
The Globe and Mail, December 6, 1997, p. D12.

Implementing the Legislation

All of the provincial statutes authorize provincial commissions or boards to deal with human rights complaints. The commission has the power to hear complaints as well as to investigate and adjudicate. In many provinces, the commission also has the right to initiate the process. After the appropriate procedure has been followed, it falls to the discretion of the board to decide on and apply the remedy. Usually, the board has the right to levy a fine or issue an injunction against the perpetrator. These remedies are within the discretion of the board. They are not within the control of the complainant, as is the case in a civil tort action. We will look in more detail at the role of commissions and tribunals in Chapter 6 of the text. It should be pointed out, as is suggested in the above excerpt from the *Globe and Mail*, that claimants dissatisfied with the decision of a human rights tribunal have limited access to appeal the decision. A court will normally only review the matter if it is clear that the decision-makers have failed to give the complainant a fair hearing and not on whether the complaint itself has merit.

FEDERAL HUMAN RIGHTS STATUTES

The first federal human rights statutes were designed to prohibit discrimination in restaurants and other service industries. In 1977 the federal government passed the *Canadian Human Rights Act*,[4] which corresponds with the provincial acts, prohibiting discriminatory practices between individuals in those areas within federal jurisdiction, such as the broadcast industry, national parks and airlines.

The *Canadian Bill of Rights*

All the provincial and federal statutes in place could do nothing to protect individuals against discriminatory conduct on the part of government. Officials may have been governed by provincial human rights legislation or the federal *Human Rights Code* and could be charged if found in violation, but nothing prevented the government from amending, appealing or simply overriding the provisions of human rights legislation with another statute. In fact, specific provisions existed that protected government officials from being held responsible for such wrongful conduct. To prevent federal and provincial governments from introducing statutes that violated fundamental rights and freedoms, a sure-fire method was needed to restrict the kind of legislation that could be passed.

In reaction to the treatment of Japanese-Canadians during World War II, as well as to other injustices that took place after the war, especially in relation to the Cold War anti-communist scare, Canadians began to feel that some means should be found to guarantee the rights of citizens. The CCF, predecessor of the New Democratic Party, first introduced a motion into Parliament for the establishment of a bill of rights for Canada. The move was unsuccessful, but the matter continued to be studied by various parliamentary committees. In 1957, the Conservatives, under John Diefenbaker, came to power. In 1960, they fulfilled an important campaign promise by enacting the *Canadian Bill of Rights*.

Preamble

The *Canadian Bill of Rights* begins with a preamble that affirms the Parliament of Canada's commitment to the "supremacy of God, the dignity and worth of the human person and the position of the family in the society of free men and free institutions." The *Bill of Rights* was created to enshrine the principles of "human rights and fundamental freedoms." While this preamble has no authority as legislation, it does set the tone for the following binding provisions.

Section 1 recognizes certain basic rights that should be shared by everyone and should continue without discrimination "by reason of race, national origin, colour, religion or sex." These rights are:

a. individual rights to life, liberty, security of person, the enjoyment of property, and the right not to be deprived thereof except by due process of law;

b. the right of the individual to equality before the law and protection of the law;

c. freedom of religion;

d. freedom of speech;

e. freedom of assembly and association; and

f. freedom of the press.

An Overriding Statute

The second and perhaps most important section of the *Bill of Rights* declares that any Canadian statute must be "construed and applied" in such a way that it not take away from (abrogate, abridge or infringe) those rights and freedoms recognized in the *Bill of Rights*. The areas to which this principle particularly applies are then listed. These are more particular expressions or expand the rights listed in section 1, such as freedom from arbitrary detention, imprisonment, exile, and cruel and unusual punishment. Under the Bill, a person arrested or detained has the right to be informed of the reason for such arrest or detention, the right to retain and instruct counsel, and the right to be brought before a judge within a certain time after arrest. The *Bill of Rights* contains a provision prohibiting a court or any other tribunal or board from compelling a person to give evidence without benefit of counsel, and another protecting against self-incrimination, as well as the right to a fair hearing according to the principles of fundamental justice. When charged with a criminal offence, a person has the right to be presumed innocent until proven guilty. The *Bill of Rights* sets out that an arrested person has the right to a reasonable bail and to the services of an interpreter, if needed.

Limitations of Bill of Rights

While the *Bill of Rights* provides a guideline by which all federal statutes must be interpreted, there are several important limitations on its operation. The first limitation is that the Bill is federal legislation and applies only to federal law, including federal statutes, regulations and the conduct of federal officials. The second limitation is that the provision allows the federal government to override its provisions simply by stating that the new legislation applies notwithstanding the *Canadian Bill of Rights*. The third limitation is that, because it is federal legislation, it can be amended or repealed simply by parliamentary enactment of further legislation. The Bill was not, and could not be, entrenched as part of the Constitution. As a result of this status at law, the courts were very reluctant to interpret it liberally, as overriding legislation.

Because the *Bill of Rights* is only a federal statute, there are considerable difficulties in its application. First, it is questionable how it should affect legislation already in place. There were similar difficulties with rules of statutory interpretation for statutes that were passed after the *Bill of Rights*. It was finally decided under the *Drybones* case[5] that the human rights sections of the *Bill of Rights* made inoperative any legislation passed beforehand that was inconsistent with it. In that case, the federal *Indian Act* made it illegal for an Indian to be intoxicated off the reserve. The Supreme Court declared that that section of the *Indian Act* was inoperative because the racial classification "Indian" was a breach of paragraph 1(b) of the *Bill of Rights*. This led to other, albeit unsuccessful, challenges of the use of the term "Indian" in other sections of the *Indian Act*.[6] The court also specified a method by which such inconsistent legislation must be passed. It must be enacted with a declaration that it is to stand "notwithstanding" the *Bill of Rights*. The *Drybones* decision was the only time the Supreme Court of Canada used the *Bill of Rights* to declare a statute inoperative.

Another serious limitation on the effectiveness of the *Canadian Bill of Rights* has been in the judicial interpretation it received in the courts. Over the years, the tendency has been to find a way around applying the *Bill of Rights* to federal legislation. Although the Bill was intended to apply to both past and future enactments, the Supreme Court has generally, with the exception of the *Drybones* case referred to above, refused to apply it to cases that deal with legislation in place before its passage. The *Bill of Rights* has been interpreted very narrowly and has become little more than a statute setting out rules of construction for legislation and regulations. In 1970 and 1971, amendments were made to the Bill to try to make it more effective, including the requirement that all federal regulations be vetted by the clerk of the Privy Council to ensure that they do not "trespass unduly" on the rights and freedoms set out in the Bill. It soon became clear, however, that something more was needed. It was not long before the federal and provincial governments were involved in conferences to design a bill of rights that could be broadly interpreted and entrenched in the Constitution. Although it has been largely overshadowed by the passage of the *Charter of Rights and Freedoms* in 1982, it must be emphasized that the *Bill of Rights* is still law in Canada and contains important provisions with respect to the interpretation of federal law.

Due Process

The only provisions of the *Bill of Rights* that are broader than the Charter and thus have force today are the due process clauses that relate to property (paragraph 1(a)) and paragraph 2(e), which extends the right to a fair hearing for the determination of rights and obligations. Paragraph 1(a) of the Bill states that Canadians have the following human rights: the right to "life, liberty, security of person, enjoyment of property and the right not to be deprived thereof except by due process of law." The *Charter of Rights and Freedoms* contains no such guarantee in relationship to property rights. Paragraph 2(e) states that "no law of Canada shall be construed or applied so as to deprive a person of a fair hearing in accordance with the principles of fundamental justice for the determination of his rights and obligations." While section 7 of the Charter provides that everyone has a "right to life, liberty and the security of person and the right not to be deprived thereof, except in accordance with the fundamental principles of justice," it says nothing about the right to have a hearing to determine those rights and freedoms. With the exception of these two sections, the *Bill of Rights* no longer has any practical significance. When the *Constitution Act, 1982* was enacted, it included a list of other acts that had constitutional standing, including several federal acts. The *Bill of Rights* was not numbered among them. For our purposes, the *Bill of Rights* must be viewed as important because it set the scene for the passage of the *Charter of Rights and Freedoms*. It was a stepping-stone in the process of entrenching fundamental rights and freedoms in the Constitution.

INTERNATIONAL HUMAN RIGHTS LEGISLATION

Before we continue our discussion of Canadian human rights laws, it is worth noting that Canada is bound by a number of international human rights treaties. In 1976 Canada became a party to the *International Covenant on Civil and Political Rights*. Because it is a treaty, it is not a part of Canada's domestic law and, therefore, it is not enforceable in the courts. However, it does apply to relations between the countries that have signed the covenant. Not only are the rights set out in the treaty very similar to those later entrenched in the *Charter of Rights and Freedoms*, but also the language used and the interpretations applied to the Covenant have been very influential and persuasive in decisions based on the Charter.[7]

THE *CANADIAN CHARTER OF RIGHTS AND FREEDOMS*

After a long series of conferences dealing with constitutional reform, the process culminated in the passage of the *Constitution Act, 1982*. The first purpose of this act was to sever the ties Canada had with Great Britain and to give the government of Canada sole responsibility for changing or amending the Constitution. Thus the Constitution was "patriated" and the last vestiges of colonialism were eliminated, with the single exception that the Queen of England remained the Queen of Canada. The second major feature of the Constitution Act was the inclusion of the *Canadian Charter of Rights and Freedoms*.

Its Limitations

The main feature of the Charter, its main advantage and, in a curious sense, its main limitation, is the fact that it only applies to the dealings of government. It does not attempt to control the relationships between individuals, but rather to control the relationships between individuals and government institutions. Section 32 of the Charter makes it clear that the provisions are limited in their application to government institutions. The demarcation between where governmental function ends and interpersonal relationships begin is often not clearcut. Thus, there is some question as to just what functions of government the Charter affects. For example, does the Charter apply to Crown corporations carrying on normal corporate business in competition with other corporations? The answer must be determined by examining the function of the Crown corporation or government agency to determine whether it is acting as an arm of government or in a private capacity. If it has a government function, then it is likely that the Charter applies.

Its Scope

Even with this limitation, however, the *Charter of Rights and Freedoms* does have an impact on human rights, not only within the provinces but also in interpersonal relationships. The provincial human rights legislation designed to regulate these interpersonal relationships is an act of government, or a statute. The terms of these provincial human rights codes must not be inconsistent with the provisions of the Charter. Therefore, while interpersonal relationships may not be directly controlled by the Charter, they are indirectly affected by it because of the Charter's overriding control of legislative enactments, including the provincial and federal human rights statutes.

There is another important consideration. Although section 32 of the Charter indicates that it applies to legislative or parliamentary bodies and the statutes created by them, it also applies not only to the regulations created by government agencies, but also to the conduct of government officials employed in these agencies. Government officials derive their authority from provincial or federal enactment; in fact, they must be able to point to a statute to authorize everything they do. If they are acting in a way that is inconsistent with the Charter, then either they are doing something unauthorized or the statute itself, or part of it, is invalid under the Charter. While the direct effect of the Charter on government institutions is extremely important, its indirect impact on all elements of society that rely on statutory authority broadens the impact of the Charter considerably.

The Role of the Courts

The Charter's greatest impact may be the way it affects the traditional concept of parliamentary supremacy and the role of the courts. Prior to 1982, Canada followed the British example, in which parliament was supreme and, subject only to the division of powers between federal and provincial governments, had the power to do anything it wanted within its sphere. With the passage of the Charter, Canadian courts have gained some veto power over laws enacted by parliamentary bodies. Traditional parliamentary supremacy dictated that when parliament passed a statute, it overrode prior judge-made law. Now, however, the courts have the power to declare that certain enactments are beyond the power of both the federal and the provincial governments. Thus, the courts now have the power to override parliament in determining law in this country.

To fully appreciate the increased status of the courts, there are two other features of the *Charter of Rights and Freedoms* that must be understood. First, the *Constitution Act, 1982* is now entrenched as the supreme law of Canada. Section 52 declares that the "Constitution is the supreme law of Canada and any law that is inconsistent with the provisions of the Constitution is, to the extent of the inconsistency, of no force or effect." This section also declares that the *Canada Act*, which includes the *Constitution Act, 1982*, which in turn includes the *Charter of Rights and Freedoms*, is part of that Constitution. As such, the provisions of the Charter, as well as other constitutional provisions, must be adhered to. They override other inconsistent enactments and can only be changed in the way provided in the Constitution itself; that is, by following the amending process set out in Part V of the *Constitution Act, 1982*.

The second major feature that contributes to the power of the courts is the broad terminology used to set out the basic rights and freedoms contained in the Charter. The courts have traditionally interpreted statutes in a very narrow and restrictive way, leading legislators to be very precise and specific when they draw up the statutes. The Charter, however, is composed of broad, sweeping terms and generalizations. It is left to the courts to determine their meaning. The courts were put in the position of either having to reject the provisions of the Charter out of hand because they were too vague, or having to rise to the challenge of interpreting its provisions, thus creating a new body of law. Because the Charter is an entrenched, constitutional document, it could not be treated as an ordinary statutory enactment. Therefore, the courts have chosen to embark on the process of constitutional interpretation, which has created and will continue to create new law. Thus, a fundamental change in the nature of Canadian governmental institutions has occurred, which not only places more power and authority in the courts as the final arbiters of an individual's rights, but also limits the supremacy of Parliament and the legislative assemblies. Canadian courts now look more like the activist American courts, which provide a check on the power of Congress and the president.

Qualifications

Section 1

There are two extremely important qualifications on the application of the Charter, which are set out in sections 1 and 33. The first section states that the Charter guarantees the rights and freedoms contained therein, "subject only to such reasonable limits prescribed by law as can be demonstrably justified in a free and democratic society." Simply stated, the freedoms and rights, although expressed in sweeping and unqualified terms, are not absolute. Legislation passed by federal and provincial governments that limits rights and freedoms would be valid if it could be demonstrated that such legislation was reasonably justified. For example, the Charter guarantees freedom of expression, but few would question the prohibition of libel, slander or hard-core pornography. While enshrining the basic nature of freedom of expression, the Charter allows for valid laws restricting that freedom if it infringes on the rights of others. In *Hill v. Church of Scientology*[8] the Supreme Court of Canada made it clear that they would not follow the American approach of overriding defamation in the name of free speech when public officials were involved. They allowed a defamation award in favour of a federal employee who had been defamed by representatives of the church. The rules of defamation were a reasonable limitation on freedom of expression.

Another example of the need, at certain times, to set limitations on rights is the *Emergencies Act* (formerly the *War Measures Act)*. In the future, it is likely that invoking the powers under the various parts of the *Emergencies Act* will be challenged under the Charter. It would then have to be established to the satisfaction of the courts that the emergency was threatening enough to justify such a restriction of basic rights.

The American *Bill of Rights* does not contain a provision like section 1 of the Charter. As a result, the US Supreme Court had to create such a clause through judicial interpretation that allowed for reasonable qualifications on the listed basic rights and freedoms. There is little debate, then, that a limitation on the absoluteness of the rights set out in the Charter was necessary. The problem for the courts is how to determine when such a qualification is reasonable. This problem faced the Supreme Court of Canada in the *Oakes* case.[9] Under the *Narcotics Control Act*, once a person is found guilty of possession of a prohibited drug, the onus shifts to him or her to show that he or she didn't have the drug for the purpose of trafficking, a much more serious offence. This provision clearly infringed the protection of the presumption of innocence found in paragraph 11(d) of the Charter. In the *Oakes* case the Supreme Court had to decide if an infringement such as this reverse onus clause was reasonably justified. The court developed a two-pronged test that had to be satisfied to have section 1 operate. The test requires that the infringing law has as its objective a purpose that is sufficiently important to justify infringing the Charter right, and secondly that the means used to accomplish this objective are reasonable. Whether the exception is reasonable requires that the law in question be carefully designed to accomplish the goal stated, that it go no further than is necessary to accomplish that goal, and finally that there be a proportionate effect, which means essentially that the solution isn't worse than the problem. In applying this test, the court decided such a reverse onus clause was not reasonably justified and therefore was not valid in criminal matters.

Section 33

The second major limitation is the "notwithstanding clause," which states:

> Parliament or the legislature of the province may expressly declare in an Act of Parliament or the legislature as the case may be, that the Act or a provision thereof, shall operate notwithstanding a provision included in section 2 or sections 7 to 15 of the Charter.

Invoking this term allows a government to enact legislation that contravenes or overrides the noted sections. It may seem a relatively minor qualification until one considers that section 2 covers fundamental freedoms, sections 7 to 14 contain legal rights, and section 15 is concerned with equality rights. Only democratic rights, mobility rights, language rights, minority language education rights and some other sections of the Charter cannot be touched by the legislatures.

The framers of the Charter felt that political pressure, which plays such an important role in the democratic process, would discourage a government from invoking this clause except in rare and extenuating circumstances. In 1989 the government of Quebec used the notwithstanding clause to override the equality rights of the Charter in order to permit only French-language business signs in Quebec.[10] This caused an outcry in the rest of the country because it set a precedent that seemed to allow governments to opt out of these sections of the Charter at will. This one event played a significant role in the failure of the Meech Lake Accord.

Note, however, that the notwithstanding clause does not give provincial legislatures the power to pass laws that they would not otherwise have under the *Constitution Act, 1867*. For example, matters dealing with freedom of religion clearly fall within federal power. Any attempt to override the Charter using the notwithstanding clause in this area would have to be done by the federal, not the provincial government.

Sunset Clause — Subsection 33(3), referred to as the "sunset clause," puts one significant limitation on the operation of the notwithstanding clause. It states that, when legislation is passed overriding Charter rights through the use of section 33, the operation of that statute will cease after five years. In effect, this subsection requires the overriding statute, if it is intended by the government to continue over the years, to be renewed every five years through the passage of new legislation. This ensures that the matter will again come up for debate on the floor of the legislature or Parliament. While this process does not overcome the criticism levelled at the notwithstanding clause, it does go some distance to ameliorate its negative effects.

While section 33 seems to be a devastating retreat from the protections set out in the Charter, it must be remembered that these rights are only as valid as the will of democratic institutions to adhere to its provisions. Many countries that are considered oppressive totalitarian states have in their constitutions basic protections covering civil rights. The protections are ineffective, because these countries lack the democratic traditions and requisite will to make them effective. Ultimately, therefore, the protection of basic civil liberties depends on the will of the government more than on any enacted legal summary of those rights. Because section

33 merely reconveys the power to protect civil liberties to the parliamentary level of government rather than to the courts, it may not be as great a threat to the operation of the Charter as it appears. We must rely on either our judges or our elected representatives to protect our basic rights and freedoms, while realizing that either can let us down. Section 33 restores some of the aspects of parliamentary supremacy that other terms of the Charter took away.

Terms of the Charter

Fundamental Freedoms

The basic rights and freedoms set out in the Charter can be divided into separate categories. The first category includes fundamental freedoms. These are set out in section 2, which provides for freedom of conscience and religion. Freedom of religion is the right to hold personal religious beliefs and ideas about a supreme being. Freedom of conscience is an expansion of that right, and relates to ideas and principles that may not be based on the belief in a supreme being. The protection extends to the right to practise those beliefs in worship and other activities associated with the religion or conscience, as long as they are not illegal in their nature. Paragraph 2(b) provides for freedom of thought, belief, opinion and expression. It includes freedom of the press and other media of communication. These principles are fundamental to a free, democratic society, and their protection is vital. It should be emphasized, however, that there are many limitations on freedom of expression and freedom of speech. Laws against libel, slander, obscenity, hate and pornography put reasonable boundaries on freedom of expression.

There are fewer limits imposed on the freedom of the press, because an unfettered press is essential to a democratic system. Even the press, however, may have limits placed on its freedom of expression, providing those limits are reasonable. Thus the normal rules of defamation apply to the press as well as to private individuals. In contrast to the United States, if an individual is defamed, whether or not malice is involved, the media outlet will be held liable and be required to compensate the defamed individual.

Paragraphs 2(c) and (d) of the Charter provide for freedom of peaceful assembly and freedom of association. These provisions protect the right of people to gather and associate in groups and to meet as they wish. However, riotous assemblies or violent activities cannot be supported under these provisions. Many jurisdictions have in place legislation restricting certain kinds of people such as managers from joining trade unions. Some employees, such as those in essential services, may have their right to strike or picket restricted. These statutes now must qualify as reasonable limits to the fundamental freedoms of association and assembly.

Democratic Rights

The second category of rights protected by the Charter is the democratic rights set out in sections 3, 4, and 5. While it is likely true that basic democratic rights were covered by constitutional convention before the Charter was enacted, the Charter enshrines them as constitutional principles. The rights contained in these sections cannot be overridden with the operation of section 33. For the first time, the right to vote is guaranteed for all citizens of Canada. Historically, particular groups of people have been excluded from voting in federal and provincial elections, including Asians during the first half of this century, women before 1920, and young people today. In *Sauve v. Canada*[11] the court had to decide whether the practice of denying prisoners in federal penitentiaries the right to vote could be justified under section 1. This denial clearly infringed their rights under section 3 of the Charter, and the court found that such an infringement could not be reasonably justified under section 1. For such an exclusion to be valid today, it would have to be a reasonable limit within the context of section 1. This may justify the exclusion of those who are under age or mentally incompetent. Section 3 specifically limits the right to vote to Canadian citizens. This right, as well as the limitations on it, pertains only to federal and provincial elections. Municipal elections are not covered by this provision. Section 3 also provides that all Canadian citizens have the right to be candidates in elections. Prior to the passage of the Charter, provincial and federal civil servants were prohibited from participating in political activities. They now have the right to be candidates and to participate fully in the political process.

Section 4 provides that elections must be held at least every five years, except in times of "real or apprehended war, invasion or insurrection." Even then, the continuation of the government without an election must not be opposed by more than one third of the members. Within this restriction, at both the provincial and the federal levels, the party in power has the right to determine when an election shall take place and can choose the most advantageous time.

Section 5 provides that "there shall be a sitting of Parliament and of each legislature at least every twelve months." This simply assures the parliamentary process and prevents the abuse of power by a governing body. However, there is no description as to what this sitting must consist of; therefore, the process could be abused if the parliamentary assembly permitted the government to do so.

Mobility Rights

Section 6 states that "every citizen of Canada has the right to enter, remain in and leave Canada." Subsection (2) states that every person who qualifies as a "permanent resident of Canada" can move from province to province and earn a livelihood in any province. The right of citizens to come to or leave Canada allows citizens to travel freely, subject only to the controls imposed by other nations. These laws, however, are subject to reasonable limitations. Thus, the Supreme Court upheld the right to return a Canadian citizen to (then) West Germany to face a war-crimes trial.[12] The right to interprovincial mobility refers only to people who have the status of "residents of Canada." These may be landed immigrants or other permanent residents. They also have the right to earn a livelihood wherever they so choose. Some believe that Canada's immigration policy should be tailored so that newcomers are forced to go to rural areas, rather than major urban centres. Section 6 clearly prohibits such limitations on the freedom of movement of immigrants who have obtained the status of permanent residents. Although section 6 gives each permanent resident the right to move freely within the country and to earn a living, there are some significant limitations on the free transferability of employment. Section 6 sets out some specific limitations to the mobility rights included in the section. "Any laws or practices of general application in force in a province" that justify the general licensing and certification requirements associated with carrying on professions and livelihoods in the various provinces must be complied with.

The section also permits the provinces to require a reasonable residence period before a person can obtain social services such as welfare and medical coverage. Because there are often social programs in place that are designed to encourage and help the economically disadvantaged, these programs are permitted to discriminate against people coming into the province to take advantage of the program. For example, in some areas of Canada the unemployed are allowed to collect benefits for a longer period of time. In some depressed areas, zones with favoured tax rates have been created to encourage industry to locate there. The province offering such compensatory programs must establish that it is doing so because the rate of employment within that province is lower than the rate in the rest of Canada. Affirmative action programs that attempt to right employment imbalances, while controversial, are sanctioned by subsection 6(4). For example, if there were a program in place to give preferential hiring treatment to females in a particular industry where females were under-represented, that program would be justified, even though it discriminates against men.

Legal Rights

The next major category of legal rights is those set out in sections 7 to 14. Section 7 provides that "everyone has the right to life, liberty and the security of person and the right not to deprived thereof except in accordance with the principles of fundamental justice." Life, it should be noted, is assured to "everyone," but does not include an unborn fetus.[13] Thus, there is no prohibition against abortion found in this section. Liberty, as it is used here, does not simply mean freedom from physical restraint; it is broader and includes such concepts as the right to carry on normal activities, to do what one wants, to marry, and so on. Security of person, as it is used here, extends to physical security, in the sense that any government act that interferes with a person's ability to receive appropriate medical care might be an invasion of this right. There seems, however, to be a striking omission in section 7: there is no guarantee for the security of property, as there is in the American Constitution.

Perhaps the most important phrase used in this section is the requirement that the rules of fundamental justice be followed in any attempt to take away these basic rights. Fundamental justice was defined by Fateaux C.J. for the Supreme Court of Canada in *Duke v. R.* (1972). He said that "the tribunal which adjudicates upon his rights must act fairly, in good faith without bias and in a judicial temper, and must give him [her] the opportunity adequately to state his case."[13] In Canadian law in the past, such basic rights before administrative bodies have been referred to as the rules of natural justice, which require a hearing, unbiased adjudication and "fair" procedure. The principles of fundamental justice, as outlined in the Charter, likely embody essentially the same rights as the rules of natural justice used prior to the Charter.

Section 8 provides that everyone has the right to be secure from unreasonable search and seizure. The "unreasonable" requirement assures that, when it is appropriate, the search must be authorized by law, that a warrant has to be issued by someone who has the authority to act judicially, and that the warrant be granted only if there is sworn evidence of probable cause. In situations where it may not be possible to obtain a warrant, the search and seizure would have to meet the test of reasonableness. For example, in pursuing an escaping criminal, it is unlikely that the police would have to call off their pursuit in order to obtain a warrant if this meant that the suspect would likely escape. Prior to the passage of the Charter, it was common practice for police officers to be issued "writs of assistance." These were, in effect, search warrants in blank, which authorized a search of the premises and person of anyone they had grounds to believe had committed a crime. This procedure, however, did not satisfy the requirements of the Charter, and all writs of assistance have been withdrawn.

In the case of *R. v. Feeney*[14] the Supreme Court of Canada had to deal with a warrantless search and arrest. The police investigating a recent murder went to the trailer of the accused. They knocked on the door and upon receiving no answer opened the door and found the accused asleep. They woke him and took him to where there was better light and discovered blood on his shirt. They then arrested him. At trial he was convicted of murder. The matter was appealed and at the Supreme Court of Canada level the court found that the police did not have reasonable grounds to enter the trailer in the first place and as a result the accused's section 8 Charter right against unreasonable search and seizure had been violated. The appeal of the accused against his murder conviction was allowed.

Section 9 of the Charter provides that everyone has the right not to be arbitrarily detained or imprisoned. Arbitrary detention or imprisonment refers to imprisonment that is unsupported by law, or if supported by law, where the law is not uniformly applied. Imprisonment must be based on some sort of principle or uniform standard, evenly applied. Whether or not imprisonment for an offence is severe or cruel is not the question here. The question is whether or not imprisonment is arbitrary, in the sense that it is inconsistently enforced or not based on authority.

Section 10 of the Charter states that people arrested or detained have the right to be informed why, to be told of their right to retain a lawyer, to be given the opportunity to contact one, to be allowed the right to challenge the arrest or detention on the grounds of *habeas corpus*, and to be released if the arrest is not lawful. The *habeas corpus* provision in section 10 is a reference to an ancient writ that requires the jailer to bring the arrested person before the court to show cause why the person should not be released. Section 10 enshrines this right in the Constitution, although there are other enforcement sections that will work as well. At the time of an arrest, the arresting officer is required to let the person know of the right to retain counsel. It is the arrested person's problem as to who is retained and how their services will be paid for. It is only when the arrested person clearly cannot afford counsel that there is a constitutional requirement that legal help be provided. The terms *arrest* and *detention*, in the sense in which they are used in section 10, mean some sort of compulsory restraint. Therefore, when a person cooperates voluntarily, there is no arrest or detention. When compulsion is used, or when the person being detained or arrested thinks there is no choice but to go with the police, the section 10 rights discussed above come into play.

The rights contained in section 11 are quite extensive, dealing with criminal proceedings up to and including the trial. The rights of a person so charged are set out in section 11 and can be summarized as follows:

a. to be promptly informed of the specific offence;

b. to be tried within a reasonable time;

c. not to be compelled to be a witness against himself;

d. to be presumed innocent until proven guilty, in a fair and public hearing by an independent and impartial tribunal;

e. not to be denied reasonable bail without just cause;

f. to be tried by jury if the maximum penalty is over five years;

g. not to be found guilty of an offence that was not an offence when committed;

h. not to be tried again for an offence after being found not guilty for it; and

i. if found guilty, and the punishment has been changed since the commission of the offence, to be afforded the lesser punishment.

This section applies to any person who has been charged with an offence under federal or provincial law, so long as the offence is subject to punishment.

Paragraph 11(b) provides that a person must be tried within a reasonable time. This is a new right, and has not been guaranteed before in Canadian law. Although considerable delays are common in court proceedings, this section simply provides that the delay not be unreasonable. What constitutes "unreasonable" will, of course, be open to interpretation, and the standard will be set by the courts. The Supreme Court has held that lengthy delays of eight months or more, caused by the backlog of cases in Ontario's overtaxed courts, was unreasonable delay, thus triggering the protection of this section.

In *R. v. Askov*[15] the Supreme Court of Canada found that the delay experienced by persons accused of crimes in 1983 and not brought to trial until 1986 was too long, infringing their right under Charter paragraph 11(b) to be tried within a reasonable time. The court allowed their appeal, staying the charges and thus blocking any further action against them. This decision had far-reaching effects. Because of a backlog, thousands of other cases in Ontario also had to be dropped.

Paragraph 11(c), which provides that people have the right not to testify against themselves, is an expression of the historical reality in Canadian law. In many criminal trials the accused does not give evidence. This right is restricted to proceedings involving the trial of the actual offence. This section of the Charter does not protect a person charged with an offence from being required to testify at someone else's trial, at an inquest, or at some other proceeding that does not involve the trial of the accused's offence. This section also does not protect the accused against bodily evidence, such as a breathalyser or fingerprinting, which does not involve actual testimony given by the accused.

The presumption of innocence contained in paragraph 11(d) is also a reflection of historical reality in Canadian law. There have, however, been many exceptions, which are referred to as *reverse onus* offences. In a drug-trafficking charge, for instance, it used to be up to a person caught with drugs in his or her possession to prove that the drugs were not to be sold to someone else. In these situations the accused is required to prove his or her innocence. As a general rule, this requirement is no longer compatible with the Charter and has been changed to reflect the right to the presumption of innocence in all criminal cases.[16] In the *Oakes* case discussed above, the accused was found guilty at trial of possessing a prohibited substance under the *Narcotics Control Act*. He was then required to prove that he did not have the substance for the purpose of trafficking. It is in this case that the Supreme Court of Canada ruled that such reverse onus clauses were invalid because they not only infringed the accused's right to the presumption of innocence under paragraph 11(d) of the Charter, but they could not be reasonably justified as an exception under section 1. Once the Crown has established certain facts that, without rebuttal, would prove the case, the obligation is on the accused to disprove the Crown's case. This is not inconsistent with the right set out in the Charter, because the accused is merely answering the case the Crown has established.

Paragraph 11(e) provides that the accused cannot be denied reasonable bail without just cause. The term *bail* has been replaced by *judicial interim release*. The accused can only be retained in custody if detention is necessary to ensure that he or she will show up at trial, or to protect the public. Paragraph 11(f) of the Charter guarantees a trial by jury if the offence involves the possibility of a penalty of five years or more. Alternatively, the accused can choose a trial by judge alone.

Paragraph 11(g) prohibits the court from finding the accused guilty of a retroactive offence (an act that was not an offence at the time it was committed). Paragraph 11(h) prohibits double jeopardy — that is, when a person is charged with an offence, tried, and acquitted, he or she cannot be charged again with the same offence. Many trials are stayed by the prosecution. This is not a final determination by the court, but merely the prosecution stopping the process part way through. Because the accused person has not been found not guilty, he or she can be tried again for the offence. Paragraph 11(i) provides that if there is a change in the law that reduces or increases the penalty for the offence, the accused is entitled to the benefit of the lesser penalty.

Section 12 of the Charter provides that a person has the right not to be subjected to "any cruel or unusual punishment." This provision prevents a person from being subjected to excessive punishment. The death penalty, although not used in Canada today, is likely not cruel or unusual punishment, although the practice of sentencing habitual criminals to an indeterminate sentence has been held to be cruel and unusual. Practices such as solitary confinement, whipping or paddling would also be controlled or eliminated by this provision of the Charter.

Section 13 protects witnesses from having their trial testimony used against them later. The protection against self-incrimination was embodied in the *Canada Evidence Act* prior to the Charter and is entrenched constitutionally today. Witnesses can be required to testify, but if their statements prove to be self-incriminating, they cannot be used against them in subsequent proceedings.

The final legal right contained in the Charter under section 14 provides that any of the parties to a proceeding, or the witnesses involved, are entitled to an interpreter if they do not understand the language.

Equality Rights

The next category of rights protected under the Charter is the equality rights found in section 15. These are the rights we normally think of as civil rights, which protect us from discrimination on the basis of various characteristics:

> Every individual is equal before and under the law and has the right to the equal protection and equal benefit of the law without discrimination and in particular without discrimination based on race, national or ethnic origin, colour, religion, sex, age, mental or physical disability.

Prior to 1982, the federal and provincial governments had power to pass discriminatory laws and, as Canadian history reveals, often did so. The *Indian Act*, with its prohibition against Native people consuming alcohol anywhere but on a reserve, is a prime example. That act also provided that a Native woman marrying a non-Native would lose her Indian status. This is now regarded as a clear violation of section 15 of the Charter.

It is all too easy, should disturbances erupt, to crush them in the name of law and order. We must never forget that in the long run, a democracy is judged by the way the majority treats the minority.

Pierre Elliott Trudeau, October 2, 1969

Section 15 of the Charter provides for equality before and under the law. This means that the various provisions of federal and provincial laws must be applied equally to all. This section also prohibits all forms of discrimination, and gives specific examples. Any time a distinction is made in any provincial or federal law on the basis of one of the listed categories, it can be challenged as unconstitutional. If a type of discrimination is involved that does not fall into one of the categories set out in section 15, it can still be held to be discriminatory. Of course, section 1 of the Charter allows such reasonable limits to be placed on this protection as is reasonably justified in a free and democratic society. Thus, the discrimination against children under 16 that prohibits them from driving or voting before the age of 18, or the discrimination against mentally incompetent people by which they are treated differently, would likely be justified. Historically, there has been some institutionalized discrimination in Canada; governments have discriminated against people on the basis of race, sex, age and the like. However, most discrimination takes place at the public and private level between individuals. While this kind of interpersonal discrimination is not covered under the Charter, it is controlled by the provincial human rights codes. Section 15 of the Charter does have an indirect role to play in this area, in that the provincial and federal laws must be compatible with section 15. If a provincial human rights act allows employees to be discriminated against on the basis of age, that act can be challenged under the Charter. Subsection 15(2) also authorizes affirmative action programs in Canada that are designed to correct the imbalances that have come into existence because of discriminatory practices. Thus, it has been considered acceptable for universities, for example, to give preference to qualified women applicants in an effort to achieve gender balance in their institutions.

Language Rights

Section 16 declares that English and French are the official languages of Canada and in the province of New Brunswick. Quebec has French as its official language, while the other provinces are officially English. Only in institutions of the federal government and New Brunswick do both languages have equal standing and the right to be used equally in all governmental institutions. Section 17 gives everyone the right to be heard in either English or French in all federal government proceedings, as well as in the proceedings of the government of New Brunswick. Section 18 provides that all federal government publications, in the form of statutes, records, journals, and so forth, must be published in both English and French. Section 19 guarantees the right to the use of either English or French in court proceedings in superior courts. Section 20 gives people the right to deal with government agencies in English and French, providing there is sufficient demand for service in both languages. Sections 21 and 22 make it clear that nothing in the Charter will take away any pre-existing rights to English and French, in the Constitution or by custom. These provisions in regard to language rights cannot be read separately from those embodied in the *Constitution Act, 1867*. Language rights have been essential to the nature of Canada since before Confederation, and the provisions in the Charter merely enshrine certain basic language rights to the services and procedures of government.

There are additional language rights guaranteed in other constitutional documents. For example, section 3 of the *Constitution Act, 1867* guarantees English-language rights in Quebec courts and other governmental institutions. Under the *Manitoba Act* of 1870, Manitoba is obligated to provide similar services, although it did not do so until it was challenged in the Supreme Court of Canada.[16]

Section 23 of the Charter deals with language rights as they affect education. The spoken language of a person's parents determines the language in which that person has the right to be educated. This right is available only to Canadian citizens, however. Immigrants from English- or French-speaking countries have no such guarantee. Another limitation on this right is that the provincial governments will only be required to provide minority language education where the numbers warrant. Thus the government of Alberta would not be required to provide French education where there are only a few French-speaking families in the community.

There are three categories of citizens who have the right to have their children educated in the minority language:

1. citizens whose first language learned and still understood is that of the language minority where they reside;

2. citizens who have received their primary school instruction in the minority language, providing they are still in the same province; and

3. citizens of Canada who have had any one of their children educated in that minority language. These provisions are very controversial, especially in the province of Quebec.

Section 59 of the Charter was designed to allow Quebec to opt out of, or phase in, these rights in relation to the first two categories. Quebec, however, has had its control over minority language rights severely restricted by section 23. The *Constitution Act, 1867* still provides for educational rights in denominational schools and, although the terms are primarily religious in their nature, they are also used to some extent to protect minority language rights. Language rights and minority-language education rights cannot be overridden by section 33.

Enforcement

Section 24 of the Charter provides a new method of enforcement. Prior to the Charter, the constitutionality of a particular provision or statute passed by the federal or provincial government or an action by federal or provincial government officials would come into question as that legislative provision was being enforced at a trial of the matter, or through the process of judicial review. The person being required to act a certain way because of the statute would challenge the constitutional validity of the statute or action as a collateral matter to the proceeding. When the statute or the act of the government official was unconstitutional or inconsistent with constitutional protections, it would be declared *ultra vires*. In some cases, an injunction would be granted to prohibit the government official from performing the unconstitutional act. Subsection 24(1) of the Charter, however, goes further than this: It provides that, when the provisions of the Charter have been infringed or denied, the court may give such remedy as "the court considers appropriate in the circumstances." This may empower the courts not only to declare the legislation void and to issue an injunction, but also to compensate the victim by ordering payment of damages. Of course, these remedies could only be granted if it were in the courts' jurisdiction to grant such remedies. Thus, damages could not be awarded in a criminal matter against a police officer or government official who had violated an individual's Charter rights; this would have to take place in a civil action.

Subsection 24(2) provides that, when evidence has been obtained in a way that infringes on the rights set out in the Charter, the courts may exclude that evidence and refuse to admit it. In Canada prior to the passage of the Charter, if the evidence was supported by other evidence and shown to be true, then even if it was wrongfully obtained, it was admissible in court. Subsection 24(2) changes that practice significantly, allowing the court to exclude such evidence if its admission would bring the administration of justice into disrepute. Thus, a confession that was coerced or otherwise wrongfully obtained from an individual could be excluded, even if it was supported by other evidence, such as a gun or other weapon, obtained because of the contents of that confession. Similarly, the physical evidence itself obtained by such unlawful means could also be excluded if its admission would bring the administration of justice into disrepute. In the United States, the confession as well as the physical evidence found as a result of the unlawfully obtained confession is automatically excluded. In Canada, the courts have the discretion to exclude such evidence if they believe that allowing it would bring the administration of justice into disrepute.

Aboriginal Rights

The *Charter of Rights and Freedoms* also contains a section guaranteeing the existing rights of the aboriginal people of Canada. Many provincial governments, as well as the federal government, are in the midst of land-claim negotiations or disputes with Native bands. These are based on treaty rights and other historical claims to geographical areas that are related to race and ethnic origin. Such special treatment could be challenged as discriminatory and prohibited under the Charter. Section 25 specifically sets out that the "guarantee in this Charter of certain rights and freedoms shall not be construed as to abrogate or derogate from any aboriginal treaty or other rights or freedoms that pertain to the aboriginal people of Canada." Section 26 of the Charter also states that any guarantees set out in the Charter will not affect any other rights or freedoms that predate the Charter. Note, however, that neither the Constitution nor the Charter provides affirmative guarantees of any special rights for Native peoples. These rights are in the process of being defined both in court action and through the treaty-making process. At the time of writing an important step in this process has been reached whereby the various levels of government and the Nisga'a peoples of British Columbia have reached agreement on the contents of a treaty, the culmination of decades of court action and negotiation.

Application of Charter

Finally, it is important to point out that the rights guaranteed in the Charter extend to all hearings before government agencies. Thus, administrative tribunals are covered by the Charter, including the provision that the fundamental rules of justice be followed when a person's life, liberty or security of person is threatened.

CONCLUSION

Prior to the introduction of human rights legislation, Canadians would have to rely on common law principles when they appealed to the court to have their complaints addressed.

Recognizing the role of legislators in framing and enacting laws to protect individual rights, the courts were reluctant or unable to create sweeping new laws. This deficiency became unacceptable when relatively large-scale human rights offences prompted the passage of modern human rights legislation. Provincial statutes protected individuals in private relationships, but they did not protect citizens from government action that deprived them of rights. The problem was only partially remedied by the *Canadian Bill of Rights*, which eventually gave impetus to the passing of the *Canada Act* in 1982, which included the *Canadian Charter of Rights and Freedoms*. The Charter has had a significant impact on the nation. Citizens have become more aware of their rights and more willing to challenge those who would infringe upon them. Court decisions have been made that strike down existing laws and encouraged legislators to create new laws consistent with the ideals and goals set out in the Charter. The courts have also assumed greater responsibility for ensuring that the rights of individuals and minorities are better protected. The Charter has also affected the role of judges, a topic that we will look at more closely as we examine the court system in the next chapter.

QUESTIONS FOR DISCUSSION AND REVIEW

1. Explain what recourse may have been available to a citizen in 1930 for an infringement of his or her civil rights.

2. If you were involved in a dispute with a landlord because he would not rent an apartment to you just because you were young, how would you persuade him to change his mind?

3. If an employer sexually harassed you, what recourse would you have?

4. What problems do boards and commissions, authorized under human rights legislation, have in responding to complaints?

5. Under what circumstances will a court review a decision made by a human rights commission?

6. Give reasons why the *Bill of Rights* did not accomplish what it intended.

7. What were the most significant reasons given to justify the entrenchment of a *Charter of Rights and Freedoms*?

8. What impact does the Charter have on other human rights legislation?

9. Describe the limitations of the Charter.

10. Explain the significance of section 1 of the Charter.

11. What is the effect of the "notwithstanding" and "sunset" clauses in the Charter?

12. What would you do when one of your Charter rights has been denied?

13. Describe how the Charter has affected the role of judges.

NOTES

1. Hogg, Peter. *Constitutional Law of Canada*, 4th ed. Toronto: Carswell, 1997, p. 599.

2. Hogg, p. 598.

3. *Vriend v. Alberta* (1998), 156 D.L.R. (4th) 385 (S.C.C.).

4. *Canadian Human Rights Act*, R.S.C. 1985, c. H-6.

5. *R. v. Drybones*, [1970] S.C.R. 282.

6. Hogg, p. 934.

7. Hogg, pp. 652-653.

8. *Hill v. Church of Scientology of Toronto* (1995), 126 D.L.R. (4th) 577 (S.C.C.).

9. *R. v. Oakes*, [1986] 1 S.C.R. 103.

10. *Allan Singer Ltd. v. Québec (Procureur Général)* (1988), 90 N.R. 48.

11. *Sauve v. Canada (Chief Electoral Officer)* (1995), 132 D.L.R. (4th) 136 (F.C.T.D.).

12. *Canada (Minister of Citizenship and Immigration) v. Tobiass*, [1997] 3 S.C.R. 391.

13. *Duke v. R.*, [1972] S.C.R. 917.

14. *R. v. Feeney*, [1997] 146 D.L.R. (4th) 609 (S.C.C.).

15. *R. v. Askov*, [1990] 2 S.C.R. 1199.

16. *Bilodeau v. Attorney-General of Manitoba* (1986), 27 D.L.R. (4th) 39.

FURTHER READING

Banfield, Jane, ed. *Readings in Law and Society*, Chapter 3.

Beaudoin G.-A. and E. Mendes, eds. *The Canadian Charter of Rights and Freedoms*. Toronto: Carswell, 1990.

Berger, Thomas R. *Fragile Freedoms: Human Rights and Dissent in Canada*. Toronto: Clarke, Irwin, 1981.

Brownlie, I. *Basic Documents on Human Rights*. Oxford: Clarendon Press, 1971.

Code, M.A. *Trial Within Reasonable Time*. Toronto: Carswell, 1992.

Culhane, Dara. *The Pleasure of the Crown: Anthropology, Law and First Nations*. Burnaby, BC: Talonbooks, 1998.

Kallen, Evelyn. *Ethnicity and Human Rights in Canada*. Toronto: Gage, 1982.

Milne, D.A. *The Canadian Constitution*, 2nd ed. Toronto: James Lorimer, 1991.

Schabas, W.A. *International Human Rights Law and the Canadian Charter*, 2nd ed. Toronto: Carswell, 1996.

Tarnopolsky, Walter. *The Canadian Charter of Rights and Freedoms*. Toronto: Carswell, 1982.

Wintemute, R. *Sexual Orientation and Human Rights: The United States Constitution, the European Convention, and the Canadian Charter*. Oxford: Clarendon Press, 1995.

Chapter

5

THE COURTS

Not only the making of new law and the effect of old, but the hold and the thrust of all other vital aspects of the culture, shine clear in the crucible of conflict.

Llewellyn, K. and A. Hoebel, *The Cheyenne Way*[1]

One of the most visible institutions in our legal system is the courts. Courts have the function of adjudicating between parties in civil or private disputes and of determining guilt and punishment in criminal matters. The courts are the most tradition-bound and formal of our conflict resolution mechanisms. The rules of procedure that govern the workings of the court are driven by tradition in all jurisdictions. The idea is to preserve the dignity and decorum of the institution in the process of reaching efficient and just decisions, so that members of the public can depend on its order and authority and maintain respect for the institution and confidence in its decision-making powers. The elevated bench behind which the judge sits, the black court gowns worn by judges and lawyers in some proceedings, and the formal terms used to address members of the court all contribute to the authority and dignity of the occasion. People are expected to be well dressed when attending the court and to show respect for those who officiate there. The courts are open to the public since justice "must be seen to be done." It is with great reluctance that a Canadian court will close its doors to the media or to the public because for the workings of justice to maintain their integrity they must be subject to public scrutiny. The court may in certain circumstances ban the publication of information about people involved in a case in order to protect them, as in the case of children or victims of sexual abuse, but generally an open court is felt to be essential to its function.

Another important characteristic of our courts that should be recognized at the outset is that the trial process is based on a system of evidence-gathering. Therefore, the capacity of each side to present enough evidence to persuade the court of the rightness of their claim casts them in adversarial positions — that is, one party is pitted against another, whether it is a plaintiff against a defendant in a civil matter or the state against the accused in a criminal case. The judge must hear the evidence presented by each side and then choose between them. The litigation process is based on the idea that both sides are equally balanced and each has the same access to the court; whether this is, in fact, the case often depends on the power and influence of the respective parties.

While the judge may have some discretion in applying the remedy or penalty, it is usually the case that one party "wins" while the other "loses" and there is no opportunity for the judge to exercise the kind of wisdom Solomon used in making his decisions. Although the parties are encouraged to settle their differences, there is little room for the judge to compromise or make concessions. The law must be applied regardless of whether the consequences seem harsh. The judgment must be based on the weight of evidence brought to bear in the case, and the judge has little leeway to make allowances for the weakness of one of the parties' legal counsel or the lack of resources one party brings to the action. Placing parties in contesting positions also tends to favour the stronger of the parties. When the positions of the parties may be out of balance, especially in the prosecution of offences, it is vital that mechanisms be in place to protect the weaker party. This is one reason the legal rights set out in the Charter are so important. When all of the rights are enforced as they should be, they serve to even the balance between the weak and powerful in the court.

> Any set of laws and procedures, no matter how complete, requires continuous interpretation as it is applied in practice; and in actual practice those who interpret and apply the law have found it necessary to look beyond the written statutes to an ideal of justice which is taken to be the goal of the law. Interests are recognized and secured with reference to this ideal concept of social justice.
>
> Mark McGuigan, Canadian Minister of Justice, 1983

JUDICIAL DECISION-MAKING

Courts are presided over by judges who have the responsibility for determining the law to be applied in cases brought before them. Their task also includes the search for truth and the provision for fair and just resolutions to the problems that come before them. In the process of making decisions, judges are required to follow rules of procedure to ensure that everyone who appears before them receives a fair hearing. In addition judges interpret statutes, apply common law and equitable principles, determine the extent of the protections afforded by the *Charter of Rights and Freedoms*, and otherwise determine the constitutional validity of the laws. A judge hearing a case without a jury also has the responsibility of determining, on the basis of the evidence presented, just what has occurred between the disputing parties. This is referred to as determining the facts (as opposed to determining the law). If a jury is present, it has the responsibility of determining the facts, while the judge is responsible for determining the law.

Standard of Proof

Courts are concerned either with criminal matters or with civil disputes. Although the same courts may deal with both, the procedure involved is somewhat different. A criminal case involves the prosecution, and punishment if convicted, of a person charged by the Crown or government with committing a criminal act. A civil dispute, on the other hand, takes place between private individuals: the plaintiff, who brings the action, and the defendant, who responds to the complaint. The court adjudicates between the two positions. The standard of proof required in criminal and civil actions is also different. In a criminal prosecution, the judge must be convinced "beyond a reasonable doubt" of the guilt of the accused, and the onus is on the Crown to provide evidence of guilt. A judge might be convinced that the accused likely committed the crime, but that is not good enough. If there is any reasonable doubt, the accused must be given the benefit of it and acquitted of the crime. In a civil dispute, however, it is only necessary that the plaintiff prove on the "balance of probabilities" that his or her position is correct. This means that the plaintiff must convince the court that the position he or she is advancing is more likely true than that presented by the defendant.

Function

Courts also differ in the function they perform. A court may function as a trial court or as a court of appeal. A trial court makes the first decision on a matter. It hears the evidence, receives the testimony of witnesses and hears the arguments from the plaintiff and the defendant. A court of appeal hears complaints from litigants who believe that the lower court has made a mistake in law, and had it not been for that error the case would have been decided differently. At this level, the person who is appealing the decision is referred to as the appellant, while the person responding to it is referred to as the respondent. Note that an appellant can be either the plaintiff or the defendant at the trial level depending on who is disappointed with the trial court's decision. An appeal court does not completely rehear a case. It will only review the alleged mistake made by the lower court. This mistake must relate to how the trial judge applied the law and not whether or not the factual evidence presented at trial was correct or complete. Whether or not A struck B is a question of fact; whether or not A had the right to strike B is a question of law. The attention of the judges (there are usually more than one at the appeal level) is brought to the portion of the transcript of the trial or judgment where the alleged mistake has been made, and arguments supporting or refuting the allegation are presented by both the appellant and respondent. The original plaintiff and defendant do not participate in these proceedings. The matter is conducted wholly by their legal representatives.

THE STRUCTURE OF THE COURTS

The restructured English court system of the nineteenth century was the model used by the common law provinces as they entered Confederation. The *Constitution Act, 1867* gave the provinces the power to establish and maintain provincial courts to deal with matters that fell within their jurisdiction. The Act also authorized the federal Parliament to establish "a general court of appeal for Canada" and "any additional courts for the better administration of the laws of Canada." There are lower-level trial courts in all provincial and territorial jurisdictions in Canada.

The superior trial courts of the province consist of a superior trial court, referred to as either the Court of Queen's Bench, the Supreme Court, or the Divisional Court depending on the province, and a separate court of appeal. Because each province has the jurisdiction to create its own courts, they vary in name and structure from province to province. The federal court system includes the Federal Court (Trial Division), which hears matters relating to the federal government; the Federal Court of Appeal, which hears appeals from that court and other federal bodies; and the Supreme Court of Canada, which is the highest court in the land and our court of final appeal.

FEDERAL COURTS

Federal Court of Canada

The Federal Court of Canada was established in 1971 to replace the Exchequer Court, which had originally been created under the *Constitution Act, 1867*, and to add to the earlier court's jurisdiction. The Federal Court, consisting of the Trial Division and the Federal Court of Appeal, has both a civil and a criminal jurisdiction. Under such legislation as the *Competition Act* and other special federal statutes, the Trial Division deals with special criminal offences. It also deals with civil disputes in areas that fall under federal jurisdiction, such as copyright, patent, trademark and admiralty matters. It also has jurisdiction to hear disputes when the federal government is being sued. There is still considerable debate over the extent of the jurisdiction of the Federal Court, and many of these matters can also be dealt with in the provincial court system. The Federal Court of Appeal hears appeals from the Federal Court Trial Division, but it also hears appeals and exercises a supervisory jurisdiction over federal administrative tribunals, such as government boards dealing with immigration, employment insurance, communications, broadcasting, aviation and tax matters. In addition, another federal court, called the Tax Court, was established in 1983 to deal with all disputes arising from the assessment of federal taxes. An appeal from the Tax Court also goes to the Federal Court of Appeal.

The new powers given to the court have created considerable controversy because of the uncertainty of its jurisdiction and dispute over what laws are included in the term in the Act "laws of Canada." It is accepted that the term refers to federal laws, but does it also cover provincial statutes or the common law? Numerous cases have been heard in the Federal Court where this question has been the focus of the arguments. In 1990 the *Federal Court Act* was again amended to make the right of the Federal Court to hear claims against the Crown concurrent with the provincial superior courts. This in effect has created a dual court system, and Peter Hogg asserts that this is not necessary because superior court judges in the provinces are federally appointed and their decisions are appealable to the Supreme Court of Canada. He claims that "The existence of a parallel hierarchy of federal courts cannot fail to give rise to wasteful jurisdictional disputes and multiple proceedings."[2]

According to the *Constitution Act, 1867*, judges in the Federal Court system are appointed by the cabinet and are usually drawn from the ranks of provincial superior court judges. Recent appointments to the court's trial and appeal divisions have been former members of Parliament or government employees. Because of that, questions have been raised about the judicial independence of the court when it is dealing with politically sensitive matters such as the recent cases deciding on the deportation of suspected war criminals.

The Supreme Court of Canada

The Supreme Court of Canada was established by an act of Parliament in 1875. It did not have the role then that it does now since the Judicial Committee of the Privy Council in the British House of Lords was the final court of appeal from all the Commonwealth courts. Over the years the Canadian court gained prominence as the British Parliament passed a series of acts at first restricting and then eliminating the power of the Privy Council to hear appeals from Canadian courts. In 1949 the final act was passed, giving the Supreme Court ultimate jurisdiction to hear appeals from Canadian courts. Nine judges sit on the Supreme Court according to an established pattern of representation: three judges from Quebec, three from Ontario, two from the western provinces and one from Atlantic Canada. The position of Chief Justice alternates between French- and English-speaking justices. Judges are appointed by the federal cabinet on the recommendation of the prime minister. The provinces are not consulted and have had little role in the selection of judges, but now local legal organizations such as provincial bar associations have been given some input into the selection process.

The Supreme Court hears appeals from the Federal Court of Appeal and from all the provincial courts of appeal. The court can deal with questions of constitutional, federal or provincial law. "It is the final authority on the interpretation of the entire body of Canadian law, whatever its source. [It] does not tolerate divergences in the common law from province to province, or even divergences in the interpretation of similar provincial statutes."[3] The right to hear an appeal in a civil case was abolished in 1975 and now parties in such an action must get leave to appeal. Leave may be granted by the provincial court of appeal, but because the purpose of the 1975 Act was to reduce the burden on the highest court, leave is rarely granted. The Supreme Court itself decides whether or not it will hear a case, and the determination is based on the importance to the public of the legal issue. Leave to appeal is not required in a criminal action, but the court determines whether the "question of law" at stake in the case is of sufficient merit to be dealt with by the Supreme Court. The court is not required to give reasons as to why it grants and denies leave to hear the case, but a denial is not meant to suggest that the court agrees with the lower court decision. Because the Supreme Court hears and determines upwards of 120 cases a year, the requirement of leave is a practical matter, allowing the court to control the size of the docket and to function more efficiently. The late Chief Justice Bora Laskin described the effect of the leave policy as follows:

> Now, even more in its supervisory role than in its heretofore more traditional appellate role, the Supreme Court's main function is to oversee the development of the law in the courts of Canada, to give guidance in articulate reasons and, indeed, direction to the provincial courts and the Federal Court of Canada on issues of national concern or of common concern to several provinces, issues that may obtrude even though arising under different legislative regimes in different provinces. This is surely the paramount obligation of an ultimate appellate court with national authority.[4]

A private person can challenge the validity of a federal or provincial law by first bringing a declaratory action before a provincial court, and if the matter is of sufficient importance, usually involving a Charter violation, leave may then be granted to have the matter heard by the Supreme

Court. Since the entrenchment of the Charter a large proportion of the cases heard by the court involve Charter questions, particularly on matters where the court must determine whether federal or provincial legislation is inconsistent with the terms of the Charter and thus invalid.

Procedure

A minimum of five justices usually sit on a case, and the panel is structured where possible so that the majority of the judges are from the region where the case originates (for example, the three judges from Quebec would hear a case based on Quebec civil law). That is not to say that the judges represent a region but that their experience and knowledge of the laws in that region will assist the decision-making process. The full court will sit on important constitutional cases that affect the whole nation. Often the justices hearing a case will render independent decisions, producing reasons and opinions on the matter. The opinion held by the majority of the justices forms the decision in the case. It is becoming more common for the judges to consult with one another before making the decision and then to produce a joint opinion. The judges taking the minority position will offer their dissenting opinions on the case.

Decision-Making in the Supreme Court

Judicial decision-making, particularly at the Supreme Court level, has been responding to changes over the past several decades. In their reporting of *Harrison v. Carswell* in 1976 the justices provided some insight into the role they each thought they should be playing in the administration of justice in Canada. The case was an appeal of a decision from the Court of Appeal of Manitoba in which that court had overturned a trial-level decision that a person's right to picket in a lawful labour strike took precedence over a mall owner's right to restrict people from using private property for that purpose. The Supreme Court of Canada had to decide what took priority — Manitoba's *Petty Trespass Act* or the *Trade Unions Act*. The justices had to choose between two competing interests — one rising out of long-held traditions relative to property and the other out of newer principles relative to the rights of employees engaged in legal job action. If they applied the existing rules, thereby deciding not to extend the provisions of the *Trade Unions Act* to allow such picketing on private property, the result would seem unjust but the law would remain certain. If they followed the direction of judgments in similar cases in the US, they would rule in favour of the picketer and protect the hard-earned rights of employees. Although the majority of the court held that the more conservative approach was the one to take in this instance, both sides offered their reasons for choosing the course they did. The majority held that preserving the law was of primary concern to ensure the certainty and predictability of the law. Mr. Justice Dickson, speaking for the majority, stated:

> The submission that this Court should weigh and determine the respective values to society of the right to property and right to picket raises important and difficult political and socio-economic issues, the resolution of which must, by their very nature be arbitrary and embody personal economic and social beliefs. It raises also fundamental questions as to the role of this Court under the Canadian Constitution. The duty of the Court, as I envisage it, is to proceed in the discharge of its adjudicative function in a reasoned way from principled decisions and established concepts. I do not for a moment doubt the power of the Court to act creatively — it has done so on countless occasions; but manifestly one must ask — what are the limits of the judicial function?[5]

The second argument was that if the courts took the position that they should give priority to the *Trade Union Act* they would be usurping the function of the legislature. Because the courts were not representative of the people nor responsible to them, they should not be changing the rights of individuals by changing the law rather than merely applying it.

The opposing view taken by then-Chief Justice Laskin and two others considered another role that the Supreme Court might take. They wanted the court to consider a "balancing of interests" approach to judicial decision-making. This is the course normally taken in the United States and reflects their legal realist approach to the law where they consider factors other than the law itself in making a decision. Laskin was uncomfortable with the idea that the Supreme Court could only "pay mechanical deference to *stare decisis*" and ignore "new and changing social conditions." He thought that this case demanded "a search for an appropriate legal framework for new social facts which show up the inaptness of an old doctrine developed upon a completely different social foundation."[6]

Former Justice Bertha Wilson has affirmed that there was ongoing discussion among the justices at Canada's highest court regarding their role. She recalled the decision in *Harrison v. Carswell*, which she termed a "hard case" because of the court's concern that "doing justice in the particular case may lead to the creation of a precedent which might get the jurisprudence off on the wrong track." In an article published in the *University of Toronto Law Journal*, she describes four "tensions" that the justices must grapple with when making any decision and the burden they bear when they chose one course over another.

> The first of these is the desire to do justice in the individual case and the desire to rationalize the development of the jurisprudence in the particular area. The second is the tension between attempting to achieve certainty in the law and at the same time ensuring its adaptability to social conditions which are constantly changing. The third is the tension between the 'deciding only what is necessary for the case' approach and the approach that views the Court in the role of overseer of the development of the jurisprudence. And the fourth is the tension between the judge as an individual member of the Court and the Court as an institution.[7]

Wilson recognized that the Charter had a good deal to do with the Supreme Court beginning to revise their traditionally conservative approach to judicial decision-making and assuming the role required by the Charter to become more activist in their response to preserving individual rights. The more contemporary response to the same issues is apparent in the comments made in 1996 by Canada Supreme Court Justice Jack Major.

> Some of us can remember when courts took a fairly mechanical approach. The established rules were applied without a lot of soul-searching if there was supporting authority. The purpose, rationale and effects on society were secondary to the authorities that supported the rules. Today all our courts, and I think particularly the Supreme Court of Canada for better or worse, are more willing to evaluate established doctrines and examine the rationale which underlie them... and if an established rule appears outdated or unrelated to its objectives, it should be challenged. Today, I would say that nothing appears untouchable.[8]

Supreme Court's Advisory Role

The Supreme Court also functions as an advisory body on constitutional questions and can declare the law on questions referred to it by the federal government. These are called "reference" cases and must be heard by the court. For example, in a dispute over ownership of the offshore mineral rights to the seabed under Georgia Strait (the area between the mainland of British Columbia and Vancouver Island) that took place between the government of British Columbia and the federal government, the matter was referred directly to the Supreme Court of Canada, which declared that the mineral rights belonged to the federal government.[9] A more recent example was the Supreme Court deciding on a reference from the Prime Minister that Quebec had the right in principle to negotiate a separation agreement, but at the same time it affirmed that it would require more than a simple majority of voters to approve a referendum that would ensure that the separation agreement would be finalized.[10]

PROVINCIAL COURTS

Lower Trial-Level Courts

The lowest-level courts of the provinces, called provincial courts in most jurisdictions, are considered a lower or inferior trial court, and the judges are appointed by the provinces. Their functions are generally divided among several sections, including criminal, family and youth divisions, and a civil or small claims jurisdiction (see chart). The criminal divisions operate under the *Criminal Code*, which is federal legislation that empowers provincial court judges not only to deal with less important criminal offences (referred to as summary conviction offences), such as theft under $5 000, but also to have a role to play in more serious cases. When serious, indictable offences are involved, a preliminary inquiry, conducted by a provincial court judge, usually is held to determine whether there is enough evidence to take the matter to trial. If the accused chooses to have a speedy trial, the case is treated as a summary conviction procedure, with a magistrate hearing and deciding the case. In spite of the attention given to more sensational superior court trials, the vast majority of criminal cases are handled at this level.

In addition to this criminal court function, there is a civil jurisdiction at this lowest level. The Small Claims division of the Provincial Court, or the separate Small Claims Court in some provinces, has a civil jurisdiction that is restricted to $10 000 or less, depending on the province. The procedure used is less formal, so that people can represent themselves without the assistance of a lawyer. In many jurisdictions, the court requires parties to a civil dispute to attempt a mediated settlement and attend a settlement conference presided over by a judge before the court will hear the case. Family courts deal with disputes over child custody and maintenance and support upon marriage dissolution. However, they are not authorized to grant divorces or settle real property matters. In most provinces the family court also deals with all matters relating to the *Young Offenders Act*, but some provinces have separate youth courts. There are usually other special-function courts established at this level to deal with provincial offences such as traffic violations; many jurisdictions, however, have given the power to deal with such offences to the criminal division of the provincial court.

Decision-Making at the Trial Level

While judges at this level are primarily concerned with applying the law, they have a fair amount of discretionary power in their decision-making. In small claims matters, they hear the evidence from both parties but are not obligated to enforce the rules of evidence, primarily because the parties are not usually represented by lawyers. The judge acts more as an arbitrator, who may or may not rely on precedent cases. The matter is decided on the balance of probabilities, with the judge weighing the relative merits of the case. If the decision is challenged it begins a whole new trial in a higher court which will hear the matter as if it were the first time, with the presentation of evidence according to the rules that govern that court and the reliance on precedent decisions. A judge in a criminal division is bound not to apply more than the maximum sentence allowed for the offence but has considerable discretion in rendering a judgment up to that limit. There are many options available in terms of the kind of sentence that can be applied to the situation. In family courts, judges rely on the advice of counsel, the reports of professionals dealing with the family and any pre-trial mediation processes to help them determine what is in the best interests of the family. These decisions too are customized to meet the needs of the situation.

Superior Courts

The highest trial-level courts or superior courts in the provinces are variously called the Court of Queen's Bench, the Supreme Court, the Superior Court or the Divisional Court. They have no geographical limitations (other than the province itself) and no monetary or other jurisdictional limitations, with the exception of a few matters assigned by statute exclusively to another court.

All of the provinces have now restructured their court systems by amalgamating their intermediate-level or county and district courts into the trial-level superior courts. In a sense, the district courts are retained, but not as distinct courts of intermediate authority. The judges are designated to reside in the various judicial districts of a province, but they are now superior court judges, sitting as judges of the Court of Queen's Bench or the Supreme Court, as the case may be. Thus, the advantage of having local judges at the district and county courts is retained, but without the limitations that were placed on the powers of such judges in the past. Another result of the reforms is that provinces with a separate surrogate or probate court dealing with wills and the administration of estates had this function taken over by the superior court. Some provinces have created divisions of their Supreme Court (Court of Queen's Bench level) to deal with different functions, such as a family division. In Ontario, there is a special divisional court to handle some types of appeals.

Decision-Making at the Superior Court Level

Superior court judges have very limited discretionary powers. They hear the facts in the case and listen to the testimony of witnesses. They hear the legal arguments from opposing counsel, which will include the precedent cases and the appropriate statutes that each side believes apply to the facts of the case at hand. If a judge is sitting alone, the judge will apply the law to the facts as he or she understands them. To determine the law, the judge must select which precedent case is most similar to the facts in the present case. This is called "distinguishing" the case, and once that determination is made, the judge is bound to follow the decision in that case. The judge then prepares a report on the case, which includes a summary of the facts and issues, the judgment made and the reasons for the judgment, including the case or cases used as binding precedent, the appropriate statutory provisions and a justification for the choice. If a decision at this level is challenged, the appellant must satisfy the appeal court that the trial-level judge did not follow the rules of procedure or made an error in the application of the law, whether in the choice of the precedent or in interpreting the principle established in the precedent case or statutory provision.

Appeal Courts

Every province in Canada has a court that deals exclusively with appeals from the other courts. This may be either a separate court of appeal, as is the case in British Columbia, the Prairie Provinces and Ontario, or a division of the Supreme Court, as is the case in Nova Scotia, Newfoundland and Prince Edward Island. With the recent changes in the role of the Supreme Court of Canada, the role of the provincial courts of appeal has become increasingly important. Superior court judges are appointed by the federal government from a list of candidates supplied by the provinces. Because the Supreme Court of Canada no longer automatically hears appeals from the provincial courts of appeal, the highest court in which a litigant can be sure of a hearing is the provincial court of appeal.

The justices in a provincial court of appeal hear challenges to the decisions of lower court judges, but they do not in most instances rehear witnesses, testimonies or accept new evidence. They work from the assumption that the facts are as they were reported in the trial of the matter. They respond to questions of how the law was applied to the facts and determine whether it was conducted according to the rules governing those procedures. They examine the way the precedents were selected and interpreted and establish that it was done correctly. If they find that legal errors were made that cast doubt upon the facts found by the lower court, they can send the matter back for retrial. But if the facts are clear and the error went to the legal effect of those facts, the decision of the lower court can be reversed.

TABLE 5-1   Courts of the Provinces

	Alberta	British Columbia	Manitoba	New Brunswick	Newfoundland
Appellate Court (Superior Court)	Court of Appeal	Court of Appeal	Court of Appeal	Court of Appeal • Appeal Division • Trial Division	Supreme Court
Highest Trial Court (Superior Court)	Court of Queen's Bench	Supreme Court of B.C.	Court of Queen's Bench • Family Division • Special Small Claims Procedure • Special Probate Procedure	Court of Queen's Bench • Trial Division • Family Division	Unified Family Court
Lower Trial Court	Provincial Court • Criminal Division • Youth Division • Family Division • Civil Division	Provincial Court • Small Claims • Family Court	Provincial Court • Criminal Court • Family Division	Provincial Court • Criminal • Family Division Court • Small Claims Court	Provincial Court • Criminal • Unified Family

Nova Scotia	Ontario	Prince Edward Island	Québec	Saskatchewan	Northwest Territories	Yukon Territory
Court of Appeal	Court of Appeal	Supreme Court of P.E.I. • Appeal Division	Court of Appeal	Court of Appeal	Court of Appeal for the Northwest Territories	Court of Appeal
Supreme Court of Nova Scotia	Ontario Court, General Division • Divisional Court • Small Claims Court • Family Court	• Trial Division • Estates Section • Family Section • Small Claims • General Section	Superior Court	Court of Queen's Bench • Family Law Division	Supreme Court of the Northwest Territories	Supreme Court
Provincial Court • Small Claims Court • Family Court • Criminal	Ontario Court, Provincial Division	Provincial Court • Criminal	Court of Québec • Civil Division • Criminal and Penal Division • Youth Division • Expropriation Division • Municipal Courts	Provincial Court	Territorial Court of the Northwest Territories	Supreme Court Small Claims Court

CIVIL LITIGATION

A trial is just the final step in a lengthy process that takes place between the parties to an action. The objective of the process is the uncovering of as much information about the case as possible. In a criminal action the goal is to ensure that there is enough evidence against the accused to warrant taking the case to trial. Once a criminal case is committed for trial (or the matter has been seized by the court), neither the accused nor the witnesses can withdraw without authorization from the court. The process of a criminal hearing is detailed in Chapter 7 of the text. In a civil action, the goal is to encourage the parties to settle before trial, and claimants can settle any time before the court renders its final judgment. Ideally, the effect of the efforts on both sides is the identification of the issues and the clarification of the points of confrontation so that when the matter does come before the court, it can be dealt with expeditiously. The litigation process is regulated by procedural law. The steps that must be followed in suing a person, what documents have to be filed and served, as well as the time limits involved, are all procedural matters. The procedures described here will vary to some extent not only from province to province but also between courts within a province; however, they are those traditionally used in most common law jurisdictions.

Pre-Trial Procedures

Writ of Summons

When a dispute arises between two individuals over a civil or private wrong, such as a breach of contract, the commission of a tort, or a breach of trust, a civil action can be commenced by the injured party. The first formal step is for the person bringing the action (the plaintiff) to have a lawyer issue a writ of summons. The writ of summons is the last remnant of the writ system described in Chapter 1. It is an order from the Crown informing the defendant that an action has been commenced by the plaintiff, describing the nature of the claim, and instructing the defendant to enter an appearance to dispute the matter. The writ is taken to the court registry, a fee is paid, and a seal of the court is affixed, making it an official court document. The registry creates a file and the plaintiff arranges for an authorized copy of the writ to be served on the defendant. As a general rule, the writ of summons or other initiating document must be personally served. In the case of corporations, this is usually done by registered mail to the corporation's office. If individuals are involved, however, the writ must be personally handed to the defendant. The writ of summons contains an address for service; all subsequent correspondence, even official court documents, can then be served simply by mailing them to the designated address.

Other Methods of Initiating an Action

Because some forms of action, such as a foreclosure, originated in the Courts of Chancery, a petition is another method of commencing an action. In other situations, usually where the facts are not at issue, an application is the appropriate way to commence an action. Ontario is one jurisdiction that has altogether abandoned the writ of summons as a method of starting an action. In Ontario, an action is started by filing a "notice of action." (These methods are outlined in detail in the Court Rules issued for each province.) When an action is started by an application, many of the steps designed to get at the facts, such as the pleadings and the discovery process, are eliminated. Because there is agreement as to the facts, there is no need for these procedures. Whatever method is used to commence an action, the effect is to notify the other party of the action and to let the party know that a response is necessary within a set period of time.

Appearance

Once the writ of summons or notice of action has been received by the defendant, there is a limited period of time in which an appearance must be filed with the court registry and a copy served on the plaintiff. This merely indicates that the defendant intends to dispute the claims set out in the writ. If no appearance is filed, the plaintiff can bring an application to the court for default judgment, short-circuiting the whole process and obtaining an enforceable judgment against the defendant. Therefore, prompt action by the defendant in filing an appearance is very important.

Statement of Claim

Once the appearance is filed and served, the plaintiff is under an obligation to file a statement of claim, the first of several documents, referred to as the pleadings, that set out the positions of both parties. There are time limits within which the pleadings have to be filed, but usually the lawyers work out a convenient schedule. Some jurisdictions commence an action with the issuance of a statement of claim, and have abandoned the writ altogether. In other areas, it is included with the writ of summons and served as the initial document on the defendant.

The statement of claim is prepared by the plaintiff's lawyer; it alleges the facts and makes the claim which are the basis of the action. This is not an argument of the case; evidence is not presented and the position is not argued. This is the official notice to the other side of the claim or case, to which they must respond. If a trespass to land is involved, the statement of claim would say, among other things, that at a specific time on a specific day, the defendant entered onto the plaintiff's property (specified) without permission or authority. If damages are involved, the specific damages must be alleged, along with an allegation that they were caused by the defendant. A specific claim for an amount of monetary compensation or other remedy would also be made.

All of the elements of the offence must be set out in this document. If important facts are left out and it fails to reveal a cause of action, the defendant can bring an application to the court to have the action quashed. If, for example, damages were claimed but there was no assertion that they were caused by the defendant, no claim for those losses could later be brought against the defendant at trial. Because a statement of claim is made at the earliest stage of the litigation process, most of the facts are not clearly known by the parties. The plaintiff, therefore, makes the statement of claim as broad as possible, noting any possible wrong that may have been done, thus laying the groundwork for anything that may eventually come out in the information-gathering process. For example, a trespass action might allege that the trespasser intended to cause harm, while a breach of contract claim might allege that there was fraudulent intent or an intent to cause damage even though there is little likelihood that this is the case.

Statement of Defence

Next the defendant's lawyer must prepare a statement of defence, file it with the court registry and serve a copy on the plaintiff, usually by registered mail. This document contains a specific response to each allegation set out in the statement of claim, along with a statement of the facts as understood by the defendant. Arguments to support the defendant's position are not made at this time; rather, it is an opportunity to make the plaintiff understand exactly what the defendant's stand is, so that she can anticipate what supporting evidence and arguments will be used in a later trial. Also, if the defendant thinks that she has a legitimate complaint about the conduct of the plaintiff, she can make that claim as a counterclaim in the statement of defence. This becomes, in effect, a separate action, with the defendant suing the plaintiff, but it is contained within the structure of the main action. The counterclaim is set out in the same way as the statement of claim. If a statement of defence that includes a counterclaim is served on the plaintiff, the plaintiff must file a reply to that counterclaim. This reply is essentially a statement of defence to the counterclaim. The court will be asked to judge on the merits not only of the plaintiff's claim but also of the defendant's counterclaim.

Demand for Further Information

Even after the statement of defence has been served, and a reply received if there is a counterclaim, one of the parties may feel that the pleadings are not detailed enough and that more information is needed in order to answer the allegations. In that case, a demand for particulars can be served on the other party. Alternatively, specific questions may arise that need answers. These questions can be put to the other party in the form of an interrogatory. The other party will be expected to respond to these interrogatories or demand for particulars; however, that party may refuse if he or she believes enough information has already been provided. If the party requesting the information feels strongly enough about it, he or she can bring an application to the court (an interlocutory application) and ask the judge to order that the questions be answered or the particulars be provided. This process can go on for some time, until both parties are satisfied that they have a clear understanding of the exact position of the other party. Then the pleading process is brought to an end.

Chambers Application

During this process of pre-trial maneuvring, the parties may find themselves in dispute with one another over some procedural obligation. At each stage, an application can be brought to the court to have the matter settled. Chambers applications, although they usually take place in a courtroom, are handled in a much less formal manner than an actual trial, with the judge acting as the administrator of the process rather than as the adjudicator of the actual claim itself. Thus, even before the trial, the parties in a hotly disputed or complicated matter may find themselves before a judge several times.

Discovery

Once the pleadings have been completed, the discovery process begins. The discovery of documents ensures that all important documents in the possession of either party are made available to the other side for inspection. Typically, lawyers will attend each other's offices and examine the files. Important documents that have some relevance to the case (other than privileged communications between lawyer and client) must be made available, and may be copied at this time. The objective is to eliminate surprises later at trial. The examination for discovery involves both the plaintiff and the defendant, or their representatives, making themselves available to the opposing lawyer in order to answer questions on matters relevant to the case. The parties are required to answer any questions asked that are in any way relevant to the matter being litigated. Their answers are given under oath and taken down by a court reporter. Because the litigant is under oath and responses are recorded, the responses can be used against him or her at trial.

An added cost in taking a matter to trial is the fee charged by court reporters to type up and make available transcripts of the examinations for discovery. The questions are usually far-reaching; they cover every aspect of the case, with the goal of getting as much information as possible out on the table. The case is often won or lost at this juncture because if either the plaintiff or the defendant gives false or damaging information at the examination for discovery, that statement is presented to him or her and he or she must then admit to lying under oath, either at the examination for discovery or later at the trial. If the person does make a damaging submission, it encourages him or her to settle the matter before going to trial.[11]

Procedural Delays

It often takes years to bring a civil matter to trial. While this delay is frequently an irritant to the parties, it is not only an essential ingredient in the litigation process, but also a hallmark of the system's success. Because it gets most of the information out on the table and the parties focusing on the areas of dispute, and because it involves a myriad of complex and costly procedures over a lengthy period, the parties are often persuaded to settle their differences before the matter ever comes to trial. This in turn reduces the pressure on the court system.

Pre-Trial Hearing

The final step in the pre-trial process in civil matters is the pre-trial hearing. This is a hearing held before a judge in which the lawyers for the disputing parties appear and explain the nature of the dispute and the reasons why a settlement cannot be reached. Sometimes the pre-trial hearing is merely a formal process. In some provinces, however, it has been given more weight, with the judge encouraging and pressuring the parties to settle, especially when the position advocated by one party is weak or a party is being unreasonable. The pre-trial hearing has been eliminated in some jurisdictions. For instance, it is not used in a small claims procedure but in some jurisdictions mediation is mandated or the judge will conduct a settlement hearing herself in which she facilitates or mediates the process and gives counsel to the parties relative to the legal issues of the matter.

Payment into Court

In a civil action, another important tool to encourage parties to settle before trial is the option of making a payment into court. In order to understand how payment into court works, it must be appreciated that the person who loses a court action is required to pay the court costs, including the legal expenses of the successful party. These costs, paid to the lawyers, are generally assessed on the basis of a published fee tariff and are called party/party costs. Usually the actual amount charged will be higher than this fee, because the actual rate charged by the lawyer is higher, or he or she has spent more time on the file than was anticipated in the tariff. When a judge makes an award of costs in an action, the amount awarded usually does not include all of the normal fees that the successful party must pay his or her lawyer. These fees are referred to as solicitor/client costs. In some cases, if the judge believes that the system has been abused by the losing party, the court will order that the costs be paid at the higher solicitor/client rate. Normally, however, the difference between solicitor/client costs and party/party costs must be borne by the successful party.

In a dispute, the defendant will often admit to being liable for some of the plaintiff's injuries, but may also believe that the amount claimed by the plaintiff is excessive. In a negligence claim, for instance, the plaintiff may claim $100 000 in damages for injuries suffered. The defendant may freely admit liability but believe that the actual amount of damage suffered is only $20 000. The defendant can pay that amount into court before the matter comes to trial. As soon as payment has been made, the plaintiff has the choice either of accepting the money and bringing the action to an end or of proceeding to trial. If the plaintiff remains unwilling to settle, the matter goes to trial and the judge awards less than $20 000, then it is really the defendant who has won, because he or she was willing to pay more. In these circumstances it would be unfair to require the defendant to pay the plaintiff's court costs, because the trial would have been unnecessary if the plaintiff had been reasonable. As a consequence, the plaintiff will not only receive nothing for the costs incurred after the payment into court was made, but also will have to pay the legal expenses of the other party. If more than this amount ($20 000 in this example) is awarded in the judgment, then the normal costs will be awarded to the defendant. The judge knows nothing of the amount paid into court.

Some provinces have introduced a method by which the plaintiff can put the same kind of pressure on the defendant. In such a case, the plaintiff may realize that he is asking too much and may be willing to settle for less, or the defendant may refuse to offer anything or may offer an unreasonably low amount. If it is the defendant who is being unreasonable, the plaintiff can make an offer to settle for a lesser amount. In this case, no payment of money into court would be involved, because it is the plaintiff who will be receiving the money. In the example given in the paragraph above, although the plaintiff has claimed $100 000, he will settle for $20 000. If the defendant is stubborn and refuses to pay anything or offers an unreasonably low amount and the matter must go to trial, the plaintiff will be successful if he receives more than the amount he was willing to settle for. In these circumstances, some provinces instruct the judge to award double costs; others award costs on the higher solicitor/client tariff. Since the defendant, when faced with such an official "offer to settle," knows that she can incur these higher costs, such knowledge exerts much pressure on the parties to be reasonable. The vast majority of private matters are settled before going to trial because of these pressures. If the matter cannot be settled, however, the next step is the trial itself.

The Trial

In many jurisdictions there is a considerable backlog in the courts. It is often difficult to set up a time when the court is available to hear a particular case. Not only is it necessary to find a time when the facilities and a judge are available, but also the lawyers for both parties must be able to fit the date into their schedules. The lawyers and the court registrar must find and set a trial date that is convenient for all. Scheduling is further complicated if the parties in a civil suit choose to be heard by a jury, which is only available in personal injury cases in civil actions.

The trial begins with the court clerk reading off the name of the case and calling on the lawyers to introduce themselves. At this point, there may be motions made by the lawyers. The motion could be for adjournment, perhaps because there has not been time to prepare or new evidence has come forward, or the motion could be to dismiss the case because the pleadings do not give grounds for an action. The plaintiff counsel usually makes an opening statement in which he summarizes the nature of the claim and his intentions as he brings forward evidence. The plaintiff's counsel then calls witnesses, in order, extracting evidence from them by asking them questions. When there is physical evidence in the form of documents or objects, these are brought into the trial through the testimony of witnesses, who are asked to identify the document or object presented as an exhibit. Strict *rules of evidence* govern the types of questions that can be asked. In the process of *direct examination* (sometimes referred to as the examination in chief), in which a lawyer questions his or her own witness, the lawyer is not permitted to ask leading questions — that is, questions that suggest an answer, such as, "You didn't sign that document, did you?" Generally, a witness is not permitted to testify with hearsay evidence — that is, to testify about something he or she heard someone else say.

Once the plaintiff counsel has extracted the evidence from his witness, the defence lawyer can cross-examine. The defence has more latitude in the type of questions she can pose. While she is not restricted from asking leading questions, the rules of evidence still apply to the cross-examination. The plaintiff's counsel may then raise some additional points he wants to clarify. This process is continued with new witnesses until the plaintiff is finished presenting evidence.

When the plaintiff's counsel has completed his case but the defence feels that some vital part has been omitted, defence may make a motion for dismissal. If no other evidence is presented and the judge feels some vital point has been left out, the judge has no option but to dismiss the action, which means there is no case for the defendant to respond to. On the other hand, if the defence lawyer believes that the judge could decide in the plaintiff's favour but that the case is very weak, she can bring an insufficient-evidence motion, in effect telling the judge that she does not believe there is enough of a case to warrant presenting a defence. An insufficient-evidence motion is different from a no-evidence motion, because the judge is actually being asked to pass judgment on the merits of the case. In effect, the judge is being asked to rule that the plaintiff has failed to satisfy the burden to persuade the court, on the balance of probabilities, that the defendant is liable in the circumstances. Usually, however, the defence proceeds to make her opening statement call her witnesses at this time, just as the plaintiff called his in the first part of the trial. The plaintiff will also have the opportunity to cross-examine these witnesses.

When both sides have completed calling their witnesses, the plaintiff will sum up his case and make his argument to the court. Then the defence lawyer will do the same. They will, typically, summarize the facts as they believe they have been established by their witnesses, and they will make their arguments in law, supporting the position they advocate to the judge.

The Jury

If a jury is involved, the process is just a little different. During the trial, if there is a dispute about whether some evidence ought to admitted under the rules of evidence, the judge usually excuses the jury and holds a *voir dire*. This is a trial within a trial, in which the questionable evidence is presented in the jury's absence and the lawyers make their legal arguments as to why the evidence ought or ought not to be presented to the jury. If the judge agrees it is the kind of evidence that the jury ought to hear, they will be brought back and the evidence presented to them. If the judge does not agree that the jury should hear the evidence, the jury will be called back and the trial will proceed with no reference to the excluded evidence.

Another major difference occurs when a jury is involved in a trial. At the trial's conclusion, the lawyers generally direct their arguments to them rather than to the judge. When the lawyers' closing arguments are finished, the judge makes his or her charge to the jury, summarizing the legal issues and principles involved and explaining to the jury what they must find as facts in order to decide for or against the claims made by the plaintiff and the defendant. The jury then retires to deliberate on the matter, returning later to render its judgment. It must be emphasized that the presence of a jury in a civil case is very rare; when a jury is used, its function is quite restricted. The option of holding a jury trial is most often chosen when the claim is for personal injury, usually relating to a vehicle accident. Juries have awarded huge damages when their sympathies for the plaintiff have been aroused, particularly if the defendant is an insurance company or a car manufacturer, which is perceived to have deep pockets or is well able to bear the costs of the injury. The practice of juries making such large awards is much more common in the United States than in Canada, however.

In civil or criminal matters, the jury decides questions of fact, not questions of law. A question of fact deals with the events giving rise to the complaint. In a tort action, for example, one involving personal injuries suffered in an automobile accident, questions of fact might be whether or not: the defendant was driving the car; had been drinking; the street was wet; the driver was driving at an excessive rate of speed; the car had defective brakes or lights; the driver was speeding or driving in an erratic manner; the plaintiff was injured as claimed; that injury was caused by the conduct of the defendant; and the plaintiff was able to work. In these circumstances it is up to the judge to deal with questions of law, such as what constitutes negligence, what would be the effect of a determination that the plaintiff was also negligent, and whether the defendant or the plaintiff failed to live up to provincially imposed motor vehicle standards, such as having functioning brake lights or tail lights or wearing seat belts. In other words, what actually happened is a question for the jury, but what rules should be applied are questions for the judge.

Judgment

If a jury is involved in a trial, it will deliberate, then return and render its decision. If a judge is sitting alone and the situation is a complex one, she will often reserve judgment (take time to render a decision). The judge will reach a decision, deciding between the plaintiff and the defendant, write up her reasons, and give the judgment to the lawyers of the parties at a subsequent date. When a dispute goes to trial, the judge will normally be asked to render a judgment that is combined with an appropriate remedy to rectify the injury or damage. In civil cases, there are many different remedies the court can apply.

Damages
Damages are an order by the court that one party pay monetary compensation to the other. A distinction must be drawn between special and general damages. **Special damages** are ordered by the court to compensate for specific, accountable expenses, such as wages actually

lost and cost of medication, as well as other expenses for which receipts can be produced. **General damages** are ordered by the court to compensate for losses that cannot be specifically accounted for, such as pain and suffering and loss of future wages. Damages are just one form of remedy available.

In different types of civil actions, some equitable remedies may be available, such as **specific performance** (when a person is ordered to perform as required by a contract) and an **injunction** (when a wrongdoer is ordered to discontinue his wrongful conduct). Otherwise the court can order a common law remedy. When property has been wrongfully withheld, the court has the power to order that the property be returned to its rightful owner. In some cases, **punitive damages** (designed to punish the wrongdoer rather than compensate the victim) may be available. On rare occasions, the court is simply asked to make a **declaratory judgment** — that is, to declare the law, even though there may be no order accompanying the declaration. Because there is always a delay between the action complained of, the court decision and the ultimate payment, all jurisdictions require that interest be paid on the outstanding claim. In some circumstances that interest award is restricted to the period after the judgment has been obtained. Of course, the judgment will also include a monetary award for costs, as discussed in the previous section.

The decision is a public document. If it contains some important principle of law or is otherwise interesting, the decision containing the reasons may be published as a reported case in the law reports. Thus, decisions become available for study or for citation in other cases, adding to that body of precedent-setting cases that form the foundation of the common law system.

Small Claims Courts

Variations of the pre-trial and trial procedures described above apply in most jurisdictions at the superior court level. At the small claims court level, however, the procedure is much simplified. The small claims court is the court that will hear claims when the amount being contested is under $10 000, or less in some jurisdictions. The action is usually initiated by the plaintiff, who simply files a document, which is served on the defendant, stating the nature of the complaint. Pleadings and examinations for discovery are dispensed with, although mediation is mandated in some jurisdictions and in British Columbia a settlement hearing is conducted. The next stage is the trial itself. While at the superior court level the judge acts somewhat like an umpire with the lawyers championing their clients' causes, at the small claims level the judge, by questioning the parties and witnesses, takes on a more active role in making sure that all of the information comes out. The presence of lawyers is discouraged by restricting claims for legal costs. Usually the judge will make her decision on the spot, but sometimes, even in small claims court, she will reserve her judgment and deliver it later.

Appeal

If either party is dissatisfied with the decision of the trial court, that party may have the right to appeal. If the judge made an error in stating the law in his reasons for his decision, or if the finding of fact at trial was based on evidence that should not have been admitted, those matters can be appealed. Whether that evidence should have been admitted or not is, of course, a question of law rather than a question of fact and, thus, can be the subject of an appeal. As a general rule, it is only questions of law or errors in law that can be challenged through the process of appeal. The person launching the appeal is referred to as the appellant, and could be either the plaintiff or the defendant in the trial, depending on who is dissatisfied with its outcome. The other person in the action is referred to as the respondent. In order to launch an appeal, the appellant must not only register the notice of appeal with the appropriate appeal court but also serve a copy on the respondent within a short period of time.

Usually the provincial Court of Appeal deals with appeals, but if the trial being appealed is from the small claims level of the Provincial Court, the appeal might be put to a judge at the Supreme Court (or Court of Queen's Bench). In Ontario such an appeal usually goes to the Divisional Court, a section of the General Division of the Ontario Court. It should be noted that this would be a new trial, not a true appeal as described below. The appellant must prepare an appeal book, containing a table of contents, all of the pleadings, the notice of appeal, the judgment of the trial court and reasons, as well as other information, such as a transcript of the evidence given at trial and any motions made. Also normally included is a *factum*, which sets out a statement of the facts, the issues, the arguments, the understanding of law upon which the complaint is based, and references to relevant cases and statutes. The respondent will also normally file a factum, summarizing things from his or her perspective. This information is examined by the appeal judges before the hearing. There can be one, three or five judges sitting on an appeal; there is always an odd number to ensure that, if they don't agree, there is no deadlock.

The appeal is not a complete rehearing of the case; rather, it is an examination of the appellant's complaint in relation to the trial process. Usually, the complaint is directed at some specific error of law, such as an error made by the judge regarding the reasons for the decision, or the admissibility of some evidence the appellant claims should or should not have been admitted. If a jury was involved at the trial level, the complaint might deal with the words the judge used to direct the jury. The appeal court assumes that because the trial judge and/or jury saw the witnesses and heard their actual testimony, they are in the best position to determine the facts. After reading the material and hearing the arguments, the appeal judges will then render their decision. The appeal judges' decision might affirm the lower court decision. If they agree that an error has been made, however, they might either overturn the decision, thus reversing the outcome and giving judgment to the other party, or send the matter back for retrial. If one of the parties disagrees with the appeal court's decision, the matter could be appealed again if there is a higher court to appeal to. This court would normally be the Supreme Court of Canada, but as explained above, only appeals that have been given leave may proceed that far.

Enforcement

Once the decision of the final court has been rendered, the process of recovery for the victor begins. It may well be that the defendant, if she is the losing party, and who is now referred to as the judgment debtor, will simply accept the judgment and make the appropriate payment to the other party. On the other hand, the defendant may not be able to do this because of lack of funds, or she may simply refuse to cooperate. There may be many other creditors and judgment holders (referred to as judgment creditors), each with a claim against the assets of the judgment debtor. The plaintiff then, if successful, must take steps to enforce the judgment.

If the judgment debtor has no money and no assets, it is usually senseless to incur the expense of trying to enforce the judgment. Sometimes, however, there are good reasons to obtain a judgment, even when the person being sued has no assets. If circumstances change in that person's life — for example, if she gets a good job, wins a lottery or inherits an estate — the judgment could then be enforced against her. For this reason, it may be worth going through the process; however, it is a judgment call and a risk; the cost of bringing the action may never be justified by what is actually collected. When a debtor is unable to pay, it is referred to as a dry judgment. In these circumstances, the plaintiff not only will be unable to collect the judgment from the judgment debtor but also will have to bear his own legal costs, because these cannot be collected from the debtor.

Examination in Aid of Execution

In the not-too-distant past, a person who could not pay his debts was sent to a debtors' prison. Today, debtors in Canada are not imprisoned unless they have committed some other kind of offence, such as fraud or contempt of court. A debtor who *cannot* honour the court order will not be jailed, but a person who *refuses* to honour the court order could find himself behind bars. The process of having an examination in aid of execution is usually the first step in enforcing a judgment. In this process, the successful judgment creditor will bring an application before a judge (or in some cases another officer of the court, such as a clerk or registrar) to have the judgment debtor brought before an officer of the court. The judgment debtor will then be examined by the judgment creditor's lawyer regarding his assets. The lawyer can ask questions about wages, other income, cars, property, boats, vacation property, safety deposit boxes, inheritances, bank accounts and so on. These questions are designed to determine what assets the debtor has and where they are located, in order to satisfy the judgment and to make them available to the judgment creditor. These questions must be answered under oath. Once the assets of the debtor are determined, the court can issue an order to seize them if they are not surrendered voluntarily.

Other Remedies and Limitations

The seizure of money from bank accounts and wages in order to pay a debt is called **garnishment**. The person holding the money, or *garnishee*, is required under this order to pay the money over to the court rather than to the debtor. However, only a portion of a person's wages can be garnisheed; the debtor is left with enough to live on. If real property is involved, the judgment is registered with the appropriate land registry district. It can be enforced by having the property sold if the debt is not paid. Usually, the presence of such a judgment against the property will put great pressure on the debtor to pay, because it will be very difficult to sell, mortgage or otherwise deal with that property while the judgment is registered against it. If there are others with a prior secured interest against that property, such as a mortgagee, they will still have a prior claim.

Cars, stereos, household articles and personal possessions can all be seized to satisfy the judgment; there is legislation in each province, however, to protect the debtor's livelihood by limiting the amount of assets that can be seized in this way. In Ontario, the *Creditors' Relief Act* puts a limitation on just what can be seized, as well as stating that the proceeds from the sale of seized goods must be made available to all the creditors who have a claim. In all jurisdictions, food, clothing, bedding, furniture, tools needed to perform a trade, fuel, and motor vehicles used in the course of employment are, to differing extents, exempted from seizure. When a judgment is involved, the seizure and sale of these goods is normally performed for a fee by government officials. Interest must be paid by the judgment debtor on the amount owing, from the time the debt was first incurred to the time of judgment (pre-judgment interest) and from judgment until ultimate payment (post-judgment interest).

Costs

The costs of taking a person to judgment and enforcing that judgment can be very significant and must be taken into consideration when contemplating such an action. Although there is the provision for the loser of a court action to pay the costs of the winner, this is usually not enough to cover all the legal expenses of the successful party. There is also the problem of whether or not the person who loses the action has the assets to cover the amount of the judgment. As well, there can be further expenses involved in trying to collect the judgment. The possibility of losing must also be taken into consideration. The losing party will not only fail to obtain compensation for his own legal costs but will also be required to pay the costs of the winning party.

On the other hand, if a person chooses to delay suing, there is a risk that the limitation period will pass. A person with a civil claim must launch a court action by issuing the writ of summons or other originating document within a specified period of time from the commission of the act complained of. Usually this time is set by provincial statute. It might range from two years for a tort action, such as negligence, to six years for an action to collect a debt. If an action has not been started by that time, it will be too late to sue. To satisfy this time limit, it is only necessary that a writ be filed. The writ does not have to be served for up to a year from the time of issuance. Costs of court settlement may outweigh returns.

Bankruptcy

Finally, the debtor has another way out: He or she can declare bankruptcy under the federal bankruptcy legislation. Simply put, the bankruptcy legislation provides a process for a debtor, hopelessly encumbered by debt, to be released from his obligations. Insolvency means that a debtor cannot pay debts as they come due, but bankruptcy means something quite different. In a bankruptcy, the debtor either voluntarily assigns personal assets to a trustee (called an assignment in bankruptcy) or an application is brought to the court by the creditors to forcibly convey those assets to a trustee (called a receiving order). The trustee then is charged with getting as much money as possible out of those assets for the benefit of the creditors. Recent changes to the bankruptcy legislation of Canada allow the debtor to seek the protection under the act by making a proposal to his creditors. This prevents them from seizing property to satisfy a debt or judgment for a set period of time, giving the debtor time to rearrange his affairs.

Not all the assets of the debtor are taken in this process. Certain assets are exempt, such as bedding, specified furniture, and food; these remain the property of the debtor. These are the things needed to carry on a basic level of life and to earn a living. If the debtor hasn't committed any fraud or other wrongful conduct such as trying to hide assets from the trustee and creditors, after a period of time an application can be brought to the court for the debtor to be relieved of his debts. This is called discharge of the bankruptcy. In a first-time consumer bankruptcy, such a discharge is automatic unless a creditor objects. When the court grants such discharge, the bankrupt no longer owes anything to the creditors, even if they have not been paid off from the sale of the assets. When the bankrupt's assets cover too small a portion of the outstanding debts the court will often grant a conditional discharge. This condition will require more payments to be made by the debtor even after discharge.

After the discharge, the bankrupt starts fresh and those creditors no longer have any claim against him. Even if there is an outstanding judgment, it comes to an end. Only ongoing obligations, such as a court order for the payment of maintenance, will survive the discharge of the bankruptcy. If, subsequent to discharge, the discharged bankrupt comes into a fortune by winning a lottery or inheriting an estate, the pre-bankruptcy creditors will have no claim against him, and there is no obligation on him to make that money available to satisfy those old debts. The purpose of this system of bankruptcy is to allow a person who could be a productive member of society to start afresh. It makes no sense for such debtors to be encumbered for the rest of their lives, facing impossible debt with no hope of getting out from under it. The primary interest of most creditors is to get as much as they can from the situation, not to ruin the debtor. The bankruptcy process allows a potentially useful member of society to start again, while ensuring that the creditors are protected as much as possible by transferring the assets of the debtor to the trustee, who manages them to the benefit of those creditors. It should be noted that recent changes in the law may allow debts owed to the government such as student loans to survive bankruptcy.

CRIMINAL PROCEDURE

A primary distinction between a criminal action and the civil action described above is the parties involved. In a civil action there are two private parties (even if the government is one of them, it is acting as a private party), and the role of the court is to adjudicate between them. In a criminal matter, however, the government or state, referred to as the Crown, is one of the parties. The Crown then prosecutes the accused, and the role of the court is to adjudicate between them. To protect the rights of the accused, the court must be independent of the influence of government, and procedural regulations seek to guarantee that the rights of the accused are protected. Because this process is so tied to the criminal law itself, we will deal with criminal procedure in Chapter 7, which is devoted to criminal law.

COURT PERSONNEL

The most prominent personnel involved in the legal system are the judges and the lawyers. In Canada, lawyers act as both barristers (lawyers who represent their clients in court) and solicitors (lawyers who undertake the paperwork required by the legal system), although most specialize in one aspect of the law or the other. Judges are almost always selected from the ranks of lawyers. The functions these professionals perform have been described throughout this text. A number of other people associated with the legal system, however, often go unnoticed. Many common law jurisdictions have notaries public, who offer legal services but are independent of the legal profession. Notaries take oaths, swear affidavits when they are required to satisfy governmental procedure and requirements, and also provide some basic legal services, such as transferring the title of houses, witnessing official documents and so on. Because all lawyers are also notaries and the number of lawyers has greatly increased in recent times, the need for this separate profession is no longer as great as it once was.

Law Practice

In the law office, a number of people may be employed to assist lawyers in carrying out their responsibilities. Historically, these services were performed by legal secretaries or articling clerks. Legal secretaries are people with secretarial skills who specialize in the services required to assist lawyers in preparing and filing documents, completing real estate transactions, and the like. Training for such a career is often provided by vocational institutions and colleges. The articled clerk is a law student who, upon graduation from law school, is required to serve a period of time as an apprentice in a legal firm before being called to the bar and practising. Paralegals are often added to this complement. They specialize in some aspect of legal practice, such as legal conveyancing, the documentation involved in litigation, the preparation of other documents, and so forth. Paralegals, who are trained in colleges or on the job, are becoming indispensable in major law offices, but the responsibility for their work rests on the lawyers.

Associated Agencies

In addition, private companies offering services to lawyers are often set up. For example, title-search companies register and search the documentation associated with real estate transactions, a service for which lawyers pay a fee. Justices of the peace are judicial officials, usually taken from the ranks of clerks or other experienced people and given the responsibility of swearing out information forms, laying charges, taking oaths, and serving other specified judicial functions as set out in the *Criminal Code* and other federal legislation. Typically, these officials can also adjudicate provincial offences under provincial legislation, and have powers as designated within that legislation.

Courthouse

The court system also employs a large number of clerical and administrative personnel. Because it is under provincial jurisdiction, the various offices and officials are created under the provincial *Judicature Act* or its equivalent. Typically, the person in charge of the organizational aspects of the court structure, the one who makes sure that cases are scheduled, is referred to as the Court Registrar, although the Chief Justice of the court in question has ultimate authority. Registrars also have a judicial function in determining, after the judgment has been rendered, the amount of the costs and how they are to be distributed, in accordance with the judge's decision. An extension of the Court Registrar function is now done by Masters. These are lawyers appointed to deal with, among other things, matters under the *Bankruptcy Act* or when there is a complaint about a lawyer's fees.

Courtroom

Besides the judge and the lawyers in the courtroom, there is a court clerk who collects and stamps documents, marks exhibits and is generally responsible for the flow of information. The court reporter is responsible for taking down all the words of the witnesses, the lawyers and the judge during the trial, with of course electronic backup. This transcript of the trial can be very important for appeal purposes. Reporters are also used in the examination-for-discovery process. In addition to these parties, if a criminal action is involved, there is usually either a police or a sheriff's officer present. These officers, sometimes referred to as bailiffs, are responsible for maintaining order in the courtroom.

Judges

Judges are appointed by the government from the ranks of lawyers in a community. At the superior court level, judges are selected by the federal government from a list of appointees recommended by the provincial governments. Judges at the provincial or inferior court level are appointed by the provincial government. Judges have no special training for their profession other than their experience as barristers and solicitors practising in the court system and some limited instruction and training they receive when they are called and as they continue to serve. Security of tenure is important to allow judges to do their job. The independence of the judiciary is such that a judge can only be removed for misbehaviour, such as taking a bribe or speaking out in areas where his or her qualifications to serve as an impartial judge would be put into question. Removal from the superior court level is extremely rare. In most situations, a judge would resign rather than face this eventuality. A judge appointed by the federal government can remain in office until retirement (usually at age 75). Of course, if a judge becomes physically or mentally incapable of functioning, he or she can be removed from office.

There are several limitations on a judge's freedom, compared to other citizens. A judge must avoid anything that creates a conflict of interest. He or she must give up directorships or other management positions in corporations and business ventures. A judge must also be very careful when speaking on public matters that he or she may later be required to adjudicate. If charged with traffic or other minor offences, a judge is expected not to contest the charge, in order to avoid embarrassing colleagues by having to appear before them.

A judge's salary is set by government and is usually considerably less than what could be earned by an experienced practising lawyer. Monetary gain is not usually an incentive for accepting a judgeship, but the status awarded judges is great. Such an appointment is often considered the apex of a legal career.

Lawyers

Lawyers must be members of the bar association of the province in which they practise. The bar associations or law societies are officially recognized professional bodies made up of practising lawyers within the province. Each is a self-governing body, responsible not only for setting the standards for admission and continued practice but also for disciplining members who fail to meet those standards. The benchers of the bar or law society are members elected by the other lawyers in the province. They serve, in effect, as a board of directors of that law society. In some of the bar associations across Canada, lay benchers have been appointed in an effort to ensure that the public good is recognized. This is also a political step to increase the recognition and level of respect given to lawyers.

For a lawyer to be called to the bar and become a member of this professional body, the qualification requirements as set out by that body must be met. Usually, this involves a university law degree, which is most often preceded by an undergraduate degree; thus, most lawyers have undergone at least seven years of university. Most law schools reserve the right to admit mature students directly into the program, although most require a minimum university experience of two or three years. After attaining an LL.B. degree, the graduate must serve as an articling student. During this time, the student must take courses provided by the law society and write examinations, usually referred to as bar exams. Upon successfully completing the articling process and the bar exams, as well as meeting the other qualifications set down by the law society, the student will be admitted as a member of the bar.

In Canada, lawyers are called to the bar as both barristers and solicitors. Some choose to practise primarily as advocates in the courtroom, but others may choose to fulfill their role as solicitors. These distinctions are not imposed on them; they are free to function in either area if they so wish.

The lawyer may go into business as a sole practitioner, undertaking everything from transferring real estate to criminal defences. Partnerships offer a different alternative, allowing the lawyer to specialize in a particular area of the law. While most lawyers practise in the legal system, many others devote their professional lives to such fields as education, business and government.

Normally lawyers in practice charge an hourly fee for their services, or they charge at a set rate for the job being done. In the last 20 years the practice has developed of charging a contingency fee. Here the lawyer represents the plaintiff, usually in a negligence action where there is no doubt of the liability of the defendant, and receives as his or her fee a percentage of the award of damages given to the plaintiff. This is usually up to 35 per cent if the matter goes to trial. The lawyer is not paid if the action fails. Initially this practice was resisted because it seemed to encourage litigation. However, because it allowed people who could not otherwise afford it to seek satisfaction of their rights in court, the contingency fee came to be recognized as the poor man's key to the courthouse. Still, the use of contingency fees is prohibited in several provinces, notably Ontario.

Because the practice of law is a business, advertising has become an important component of it. Until recent times, advertising was considered to be beneath the dignity of lawyers. They were prohibited from doing anything more than listing their phone numbers in the telephone book. This position has now largely been abandoned; today, in most jurisdictions, it is common for lawyers to use some form of advertising.

As is the case with any profession, lawyers are bound to a strict standard of professional ethics. While these standards are defined in various canons of legal practice, each law society sets out specific standards of conduct for their members, which may not be violated. One of the important functions of a provincial law society is to discipline any of its members who have contravened these ethical standards. One of the primary requirements for lawyers is that they must avoid conflicts of interest. Thus, if members become involved in the business affairs of their clients or act for both sides in a matter that potentially involves a dispute, they have violated that ethical standard. A common reason for disciplinary action against a lawyer, usually involving disbarment (the lawyer is stripped of membership in the law society and of the right to practise law), is the misuse of trust funds. Lawyers often have large sums of money entrusted to them. They must keep a separate bank account to handle these funds. Because the amounts in these accounts are often large, there is a great temptation to use these monies for personal or other unrelated purposes. Such conduct is in clear violation of legal ethics and of the law. Depending on the province, interest from monies held in the trust accounts of law firms may be turned over to provincial law foundations, which administer the funds to promote a variety of public legal education services.

Lawyers often face an ethical question as to whether they should defend someone who admits to having committed the offending act. In fact, the lawyer has a duty to represent anyone in need of legal representation. It is not the lawyer's function to prejudge the case. The litigation process is based on an adversarial model, with both sides making every effort to present their clients in the best light. As long as both sides are trying, the legal system is balanced; therefore, the judge or jury will be able to reach a proper decision. If a lawyer prejudges a case and as a result does not represent the client well, the system becomes skewed and justice is not served.

At the same time, lawyers have a duty to the court. They must assist clients neither to lie nor to mislead the courts. Many lawyers, if they know their client is likely to lie, will still represent the client to the extent of ensuring that the Crown fulfills its obligation to prove the per-

A Discussion Between Samuel Johnson and James Boswell, 1768

Boswell: I asked him whether, as a moralist, he did not think that the practice of law, in some degree, hurt the nice feeling of honesty.

Johnson: Why no, Sir, if you act properly. You are not to deceive your clients with false representations of your opinion: you are not to tell lies to a judge.

Boswell: But what do you think of supporting a cause which you know to be bad?

Johnson: Sir, you do not know it to be good or bad till the Judge determines it. I have said that you are to state facts fairly; so that your thinking, or what you call knowing, a cause to be bad, must be from reasoning, must be from your supposing your arguments to be weak and inconclusive. But, Sir, that is not enough. An argument which does not convince yourself, may convince the Judge to whom you urge it; and if it does convince him, why, then, Sir, you are wrong, and he is right. It is his business to judge; and you are not to be confident in your own opinion that a cause is bad, but to say all you can for your client, and then hear the Judge's opinion.

Chapman, R.W., ed. *Boswell: Life of Johnson*, 3rd ed. Oxford: Oxford University Press, 1970, p. 388.

son guilty. They will cross-examine Crown witnesses, make sure that the proper procedures are followed, and take advantage of any errors or omissions that benefit their clients. They will even call witnesses who can give evidence reflecting favourably on their clients. But they will not be party to putting their clients, or any other witnesses, on the stand knowing they will lie and mislead the courts. If lawyers make this clear to their clients, and their clients agree to these terms, then the lawyers have acted ethically in the eyes of the legal profession.

CONCLUSION

The most prominent institution in the judicial system is the courts. The regulations that determine their structure and govern their operation have been established by tradition and convention, and are set out in the Constitution and federal statutes. The integrity of the court relies on the judiciary adhering to the rules of procedure and practices that engender the respect and confidence of the public. The purpose of the courts is to administer the law as it is set out in the Constitution, legislation, the common law and equity, and the goal is to resolve disputes justly and fairly. While there may be instances when these objectives run counter to each other, maintaining the consistency and predictability of judicial decisions is paramount. The various levels within the court hierarchy and the standards that regulate the profession work to ensure that this characteristic is retained within the system. The product of the pursuit of these goals is a system that is complex, expensive to operate and much encumbered because of the time and energy expended on formal dispute resolution. Much contemporary debate about the judicial system centres on the need for reform and alternative forums for managing and resolving conflicting claims. That is the topic of the next chapter of this text.

QUESTIONS FOR DISCUSSION AND REVIEW

1. Propose the response a Supreme Court justice might make to a request to conduct an appeal hearing in private.

2. Consider some of the negative implications of the adversarial model of dispute resolution.

3. Discuss the change in the role of judges as a result of the *Charter of Rights and Freedoms*.

4. Describe the process by which an individual might challenge a government agency that she feels has violated her Charter rights.

5. Outline the stages of civil litigation and suggest why they are so complex.

6. Discuss the implications of the judicial system's commitment to preserve legal rights for individuals accused of crimes.

7. Suggest advantages and disadvantages of having a case heard by a jury or by a judge alone.

8. It is said that the judicial system has become mired in a backlog of cases and is too expensive for the average person to access. Comment on those claims and suggest ways it might be reformed.

9. Explain some of the reasons for the delay present in civil litigation and indicate any justification for it.

10. Consider the ethics of acting as defence counsel for a person who has committed a heinous crime and what restrictions should be placed on his or her actions in the process.

NOTES

1. Llewellyn, K. and A. Hoebel. *The Cheyenne Way.* Tulsa: University of Oklahoma Press, 1941, p. 28.

2. Hogg, Peter. *Constitutional Law of Canada.* Toronto: Carswell, p. 186.

3. *Ibid.*, p. 217.

4. *Harrison v.* Carswell, [1976] 2 S.C.C. 200.

5. Coval, S.C. and J.C. Smith. "The Supreme Court and a New Jurisprudence for Canada." *The Canadian Bar Review*, Vol. LIII, 1975, p. 824.

6. *Ibid.*, p. 825.

7. Wilson, Bertha. "Decision-Making in the Supreme Court." *University of Toronto Law Journal*, Vol. 36, 1986, p. 227.

8. Daisley, Brad. "Litigators Must React to Courts' New Attitude Towards Precedent: Major." *The Lawyers Weekly*, August, 1996, p. 6.

9. *Reference Re Offshore Mineral Rights of B.C.*, [1967] S.C.R. 792.

10. *Reference Re Secession of Quebec* (1998], 161 D.L.R. (4th) 385.

11. Some provinces have eliminated the examination for discovery process. In all jurisdictions, in the more simplified processes in place in small claims actions, the involved procedures discussed above, including the discovery process, are eliminated.

FURTHER READING

Banfield, Jane, ed. *Readings in Law and Society.* See especially Bertha Wilson, "Decision-Making in the Supreme Court," pp. 124–129, and Peter H. Russell, "Basic Structure of Canadian Courts" and "The Supreme Court of Canada," pp. 89–102.

McCormich, Peter and Ian Greene. *Judges and Judging.* Toronto: James Lorimer, 1990.

Morton, F.L., ed. *Law, Politics and the Judicial Process in Canada.* Calgary: University of Calgary Press, 1987.

Russell, Peter H. *The Judiciary in Canada.* Toronto: McGraw-Hill Ryerson, 1987.

Snell, James S. and Frederick Vaughn. *The Supreme Court of Canada.* Toronto: The Osgoode Society, 1985.

Strayer, Barry L. *The Canadian Constitution and the Courts.* Vancouver: Butterworths, 1983.

RESOLVING DISPUTES OUTSIDE THE COURTS:

Administrative Tribunals and Alternative Methods of Dispute Resolution

Chapter 6

INTRODUCTION

The focus of the text thus far has been on the common law system inherited from Britain, and it was suggested at the beginning that that system developed because of the need to find a practical and predictable way to resolve disputes. As we have traced its development, we have found that law has come to serve many more purposes than simply as a dispute resolution mechanism. The common law protects individual rights and personal interests in land and property. It provides a means for punishing behaviour that causes injury or loss and provides compensation. Statutory law sets out to order society in highly sophisticated ways. It regulates the economy; it regulates business and industry; it protects consumers; and it determines rights and obligations. In the process of overseeing that laws are implemented fairly and uniformly, modern courts have to deal with a wide range of matters. As our population grows and the diversity and complexity of social and commercial activities increase, the courts are hard-pressed to keep up with the demands placed on their services.

The current system has been criticized because of its inefficiency, expense and inaccessibility, and perhaps it is too much to expect that the adversarial court-adjudicated method of resolving the multitude of disputes that such complex societies engender would be adequate, particularly when that method is fraught with formality, exclusivity and manned by a closed body of professionals trained primarily in the law who do the work of the court.

The courts are not always the best forum in which to have disputes between individuals and institutions resolved. Taking a case to court is a costly and time-consuming process. It also takes control of the matter in dispute away from the parties involved, and sometimes imposes a solution that is in the best interests of neither party. The formal structure of the courtroom, as well as its apparent inaccessibility to some groups in society, also tend to discourage many from defending their rights. As a result, alternative methods of dealing with disputes have been developed that play an increasingly important role in our legal system.

> Lengthy delays in civil cases favour affluent litigants over those with modest means. Delays distort the financial effects of the ultimate verdict on the parties and may impose severe emotional strain. Perhaps the answer is increased use of arbitration and mediation.[1]
>
> Chief Justice Brian Dickson of the Supreme Court of Canada, 1987

ADMINISTRATIVE LAW

We live in a heavily regulated society. Statutory law has been enacted to affect many aspects of our personal, social and professional lives. The statutes are complex and far-reaching and establish all of the agencies and departments set up to conduct the business of government. Public programs are designed to fill needs that are not met by private enterprises. When a need is identified, a policy is defined by members of legislatures and government bureaucrats and a statute is written to address the problem. Often the statute provides for a body to administer it and authorizes the passage of additional regulations necessary to set in place the policies of the agency. This is a new legal framework operating outside of the court system, with the responsibility for implementing the policies of the government and providing a means for resolving conflicts arising from the implementation of those policies and when individuals affected by them have a complaint.

In addition to the courts described in the previous chapter, there are other government bodies that have an adjudicative function. These bodies often look and act like courts; they are, however, part of the executive branch of government. The function of government is divided into three branches: the **judicial** branch, which includes the courts with their adjudicative process; the **legislative** branch, which in Canada includes both the federal Parliament and the provincial legislative assemblies; and finally the **executive** branch, which is responsible for implementing the law and includes the various departments of government. The employment insurance commission, the taxation branch, the workers' compensation board, the consumer and corporate affairs department, forestry, the police, the military, the postal services, and, in fact, almost all government agencies that individuals have any contact with are part of this executive branch of government.

The executive branch of government, whether at the federal or provincial levels, regulates and includes the employees within its jurisdiction. These employees, in turn, have contact with citizens through government agencies, offices, and departments. Disputes sometimes arise as a result of these contacts. In the past the place for the resolution of such disagreements was in the courts. It became apparent, however, that it was more efficient and practical to establish mechanisms within the various government departments to handle such disputes. Thus, if a citizen has a dispute with the employment insurance commission as to whether she is entitled to unemployment insurance payments, she can challenge the decision by taking it to an appeal board set up under the auspices of the employment insurance commission. This board functions like a court but it is not part of the judicial branch of government at all. Rather, it is an **administrative tribunal** set up under the government bureaucracy, and it is part of the executive branch. The distinction is very important because the function of the executive branch of government, and any agency set up under it, is to facilitate and implement government policy. Even if that policy is inconsistent with the law or the interests of citizens, it is quite possible that the government interests will prevail. Citizens who have a disagreement with how the policy is implemented or whose rights are infringed by the agency's administrators must turn to that body for redress. In that decision-making process, as in a court, great care must be exercised to ensure that decisions are made impartially and free from discriminatory bias. The function of the court, on the other hand, is to apply the law, independent of government policy.

Administrative Tribunals

Although administrative tribunals are not courts of law, their impact on the parties involved can be every bit as important and significant as that of the courts. The right to receive compensation for a work-related injury or getting permission to build a shopping mall depends on the decisions made by government agents functioning as decision-makers. Thus, the power of workers' compensation boards and municipal councils and other bodies like them can be extremely important to the parties that appear before them. In fact some legal professionals have suggested that some administrative tribunals have become as formal and adversarial as the courts, and that essentially there has just been a change in the judges.[2]

The range of situations that are dealt with by bodies functioning like tribunals is extensive. Commissions struck by the government to conduct public inquiries can have a serious impact on the career of a person named in the investigation, and the officials must be careful not to go beyond their jurisdiction when implicating people who are involved in the subject matter of the inquiry. The Royal Commission appointed to head the inquiry into the distribution of blood products by the Red Cross was specifically ordered by the Supreme Court of Canada not to name the people who they may have determined were responsible for the decisions that resulted in not adequately testing for contaminated blood. Had they released the names, the action could have been challenged by a court as having gone beyond the jurisdiction of the Commission. The BC Supreme Court awarded a civil servant legal costs and the government was prompted to settle a civil suit because the court decided that the Commissioner of a public inquiry had "gone beyond the jurisdiction of the commissioner" when he criticized her performance. As an indirect result of the criticism, she lost her job and her professional reputation was maligned.[3] This is an example of the recourse available to people who have suffered losses because of their treatment at the hands of an officer of the government. The courts maintain a supervisory role when government or its agencies function beyond the scope of their powers.

Because there are as many different forms of tribunals as there are government bureaucracies, it is difficult to describe their structure and procedures. It can be said, however, that whenever a government administrator takes on a judicial or quasi-judicial function making a decision affecting the rights of others, some basic rules of procedure, sometimes referred to as **due process** or the **rules of natural justice**, must be followed. A government representative or board, functioning as a judge, is required to follow some basic rules and procedures when making such decisions as whether or not a citizen should get an employment insurance cheque or a union should be certified. If they fail to follow those rules, the judicial branch of government has reserved the right to supervise the process and review the decision based on the principles established in the concept of the rule of law.

These regulators may be individual government employees or members of administrative tribunals serving on a full- or part-time basis as employees of the government. As such they are subject to political will. Their job is to implement the policies of the agency and to conduct hearings and make decisions according to the rules and procedures set out in the legislation. A decision-maker should have some autonomy to ensure that the decision is unbiased. One of the problems with administrative tribunals is that their commitment to uphold the policies of the department that pays their salaries is sometimes in conflict with responding to the needs of individuals who feel they have been harmed by those policies.

The Rule of Law

Since Canadians are governed by a principle called the rule of law, the powers held by government bureaucrats or boards must be set out in legislation. Such bureaucrats or boards must be able to point to some source of authority in the law that grants them the power to make decisions that affect the citizens or bodies appearing before them. Supreme Court Justice Beverley McLachlin has summarized the various definitions of this concept that have been offered by jurists over the years and applied them to administrative tribunals and the way they use their discretionary power. She suggests that the "principles of general application should apply to all public decision-making in a democratic society. We expect our administrative tribunals to be bound by the law, to render decisions in an equal and predictive manner and to act in accordance with law and social values."[4] She adopted a list developed by Professor G. Walker, who identified 12 basic "requirements" of the rule of law that serve to remind us of the essential characteristics of an effective judicial system.

1. Freedom from private lawlessness (coercion).
2. Government under law: the state must be bound by the ordinary law.
3. Ordinary (substantive) law should possess certainty, generality and equality.
4. Mechanisms must ensure the congruence of law with social values.
5. The effective and impartial enforcement of law and order (against private coercion).
6. The enforcement, through procedures and institutions, of government under law.
7. The assurance of the independence of the judiciary.
8. A system of legal representation: an independent legal profession.
9. The application (and enforcement) of the principles of natural justice.
10. The accessibility of the courts.
11. The assurance of "impartial and honest" law enforcement.
12. An "attitude of legality": the application of law in spirit as well as in letter.[5]

She went on to assert that "the modern concept of the rule of law provides a structure of legal and political values applicable not only to the courts, but also the administrative decisions of governments."

Administrative tribunals then cannot act in an arbitrary manner, but must point to some source of authority to support their exercise of power and then act consistently in the exercise of that power. Thus, if an officer working in the employment insurance commission denies a payment to a claimant, the claimant can appeal that decision to a board set up to hear such appeals. The decision-maker must be able to point to legislation, or to an authorizing regulation properly passed under that legislation, that bestows such power. Similarly, in a workers' compensation board hearing that denies a person the right to receive workers' compensation benefits, the decision-maker must be able to point to some legislative authority, or to regulations passed under that authority, that supports the exercise of such power. These are questions of jurisdiction.

The Charter of Rights and Freedoms

Even then, it may be possible to challenge the legislation itself as unauthorized under the constitutional division of powers in the *Constitution Act, 1867* or on the basis that it violates the provisions set out in the *Charter of Rights and Freedoms*. If a government administrator exceeds the authority given under the legislation or if the legislation is invalid because of either the Charter or the constitutional division of powers, the administrator's acts can be challenged. Even if the legislation and regulations authorizing the decision are valid and the decision-maker has acted within the powers granted under them, the administrator is still obligated to exercise the power according to certain basic procedural rules. The decision-maker must adhere to them at least whenever a decision is made that affects a person's basic rights.

The Rules of Natural Justice

The role of an administrative tribunal is to deal with individual problems when and where they occur. Such tribunals have the power to assess and levy fines, withhold payment of money, grant or refuse refugee status, approve an immigration application or determine whether a prisoner will be paroled. Most often the decision involves the determination of that person's legal rights, and often there is no right of appeal. Even then, where the process has been conducted improperly the complainant can still turn to the courts. These administrative tribunals are required to conduct any hearing according to the rules of natural justice.

Rules of natural justice are basically the rules of fair play, and primarily embodied in the idea of having a fair hearing. In fact, what constitutes a fair hearing may vary with the nature of the matter discussed. It may involve no more than allowing the interested party to write a letter describing his or her position. In other situations, it may require having the opportunity to appear before the decision-maker or cross-examine a witness. It is vital, however, that the person about to be affected by the decision be notified of the hearing ahead of time, and the full extent of the complaint must be detailed in that notice.

Sinkovich v. Strathroy (Town of) Commissioners of Police[6]

The Ontario Police Commission was asked to investigate the Strathroy Police Department because of a number of complaints that the Police Board had received about the management of the Department. The Commission held an inquiry and notified the Police Chief, Mr. Sinkovich, that he was to appear before it having been told only that the Commission was looking at the management and administration of the force. It turned out that it was the competence and personal conduct of the police chief himself that were being reviewed. His performance was found to be unsatisfactory and the commission recommended that he be dismissed.

Mr. Sinkovich complained and brought an application to the court that the decision of the Ontario Police Commission and the resulting report be quashed. The court agreed, saying that the only time a police chief could be terminated was after a proper hearing of the Board or after an inquiry of the Ontario Police Commission. Since Mr. Sinkovich wasn't given proper notice of the inquiry or told his position was in jeopardy, that inquiry was not properly conducted.

This case illustrates that in order for a proper hearing to take place, a person must be notified of that hearing, and a significant aspect of such notification is for him or her to be told the nature of the charges to be dealt with so that he or she will have an opportunity to respond. Notice and a fair hearing are central to the rules of natural justice.

If a municipal council informs an individual that a hearing is being held to consider whether or not a building permit will be suspended but does not state the nature of the complaint that prompted the hearing, the builder has not been given sufficient notice of the hearing because he has been given no indication of what to respond to. There are no formal requirements of how the hearing should proceed, only that the respondent be given a fair opportunity to be heard. Thus, there is no obligation to follow strict **rules of evidence**. There is an obligation, however, that the decision be made by the person hearing the evidence. Thus, if a hearing is held and the complainant gives evidence and presents witnesses but for some reason one of the members of the panel or board hearing the complaint is then changed, the panel or board must start all over again or make its decision with reduced numbers because the new member will not have heard all the evidence.

As well, the person making the decision must be **impartial**. When adjudicating between two people, for example, in a landlord and tenant dispute, if it can be shown that the decision-maker is somehow biased or has an interest in the outcome of the dispute (e.g., a cousin owns the building), that will be enough to overturn the decision. The decision-maker is no longer impartial. In some types of disputes, however, the role of the decision-maker or administrative tribunal is not to adjudicate between two parties appearing before them, but rather to hear a complaint laid against the conduct of the government agency itself. In this case, it is not a valid argument to state that the decision-maker is biased because he or she is employed by that government agency.

Other Curbs on Administrative Powers

Administrative tribunals are also subject to the terms of the *Charter of Rights and Freedoms*. If a person appearing before a government administrative tribunal or agency believes that his personal rights have been violated under the *Charter of Rights and Freedoms* or there is a problem with jurisdiction or due process, it is possible to apply for a judicial review. Court challenges to administrative action may be based on infringements of Charter rights such as the denial of liberty or security of the person or when the tribunal acts contrary to the principles of fundamental justice as set out in section 7 of the Charter.

Another factor that may result in judicial review is if the tribunal fails to act in a reasonable way (for example, its findings must be supported by facts or there must be sufficient legal evidence presented at the hearing to justify the decision). It is possible, however, for the tribunal to defend the seemingly unreasonable action on the grounds that it can be justified under section 1 of the Charter as a "reasonable limit prescribed by law."

There are a number of other requirements that must be met for an administrative decision to be beyond judicial review. The decision-maker must be properly appointed and must act within the authority granted by the statute. The members of the tribunal must be able to point to a specific term of the applicable statute to justify their action. In other words, they must function within the scope of the law and the jurisdiction they have been given. If the decision-maker is not authorized to act under the legislation or regulations, has exceeded authorized power, has not conducted the hearing in an impartial way or has not followed the rules of natural justice, then the individual has the right to turn to the courts for redress. If the decision-maker is functioning within the proper jurisdiction and the process is procedurally fair, the courts are generally reluctant to interfere with the decision. But if the decision incorporates a remedy beyond the decision-maker's power to grant, it will also be reviewable on the grounds of jurisdiction.

Administrative Discretion

It is well to remember at this point that for the most part the members of administrative tribunals are appointed because they have an expertise in the area and experience dealing with the legislation. Decision-making processes are subject to rules and guidelines developed to deal with the specific kind of problems that arise. As administrative decision-making has become more prevalent, so have the number of methods and devices available to assist in the application of the principles behind the rule of law. But they are not bound to the same rules of procedure that govern the courts, and to impose "strict judicial standards would impair the efficiency of administrative agencies, and a failure to recognize the particular expertise of administrative agencies may result in inappropriate decisions on matters of substance."[7] It is also important to recognize that any decision-maker must be able to exercise some discretion in order to come to effective, fair and just conclusions. That discretion must be used according to the framework standard to the agency, the jurisdiction and to accepted societal norms. As long as the decision is made within the parameters of the rule of law and the rules of natural justice and the policies set out in the legislation, the decision-maker is free to make a decision and the agency to implement it.

Judicial Review

The laws associated with judicial review are designed to ensure that administrative agencies conform to the rule of law. The courts will review a decision made where the procedure was inconsistent with those well-established principles. The power of the court to review provides a balance to the discretionary power given to government appointees. The court's supervision helps to ensure that government does not exercise its power arbitrarily. The review process is quite complex. It is unlike an appeal in that it is an exercise by the courts of a supervisory jurisdiction over any kind of adjudicative or judicial process that takes place within their jurisdiction.

The courts will consider a number of complaints against a decision made by an administrative tribunal. They will first look to the jurisdiction of the tribunal and determine that it was operating within its territorial jurisdiction as set out in sections 91 and 92 of the *Constitution Act, 1867.* Then they may determine whether the tribunal was acting under appropriately passed legislation within that jurisdiction. The next step is to decide whether the actions of the tribunal infringed on any rights set out in the *Charter of Rights and Freedoms.* The final concern of the courts is whether or not the hearing and decision-making process was conducted according the rules of natural justice. If any of these conditions are not satisfied, the courts may assume their responsibility to review the decision and apply remedies.

Court Powers

When the court believes that an injustice has taken place, it has an inherent right to intervene. In the exercise of its supervisory power, the court relies on prerogative writs to apply a remedy. These are ancient remedies traceable to the prerogative power of the Crown, mentioned in Chapter 1. There are four main writs in use today. The writ of *habeas corpus* is used when there is concern that a person is being improperly detained. This writ is primarily used in criminal matters, but it is also used in immigration and child custody cases or when people have been institutionalized for mental health reasons. The court will examine the decision to determine whether the custody meets the conditions described above. The main prerogative writs used by courts in their supervisory capacity are certiorari, mandamus or prohibition. Typically, a person applying for judicial review will ask for an order of *certiorari* when he or she wants the decision of the government administrator quashed or declared of no effect. The petitioner may ask for an order of *mandamus* to force the decision-maker to make a decision if the decision-maker has a duty to make a decision and has not done so. An order of **prohibition** may be granted when the claim is that the administrators should be prevented from making a decision or becoming involved in the process because they are exceeding their jurisdiction.

The court also has the power to make a **declaratory judgment**, which means it will declare the law that applies in the situation. When the impact of an unfair decision has already been felt, the complainant may be entitled to compensation that can be assessed and granted by the court. In addition to these remedies, the court may also issue the more common remedy of an injunction to prevent the government administrator from doing something unlawful or interfering with an individual's rights.

Damages may also be available in some circumstances. In many provinces, these tools have been amalgamated by statute into one procedure that greatly simplifies the process of judicial review.[8]

Privative Clauses

The courts have always been protective of their supervisory right over other adjudicative bodies, and legislators have been just as keen to stop courts from interfering. Many statutes that empower administrative tribunals now contain clauses that attempt to prevent courts from exercising their supervisory role. They are referred to as **privative clauses**. The legislation creating a government agency, such as the Labour Relations Board or Workers' Compensation Board, will often contain a clause saying that no decision of that board is reviewable by any court of law and no order of *certiorari*, prohibition, *mandamus* or declaratory judgment can have any effect against the decision of a board. While it may appear to be quite clear and concise, and under the principle of parliamentary supremacy seems to override any right of judicial review, the courts have always treated such privative clauses with a certain amount of resistance. Judges carefully read such clauses, looking for any kind of inconsistency or ambiguity, and should any be found, will interpret them in such a way as to give the courts power to review if they wish to do so. Therefore, one should not automatically conclude that the courts will have no power in the face of such a provision.

Administrative Process

Madame Justice McLachlin concludes her overview of the supervisory role of the courts in administrative decision-making by saying:

> The task of the courts in relation to administrative decision-makers is to provide society with assurances that the fundamental values associated with the rule of law are being respected in administrative decision-making. On the legal side, it is the traditions associated with an independent judiciary, established principles and the appeal process that ensure that the courts do not stray from the rule of law. On the administrative side, growing traditions and legislative limitations are effectively incorporating the same values. As a last resort, the courts stand as independent tribunals to which the citizen may appeal on (the hopefully infrequent) occasions when violations occur, who will hopefully ensure that discretionary power, wherever it is exercised, is exercised in accordance with the values underlying the rule of law.[9]

The field of administrative law is complex and involved. The expression "You can't fight city hall" finds its justification in the delay, technicality, difficulty and formality associated with this judicial review process. Costs are often prohibitive for private citizens. It is important to recognize, however, that when individual rights of citizens are trampled by abusive power exercised by government officials, these avenues are provided for redress.

There are some important advantages to having administrative tribunals resolve disputes besides reducing the burden on the courts. People appointed to serve on tribunals are specialists in the area, with a knowledge of the legislation, its goals and the way it was meant to be implemented. They are familiar with prior decisions and they are not restricted by judicial rules of evidence as they gather information about a case. The process is less formal than in the courts and is not as affected by scheduling problems. It is more efficient and less costly than a court-adjudicated decision. Generally the decision-making processes are open to public scrutiny and criticism, and public pressure can have some effect in getting the legislation amended.

ALTERNATIVE METHODS FOR DISPUTE RESOLUTION

So far in this text we have looked at the processes set in place by the Constitution and the executive branch of government to adjudicate disputes in both the private and public sectors. The traditional judicial system has evolved over centuries in an effort to find a reliable, predictable and effective way of resolving the conflicts between individuals and between people and society's institutions. Administrative tribunals have become important as they have assumed the responsibility of settling claims between citizens and government, relieving the courts of a heavy burden. There are other ways of handling conflict, and the rest of this chapter will examine some of them and point out some of the advantages and disadvantages of these alternatives.

Problems with the Judicial System

The courtroom is a formal place, governed by rules and procedures designed to protect the rights of parties, maintain the dignity of the court and ensure that justice is appropriately administered. Its hours of operation are usually limited to normal business hours or, in some instances, are shorter. Business attire is expected. Proceedings are lengthy and frequently delayed. In most Canadian courtrooms the official languages are limited to English and French, and Canadians of other languages must depend on translators, if indeed they are available. It is an unusual case where parties can avoid using the services of lawyers. The pre-trial proceedings are complex and arduous. The processing of documents is laborious and time-consuming, requiring the services of numerous court officers. Scheduling a trial date is often a problem. Court space is limited, and the schedules of courtrooms, judges, counsel and support staff must be coordinated. In some jurisdictions, parties can wait up to a year or more to get a hearing which itself may take weeks or months depending on the issue at stake. Then parties may have to wait months before a decision is rendered, only to go through a similarly time-consuming process if the matter is appealed by either party.

The costs of court action are often prohibitive, making the justice system available only to those who can afford it. Lawyers' fees, document processing fees and court time all cost money, and for an uncertain end. If a jury is used in a civil action, this adds to the time and cost of the trial. All of the time spent in the pre-trial and court process is time lost from normal business, professional and personal life.

In most cases, the court must decide wholly in favour of one side or the other, deciding from precedent how a case should be settled. Usually that means that one party has lost all and often may be required to assume the court costs as well as pay the judgment, which may be enough to put the loser into bankruptcy. This process almost certainly guarantees a complete breakdown in the business, social or personal relationship between the parties, precluding the possibility of future productive association.

It is these very factors, perhaps consciously encouraged by the system, that discourage people from ever taking a case to court. The first visit to a lawyer may inform a prospective plaintiff that the cost of the proceedings may be higher than any potential gains and that it may in fact be impractical to proceed. Many steps in the pre-trial proceedings are designed to help the parties reassess their positions before going to trial. The vast majority of cases are settled before trial, many of them on the courthouse steps, as parties recognize the vulnerability of their positions and the prospect of losing more than they are willing to settle for.

All of this frustration inevitably leads to the conclusion that there must be another way to resolve legal problems. Readers will likely be glad to hear that indeed there are other ways that are coming into prominence as the limitations of the court system become more apparent. In this chapter we will discuss several of them, as well as the advantages and disadvantages of turning to alternative dispute resolution mechanisms.

First Nations Justice Issues

The Dean of Law at the University of Victoria, David Cohen, reported in a conference in 1998 that law hadn't changed much in the last decade of the century, except in three areas. The first was as a result of the entrenchment of the Charter, the second was with the growth of alternative dispute resolution, and the third was with Native justice issues and particularly land claims.[10] We have mentioned Native justice issues in previous chapters, but Cohen's remarks about the formal and informal methods that have been used to attempt to address Native claims invite some comparisons between the role and effectiveness of traditional and alternative methods of resolving disputes.

The First Nations people in Canada have been seeking ways to clarify ancient treaties, renegotiate them or create new ones in order to gain a more just place in Confederation. In British Columbia Native groups have been pursuing their claims to land ever since territory was taken from them without the benefit of treaties in the nineteenth century. Unlike in the rest of

Canada, few treaties were drawn up in British Columbia, essentially because England had run out of funds to compensate Native people for their land. With the passage of the *Indian Act* in 1908, the Native people of BC were dealt with much as all the other First Nations people in Canada despite the lack of treaties. All Native people were relegated to live on reserve land, tribal governments were disbanded, children were sent to residential schools, and all were subjected to the narrow restrictions of the *Indian Act*. Most chafed under the federal government's administration of the terms of the Act and the loss of territory and rights they felt belonged to them. Ongoing efforts were made in the early part of the century to negotiate through the differences, but the *Indian Act* served to render them powerless in that forum. Having met with no success in the negotiation process, the Natives reconciled themselves to fighting the governments and their policies through the court system even though the process and the principles of the justice were foreign to their traditional ways of dealing with conflict.

In 1969 a court action was launched against the BC Attorney General by Frank Calder, a Nisga'a and the first Native member of the province's legislative assembly. The band wanted title to the area surrounding their reserve, claiming that the Nisga'a had used it throughout time and their claim to it had never lawfully been extinguished. Not surprisingly, the Nisga'a lost at the provincial trial and appeal levels. The case went to the Supreme Court of Canada, and six of the justices hearing the matter were evenly split on the issues. The seventh judge cast the deciding vote against the Nisga'a, but based his decision on a legal technicality. The decision was seen as a moral if not a legal victory for the Nisga'a because for the first time it was recognized that Native people did have some claim on their traditional lands.

There followed a long series of federal government initiatives to settle land-claim disputes, but because the BC government, which controlled the land in question, would not acknowledge the entitlement, for many years the issues remained contentious. The Natives hoped that the decision in the case would spur more fruitful land-claim negotiations between themselves and the federal and provincial governments. This was not to be, and so the Gixsan and Witsuwit'en bands from an area adjacent to the Nisga'a launched another action in 1987 known as *Delgamuukw v. British Columbia and the Attorney General of Canada* to have "ownership and jurisdiction" over their traditional lands. The trial-level judge dismissed their claims. When the case went to appeal, the BC Court of Appeal ruled against the appellants, who had replaced their claims to "ownership and jurisdiction" with "aboriginal title and self-government." The Court of Appeal dismissed the claims, giving reasons that discounted the reliability of oral history and therefore the primary source of evidence submitted by the appellants. It was clear that the BC courts and the Native people spoke different languages, each depending on understandings of law and justice that were incompatible, and that the courts could not deal with the issues to the satisfaction of either side. In a decision rendered in December 1997 the Supreme Court of Canada overturned the BC Court of Appeal decision and ordered a new trial. The court's reasons, set out by Chief Justice Lamer, challenged the way the trial and appeal courts failed to recognize the value of oral history. He stated:

> Many features of oral histories would count against both their admissibility and their weight as evidence of prior events in a court that took a traditional approach to the rules of evidence. The most fundamental of these is their broad social role not only "as a repository of historical knowledge for a culture" but also as expression of the 'the values and mores of [that] culture.' Notwithstanding the challenges created by the use of oral histories as proof of historical facts, the laws of evidence must be adapted in order that this type of evidence can be accommodated and placed on an equal footing with the types of historical evidence that courts are familiar with, which largely consists of historical documents.[11]

The Delgamuukw case took years of effort to bring to trial. Rooms full of documents were carried into the court, representing the labour of many lawyers working full-time at government expense. Evidence-gathering had to span two distinct cultural views and distinctive ways of recording history. The task of analyzing cultural evidence and testimony was given to middle-class Caucasian men whose training was in a form of law foreign to the plaintiffs. The courthouse itself, in the midst of a large urban centre far removed from the area at the centre of the conflict, was an alien environment to most of the people giving testimony. The legal costs were enormous, not to mention the personal toll the process took on the professionals and Natives alike. The frustration of having the case decided within the narrow constraints of Canadian law as it is administered in provincial courts with no consideration of the traditional laws of the Native people made most wonder if fairness or justice had in fact been achieved.

The effect of this decision and the stated goal of the Supreme Court decision was not to conduct a new trial of the matter but to finally draw the BC government and the Natives to the bargaining table to negotiate a settlement of the land-claim dispute. What has taken many years in the courts, for an inconclusive end, has provided the political will for the parties to negotiate through their differences and a recognition that putting such a sensitive matter in the hands of courts was really an abdication of decision-making responsibility. The courts forced government's hand, but it is clear that the decisions being made at the negotiating table are likely to have a more positive effect than could ever have been possible in a court-imposed decision because both sides are now participating in the process and both have agreed that a settlement of the dispute is the most important concern. Political opponents of the proposed treaty are taking the matter back to the court, however, and it remains to be seen whether the negotiated treaty can withstand these new court challenges.

What is Alternative Dispute Resolution?

There are a wide variety of dispute resolution mechanisms, some of which have been in use since the beginning of time. The new methods are based on old ideas and practices, some of which find their roots in pre-industrial cultures like those of First Nations people prior to European contact. They are products of the premise that people should first try to solve their own problems, if necessary seek the assistance of a neutral third person, or call on the community that is affected by the problem to reach a solution that satisfies everyone. These methods remain within the control of the people who have the problem, they remain private, and the problems are usually solved in such a way that the individuals can continue to associate with one another. The process contributes to the well-being of the community instead of detracting from it. None of these characteristics can be used to describe the court system as we know it today. Plaintiffs and defendants relinquish their positions into the hands of lawyers. The judge is rarely a member of their circle; the problems get a public airing, the decision hardly ever satisfies both parties and the only satisfaction the community gains is that it's finally over. There are some problems that require adjudication because they have complex legal questions at their heart or the conflict can only be resolved in that way. Where the legal rights are unclear or contested and where there is a great disparity in the power between the parties, it is often necessary to rely on the courts for a decision.

Not all the traditional methods of dealing with disputes are effective or satisfying. They include walking away from the problem, and that is only a temporary fix. The other way is to concede to the other party, and that too does not make for a long-term solution. Even compromise may not get each of the parties what they were looking for. It is possible too for one party to exercise power and subdue the other, which does little to enhance future harmonious relations. The ultimate and least satisfactory way to resolve an issue is to come to battle over it, with the victor taking away the spoils and the other suffering defeat. Within this range of alternatives there is room for more satisfying responses to conflict, and those methods have been identified, distinguished and developed as dispute resolution strategies that can effectively resolve disputes in business, social and private domains.

Alternative methods for resolving disputes have become more common in the latter third of the twentieth century. What began as community-based conflict resolution centres in the United States have mushroomed into a plethora of programs and institutions set up to address the problems facing the courts but have become increasingly accepted as people have been satisfied with the new dispute resolution options. The services offered by mediation and arbitration centres are numerous and varied. We will look at some that have become widely practised in Canada, ranging across the whole spectrum of dispute resolution, from criminal diversion programs through commercial and family mediations to labour arbitration.

Sentencing Circles

Alternatives to court action are being tried in the criminal justice system. One of them is being used in the Native communities and is called a sentencing circle. Because there is a disproportionately high number of Natives in federal and provincial prisons and the rate of recidivism is high, there is a consensus that sentencing Natives to prison serves no rehabilitative end, nor does it pose an effective deterrent. First Nations people have long desired some control over their justice issues, and giving some of that responsibility back to them is finally beginning to take place. In some jurisdictions, when a Native person has been convicted of a criminal offence, the jurisdiction has allowed a community-based group to assume the responsibility of sentencing the offender. While a court-appointed judge will preside in the circle and affirm the final decision, the judge's role is primarily that of facilitator as the members of the sentencing circle attempt to reach a consensus as to the best way for the offender to be held accountable for his or her offence. The circle may include the offender and his or her family, a probation officer, social workers, and other supportive people. It may also include the victim and his or her family as well as band leaders. The group members are given some flexibility as to how they will deal with the situation, and will take into consideration the needs of the victim and the community. They decide on a sentence that will have the greatest likelihood of rehabilitating the offender and deterring him or her from re-offending. The process has been found to be a positive step in Native communities to overcome some of the social problems they face and provide more productive ways of addressing harmful and self-destructive behaviours. This process is also helping to prepare First Nations peoples to assume more responsibility for their own justice issues.

Diversion in Criminal Justice

Even the use of diversion for people convicted of crimes in youth and criminal courts as alternatives to prison sentences is a form of alternative dispute resolution. These Alternative Measures Programs are usually administered by the Crown prosecutor's office. The prosecutor may encourage first-time offenders to participate in the program by removing the threat of incurring a criminal record. Offenders who plead guilty of less serious offences may be eligible for programs that allow them to reconcile with or make restitution to the victim of their crime. They can be given other means to repay society for their misdeeds by doing community service hours, or even discouraging others from following a similar course by speaking to youth groups or treatment programs. Even plea-bargaining is a form of negotiation where the offender is persuaded to plead guilty to a lesser offence rather than risk being convicted of a more serious charge in court. These measures are covered in more detail in the next chapter.

Alternative Dispute Resolution Mechanisms

The methods which will primarily be used in civil matters, including family breakdowns, contractual and other business disputes, fall into several distinct categories which can be placed on a scale, ranging from those in which there is no outside intervention to those where an outsider imposes a decision.

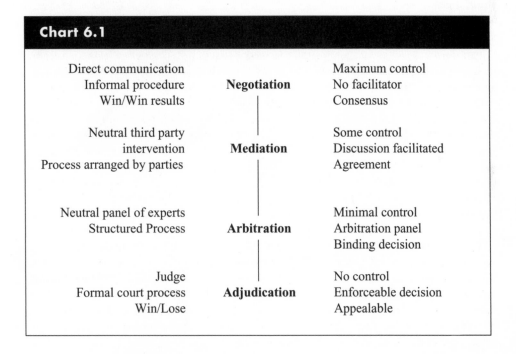

Chart 6.1

Direct communication	**Negotiation**	Maximum control
Informal procedure		No facilitator
Win/Win results		Consensus
Neutral third party intervention	**Mediation**	Some control
		Discussion facilitated
Process arranged by parties		Agreement
Neutral panel of experts	**Arbitration**	Minimal control
Structured Process		Arbitration panel
		Binding decision
Judge	**Adjudication**	No control
Formal court process		Enforceable decision
Win/Lose		Appealable

The scale also describes the level of control that is being relinquished by the parties to the dispute, with the most control at the negotiation end of the range and the least at the adjudication end. There are variations on each of these processes that we will discuss as we describe each one.

Negotiation

As we suggested in our reference to the Nisga'a land-claim dispute, perhaps the biggest task in solving the problem is getting the parties to the bargaining table in the first place. But once the parties agree to negotiate, success depends largely on their will to resolve the matter. Whether the dispute is between two neighbours or two nations, the negotiation process is fundamentally the same. The two parties or their representatives sit down and talk over the problem. They lay out the issues, describe their respective positions, make demands and offer concessions. They work together to come to some mutually agreeable solution. This is the simplest form of ADR, requiring only a willingness to solve the problem, limited preparation and no outside intervention. Of course the process may become more complicated. Thus the parties in the land-claim dispute included many government officials and a variety of representatives from the Native tribal councils. Doubtless the parties listened to many hours of testimony describing the claims of both sides, considered historical evidence, reports of the court hearings and comparable settlements in other jurisdictions. The idea is that the parties themselves sat down together and worked through all the problems until they came to a mutually satisfactory agreement. In this case it was the signing of a historic treaty that needs only the ratification of the legislature and approval of the federal government to become effective.

If the negotiation process results in an agreement, then that bargain has the same legal validity as any contractual agreement. The parties to a negotiation may be competing institutions, managers and employees, groups of people or single individuals. The parties to the dispute may be engaged in the process themselves or they may be represented at the bargaining table by agents. In the land-claim case the will to come up with a settlement was generated by social pressure to finally dispense with a matter that has been on the national agenda and social conscience for far too long. Negotiation may also be a requirement of the contract that the disputants are party to. In many international commercial agreements, one of the terms will require parties to attempt to negotiate through their differences first rather than turning the matter over to the courts. This is particularly important when maintaining the privacy of the dispute is a pressing economic concern.

Often it is in the best interests of companies to negotiate with the people who will be affected by their activities. MacMillan Bloedel, a forest products company in British Columbia, owned a large tract of land on Galiano Island. The company decided to log part of the land and commit the rest to resort and residential development. Its proposal was not well received by Island residents, who formed a group called Clear Cut Alternatives. The company agreed to the formation of a multi-party council to discuss the issues. Council members were able to come to an agreement about how the logging plan was to proceed, although they were unable to settle their differences on the other parts of the development. But negotiation can go a long way toward preserving working and social relationships and provide lines of communication that can benefit both sides of issues.[12]

Consensus-Building

This term may be used to describe a form of negotiation in which the objective is primarily to improve the relationship between two groups who are normally opposed to one another, as for example environmentalists and resource managers. The process seeks to foster understanding between the parties that will enable them both to work toward the goals they have in common and offset the negative consequences caused by head-on confrontation, as is the case when protestors create blockades on logging roads or spike trees. It is not primarily concerned with decision-making but provides a peaceful way for both sides to come to terms with the problems and begin the process of solving them.

Mediation

Perhaps the most common mechanism for resolving disputes outside the courtroom is mediation, sometimes referred to as conciliation. This is the method that has seen the most dramatic increase in acceptance in the last few decades. When the parties are unable to come to an agreement on their own, they might turn to mediation, which relies on the intervention of a neutral third party whose task it is to facilitate the negotiation process. A mediator is a person skilled at facilitating communication. A mediator must be selected and agreed upon by both parties and may be a person with some expertise in the matter under dispute. The mediator's job is to bring the parties to the table, giving each of them an opportunity to present their case, including evidence, claims and concerns. In most mediation situations, the mediator has some power to extract information from the parties, for example by asking for an auditor's report. When the mediator is satisfied that all of the information pertinent to the dispute has been presented, he or she will hold a private session with each of the parties to determine their major concerns, demands, limitations and the areas where each might be willing to make concessions. The mediator will discuss these positions with the other and then call them back to the table. The mediator will present the information gained during the private sessions and encourage the parties to agree. The mediator may suggest areas of compromise, but has no authority to make decisions or impose a settlement. The goal is to enhance communication between the parties and help them come to an agreement. If an agreement is reached, the parties have a moral obligation to honour it, and it may be that a contractual arrangement can conclude the agreement. In some jurisdictions and in some areas such as divorce and custody actions, the court will use the mediated agreement to help decide the issue at trial.

Mediated settlements have shown a high success rate, and this can be attributed to a number of things. Because the solution is created and agreed to by the parties to the dispute themselves, it is more likely to work for them. It is usually a win/win situation with each party gaining something from the process and neither losing everything. Mediation is a focused process and can resolve problems quickly, often in one or two sessions. The hearing can be arranged at the convenience of the parties and with little delay. The cost is minimal, requiring the services of a mediator (who may or may not be a legal professional) and a place to meet that is at the parties' discretion. The whole process is conducted in private, and so concerns that the personalities or issues will be revealed to the public are alleviated. In some situations such as labour negotiations the mediator may have the power to file a report that can be made public. The effect is to embarrass a party that is being unreasonable. The potential of this happening puts extra pressure on the parties to settle their dispute.

Family Mediation

One of the areas where mediation has been particularly effective is in divorce and custody disputes. Traditionally families had to turn to courts to determine the distribution of property, child support and custody arrangements. Frequently, a court-imposed decision brings further emotional pain to the situation and contributes to the destruction of any possibility of the parents preserving a relationship that is in the best interests of the children. Enforcing court decisions was also a problem because a non-custodial parent often resents the arrangement and is unwilling to make required support payments, which then have to be enforced by the courts. Mediation has been used as a way to help divorcing parents make concessions and come to an agreement that both can live with and support. Mediation allows the family to preserve their assets to meet their own obligations rather than paying them out for lawyers' fees and court costs. The parties do not have to finalize an agreement until they have obtained independent legal advice. If either party is dissatisfied with the process, he or she is free to end it at any time, and any admissions that have been made in the course of the mediation are considered private and cannot be used against him or her in a court proceeding. A mediated agreement is influential on the court, and the court can use it to make a binding order.

Hospital Mediation

Mediation is becoming the dispute resolution mechanism of choice in many settings. It may be helpful to contrast two similar situations, each handled by a different method, and determine the merits of each approach. A recent newspaper article reported that the president of the Canadian Medical Association had been found guilty of unprofessional conduct. The doctor was accused of failing to properly diagnose and treat a young person who died from botulism. In this case the Yukon Medical Council was acting as an administrative tribunal (acting under legislated authority), with the responsibility of determining if the patient had been treated according to the standards expected of a member of the profession. Upon making its decision against the doctor, the Council fined him $5 000 and ordered him to "attend a clinical competence course and suffer a published reprimand."[13] Both the doctor and the patient's father are appealing the ruling to the Yukon Supreme Court. The father has proceeded with a suit against the doctor, nurses and hospital, charging them all with malpractice. The doctor claims that there was no reasonable basis for the charges against him, and is arguing that the decision was invalid because "the council erred in assessing his credibility and failed to properly apply the evidence before it, relying too much on their own expertise."[14] At this stage there is little information available about the circumstances of the death, but a few things are certain: the reputation of a respected doctor has been tarnished; a hospital and several of its staff face a long round of malpractice litigation; relatives of the victim remain uncertain as to the cause of their loved one's death and also face a protracted legal struggle to get to the truth; the procedures and conclusions of the Medical Council have been thrown into question; and the head of the Canadian Medical Association has been compromised.

Contrast this with a case reported in *Law Now* by Peter Portlock, the Executive Director of the Alberta Arbitration and Mediation Society in Edmonton and a former hospital ombudsman.[15] In this case a patient being treated in hospital after suffering a heart attack seemed to be making a good recovery when he had another heart attack and could not be revived. The wife of the patient had been assured by his surgeon just an hour before the fatal heart attack that he was doing well and would be released shortly. When the hospital staff were called to treat the victim, they were very aggressive in their intervention efforts and almost forceful in the way they removed her from the scene. She was distressed by her husband's death and by the harsh way she had been treated by the staff, and advised the hospital that she was considering retaining a lawyer and pursuing a suit against her husband's doctor and the medical team that attended at the bedside. The hospital administrator suggested to her that there was a mediation program in place that might help to allay her concerns. Portlock comments on the appropriateness of this strategy for a health-care setting.

> In a hospital, [the choice of mediation] may not always right the perceived wrong, but it can at the very least provide an understanding of the *how* and *why* of what occurred, and may often lead to an institutional response that will minimize, if not eliminate, the likelihood of the same

thing ever happening again. Mediation offers the guarantee of honest disclosure of the facts. It promotes communication because the breakdown of communication seems so often to lie at the heart of disputes. There is an advantage also in emphasizing the neutrality that mediation assures by involving a mediator who has no clinical bias and no professional axe to grind.[16]

In this case the physician and a member of the intensive care team were able to sit down and talk to the patient's wife, explain the unpredictable nature of heart disease and describe the intervention strategies that are usually used in such instances. They were able to apologize and explain the rough treatment that she had watched her husband receive and express their sorrow at her loss. The bereaved wife was able to express her pain at her loss and her confusion about why it happened as it did, and in the process she helped the doctors and the hospital staff to be more sensitive in their dealings with patients and their families and to be more communicative about the medical issues they were dealing with. Everyone went away from the mediation process feeling as though they had gained something positive from the experience. They are not still engaged in a public courtroom contest and each is better able to continue with the business of their lives.

It is fair to point out here that not all the comments about mediation in a hospital setting are supportive. The process may be set up to gain an easy out for doctors and hospitals to avoid malpractice litigation.[16] This may be a case where the power balance is strongly in favour of the hospital and the complainant may not be fully aware of what he or she is sacrificing when agreeing to the mediation alternative. There is no guarantee that, if there has been professional misconduct or negligence, the person responsible will be held accountable by the professional body or that necessary changes will be made in practices and procedures. The victim may gain the satisfaction of an apology, but this may not be adequate compensation for real injuries.

Opposition to Mediated Settlements

In contrast to a court action, the spirit of the mediation process is non-adversarial, even when the parties are on opposite sides of the issue. The goal is to bring them closer together in their positions, to see the other's point of view and to compromise where possible. This contrasts with the adversarial nature of the traditional process, which requires each side to dig up as much negative information as possible about the other to make the opposing party look bad. Lawyers are skilled at asking incriminating questions, finding inconsistencies and removing facts from their context. Because lawyers are trained to get at this kind of information, they may not be the best people to act as mediators, unless they can take off their adversarial hat and have a sincere interest in agreement rather than seeing one side win at the expense of the other.

When mediation was first introduced as a viable alternative dispute mechanism, there was considerable resistance from lawyers, who were possibly seeing this as a threat to litigation, the bread and butter of their profession. There was also concern voiced among the profession that untrained people could call themselves mediators and complainants would remain unaware of their legal rights. There were no professional associations in place to set standards or monitor practice. As mediation's acceptance by the public has grown, law firms have begun to offer mediation services, designating some of their staff to offer mediated resolutions to problems. But a person in search of a mediated settlement should be careful, when selecting a lawyer/mediator, to ensure that the lawyer/mediator is not so fixed in the skills of adversarial combat that he or she skews the mediation process in favour of one side over the other. Good mediators must first and foremost be good communicators and facilitators and not too easily persuaded by the best "legal" argument. It may also be true that because the standard pre-trial process is designed to encourage settlement before trial, many litigators have adopted mediation skills and apply them even when the parties have every intention of taking the matter to court. One other difficulty with mediations conducted by lawyers is that clients may end up paying high lawyer fees and become subject to the very costs they might have been trying to avoid by not going to court.

The legal profession is also and perhaps justifiably concerned that mediated settlements may not offer the best "legal" solution — that because they do not resolve legal problems, they may not be enforceable in court if the matter ends up there. It may be that a person who seeks a mediated settlement should have the agreement reviewed by a lawyer to be sure that the legal issues have been properly dealt with.

Mediation Not Always Appropriate

There are some disadvantages to mediation, and clearly it will not work in every dispute. First, the parties need to be in an equal bargaining position. If one party claims that the other owes a substantial amount of money, or if one of the parties is dominant or has been in the position of controlling the other, mediation may not be a suitable option. The parties must be willing to disclose information or allow the mediator the right to seek information. If there are complex legal issues at stake, mediation will not normally work. A mediated settlement will not, of course, set a precedent, so if the matter concerns an issue that should be resolved in such a way as to affect public policy or the law, it should be dealt with by the courts. The rights of the parties are not as well protected in a mediation setting as they would be in a court since they are not subject to rules of evidence or other procedural rules that ensure a person gets a fair hearing. If any of these situations exist, mediation may not be a suitable alternative.

Mini-Trial

Another method of dealing with disputes in a variety of settings has developed in recent years. This method, called a **mini-trial**, has been used on an experimental basis in BC and Alberta. A judicially supported form of the process has been used in BC as a pre-trial device to promote settlement in litigation. It is not a conventional trial but an abbreviated hearing that combines all the processes we have discussed so far. Private mini-trials arranged independently of the court system have been used to resolve such matters as patent disputes, commercial disputes and disputes within or between government departments or businesses.[17] The process works best when the applicable legal rules are reasonably clear and when the parties are committed to finding a solution and volunteer to participate in the process. A mini-trial may be used to deal with such difficulties as harassment, personality conflicts between employees, or disputes between managers. If company executives propose to settle the matter in a mini-trial, they will ask the concerned parties to participate and perhaps have them recommend a neutral adviser. The adviser may be called on to organize the proceedings, hear testimony, review documents, call on experts to report, and render an opinion. If the matter has legal implications, lawyers can present arguments or elaborate on the relevant laws and give their opinion as to the likely outcome if the matter were to go to court. The parties would be given the opportunity to explain their positions and respond to questions by the adjudicators or lawyers. The adviser may suggest a settlement but has no power to impose one. The goal is to acknowledge the conflict, hear the facts, and either encourage the parties to settle their differences or give them a basis for deciding whether it would be worthwhile to pursue a court action.

Arbitration

Arbitration has a long history. Evidence of this kind of dispute resolution can be traced as far back as Greece and Egypt. Despite the effort we have made here to track the development of the judicial process, it should be recognized that jurists and parliamentarians alike have recommended that people try to solve their own problems. An *Arbitration Act* was passed by the English Parliament in 1698. The Act arranged for the enforcement of arbitration orders. "Whereas Court orders have contributed much to the disputant's peace of mind, after submission to Arbitrators. Merchants and Traders desiring to end Controversy by Arbitration shall be able to enforce the Award by Court Order. Disobedience or neglect to perform shall be Contempt of Court and Imprisonment."[18]

Arbitration has been used to settle some international cases involving Canada. The dispute over where the Canada/US boundary would run in the Strait of Juan de Fuca was arbitrated by the Emperor of Germany in 1890. But perhaps the most formal application of the method was its use in the resolution of labour conflict. When labour unrest created social and economic upheaval in the first few decades of the twentieth century, something had to be done to resolve the conflict and address the concerns of employees and managers. The Americans' had enacted an innovative piece of legislation called the *Wagner Act*, one of the goals of which was to set up a negotiation process for workers represented by unions and managers to resolve their differences and create agreements that would bring peace to and regulate the labour environment. A form of that act was adopted in Canada in 1944 and it introduced the concept of arbitration as the primary means to resolve labour disputes.[19] As part of the employment contract, the parties would agree to a form of dispute settlement that included the requirement that they put their claims and demands before an independent person or tribunal and be bound by the decision of the arbitrator(s). This process has been instrumental in keeping union and management disputes at manageable levels. But in its development, labour arbitration has taken on some of the trappings of the court, with rules of procedure and the application of precedent. While the decisions of arbitrators are binding, in some cases courts have reviewed the decisions of arbitration panels, thus requiring them to follow the requirements of due process.

Arbitration has become a process used in other kinds of disputes as well. When businesses have a conflict or disagreement over an issue, they may resort to an arbitrated settlement in which they agree to be bound by the decision of an outside party. Those injured when industrial polluters have damaged the environment have taken their claims to arbitration tribunals to determine the compensation that should be awarded them.[20] The Arbitration and Mediation Institute of Canada was created in 1976 to encourage the use of arbitration and mediation. It spearheaded the development of the Federal Construction Dispute Advisory Board, which has saved the construction industry millions of dollars in court costs.[21] Another area where the Institute has served to introduce arbitrated settlements is in new vehicle disputes. The Canadian Motor Vehicle Arbitration Plan (CAMVAP) is in place throughout Canada (with the exception of Quebec) and is designed to settle disputes between owners and manufacturers when a consumer claims a vehicle has a defect or the manufacturer has not honoured warranties. Such complaints would otherwise have to be dealt with by small claims courts. When CAMVAP becomes involved the parties agree to accept the decision of an impartial third party who listens to both sides of the case and weighs the evidence before imposing a decision.

> The arbitrators come from many different backgrounds and professions but they have four things in common: they are independent, they are impartial, they believe strongly in arbitration as an appropriate alternative way to resolve a dispute (instead of going to court), and each has been specifically trained to deal with vehicle disputes.[21]

Prior to recent amendments in the *Arbitration Act* of BC there was a high degree of judicial control over arbitration processes. Recognizing that its most positive features were lost if arbitration was limited by jurisdiction, legislators enhanced BC's ability to compete in the lucrative international arbitration industry by their amendments to the Act. With growing confidence in arbitrated settlements, there has been more attention given to the procedures used and the development of regulations and standards. But when parties opt for an arbitrated settlement, they frequently draw up their own ground rules to follow or they proceed according to terms set out in their contractual agreements. More and more contracts contain requirements that the parties must resort to binding arbitration if a dispute arises. Whether it is set out in a contract or not, the disputing parties determine who will be on the arbitration panel and when and where the hearing will take place.

Process

When a three-person panel is involved, the process begins by each party selecting an individual to represent them on the panel and then a third neutral person is selected either by the representatives or the parties themselves. Usually the parties will select people who have a special expertise in the area of the dispute. The third person may have mediation and negotiation skills, but otherwise is a neutral, objective voice in the matter. The panel members will gather information from each side, hear witnesses, examine evidence and weigh the positions of each side, encouraging negotiation and suggesting concessions from each side. The regulations that govern the procedure discourage attempts to delay or obstruct the proceedings, and arbitrators can make awards in the absence of one of the parties if there is a refusal to participate. Whether or not the parties actually come to an agreement on their own, the arbitrators have the right to make a decision and impose it on the parties. Usually a union agreement will call for binding arbitration. The characteristic that most distinguishes arbitration from mediation is that the decision of the arbitrator or arbitration panel is binding on the parties. Usually there is no appeal or appeal is limited to another tribunal. The parties cannot take the matter to court unless there has been something in the process itself that did not correspond to the contractual agreement that mandated arbitration.

The advantages of arbitration over court adjudication are that the matter is heard by people with special expertise and experience in the matter and the process itself can be much more efficient. A judge would have to inform himself or herself of all the special technical information about the industry, which of course would be extremely difficult if not impossible. Arbitrators may or may not concern themselves with prior decisions and usually have much more freedom to consider the economic and social factors that affect the claims of each side at the table.

An interesting case that took place in the early 1980s illustrates the advantages of arbitration over litigation. Back in the days when microcomputer technology was primarily in the hands of the two major players in the US, a Japanese company was found to have misappropriated and used for new development in Japan some of the software developed by one of the US manufacturers. The US company sued the Japanese company, and the court determined that there had been an infringement and fined the Japanese company more than $90 million. This was enough to put the defendant company into bankruptcy and imperil the fledgling computer industry in Japan. The two companies took the matter to an arbitration panel and it was decided that instead the Japanese company should pay the US company $90 million for the right to use the software. The result was that the Japanese company could survive, the two companies could pursue an ongoing mutually profitable relationship, important technological information could be shared, and new development was encouraged and enhanced. It was beyond the power of the courts to come up with such a creative win/win solution to the problem.

Disadvantages of Arbitrated Settlements

As with any of the alternatives there are some downsides to arbitration. It is not always a quick fix, nor does it always lead to a win/win conclusion to a dispute. An arbitrated settlement usually does not set a precedent and therefore it is difficult to predict what a decision will be. Because the hearings do not follow rules of evidence, a party could more easily compromise the evidence and it would be difficult for an arbitrator, whose powers of discovery, are limited to uncover the truth. As was stated in the discussion on mediation, it is critical that the parties in an arbitration be in a more or less equal bargaining position since a more powerful party could tip the scales in its favour based on the quantity or nature of the evidence it brings to the table. The procedure as a rule is not open to the public and thus not subjected to the scrutiny of the public or the media, and usually there are no transcripts to refer to if there is a complaint. Also, there is usually no right to appeal, and this in itself may discourage people from relying on the process. It is possible too that the process could also become protracted, making time and costs a concern.

ADR Practitioners

With the widespread acceptance of ADR strategies, it has become important to find some way to regulate the practices of people who claim to have the skills and expertise required to conduct mediation and arbitration sessions. Most areas of Canada have organizations that offer services, but there has been no coordinated effort to train, license, set standards and hear complaints for practitioners. Certainly the confidence of consumers is reinforced if a practitioner can attach a professional designation after his or her name, but as of writing there was no national body designated to monitor people who claim to have such credentials. Because of that, people who have complaints about the service they have received may have no recourse. Training programs and university-based courses are being offered regularly, and each provides some form of accreditation to those who successfully complete them. Established organizations such as the Alberta Arbitration and Mediation Society have developed codes of ethics with which they expect their members to comply, but they have no formal power to enforce those standards. As interest in the field continues to grow and as people come to rely on the methods described here, it is reasonable to assume that a national professional organization will come into being to ensure that there is uniformity and standards are in place. It is also important to provide a recourse for those who feel they have not been well served.

CONCLUSION

Used in the right circumstances, alternative dispute resolution mechanisms provide a better means of solving some of the problems in the Canadian civil justice system. Overcrowding, high costs and lack of access to the courts make these alternatives essential. Thomas Heintzman, a lawyer writing in the *National*, a journal published by the Canadian Bar Association, encourages lawyers to accept and become experts in ADR, which he feels is at the heart of the reform movement in the justice system. "A fair and inexpensive dispute resolution system here in Canada will contribute as much to Canadian economic competitiveness as fair and inexpensive educational or medical systems. We have to offer the most comprehensive and the best ways of resolving disputes, both inside and outside the courts."[22]

This concludes our discussion on the institutions that make up the parts of our justice system. Next we begin an examination of the major substantive areas of law. Keep in mind the various procedures that are in place to help people resolve their legal claims as you learn some of the laws that have an impact on your personal, social and commercial endeavours.

QUESTIONS FOR DISCUSSION AND REVIEW

1. Consider the difficulties that the courts are facing in dealing with civil suits.

2. Discuss the accuracy of the statement that in many cases "administrative tribunals are just another kind of judge."

3. If we hold to the principle of parliamentary supremacy, should the courts have any supervisory role in the function of administrative tribunals?

4. Suggest some circumstances where you might be grateful for the "rule of law."

5. Discuss the advantages and disadvantages of having a matter heard before an administrative tribunal rather than a court.

6. Negotiating an agreement has some advantages. What are they?

7. Outline the skills that an effective mediator should bring to the effort to resolve a dispute.

8. A mediated settlement is not binding on the parties, but what positive effects can it have in dispute resolution?

9. Some of the strategies and goals used in labour relations are influencing current methods of arbitrating disputes. List them and describe why they are effective.

10. Imagine a situation where you have a disagreement with the manufacturer of a product that has caused you an injury, and set up the most effective and satisfying way to have the dispute settled.

NOTES

1. Dickson, Brian, the Honourable Chief Justice. Quoted in *Law Now*, April/May 1997, p. 11.

2. Cohen, David, Dean of University of Victoria Law School. Remarks at a conference for law teachers, Vancouver, BC, October 23, 1998.

3. Brook, Paula. "The Second Victim in the Matthew Vaudreuil Case." *Vancouver Sun*, November 4, 1998, p. A15.

4. McLachlin, Beverley, The Honourable Madame Justice. "Rules and Discretion in the Governance of Canada." *Saskatchewan Law Review*, Vol. 56, 1992, p. 168.

5. Walker, G. *The Rule of Law: Foundation of a Constitutional Democracy*. Carlton, Australia: Melbourne University Press, 1988, pp. 23–42. Quoted from article by Madame Justice McLachlin.

6. *Sinkovich v. Strathroy (Town of) Commissioners of Police* (1988), 51 D.L.R. (4th) 750 (Ont. H.C.J. (Div. Ct.)).

7. McLachlin, p. 179.

8. *Judicial Review Procedures Act*, R.S.O. 1980, c. 224.

9. McLachlin, p. 179.

10. Cohen, David, Dean of University of Victoria Law School. Remarks at a conference for law teachers, Vancouver, BC, October 23, 1998.

11. *Delgamuukw v. British Columbia*, [1997] 3 S.C.R. 1010.

12. Swanson, Elizabeth. "Environmental Conflict." *Law Now*, April/May 1997, p. 17.

13. Killick, Adam. "Top Doctor's Conduct Censured." *Vancouver Sun*, October 17, 1998, p. 4.

14. *Ibid*.

15. Portlock, Peter L. "Code Green Dispute Resolved Through Mediation." *Law Now*, May 1994, pp. 9–12.

16. *Ibid*.

17. Shone, Margaret. "The Mini-Trial." *Law Now*, May 1994, p. 20.

18. Geddes, William J. "From Athens to AMIC — The History of Alternative Dispute Resolution," in *Law Now*, April/May 1997, p. 9.

19. Wartime Labour Relations Regulations of 1944, P.C. 1003. These terms are now embodied in the *Canada Labour Code*, R.S.C 1985, c. L-2.

20. Swanson, p. 15.

21. Geddes, p. 11.

22. Heintzman, Thomas, Q.C. "Where to Go with ADR." *National*, March 1995, p. 4.

FURTHER READING

Banfield, Jane, ed. *Readings in Law and Society,* 6th ed. Toronto: Captus Press, 1995. See particularly John Evans, Hudson N. Janisch, David J. Mullan and Richard C.B. Risk, "The Administrative State and the Rule of Law," pp. 107–124, and Jonathan Rudin, "Native Alternative Dispute Resolution Systems: Historical and Cultural Perspective," pp. 246–251.

Cole, Jade C. *A Discussion of the Potential Cost-Effectiveness and Efficiency of ADR* (Technical Report). Ottawa: Canada Department of Justice, May 1993.

Culhane, Dara. *The Pleasure of the Crown: Anthropology, Law and First Nations.* Burnaby, BC: Talonbooks, 1998.

Edelman, Lester and Frank Carr. "The Mini-Trial: An Alternative Dispute Resolution Procedure." *The Arbitration Journal*, March 1987, Vol. 42, No. 1.

Evans, John, Hudson N. Janisch, David J. Mullan and Richard C.B. Risk. *Administrative Law*, 4th ed. Toronto: Emond Montgomery Publications, 1995.

Huber, Marc. "Legal Update — Alternative Dispute Resolution." *Canadian Lawyer*, January 1995, pp. 36-43.

Law Now — A publication of the Legal Resource Centre, University of Alberta. See especially May 1994 and May 1997.

McLaren, Richard H. and John P. Sanderson. *Innovative Dispute Resolution: The Alternative*. Toronto: Carswell, 1994.

Persky, Stan. *Delgamuukw: The Supreme Court of Canada Decision on Aboriginal Title*. Vancouver: Greystone Books, 1998.

Pirie, Andrew J. and Dinah J. Stanley. "Dispute Resolution and You: What You Need to Know!" Victoria, BC: University of Victoria, Institute for Dispute Resolution, [1994].

Chapter

7

CRIMINAL LAW

INTRODUCTION

The rest of the chapters in the text are concerned with substantive areas of law, and we begin with a look at the type of law that is most apparent in our society. Even if we have not personally come in contact with the police or courts because we have been charged with a crime, we know from our exposure to the media that criminal law is a major concern of the justice system. We get the sense that criminal activity is rampant and the fear of becoming a victim of crime causes us to guard our own activities. We invest much of our government resources in the prevention, apprehension and punishment of criminal activity. Whether or not crime is on the increase, one of the measures of our humanity and civilization is the way we deal with people who are suspected or have been convicted of committing a crime. The primary legislation that provides for the regulation of criminal activity is found in the *Canadian Criminal Code*, which is a compilation and summary of principles and decisions made throughout English common and statute law and Canadian judicial history. Some additional criminal law is set out in other federal statutes such as the *Narcotics Control Act*. Once we consider what constitutes a crime and how it differs from other forms of wrongdoing, we will examine the principles and procedures that govern how we deal with such behaviours.

NATURE OF A CRIME

A crime is any form of human activity that the law defines as such. Under the Constitution only the federal government has the authority to enact criminal law legislation. The *Canadian Criminal Code* (CCC) and several other federal statutes determine what constitutes a crime in Canada. Provincial and municipal governments have the power to determine the law with respect to speeding and other traffic violations. These are called provincial offences and because of their penal nature are sometimes referred to as quasi-criminal law, but the regulation of such offences cannot overlap the federal criminal jurisdiction. The information contained in this chapter has come primarily from the *Canadian Criminal Code*, although reference to specific sections has been limited to facilitate readability.

Is All Immoral Activity Criminal?

Criminal laws are concerned with conduct that is morally unacceptable to society, but not all the behaviours that most of us consider immoral are crimes. Criminal laws are rules designed to order society rather than to dictate and control its morals. Immoral activity is prohibited when Parliament determines that it sufficiently infringes the freedom or privacy of a person, or poses a general threat to the state. For example, sexual acts outside of marriage are criminal only if one party is under age, or does not consent, or the act is performed in public, upsetting the sensibilities of others. The study of law is therefore the study of what the law is rather than what it ought to be. Once criminal law is understood, then we can apply moral and ethical standards to determine whether new categories of prohibited behaviour ought to be created or some old prohibitions removed.

The Difference between Criminal and Civil Wrongs

Criminal wrongs are those activities regulated by the *Criminal Code* and related federal statutes. Civil wrongs (torts) are those acts, either intentional or unintentional, that cause harm or injury to another person or their property. A tort is a private, civil matter between the victim and the offender. A crime is a public matter between the accused and the state. Therefore, criminal acts are offences against the state. In a civil matter, the victim usually applies to the court for compensation from the offender. In a criminal matter the state prosecutes the offender in order to seek punishment and protection for society. Some conduct, for example a sexual assault, can give rise to both a criminal prosecution of the accused and a civil lawsuit by the victim for compensation for injuries suffered at the hands of the offender.

FOUNDATIONAL PRINCIPLES OF CRIMINAL LAW

There are some foundational principles that have been important to the development of criminal law. The basic purpose of criminal justice is to protect all members of society from seriously harmful and dangerous conduct.[1] In previous chapters we have emphasized that a primary goal of law is to protect the fundamental human rights that are essential to the preservation of a free and democratic society. In the process of enforcing criminal laws, the state is obligated to act in such a way as to interfere with individual rights and freedoms as little as necessary. Individual rights are of particular consequence in the administration of criminal justice. When the state is in the process of depriving a citizen of some of those fundamental rights, it must do so only after subscribing to all the principles of fairness and justice that we have raised in other chapters. Some of them have already been discussed in a different context, but as we apply them in criminal matters, it will be seen that they take on added significance.

Rule of Law

The rule of law is a significant principle applicable to all areas of law. In terms of criminal law it means that an act is only a criminal offence if it has been so declared by Parliament. The Code makes it clear that a person is not guilty of an offence unless he or she has been convicted, and that person is not liable to any punishment greater than that prescribed in the Code or other federal legislation (CCC 6.1).

Under the rule of law people must be able to know what actions the law prohibits. A person can only be punished for the commission of a crime if, at the time it was committed, it was recognized as a crime under the Code or other federal statute. For example, under paragraph 11(g) of the *Canadian Charter of Rights and Freedoms* (discussed in Chapter 4), Parliament cannot designate an act a crime and apply the law retroactively to actions carried out in the past.

The rule of law also includes the principle that no one is above the law and that all people are equal before the law. Police officers or other government officials who act contrary to the *Criminal Code* can be convicted of a crime. For example, a police officer who uses excessive force in arresting or detaining a suspect can be convicted of criminal assault.

Certainty of the Law

The Charter requires that the law must be certain, not vague (section 7). The courts will declare a criminal law void if it is described in terms that are so vague and lacking in precision that the public cannot know what actions are prohibited. The legislators who draft statutes frequently use words such as "reasonable" or "probable" or "likely to," which are often ambiguous and open to interpretation. Any vagueness or ambiguity in the law must be interpreted to the benefit of the accused. Despite this the Supreme Court has been reluctant to strike down provisions of the Code showing such imprecision, and has done so only in limited circumstances. For example, in the 1992 case *R. v. Nova Scotia Pharmaceutical Soc*iety[2] the court held that the use of the word "unduly" in a charge of conspiracy to prevent or lessen competition was not too vague.

Procedural Protections of the Charter

Because the *Charter of Rights and Freedoms* is part of the Canadian Constitution, all other laws must comply with its provisions, including the Code. Sections 7 to 14 of the Charter set out the rules relating to due process and procedural fairness in criminal prosecutions. These rules ensure that people who are suspected of committing a crime or who are arrested and charged with a criminal offence are treated fairly.

The rights protected by sections 7 to 14 include the following:

- life, liberty and security of the person
- security from unreasonable search or seizure

- not to be arbitrarily detained or imprisoned
- be informed promptly of reasons for arrest
- retain and instruct counsel without delay and to be informed of that right
- *habeas corpus*, to have the validity of detention determined
- be informed without unreasonable delay of the specific offence
- be tried within a reasonable time
- not to be compelled to be a witness in proceedings against that person in respect of the offence
- be presumed innocent until proven guilty according to law in a fair and public hearing by an independent and impartial tribunal
- not to be denied reasonable bail without just cause
- (except under military law) to the benefit of trial by jury where the maximum punishment for the offence is imprisonment for five years or more
- not to be found guilty unless at the time the act constituted an offence
- not to be tried or punished again for the same offence
- not to be punished more severely than the punishment provided at the time of the offence
- not to be subject to any cruel or unusual treatment or punishment
- for a witness, not to have any incriminating evidence given in one proceeding used to incriminate the witness in another proceeding, except in a prosecution for perjury or for the giving of contrary evidence
- for a witness or party who is deaf or does not understand the language, to the assistance of an interpreter.

The Charter allows the government to qualify the rights it creates. Section 1 of the Charter says that other laws may limit Charter rights so long as those laws are reasonable and can be justified in a free and democratic society. For example, laws against pornography and hate propaganda can be reasonable limits on freedom of expression because they prevent harm to individuals and groups. Also, section 33 of the Charter allows Parliament or the provincial legislatures to make a particular law, exempt from certain sections of the Charter, including those outlined above, but such a law would have to be reviewed after five years. This clause is rarely used but in effect would allow Parliament to pass a law revoking some or all of these rights — in the case of an insurrection, for example.

Actus Reus — Commission of an Unlawful Act

Actus rea is the physical action that constitutes the crime, and there must be some evidence of that unlawful conduct. In most crimes, the act that constitutes the crime is obvious. In some instances, however, the legal description of the act is vague or the act committed in a particular case is minimal and so the court must determine if the offence has been committed. For example, just what activities constitute soliciting for the purposes of prostitution in a public place has been subject to much judicial analysis. Also several cases have been heard to determine just how much marijuana a person needs to have on his or her person to qualify for a conviction for the crime of "possession" of a prohibited substance.

It is possible to commit a crime by failing to do something that the state expects of us. Criminal responsibility for **omissions,** or the failure to act, is limited to cases where there is a legal and not merely a moral duty to act. Section 215 of the Code is an example of the creation of such a legal duty. It states that parents have a duty to provide necessaries of life for a child under the age of 16 years.

In general there is no *actus reus* unless the act is the result of a willing mind at liberty to make a definite choice or decision. One example of where there is no *actus reus* because of an absence of will to commit the act is called **automatism**, describing unconscious, involuntary behaviour. If the person is not conscious of what he is doing, there is no *actus reus*. In the 1994 case of *R. v. Daviault*[3] the Supreme Court of Canada held that in a sexual assault the court must consider the possibility that extreme drunkenness could amount to automatism. Extreme intoxication akin to automatism must be established by the accused only on a balance of probabilities (CCC 16).

Another determination that the court must make to determine if *actus reus* is present is called **causation**. Did the action of the accused actually cause the resulting injury or death of the victim, or was there some intervening cause that broke the link between the act and the resulting injury? If Joe shoots Sam, who then dies of the inflicted injuries, there is no difficulty establishing the *actus rea* for murder. If the resulting wound was not serious but Sam dies because of a carelessly performed surgical procedure to treat the wound, what caused his death—the shooting or the surgery? Is Sam guilty of assault causing bodily harm or is he guilty of murder? Would the death not have taken place "but for" the conduct of the accused?

In the 1993 case of *R. v. Harbottle*[4] the accused held the victim while his companion strangled her. The Supreme Court upheld his conviction for first-degree murder, finding that his actions were a substantial and integral cause of the death and that there was no intervening act of another which resulted in the accused no longer being substantially connected to the death of the victim.

Mens Rea — The Requirement of Intention

Mens rea is the requirement that a guilty mind be behind the act that constitutes a crime. A guilty mind implies that the act was willful or intentional. The Crown must prove that the accused either intended to do the act knowing its consequences or proceeded to do it with reckless disregard for the consequences, as in driving a vehicle while intoxicated. As a general rule, accused persons are presumed to intend the natural consequences of their conduct. The court can also draw conclusions as to the existence of *mens rea* from the circumstances surrounding the act.

The Code requires different **degrees of intent** for different offences. For example, the crime of assault requires just a general intent to do wrong, whereas robbery requires a specific intent to use force to steal another's property. If the accused is too intoxicated to know that the goods he is taking do not belong to him, he does not have the required intent to commit robbery, although he may have sufficient intent to commit assault.

A distinction must be made between *mens rea* and motive. **Motive** is the reason why the accused committed the act. Good motives do not excuse criminal conduct. However, the court may use evidence of motive to determine the intentions of the accused, and such evidence may also be taken into account in sentencing. The motive of a person who murders another because of a belief that that person is about to harm someone else would likely influence the court to look more leniently on the crime than would the motive of a person who kills someone in the process of robbing him.

The court must decide whether to apply a **subjective or objective test** to prove that the accused intended the unlawful conduct. The subjective standard takes into account the personal circumstances of the accused and seeks to determine what was actually in his or her mind when the act occurred. The objective standard is the one expected by society and is based on the assumption that the person was or ought to have been aware of that standard. The distinction is whether one was aware that he was committing a criminal act or whether he should have been careful to avoid such an act whether he was aware that it was a crime or not. While the subjective standard is used for most crimes, some require that the prosecution prove an objective test of intention, such as "reasonable care" or "reasonable steps." In the 1993 case of *R. v. Creighton*,[5] the accused was convicted of manslaughter after injecting the deceased with cocaine. The Supreme Court held that the prosecution must prove a marked departure from the standard of care of a reasonable person to convict the accused of a crime that requires intention be proven by an objective test.

In general, the onus is on the prosecution to prove that the accused had the required intention to commit the criminal act, although this is usually presumed from the circumstances. If a person makes a **mistake of fact** and as a result commits a crime, the accused has a defence that she did not have the required intent to commit a criminal act. If you take goods thinking that they belong to you but in fact they belong to someone else, you do not have the requisite intent to be convicted of theft. Should a driver who relied on his speedometer, which he reasonably believed to be accurate, be convicted of speeding when his speedometer turns out to have been faulty? Some public welfare or regulatory legislation imposes strict liability on the accused. That is, if the prosecution proves that the driver was speeding, his lack of intention to speed due to a mistake of fact is not a defence.

In some offences **recklessness** or **willful blindness** is the basis for criminal liability. Recklessness is subjective in that the prosecution must prove that the accused was aware that his conduct could result in the prohibited act occurring but nevertheless persisted despite the risk.

In the 1978 case of *R. v. City of Sault Ste. Marie*[6] the Supreme Court identified three categories of offences:

1. **general** criminal offences in which the prosecution must prove *mens rea*;

2. **strict liability** public welfare or regulatory offences where the Crown must prove the act, but the accused must prove a mistake of fact was based on a reasonable belief; and

3. offences of **absolute liability**, which means that the Crown does not have to prove intention. The proof of the unlawful act is sufficient to convict and the defence of mistake of fact is not available.

Following the introduction of the Charter, the Sault Ste. Marie case and the categories it set out became a minimum constitutional standard for determining fault when the offence was serious enough to warrant a sentence of incarceration. Strict liability offences require an element of **reverse onus**, meaning that the accused must prove that he or she didn't intend to commit the offence rather than the Crown having to prove intention. In general most crimes will fall within category 1 and the prosecution must prove subjective intent. Category 2 applies to most reverse onus public welfare or regulatory offences; the prosecution must prove the objective standard of intent but the defence of reasonable belief in a mistake of fact or due diligence is available. In a very few cases that do not involve a threat to liberty, category 3, absolute liability, may apply. In the 1986 case of *Reference Re Section 94(2) of the*

Motor Vehicle Act (B.C.)[7] the Supreme Court of Canada held that because absolute liability offends the principle that a person is innocent until proven guilty, there is a presumption against legislatures intending to pass absolute liability legislation.

Burden of Proof

Because the Charter and the Code establish that a person must be considered innocent until proven guilty, it is up to the prosecution to prove evidence of each of the elements of the offence, and the required standard of proof is **beyond a reasonable doubt**. It is not enough for the prosecution to convince the judge that its position is likely to be true, because the benefit of any doubt must be given to the accused.

Reasonable Doubt

R. v. Bisson[8]

This case considered whether the trial judge misdirected the jury as to the meaning of "beyond a reasonable doubt" by comparing it to the degree of certainty used to make decisions in everyday activities. The trial judge explained that a reasonable doubt is that degree of certainty which one uses every day in important activities. He then gave an example relating in detail the steps which should be taken in order to determine the level of oil in an automobile. He suggested that when the proper checks had been done, a person could feel certain "beyond a reasonable doubt" that there was enough oil in the car to enable it to run without damage. The accused was convicted.

The Court of Appeal upheld the conviction but the Supreme Court of Canada allowed the appeal and directed a new trial.

The Supreme Court found that examples of what may constitute proof beyond a reasonable doubt may tend to indicate to a juror that the decision as to whether guilt has been proven beyond a reasonable doubt can be made on the same basis as would any decision made in the course of daily routines. Often those "everyday" decisions in life are reached by utilizing a standard of probability. They are based upon experience and a consideration of routine risks and commonplace alternatives. To suggest that jurors may apply examples from everyday life in determining proof beyond a reasonable doubt can thus be misleading and may well lower the requisite standard.

Secondly, examples tend to be applied subjectively. The consideration of an example will often vary with the life experiences and background of every individual juror. The example used in this case seemed to suggest to jurors that they can apply the same standard they would use in everyday, routine decisions to determine guilt beyond a reasonable doubt.

Since the directions of the trial judge gave rise to a reasonable likelihood that the jury misapprehended the standard of proof, the Supreme Court set aside the verdict and ordered a new trial.

Ignorance of the Law Is No Excuse

In Canada we are required to know and obey the law. Ignorance of the law by a person who commits an offence is not an excuse for committing that offence (CCC 19).

RULES OF EVIDENCE

The court convicts an accused on the basis of **admissible evidence** relating to each of the elements of the offence. The kind of evidence that can be admitted at trial is based on rules that ensure that the court considers relevant facts that are not misleading. For example, a witness can only testify as to what she knows from her own experience. She cannot testify as to what someone else told her. This is called hearsay. Also, she cannot give her opinion about matters, except in limited circumstances. If the admissibility of evidence is questioned, the judge holds a *voir dire* or trial within the trial in the absence of the jury. The judge hears the evidence and decides whether the evidence is admissible. The jury is brought back and only hears the evidence if the judge has determined that it is admissible.

Compellability is another factor that the defence must consider. An accused is not compelled to testify against himself or herself. The failure to testify cannot be commented upon by the judge or Crown counsel. If the accused does testify, he or she is required to answer all relevant questions. Similarly, competent witnesses must answer questions. However, if a witness believes the answer might incriminate her, she can invoke the protection of the *Canada Evidence Act*. The witness is still compelled to answer, but the answer given cannot be used in evidence against her in any subsequent criminal proceeding, except in a prosecution for perjury. A spouse is not considered a competent witness against her husband or his wife and cannot be compelled to testify except in certain cases.

Competency and Compellability of a Spouse — Exception to the Hearsay Rule

R. v. Hawkins[9]

As the result of an internal investigation, the Crown believed that a police officer had provided a former president of a motorcycle club with confidential information concerning police surveillance of the club in return for money. The key figure in the Crown's investigation was the officer's girlfriend.

At the preliminary inquiry, the girlfriend made a number of statements under oath and cross-examination which incriminated the officer. However, shortly afterward she testified again and recanted key portions of her previous statements. Following the completion of the preliminary inquiry, and prior to trial, the officer and his girlfriend were legally married.

The trial judge decided that the officer's wife was now not competent or compellable to testify against him. The Court of Appeal held that she was not competent to testify but that the evidence could be admitted under an exception to the hearsay rule and ordered a new trial. The accused appealed.

The majority of the Supreme Court judges held that the appeal should be dismissed. The wife was not competent or compellable to testify at trial. However, the wife's testimony at the preliminary inquiry could be read into evidence at trial because of an exception to the hearsay rule. Under this exception, a hearsay statement is admissible if it meets the separate requirements of "necessity" and "reliability."

Confession

If the accused makes a voluntary confession, for example at the time of arrest, the statement can be used against him, subject to certain safeguards. The Crown counsel must prove that the confession was freely and voluntarily given. The arresting officer must not intimidate or threaten the accused or offer inducement for the confession. The officer must caution the accused that he is not required to make a statement and that if he does it may be taken down and used against him. The Charter also requires that the officer inform the accused of his right to counsel, including how to access legal aid.

Illegally Obtained Evidence

The judge can rule that a statement or other evidence is not admissible if it was illegally obtained. For example, if the arresting officer conducts a search without a warrant the evidence obtained may be inadmissible in court. The judge must determine whether the admission of the illegally obtained evidence would bring "the administration of justice into disrepute" (Charter, subsection 24 (2)).

Illegally Obtained Evidence

R. v. Feeney[10]

In this case from British Columbia, police investigating a recent murder entered the accused's home (an equipment trailer) without permission. They knocked, received no answer, entered the trailer, awoke the accused and took him to the front of the trailer for better lighting. When they saw blood on his shirt they arrested him.

The accused was convicted of second-degree murder at trial, and his appeal to the Court of Appeal was unanimously dismissed. He appealed to the Supreme Court of Canada on the grounds that the police violated the Charter right to be secure from unreasonable search or seizure (section 8) and the right on arrest or detention to retain and instruct counsel without delay and to be informed of that right (paragraph 10(b)).

The majority of the Supreme Court judges held that the appeal should be allowed. The court found that the arresting officer did not believe he had reasonable grounds to arrest prior to the forcible entry. The test that must be met is that a reasonable person, standing in the shoes of the officer, would have believed that reasonable and probable grounds to make the arrest existed at that time.

The court held that the test for warrantless searches must be adjusted to comply with the Charter values, which increase the importance of the legal status of the privacy of the home. In general, the privacy interest now outweighs the interest of the police and warrantless arrests in dwelling houses are prohibited. However, in cases of hot pursuit, the privacy interest must give way to the interest of society in ensuring adequate police protection.

New Developments

New developments in science and technology create new challenges for the court regarding the admissibility of evidence. For example, DNA testing can now determine whether an accused was at the scene of the crime, and alcohol or drug blood testing can determine whether a driver was impaired prior to an accident. Technology also makes possible the electronic interception of otherwise private conversations. The Code provides for the circumstances in which a judge can grant a warrant for taking a blood sample, demanding a breath sample or installing a telephone wiretap.

Charter of Rights—Blood Sample

R. v. Knox[11]

The police officer in charge of a serious traffic accident formed the opinion that the accused was impaired and demanded, pursuant to subsection 254(3) of the Code, that he provide a blood sample. (The accused was in a hospital and the nearest breathalyzer machine was some distance away.)

The standard demand, which was read to the accused from a printed card, made no mention of the subsection 254(4) requirements that assurances be made that the blood samples would only be taken by a qualified medical practitioner who was satisfied that taking the samples would neither harm the suspect's health nor endanger the suspect's life.

Having found that the accused did not give his consent to the taking of the blood sample, the trial judge excluded the blood alcohol evidence. He subsequently acquitted the accused. The Court of Appeal reversed the acquittals and ordered a new trial.

At issue before the Supreme Court was: (1) whether the accused's consent was an essential element to be proved by the Crown in obtaining the accused's blood sample pursuant to subsection 254(3) of the Code; and (2) whether the standard blood sample demand read here met the requirements of subsection 254(4), and if not, what were the ramifications.

The Supreme Court dismissed the appeal. The court held that the Crown is not required to prove the consent of the accused to the giving of a blood sample.

The standard demand form read here was deficient in that it did not make the assurances required by the Code. The taking of the sample absent these assurances would contravene sections 7 and 8 of the Charter. The issue is whether the admission of the blood sample results could bring the administration of justice into disrepute under subsection 24(2) of the Charter.

The court found that if an accused actually complies with a blood sample demand in the absence of the medical assurances, adducing the evidence of the blood sample is unlikely to bring the administration of justice into disrepute. This is particularly true when the conditions stipulated by the provision were in fact met.

DEFENCES

Depending on whether the prosecution has proven his or her case, the accused can decide whether to present a defence or let the case go to judgment without one. While there is no obligation for an accused to testify in his or her own defence, there are specific defences that can be raised on his or her behalf. They include mistake of fact (i.e., no *mens rea*), necessity, self-defence, compulsion, insanity, intoxication, consent and provocation.

Mistake of Fact — No *Mens Rea*

If the accused proves that she was honestly mistaken as to an essential element of the offence, she has the defence of mistake of fact. For example, an accused charged with possession of cocaine may prove that she honestly believed that the substance was sugar.

Necessity

Necessity is a defence based on an excuse in which the accused argues that the circumstances compelled him to commit the unlawful act. For example, in a case of perceived road rage, speeding away from someone you think is pursuing you is committing an unlawful act and you may be ticketed, but a defence of necessity may excuse you because it was realistically unavoidable. In the 1984 case of *Perka et al. v. R.*[12] the Supreme Court of Canada limited the defence to circumstances of urgency in which there is no reasonable legal alternative.

Self-Defence

The Code provides a defence when a person is assaulted or threatened with assault and the force used to repel the attacker is no more than is necessary to defend oneself (sections 34 and 37). Self-defence is based on necessity and each case is therefore determined on its facts. For example, in the 1990 case of *R. v. Lavallée*[13] the accused wife shot her husband in the back of the head as he left her room. The Supreme Court of Canada held that the history of assaults by the husband against the wife could be considered in determining whether in her circumstances it was reasonable for her to apprehend death or grievous bodily harm even though the physical assault was not actually in progress.

Self-Defence — Battered Wife Syndrome

R. v. Malott[14]

The accused was convicted of second-degree murder after shooting her abusive common law husband to death. The case examines the elements of self-defence in relation to the battered wife syndrome. The Supreme Court held that the trial judge's charge to the jury adequately dealt with evidence of battered woman syndrome.

The accused wife and the deceased husband had lived together in a common law relationship for 19 years and had two children. The deceased abused the accused physically, sexually, psychologically and emotionally. She had gone to the police, but the deceased was a police informant on drug deals and the police told him of her complaints, resulting in an escalation of his violence toward her. A few months before the shooting, the deceased separated from the accused, took their son and went to live with his girlfriend. The accused and deceased had continuing contact.

On the day of the shooting the accused took a pistol from the deceased's gun cabinet, loaded it and carried it in her purse. After driving to a medical appointment with the deceased, she shot him to death. She then took a taxi to his girlfriend's home, shot her and stabbed her with a knife. The girlfriend survived and testified as a Crown witness.

At trial, the accused testified to the extensive abuse that she had suffered, and the Crown conceded that she had been subject to terrible physical and mental abuse at the hands of the deceased. The accused led expert evidence to show that she suffered from battered woman syndrome. Despite this the jury found her guilty of second-degree murder in the death of the deceased and of attempted murder of his girlfriend. The Court of Appeal affirmed the convictions and the Supreme Court of Canada dismissed the appeal.

Pursuant to subsection 34(2) of the Code, there are three elements of self-defence where the victim has died: (1) the existence of an unlawful assault; (2) a reasonable apprehension of a risk of death or grievous bodily harm; and (3) a reasonable belief that it is not possible to preserve oneself from harm except by killing the adversary. The Supreme Court held that the trial judge properly charged the jury with respect to the evidence on battered woman syndrome and it was a matter for the jury to determine whether the accused in fact acted in self-defence.

Compulsion

This is an example of a defence based on the accused not having the capacity to form the intention to commit the unlawful act because of a threat or coercion, for example, having a gun held to his head. Compulsion is an excuse for criminal conduct. The compulsion must be by way of threats of immediate death or bodily harm, and the person being threatened must believe that those threats will be carried out. The defence is not available for murder, attempted murder and some forms of treason.

Insanity

A person is not criminally responsible for an act or the failure to act while suffering from a mental disorder "that rendered the person incapable of appreciating the nature and quality of the act or omission or of knowing that it was wrong." Insanity is another defence based on the incapacity of the accused to form the required intent. The accused has the burden of proving the defence on the balance of probabilities.

Insanity — Charge to Jury

R. v. Jacquard[15]

At trial the jury convicted the accused of first-degree murder for killing his stepfather. At trial, the accused admitted that he had fired the gunshots that caused the death of his stepfather, but pleaded not guilty on the grounds that (1) he was not criminally responsible for his act by virtue of his mental disorder, and (2) he lacked the requisite intent to kill his stepfather.

Defence psychiatrists testified that the accused suffered from a mental disorder at the relevant time, as a result of which he neither understood the nature or quality of his acts nor was capable of forming the intent to carry them out.

In his lengthy charge to the jury, the trial judge reviewed extensively the evidence of the accused's mental disorder as it related to his defence under section 16 of the Code. When subsequently discussing the issue of planning and deliberation, a necessary part of the offence, the trial judge chose not to repeat himself, indicating to the jury that in considering whether the murder was planned and deliberate they should consider all the circumstances and all the evidence. The issue here was whether this was good enough or whether the judge should have also told the jury to consider the claim of mental disorder when looking at this stage as well.

The accused appealed on the ground that the trial judge's instructions did not make it clear to the jury that the burden of proof on the issues of intent and planning and deliberation was on the Crown, and that the evidence relating to the accused's mental disorder ought to be reconsidered in relation to those issues. The accused also submitted that the trial judge misdirected the jury with respect to consciousness of guilt when he commented to them that the fact that an accused tries to hide or destroy evidence can be indicative of consciousness of guilt.

The Court of Appeal and the Supreme Court dismissed the accused's appeal. The Supreme Court held that as long as an appellate court, when looking at a trial judge's charge to the jury as a whole, concludes that the jury was left with a sufficient understanding of the facts as they relate to the relevant issues, the charge is proper. The judge's instructions to the jury to consider all the circumstances when considering the case with respect to the matter of intent, planning and deliberation were good enough since the claim of mental disorder had already been raised.

Intoxication

The burden is on the prosecution to prove that despite self-induced intoxication the accused formed the required intent to commit the offence. This usually is not a problem where only general intent is needed but can be a difficult problem in those situations where specific intent is required. The accused may be able to establish that he or she did not have the specific intent required for conviction of the alleged offence.

In the 1994 case *R. v. Daviault* the accused, a chronic alcoholic, sexually assaulted a partially paralyzed 65-year-old complainant while intoxicated. Expert testimony indicated that the accused might have suffered an episode of amnesia-automatism or "blackout" in which he had no awareness or memory of his actions. The Supreme Court ordered a new trial on the basis that self-induced intoxication resulting in a state similar to automatism was a defence in very limited circumstances to a crime requiring general intent. Following the decision, Parliament passed an amendment to the Code purporting to remove the defence of intoxication in assault cases.

Consent

Consent is a valid defence if the victim consented to the action taken against him, for example a punch in a boxing match. However, no consent is obtained where the victim submits because of force, threat, fraud or abuse of authority or even when the blow in a boxing match is not within the regulations governing the game (CCC 265). No person is entitled to consent to have death inflicted on them (CCC 14). Consent is also not a defence to a sexual assault or abduction committed against a person under 14 years of age (CCC 150.1, 286).

Consent to an assisted suicide is a difficult area raising issues about a dying person's consent to medical treatment. A person can leave a living will indicating that extraordinary medical measures should not be taken to save him or her if unconscious and dying. But is removing a feeding tube assisting the person's death? And when can a person, with the consent of the patient, administer drugs that will speed death? In the 1993 *Rodriguez* case[16] the Supreme Court of Canada decided that the Code provision against assisted suicide took precedence over the individual's Charter section 7 right to life, liberty and security of the person.

Consent to sexual activity is another challenging area. Consent means the voluntary agreement to engage in sexual activity. No consent is obtained if the agreement is expressed by another person or if the person is incapable of consenting. Consent is also not present when the accused induces the consent by abusing a position of trust or authority. Any expression indicating lack of agreement to engage in the act or continue the act will constitute no consent (CCC 273.1). In the 1998 case of *Cuerrier*[17] the Supreme Court of Canada decided that failure to disclose that the partner had HIV could constitute fraud, negating the other partner's consent to sexual activity.

Provocation

Provocation is not a defence to a charge of murder, but the existence of provocation can reduce a charge from murder to manslaughter. For a reduction to manslaughter to take place, the person must have acted in the heat of passion caused by sudden provocation. Provocation is an insult or wrongful act sufficient to deprive an ordinary person of the power of self-control (CCC 232). Provocation, including blows, words or gestures, can be a defence to an assault (CCC 34).

PARTIES TO THE OFFENCE

In a civil trial there are two private parties. In a criminal trial the Crown prosecutes the accused. The Crown counsel decides who is a party to the offence — that is, who to charge with the offence. Every one is a party to an offence who actually commits it (CCC 21–24).

Accomplice

The Crown can also charge a person who aids or abets in the commission of an offence. When two or more people form a common intention to commit a crime and any one of them carries out the crime, it is assumed that each of them ought to have known that one of them would probably commit the crime and is, therefore, a party to it. An **accomplice after the fact** is someone who knows a person has committed an offence and receives, comforts or assists that person for the purpose of enabling an escape. Such accomplices can also be charged with the commission of an offence.

Attempt

A person can be a party to a crime even if the parties were unsuccessful in actually committing the offence. If the accused showed intent to commit an offence, anything done toward carrying out that offence is an attempt. Activities done in preparation, however, do not qualify as part of the attempt. The judge, not the jury, decides whether the act was preparation or if it was a substantial initiation of the commission of the offence sufficient to convict for attempt.

Counselling

Even if an offence is not committed, a person who counsels committing an offence is guilty of an offence (CCC 464). Even if the offence is committed in a different way from that which was counselled, the person is a party. Counselling includes procuring, soliciting or inciting to commit an offence.

Conspiracy

Conspiracy is another offence for which a person who does not actually commit the crime can be a party. Conspiracy is a criminal charge whereby two or more people enter into an agreement to commit a crime. The Crown counsel must prove there was a common goal or design to commit a crime. It is not necessary that either party take steps toward the actual commission of the crime (CCC 465).

Joinder of Accused

The Crown counsel can decide to join the cases of two or more parties, meaning that the trials are heard together. However, the evidence against only one of the parties cannot be used to convict another party. If there is a jury, the judge can order that each accused have his or her own trial (CCC 591).

TYPES OF OFFENCES

The Code divides criminal offences into two categories: summary conviction offences and indictable offences. Some "hybrid" offences may be either summary or indictable; the Crown counsel decides the category when laying a charge. **Summary offences** are less serious offences. The procedure followed is simple. The accused can send a counsel or agent to appear at trial in his or her place and an accused who is in prison can appear by video (CCC 800). Everyone who is convicted of a summary offence is liable to a fine of not more than $2 000 or to imprisonment for six months or both (CCC 787). **Indictable offences** are more serious crimes and involve a more complex procedure. The accused must appear personally in court. For less serious indictable offences the accused is tried by a judge alone in the provincial court (CCC 553). For more serious indictable offences the accused can choose trial by judge alone in the provincial or higher court, or judge and jury. For some very serious offences the accused must be tried by a higher court judge (CCC 469). In a **hybrid or dual procedure offence** the Crown counsel can decide whether to charge by way of summary conviction or by indictment. Usually for a first or minor violation, the Crown will charge by way of summary conviction. The offence is treated as indictable until the first appearance, and therefore the accused must appear in person.

CRIMINAL PROCEDURE

Criminal procedure is the set of rules by which the state, referred to as the Crown in Canada, brings a person accused of a crime to trial, hears the case of the prosecution and defence, determines a verdict and passes and enforces a sentence if the accused has been convicted.

Pre-Trial

Search Warrants

When it is suspected that a crime has taken place, investigating officers must sometimes search persons or premises to obtain evidence to support a criminal charge. Officers can provide information on oath to a minor judicial official called a justice of the peace that they have reasonable and probable grounds to search for evidence. If the justice is satisfied, he or she will issue a search warrant (CCC 487). In certain circumstances a warrant can be issued by telephone or fax. The Charter establishes the right to be secure from unreasonable search or seizure and peace officers can search without a warrant in only limited circumstances. The major exceptions relate to searches for drugs, alcohol or illegal weapons. For example, under the *Narcotics Control Act* a peace officer may search without a warrant any premises that is not a dwelling place or any person found in that place (sections 8, 10 and 11).

If officers search without a warrant, the court may hold that the evidence they obtain is inadmissible at the trial of the accused. For example, in the 1997 case *R. v. Feeney* (see p. 151) the Supreme Court of Canada held that the shirt of the accused, which was soaked in the murder victim's blood, was not admissible as evidence because the police did not have a search warrant or other lawful excuse to enter his trailer.

Search and Seizure

R. v. Caslake[18]

In this case the police conducted an inventory search of the car of the accused following a lawful arrest. The search was conducted pursuant to police policy and without a warrant or permission. The issue is whether the search infringed the Charter right to freedom from unreasonable search or seizure. The Supreme Court dismissed the accused's appeal.

A search, to be reasonable under section 8 of the Charter, must be authorized by law; the law itself must be reasonable, and the search must be carried out in a reasonable manner. Once the accused has demonstrated that the search was warrantless, the Crown has the burden of showing that the search was, on the balance of probabilities, reasonable.

To be lawful the search must meet three conditions. First, a specific statute or common law rule must authorize the search. Second, the search must be carried out in accordance with the procedural and substantive requirements of the law. Third, a search must not exceed its scope as to area and the items that the authority granted.

The police must be able to explain, within the purposes of protecting themselves, protecting the evidence, discovering evidence, or by reference to some other valid purpose, why they conducted a search. They do not need reasonable and probable grounds. However, they must have had some reason related to the arrest for conducting the search, and that reason must be objectively reasonable.

In this case the police officer's purpose in conducting the search was to inventory the contents of the vehicle. The court determined that this fell outside the bounds of the legitimate purposes of search incident to arrest and therefore the accused's Charter rights were infringed. However, the Supreme Court held under subsection 24 (2) of the Charter that the evidence should not be excluded. The breach was not serious. The unobtrusiveness of the search, the individual's low expectation of privacy in the area searched, the existence of reasonable and probable grounds and the good faith of the police all pointed in favour of admitting the evidence. Finally, excluding the evidence would have a more serious impact on the repute of the administration of justice than admitting it, for the prosecution had no case without the evidence.

Arrest Without a Warrant

The power to arrest differs with the status of the person doing the arresting. Anyone may arrest a person who is found committing an indictable offence, is believed to have committed an offence, or who is escaping from and is being pursued by police officers. A peace officer, which is a category that not only includes police but others such as prison guards, may arrest without a warrant a person who on reasonable grounds he or she believes has committed or is about to commit an indictable offence. The police officer may not arrest for a summary conviction offence unless he or she observes the accused committing the offence.

Laying the Information

Anyone who on reasonable grounds believes that a person has committed an offence may lay an information (a document in writing and under oath before a justice of the peace) to begin the process. Usually the police or the Crown counsel lays the information. The justice hears the information of the informant and, where there is sufficient evidence, issues a summons or a warrant for the arrest of the accused. The police then either arrest the accused or serve the summons.

Compelling Appearance of Accused and Interim Release

An accused may be compelled to appear in court by an arrest warrant, an appearance notice, a summons, a promise to appear, a recognizance without sureties, an undertaking or a judicial interim release. Once the accused is arrested, he or she can be released prior to trial by the arresting officer, the officer in charge, a justice of the peace or a judge. An accused who is not released by the arresting officer or officer in charge must be brought before a justice within 24 hours. The justice determines whether to release the accused on his promise to appear or on an undertaking with conditions set by the justice, which may include a surety which involves the deposit of money that is returned when the accused appears for trial. Where the Crown counsel shows cause why the accused should be detained, he remains in custody.

Plea and Election

When the accused first appears in court, the information is read to him and he is asked whether he pleads guilty or not guilty. If the accused pleads not guilty he is given a date for the trial. A summary conviction offence, or an offence where the Crown counsel chooses to treat a hybrid offence as a summary conviction offence, is dealt with in a simple procedure before a provincial court judge. If the Crown is proceeding by indictment, the accused can choose or elect to have a trial by provincial court judge alone, by higher court judge alone or by judge and jury. In a murder charge the accused must be tried by judge and jury.

Preliminary Inquiry

When the trial is by indictment before a higher court judge or a judge and jury, the defence has a right to a preliminary hearing. This is a hearing held before a provincial court judge in which the prosecution must present the evidence and witnesses testifying under oath to establish whether or not the Crown has a sufficient case to warrant a trial. The accused can call witnesses but it is usually in his best interests not to reveal his defence. The judge will decide whether there is sufficient evidence to proceed to trial; if there isn't, the accused will be discharged.

Jury Selection

When a jury trial is involved, the Crown counsel and defence counsel must select the jury members from a panel. The accused or the prosecutor may challenge (reject) a potential juror without cause four or more times depending on the seriousness of the offence. Either may challenge with cause for a number of reasons, including that the juror is biased toward either side.

Interference with Jury

R. v. Latimer[19]

In this case the accused was detained for questioning by the police following the death of his severely disabled daughter. He was convicted at trial of second-degree murder. He appealed on several grounds, including that the Crown counsel interfered with prospective jurors. The Court of Appeal dismissed the appeal. Subsequent to the Court of Appeal's judgment, the defence brought fresh evidence that Crown counsel at trial had interfered with the jury.

The affidavit indicated that the Crown counsel at trial and an RCMP officer prepared a questionnaire asking prospective jurors for their views on a number of issues. This questionnaire was administered by RCMP officers to 30 of the 198 prospective jurors and also led to some unrecorded discussions with prospective jurors, which went beyond the exact questions posed in the questionnaire. Of the 30 prospective jurors who were administered the questionnaire, five served on the jury which convicted the accused.

The Supreme Court of Canada allowed the appeal and ordered a new trial. The court held that the actions of Crown counsel in interfering with prospective jurors were a flagrant abuse of process and interference with the administration of justice. Given the interference with the jury, a new trial was ordered.

Trial

The Crown counsel must prove beyond a reasonable doubt each element of the offence, and the accused is entitled to make a full answer and defence. The obligation is on the Crown to prove its case. If it fails to do so, the accused does not have to provide a defence; the judge dismisses the case for lack of evidence. The accused must be present during a trial of a charge by indictment. However, when the judge and the counsel agree the accused can appear by video link. The judge can order the removal of an accused who is disruptive.

The Crown presents its case first. The Crown counsel and the accused, usually through his lawyer, examine and cross-examine witnesses who testify under oath. If the accused admits to any of the facts alleged against him, the Crown then need not prove the admitted facts. The judge makes decisions as to whether particular questions are allowed and whether specific evidence is admissible. The Crown or accused can object to the question or admission of evidence and the judge rules on whether to sustain the objection or to overrule it. The trial proceeds continuously, subject to adjournment by the judge.

At the end of the trial, the Crown counsel and counsel for the accused make summation arguments as to the law and the facts. If there is a jury, the judge gives instruction to them on technical points of the law. The jury decides the verdict of guilty or not guilty based on the facts established by the evidence. If the judge decides that the Crown did not prove an element of the offence she will direct the jury to find the accused not guilty. If there is no jury, the judge decides whether to convict or discharge the accused.

Appeal

If either the Crown or the accused believe the judge made a significant mistake in law, they can appeal to a higher court to overturn the conviction or acquittal and order a new verdict or a new trial. A sentence can also be appealed. In a summary conviction case, the appeal is to the province's superior court. In an indictable case, the appeal is to the province's court of appeal. But this is not a true appeal as it involves a complete rehearing of the case (called a **trial de novo**).Only significant issues of law, usually where there is a dissent at the court of appeal, can be appealed to the Supreme Court of Canada. The Supreme Court must give leave to appeal — that is, rule in a preliminary hearing whether the issue of law is significant enough to merit their attention. Changes to the Code made in 1997 eliminated the right to appeal if an acquittal or its equivalent were overturned by a court of appeal and a new trial ordered (CCC 691).

Sentencing

If the accused is convicted, the judge holds a hearing to decide on the sentence. Counsel for the Crown and the accused argue for a particular sentence. The prosecution will attempt to persuade the judge that the seriousness of the act, the lack of remorse, or the need to protect society calls for the maximum penalty. The defence will argue that his client has suffered enough or that there is little likelihood of reoffending. The judge can request that a probation officer prepare a pre-sentence report, which can include the offender's age, maturity, character, behaviour, attitude, willingness to make amends, and the history of previous sentences and alternative measures. The judge can also receive a statement about the impact of the crime on the victim. The judge considers the goals of sentencing, keeping in mind that incarceration is the last option to consider:

... to contribute, along with crime prevention initiatives, to respect for the law and maintenance of a just, peaceful and safe society by imposing just sanctions that have one or more of
the following objectives:

(a) to denounce unlawful conduct;

(b) to deter the offender and other persons from committing offences;

(c) to separate the offender from society, where necessary;

(d) to assist in rehabilitating offenders;

(e) to provide reparations for harm done to the victims or the community; and

(f) to promote a sense of responsibility in offenders, and acknowledgment of the harm done
    to victims and the community [CCC 718].

Discretion

The judge has a considerable amount of discretion in sentencing. A sentence must be proportionate to the gravity of the offence and the degree of responsibility of the offender. A judge
takes into consideration aggravating or mitigating circumstances when sentencing an individual. He or she compares the case at hand with other sentences in similar circumstances,
as well as the length and harshness of consecutive sentences. A maximum sentence is usually set out in the *Criminal Code*, but not a minimum sentence. A conviction does not necessarily mean the accused will go to jail. The Code requires that "all available sanctions
other than imprisonment that are reasonable in the circumstances should be considered for
all offenders" (CCC 718.2).

Penalties

A judge may impose a variety of penalties. A **suspended sentence** is a conviction, but the
sentence is suspended while the offender complies with conditions. If the judge imposes a
fine, the offender must pay the fine or serve time in jail. A **probation order** is an order
that the offender report to a probation officer and comply with other conditions for the specified time. **Restitution** is an order that the offender make restitution to the victim of the
crime. A **conditional discharge** does not result in a conviction if the offender complies
with the conditions; an **absolute discharge** is not a conviction and does not result in a criminal record. A **conditional sentence of imprisonment** permits certain offenders to serve
their time in the community. A **sentence of imprisonment** of less than two years is served
in a provincial prison and a greater term is served in a federal penitentiary.

Parole

An offender who is sentenced to a term in prison normally will not spend the whole period
of the sentence behind bars. After serving approximately one third of the sentence, the offender becomes eligible for parole. A government-appointed panel hears the application
for parole. The parole board considers factors such as the inmate's behaviour in prison, the
way the offence was committed and the danger to the community. If requests for parole are
consistently denied, the inmate becomes entitled to parole after serving two thirds of the

sentence, unless the sentence specifically stated that it was for a determined period without the possibility of parole. While on parole, the convicted person must report to a probation officer on a regular basis and maintain certain standards of conduct. Parolees can be returned to prison if they fail to abide by the conditions of the parole.

Pardon

The federal government can grant a pardon from a term of imprisonment on the grounds of mercy. Under the *Criminal Records Act* a person convicted of an indictable offence can apply for a pardon to remove a record of conviction after five years and a person convicted of a summary conviction offence can apply after three years. The person must have been of good conduct and not been convicted of a subsequent offence.

YOUNG OFFENDERS

Young people accused of committing crimes are subject to special *Young Offenders Act* procedures based on the policy that society must address the underlying causes of youth crime and respond appropriately to youth at risk of committing further crimes. The *Young Offenders Act,* a federal statute, sets out the legal rights of young people age 12 to 17 who are accused of committing federal offences. Each province has passed its own equivalent of the *Young Offenders Act* to deal with violations of provincial laws.

Guiding Principles

Section 3 of the Act lists the principles that guide dealings with young offenders. Young people are to be held accountable for their criminal acts, although not necessarily in the same way as adults. The Act recognizes that young people require age-appropriate supervision, discipline and control. Parents are responsible for the care and supervision of their children, and young people should only be removed from their care when parental supervision is inappropriate or inadequate. In the case of young offenders it is felt that the protection of society is best served by rehabilitation that addresses their special needs and circumstances.

Rights Upon Arrest

Young people have special guarantees of their rights and freedoms, particularly the right to be informed of them. A young person has an absolute right to retain and instruct counsel at any stage of the proceedings. Before agreeing to alternative measures, the young offender must be advised of his or her right to counsel. The judge can appoint counsel if the young person wishes to obtain counsel but is unable to do so.

Alternative Measures

Prior to laying a charge, the young person may be diverted from the regular procedure of the justice system. If the young offender accepts responsibility for the criminal act, Crown counsel decides whether to release the youth, proceed to trial, or divert the accused into some alternative method of punishment. The youth must consent to participate in an alternative measures program and the Crown counsel must be satisfied that there is sufficient evidence to prosecute the offence. Counsel takes into consideration the needs of the young person and the interests of society. Alternative measures might include an apology to the victim of the offence, community service or participation in crime prevention programs.

Transfer to Adult Court

In certain serious offences, the Crown can apply to have a youth 14 years and older transferred to adult court. In 1995 the federal Parliament changed the Act to require that all 16- and 17-year-old youths charged with specified violent crimes be transferred automatically to adult court, unless a youth court judge orders that proceedings take place in youth court. Those crimes include murder, attempted murder, manslaughter and aggravated sexual assault. Youths charged with crimes that are punishable by five years or more have a right under the Charter to trial by judge and jury.

Release of Information

The Act bans the publication of information relating to the identity of a young offender. A 1995 amendment increased the ability of professionals who deal with young offenders to share information. A judge can also authorize the release of information to a member of the public if there is a risk to their personal safety. In March 1999 the federal government introduced an Act to amend the *Young Offenders Act* to lift the publication ban for young offenders sentenced in adult court.

Sentencing

Sentences in youth court are called dispositions and range from an absolute discharge, which means the youth will have no record, to serving time in open or secure custody. Before sentencing, a youth worker prepares a predisposition report similar to the pre-sentence report in adult court. A youth can be fined up to a maximum of $1 000 and/or be required to pay compensation to the victim. The disposition can include conditions, for example that the youth must perform community service. The youth can be placed on probation for up to two years and be required to report to a probation officer. Open custody is often served in a community house. Secure custody facilities are usually camps in isolated areas, although some facilities have cells. In 1995 Parliament changed the maximum sentence for young offenders for first-degree murder from five years to ten years, of which a maximum of six years can be served in custody. A conviction for second-degree murder is seven years, of which a maximum of four years can be served in custody.

Parliament also clarified that custody is only imposed when all available alternatives have been considered. An order for custody is not used as a substitute for appropriate child protection, health and other social measures. A young person should be placed in a level of custody involving the least degree of containment and restraint. In less serious offences young people should be held accountable to their victims in non-custodial dispositions.

Proposed Youth Justice Act

On March 11, 1999 the Minister of Justice announced an intention to repeal the *Young Offenders Act* and replace it with the *Youth Justice Act*. Key provisions of the new Act include:

- lowering the age for adult sentencing to 14- and 15-year-old youth convicted of an offence punishable by more than two years in jail;
- expanding the offences for which a young person convicted of an offence would be presumed to receive an adult sentence;
- permitting the publication of names of all youth who receive an adult sentence and allowing the Crown greater discretion in seeking adult sentences and publication of offenders' names;
- creating a special sentence with an individualized plan for treatment for serious violent offenders who suffer from mental illness, psychological disorder or emotional disturbance;
- giving the courts more discretion to receive evidence of voluntary statements by youth to police;
- requiring all periods of custody to be followed by a period of controlled supervision in the community;
- permitting tougher penalties for adults who wilfully fail to comply with an undertaking made to the court to properly supervise youth who have been denied bail and placed in their care; and
- permitting and encouraging the use of a full range of community-based sentences and effective alternatives to the justice system for youth who commit non-violent offences.

CONCLUSION

In this necessarily brief overview of criminal law, our objective was to introduce you to the purposes and goals of the law. Because all Canadian jurisdictions are subject to the provisions of the *Criminal Code* and the enforcement of its provisions is up to government-appointed officials, the terms of the Code are explicit and the courts are bound to ensure that people accused of crimes are treated fairly and justly. This is another instance where justice must "not only be done, but seen to be done," and except in the case where the identity of the victim or a young offender needs to be protected, criminal proceedings are open to the scrutiny of the public and the media. Criminal law is a branch of public law because the government is one of the parties to the action. In the following chapters of the text we will examine in some depth various branches of private or civil law — that is, law where an individual or private body complains that another individual or group has caused them personal or financial injury. The procedures related to such actions have been dealt with under the chapter on courts (Chapter 5), and so it is important to keep in mind that such cases only come about when one party decides to sue another for financial compensation or some other equitable remedy.

QUESTIONS FOR DISCUSSION AND REVIEW

1. Police officers are often cited as saying that they are hamstrung by the Charter and can't do their jobs when they are so restricted. Do you think the Charter inappropriately restricts their powers to apprehend and arrest suspects?

2. Police officers can only arrest a person for acts that contravene the *Criminal Code* and other specific statutes. Should their powers be extended to arrest for new and unusual offences when they feel it is in the best interests of society to do so?

3. To some people, the criminal justice process seems unnecessarily complex and slow. Justify the procedures or describe how they might be made more efficient and cost-effective.

4. The protection of society is said to be the most important goal of criminal law enforcement. Is that as apparent today as it was in the past?

5. Discuss the role of the jury in a criminal trial and determine whether the jury is an important element in the administration of criminal justice.

6. A judge is bound to apply the terms of the *Criminal Code*. Should judges have more discretion to convict when it appears that police officers have overstepped their powers, especially when it is clear that the accused committed a crime?

7. Judges have considerable discretion when it comes to sentencing a person convicted of a crime. Should more guidance be provided as to the minimum sentences that can be applied?

8. A prisoner can be paroled after serving only two thirds of a sentence. What purposes does parole serve and is it justified when there is considerable risk of re-offending?

9. Young people have extra rights when they are arrested and tried for alleged criminal acts. Should they be treated like everyone else in the justice system? What justification is there for leniency?

10. Consider the various alternative measures available to young offenders and discuss their merit. Add your suggestions for ways young people might be required to right the wrongs they have committed.

NOTES

1. *Principles and Purposes of Criminal Justice: Report of the Canadian Committee on Corrections.* Ottawa: Information Canada, 1969, pp. 11–20.

2. *R. v. Nova Scotia Pharmaceutical Society* (1992), 93 D.L.R. (4th) 36 (S.C.C.).

3. *R. v. Daviault* (1994), 118 D.L.R. (4th) 469 (S.C.C.).

4. *R. v. Harbottle*, [1993] 3 S.C.R. 306.

5. *R. v. Creighton* (1993), 105 D.L.R. (4th) 632 (S.C.C.).

6. *R. v. City of Sault Ste. Marie*, [1978] 2 S.C.R. 1299.

7. *Reference Re Section 94(2) of the Motor Vehicle Act (B. C.) (1986), Reference Re Section 94 (2) of the Motor Vehicle Act* (1983), 147 D.L.R. (3d) 539.

8. *R. v. Bisson* (1998), 155 D.L.R. (4th) (S.C.C.).

9. *R. v. Hawkins* (1996), 141 D.L.R. (4th) 193 (S.C.C.).

10. *R. v. Feeney* (1997), 146 D.L.R. (4th) 609 (S.C.C.).

11. *R. v. Knox* (1996), 139 D.L.R. (4th) 1 (S.C.C.).

12. *Perka et al. v. R.* (1984), 13 D.L.R. (4th) 1 (S.C.C.).

13. *R. v. Lavallée*, [1990] 1 S.C.R. 852.

14. *R. v. Malott* (1998), 155 D.L.R. (4th) 513 (S.C.C.).

15. *R. v. Jacquard* (1997), 143 D.L.R. (4th) 433 (S.C.C.).

16. *Rodriguez v. British Columbia (Attorney-General)* (1993), 107 D.L.R. (4th) 342 (S.C.C.).

17. *R. v. Cuerrier* (1998), 162 D.L.R. (4th) 513 (S.C.C.).

18. *R. v. Caslake* (1998), 155 D.L.R. (4th) 19 (S.C.C.)

19. *R. v. Latimer*, [1997] 1 S.C.R. 217.

FURTHER READING

Hogg, Peter W. *Constitutional Law of Canada*, 4th ed. Toronto: Carswell, 1997.

Jackson, M.A. and C.T. Griffiths. *Canadian Criminology: Perspectives on Crime and Criminality*. Toronto: Harcourt Brace Jovanovich, 1991.

Mewett & Manning on Criminal Law, 3rd ed. Toronto: Butterworths, 1994.

Parker, Graham. *An Introduction to Criminal Law*, 3rd ed. Toronto: Methuen, 1987.

Verdun-Jones, S. *Criminal Law in Canada*, 2nd ed. Toronto: Harcourt Brace, 1993.

Whitley, Stuart J. *Criminal Justice and the Constitution*. Toronto: Carswell, 1989.

TORT LAW

> *Tort law can constantly underscore our*
> *dedication to individual autonomy, individual*
> *dignity, and individual worth. It can also remind*
> *us that there are more important values than dry*
> *efficiency and icy rationality.*
>
> Allen M. Linden, *Canadian Tort Law*, p. 28

A tort occurs when a person acts in an unacceptable way toward another, causing that person harm or injury. Society imposes an obligation or duty to be careful not to cause injury to others or harm to their property. The commission of a tort is the failure to live up to that duty. A breach of contract, on the other hand, is only wrongful because the agreement between the parties makes the act, or failure to act, wrongful. For example, there is nothing wrong with a person refusing to give you his automobile, unless you have a contract with him requiring the transfer of the car. However, if someone punches you in the nose or is impaired while driving and causes you injury, such conduct is inherently wrong and constitutes the commission of a tort.

Criminal law also deals with wrongful conduct or actions that are inherently unacceptable to society. A tort, however, is a civil wrong, because the victim of the wrongdoing can bring a private action seeking compensation for the injuries suffered. The civil action is a contest between the victim (the plaintiff) and the person accused of causing the injury (the tortfeasor or defendant). The same unacceptable conduct, such as an assault or a trespass, may be involved in a breach of the criminal law. In the criminal matter, however, the offence is considered so serious that it not only offends the person who was injured, but also poses a threat to society. Society, or the state, then takes steps to protect itself and to control the wrongful behaviour by prosecuting the offender. The victim of the offensive conduct is merely a witness in the resulting court proceedings. Any fines that are paid and any imprisonment imposed do not benefit the victim in any material way. The objective of determining guilt in a criminal matter is to punish the accused, whereas in tort law the primary purpose is to compensate the victim for the injuries suffered. It should be noted that the requirement to make restitution to the victim can be imposed in a criminal action today.

There is a great overlap between crimes and torts. Most crimes that involve a victim are torts as well. For this reason, people convicted of a crime often face a separate tort action, brought by the victim. For example, a person who kills another as a result of impaired driving will face a criminal trial in which he or she must answer the charge of criminal negligence. In addition, however, the estate or relatives of the victim usually bring a separate civil action, seeking damages on the basis of the tort of negligence for the loss they have suffered.

CATEGORIES OF TORTS

A tort, then, is an actionable wrong committed against the person, property or reputation of another. Torts can be broken down into a number of categories, including assault and battery, trespass to property, false imprisonment, defamation, deceit, nuisance and negligence. A perplexing problem facing those involved with the study of torts is the question of whether there is one general tort that can be committed in many different ways, or whether these categories are examples of many different kinds of torts, each having different rules and remedies associated with them. In fact, a satisfactory, all-encompassing definition of what a tort is has never been developed.

Torts have been categorized in different classes and have developed in this fashion over the centuries. The various types of torts often have distinct sets of rules and remedies that distinguish them from other torts. Today, the courts are much more willing to treat tort as a general principle. As long as the conduct complained of can be classified as socially unacceptable and wrongful conduct that causes injury to another person or to his or her property or reputation, that conduct will be actionable whether or not it fits nicely into one of these recognized categories.

Today, these categories are much less likely to be treated as restrictive by the courts; conduct not fitting into them will still likely be treated as a tort. While it must be recognized that there are different categories of torts with different rules and remedies, a general overriding principle recognizes that where wrongful conduct does not fit into one of the established classifications, the courts will treat it as tortious and provide a remedy. Because it is easier to study the subject according to these classifications, we will examine them, keeping in mind that the categories are for convenience only. When conduct does not fit into one of them, it should not be assumed that there is no actionable wrong.

Fault

A tort is not committed every time a person causes injury to another. The requirement of fault is central to tort law. The conduct causing the injury may be innocent or wrongful; only when the conduct is wrongful does it constitute a tort. Originally, only willful or **intentional conduct** resulting in injury was considered wrongful. Today, this has been expanded to include inadvertent conduct that is careless, in the sense that the conduct falls below a standard of care society considers acceptable. Such carelessness is called **negligence**, and it is only when the conduct is willful or negligent that a tort has been committed. The requirement of fault is used to determine whether conduct is innocent or wrongful. Tort law is primarily concerned with determining who should bear the loss when a person's act or failure to act causes injury to another. The function of the court is to decide when the loss ought to be shifted from the victim to the person who caused the injury or loss.

Strict Liability

There are some limited circumstances in which tort liability will be imposed even when no fault is established. Such strict liability is imposed when something dangerous is brought onto a property and it escapes, causing damage to a neighbouring property. Even if there has been no blameworthy conduct on the part of the person bringing the thing onto the property, she will be held responsible for any losses that result if it escapes. In the case of *Ryland* v. *Fletcher*,[1] water was stored in a reservoir on the property of Mr. Ryland. Unknown to him, there was an abandoned mine shaft on his property into which the water escaped through connecting shafts, causing damage to the coal-mining operation of his neighbour, Mr. Fletcher. Ryland had no reason to believe that any mining had ever been carried on under his property. His conduct was entirely innocent, but the court still found that he was liable for the damages. In Canada, the trend is to interpret strict liability as narrowly as possible. If the dangerous thing brought onto the property is a normal use of that property and is used in a normal way, there is no strict liability. Thus, electrical wiring, gas heating, or plumbing, which can be dangerous, will not lead to strict liability.

Vicarious Liability

Vicarious liability is another situation in which people can be held responsible for torts without any fault on their part and without even participating in the commission of the tort. Vicarious liability involves one person being held responsible for someone else's tortious conduct as a result of a special relationship existing between them, such as employer and employee. If an employee commits a tort while actually doing the job he was hired to do, not only is that employee responsible for the injuries caused, but also the employer can be required to compensate the victim.

As a general rule, parents are not responsible for the wrongful conduct of their children. If a parent actually contributes to the commission of the wrong, however, such as leaving a loaded gun where the child could play with it, resulting in someone being injured, then the parent will be directly liable for his own negligence. But where the parents are innocent of any wrongdoing, they will not be vicariously liable for the wrongful conduct of their children. Many jurisdictions have changed this by statute and place such responsibility on parents, at least in specific situations. For example, the *School Act* of BC states that parents are responsible for any damages caused by their children to school property.[2]

Joint Liability

In a situation in which more than one person causes an injury, all involved are responsible for it. Each one of the **joint tortfeasors,** as they are called, may be required to pay the entire amount of the judgment. This is also true in partnership organizations where partners are responsible for each other's wrongdoings. Once the victim has obtained judgment against all those participating, he can collect from whomever is more likely able to pay. He can only collect up to the full amount of the judgment; he cannot obtain a windfall by collecting the whole amount from each of the parties. As between the joint tortfeasors, the one who pays may collect a share of the compensation from each of the others. The same principles hold true when vicarious liability is involved. An employee who commits a tort in the course of his employment is not relieved of responsibility just because his employer is vicariously liable. In fact, the victim will normally sue both the employee and the employer. When judgment is obtained against both, the victim has the choice of collecting from either the employee or the employer. Usually, the employer is in a better position to pay, so the victim turns to the employer to satisfy the judgment.

Remedies

The remedy usually sought in a tort action is monetary compensation, in the form of damages. **Special damages** are losses that can be calculated with precision, such as the actual cost of replacing a damaged fender, or lost wages. **General damages** are awarded when the amount cannot be determined with such certainty. When a person receives compensation for pain and suffering, this must be an estimate and is called general damages. In rare circumstances, the court can award **punitive or exemplary damages**. Such an award is designed to punish the wrongdoer rather than compensate the victim; the plaintiff may thus experience a windfall. Another important remedy that can be applied in a tort action is the equitable remedy of an **injunction**. In the case of an injunction, the court orders the offending person to stop the wrongful conduct. In unique circumstances, more specialized remedies may be available such as **replevin**, which is an order by the court for the person wrongfully withholding goods to return them to the rightful owner.

INTENTIONAL TORTS

Torts are divided into those that involve an element of intention and those that are inadvertent (negligence). Intention, as it is used here, means that the tortious conduct complained of is the intended outcome of a willful and conscious act. When a person intends to strike another and, in fact, does so, that blow is the realization of a willful and conscious process. This constitutes intention for the purposes of tort law. Intention, then, does not require that the injury, or even the particular form of the injury, be intended; intention only requires that the conduct itself was willful. If someone intends to hit one person but hits another instead, the act of hitting is still willful; there is sufficient intention present to establish a tort. Similarly, when a person walks on someone else's property or publishes words that are defamatory, it is no excuse for that person to say she thought she was on her own property or she thought that the words she published were true. In a subsequent tort action, such mistakes would not constitute a defence.

While the claim that an injury was caused by mistake is not an adequate defence in a tort action, the claim that it was an accident might be. It is important, therefore, to distinguish between a mistake and an accident. A **mistake** occurs when the result is not what was anticipated, although the conduct leading to it was, nevertheless, willful. An **accident** involves inadvertent conduct; that is, the action itself was unintended. This may provide a defence where an intentional tort such as assault or trespass is involved, but it will not be a defence to a negligence action.

Because intentional torts require people to act willfully and of their own volition, the tort-feasor, to be found liable, must have the mental capacity to form the required intention. **Insanity** can be a defence to a tort requiring intention, but such insanity must be so extensive that the person is incapable of forming the intention to do the act. In Canada, to escape liability on the basis of insanity for an intentional tort, the defendant must have been so mentally incapacitated that he did not know what he was doing. When a mentally incapacitated person strikes another under the delusion that he is striking an attacking wild animal, this would be sufficient insanity to be an effective defence. Also, if the conduct is the result of automatism — that is, if the person has no control over what his body does, such as in the case of a seizure — there would be no willful conduct and so no liability.

For similar reasons, youth is generally not a defence when an intentional tort is involved. As long as the child is capable of forming an intent to do the act, that child can be held responsible for it. There have been several cases in which children under the age of 10 have been held responsible for intentionally injuring other people.

Assault and Battery

Although the terms "assault" and "battery" are usually used together, it is important to distinguish between them. An assault is usually thought of as an attempted battery. This is misleading, because it focuses attention on the state of mind of the tortfeasor. More correctly, assault should be viewed as conduct that causes the victim fear or apprehension of imminent physical contact. The assault, then, involves the victim's anticipation of the blow or other physical contact, regardless of whether or not it actually takes place. Battery is merely a successful assault carried through to its intended conclusion; thus, most batteries include the tort of assault. The term *assault* is often used to cover both assault and battery, but we use the term more specifically to refer only to those situations where no physical contact takes place. It is possible to have a battery in which no assault is involved, such as when a victim is kissed while sleeping or a patient is inappropriately touched while anesthetized. In the majority of situations, however, an assault is included in a battery. The legal remedies are the same, whether the conduct involved is an assault or a battery, so the distinction between the two is not usually of great importance.

Assault

It is common for an assault to take place without a battery. Pointing a gun or shaking a fist at someone, threatening to throw a stone or throwing it and missing, and advancing toward another in a hostile manner, are all examples of assault with no accompanying battery. For such action to constitute an assault, it is necessary that the tortfeasor be perceived as being able to carry out the threat immediately. If someone uses the telephone to threaten to punch a person in the nose, that does not constitute an assault because, since the parties are in different locations, there is no present ability to carry out the threat. It may be actionable as some other form of tort, but it is not an assault.

If a person points an unloaded gun at another, however, that would constitute an assault. Because the victim does not know that the gun is not loaded, she would perceive the threat to be real. It is the state of mind of the victim, involving fear or apprehension of imminent physical contact, that determines the existence of the assault. Shaking a fist at someone from the other side of a ravine would not be an assault because it would be apparent to the victim, and anyone else watching, that there was no way that the threat could be carried out. Pointing a gun at someone from the other side of a ravine, however, would constitute an assault.

If an innocent gesture is accompanied by threatening words, it may constitute an assault. For example, the common action of walking toward another becomes threatening if it is accompanied by words such as, "You dirty so-and-so, I'm going to knock your block off." In such an instance, an assault has been committed. The reverse is also true. A gesture that would normally be threatening can have the threat removed by words that accompany the gesture. If a person walks toward another with a raised fist, that might, at first, seem threatening were it not for the accompanying words, "Have you seen my new ring?"

Even words that sound threatening may, if listened to carefully, be innocent and take away from the threat of an otherwise threatening gesture. In the case of *Turberville* v. *Savage*,[3] the two parties were at a polling booth. The plaintiff touched the hilt of his sword and said, "If it were not assize time, I would not take such language from you." The defendant then drew his sword and the plaintiff did likewise. In the ensuing fight, the plaintiff lost an eye. He sued, and the defendant claimed self-defence. The court held that the words of the plaintiff, when he touched his sword, clearly stated that he did not intend to hurt or to fight with the defendant at that time. The defendant started the fight and assaulted the plaintiff; the plaintiff merely defended himself, and thus was successful in his action. When someone says, "If this weren't a police station, I'd punch you in the nose," such words may be belligerent and offensive, but no assault has taken place because the message, clearly, is that there is no intention of hitting the person at that time and in that place.

If no threat of violence is involved, the mere act of hurling insults or swearing at someone normally will not be a tort, unless it constitutes defamation. In some circumstances, however, the insult may cause the victim to have a heart attack or a nervous breakdown. In such a case, even though it does not constitute an assault, it may be actionable.

Practical jokes can be actionable if they cause mental suffering and if they result in an actual illness. In recent times, such intentional infliction of mental suffering has become actionable. In the case of *Wilkinson* v. *Downton*,[4] the tortfeasor played a practical joke by falsely informing the victim that her husband had been seriously injured in an accident and needed her help. This caused the victim great distress, resulting not only in mental anguish but also in physical illness, for which she required considerable medical attention and many weeks to recover. In this case, no assault or battery was involved, but there was an intentional attempt to cause mental distress. Although it is likely that the tortfeasor did not anticipate the extent of the victim's reaction, the tortfeasor was liable for damages. This case not only illustrates the willingness of the courts to impose liability when someone intentionally causes mental suffering that leads to physical illness, but also illustrates why it is dangerous to think of tort law as being limited to the categories outlined here. This is one area in which the courts have seen fit to expand tort law to cover new situations.

The only requirement for assault is that the victim be apprehensive, not fearful, of imminent physical contact. If a person weighing 95 pounds threatens to beat up a 250-pound wrestler, the wrestler might not be fearful. However, as long as he thinks the other person is serious, he then has an apprehension of imminent physical contact, and that would constitute an assault. (In these circumstances, however, a judge might not be too sympathetic in awarding damages.)

Battery

A battery is the actual physical contact, whether direct or indirect. The object making physical contact may be a fist, a sword, an arrow, a rock, a bullet, etc. As in other forms of intentional torts, it is not necessary that actual physical harm or injury result for an actionable tort to have taken place. In the case of *Cole v. Turner*,[5] it was held that "the least touching of another in anger, is a battery." Even such actions as touching a person's clothing, hitting a horse the victim is sitting on, or pulling a chair out from under someone about to sit down will constitute a battery.

Rude, insulting behaviour can amount to a battery if there is physical contact involved, such as taking the flower out of someone's lapel, grabbing his tie or spitting on him. Even if the physical contact is motivated by good intentions, if that conduct does not have the consent of the person being interfered with, it constitutes a battery. A doctor operating to save a person's life commits a battery if the patient has not consented to the procedure. An uninvited pat or kiss may constitute a battery, even when no harm was intended. Of course, not all forms of physical contact are batteries. When someone taps another on the shoulder to attract her attention or shakes a person's hand in greeting, no battery has taken place, unless the action is done more vigorously than custom would permit.

Defences

Conduct that would normally amount to an assault and/or battery may not be actionable if certain defences are available to the tortfeasor.

Consent

No battery has taken place when consent is present. For example, in a boxing match the boxers consent to being struck by one another. But the action must not go beyond the consent given. If one boxer were to take a club and use it to strike the other boxer, there is no consent to this conduct and it would be actionable. A number of cases have been heard in recent years involving sports-related injuries. The courts generally acknowledge that hockey players can expect to be injured while engaged in that game. However, if an injury is caused by a deliberate and unprovoked attack in violation of the rules, not condoned by the sports officials and deemed unacceptable by the courts, the offending player will be held liable for the exceptional injuries caused.

Defence of Consent

Dunn v. University of Ottawa[6]

In this case Dunn sued Lussier, a member of the opposing football team, and the University for violently and intentionally inflicting serious bodily injury beyond the scope of implied consent. The contact was between a linebacker and a receiver who had not yet caught the ball. The receiver was entitled to a "five-yard rule," meaning that no one could come within five yards of him before he caught the ball. The linebacker ignored the rule. Lussier's defence of implied consent failed chiefly because of his flagrant disregard for the rule and a clear intent to injure.

Claims against the coach failed because Lussier did not have a long record of on-field violence, and so vicarious liability claims against the university were dismissed.

When a doctor is faced with a seriously injured and unconscious patient, there is a presumption that the patient has consented to anything necessary to preserve life or health. But if the doctor goes beyond what is necessary, or if the patient has given consent for a certain type of procedure and the doctor goes beyond the bounds of that consent, an actionable battery has taken place. For example, permission to operate and repair a hernia does not imply consent to remove the patient's appendix, even if such an operation would be convenient and beneficial to the patient. A person has the right to refuse medical attention, even when it may be the only means of saving his life. A doctor who gives a blood transfusion when such a transfusion has been expressly refused commits a battery.

Battery

Norberg v. Wynrib[7]

Ms. Norberg was addicted to painkillers and began seeing Dr. Wynrib to obtain prescriptions. Dr. Wynrib demanded sex in return for prescriptions. She provided sex for a year before going into rehabilitation on her own initiative. She sued for damages for sexual assault. The claim was dismissed at trial and on appeal. The Supreme Court of Canada allowed the appeal.

The court held that the doctor's sexual conduct constituted the tort of battery, i.e., the intentional infliction of unlawful force on another person. The defence of express or implied consent did not apply in this case because of the power relationship between the parties. The concept of consent requires individual autonomy and free will. Whether a special "power dependency" exists between the parties depends upon the facts of each case. The plaintiff must prove first an inequality between the parties and then exploitation.

In this case the court held that the sex-for-drugs relationship was markedly different from what the community would consider acceptable. The injured party was addicted to painkillers, which placed her in a vulnerable position and diminished her ability to make a real choice. The respondent's medical expertise and knowledge of the appellant's addiction, combined with his authority to prescribe drugs, gave him power over her. The respondent abused his power over the appellant and exploited the information he obtained concerning her weakness to pursue his own personal interests.

Children are in a different position. A parent or guardian of a child has an obligation to act in that child's best interests. The court can intervene if life-saving medical treatment is refused on the child's behalf. In such a case, the court is entitled to conclude that the parent in not acting in the child's best interests, and it can assume control of the child and order the medical treatment, even if the child does not want it. In such circumstances, the child may be considered too young to make such a decision for herself.

Self-Defence

When a person has been threatened or attacked, she is entitled to defend herself. As long as her actions are restricted to fending off the attack, self-defence is a complete justification. The person raising the defence, however, is restricted as to how much force can be used. The victim is only allowed to use as much force as is necessary — that is, **reasonable**

force in that defence. If a 100-pound woman were to attack a 250-pound professional football player with her fists, the amount of force that the football player could use in his defence would be considerably less than if their roles were reversed. If the football player were doing the attacking, the woman defending herself could use much more force to stop the attack. In such circumstances, it might be reasonable to use a bat or some other weapon to fend off the attacker. The courts also take into consideration the passion of the moment, and will not require the victim to split hairs in measuring the amount of force to use in self-defence. However, the victim of such an attack cannot use **excessive force** in self-defence.

Damages

When a person has committed the tort of assault and/or battery, he is responsible for any damage or injury to the victim, even when the injuries suffered are unusual or unexpected. If you were to strike someone suffering from brittle-bone disease and as a result broke several bones, or if you deliberately tripped someone suffering from hemophilia, who bled to death as a result, you would be responsible for all their injury, even though you could not have anticipated their ailments.

False Imprisonment

Another tort derived from the concept of trespass to person is the tort of false imprisonment, which occurs when one person, without authority or justification, completely deprives another of his freedom of movement. There are two elements to this tort. First, there must be a total restraint of the person's liberty, and second, the restraint imposed must be undertaken without justification or authority. The imprisonment may be an arrest, whereby the victim submits or is forced to submit to the authority or control of another, in such a way that his freedom of movement is completely curtailed. In such a case, the person being so restrained is not going with the other voluntarily. On the other hand, if a police officer asks a person to come to the police station and she goes voluntarily, no imprisonment has taken place. A person held in a room from which there is no obvious or convenient way to escape has been imprisoned. If it is possible to escape without risk, then there is no imprisonment. Similarly, if the person held in a room believes that physical force would be used if he made an attempt to leave, then there is an imprisonment.

There are three ways, then, that an imprisonment can take place:

- actual imprisonment in a confined space, such as a room or a cell;
- when force is applied and a person is physically restrained; and
- when a person submits to the authority of another, thinking there is no choice.

It is important to note, however, that when a person fails to submit and escapes, no imprisonment has taken place. In *Gerner* v. *Sparks*,[8] a bailiff arrived to arrest the plaintiff, who held him at bay with a pitchfork. The bailiff then left, but the plaintiff brought an action for false imprisonment. In this case, the court decided that, in fact, no imprisonment had taken place because the plaintiff never was under the bailiff's control nor did he ever submit to his authority.

It is even possible for a person to be unaware that he is being imprisoned. In *Merring* v. *Graham White Aviation Ltd.*,[9] an employee came to the company's offices voluntarily and, while being interviewed about some thefts, was unaware that guards had been placed at the doors to prevent his escape. The employer being satisfied with the information given, the guards were withdrawn and the employee left, still unaware of their presence or function during his interview. Merring later learned of the guards' presence and sued for false imprisonment. The court held that there had indeed been an imprisonment, even though the victim was unaware of his incarceration during the interview.

The second major requirement for false imprisonment is that it be false, in the sense that it was done without authority. The power of a police officer to arrest a person is set out in the *Criminal Code*. A police officer is only justified in detaining someone when there is reason to believe that the individual has committed an indictable offence. A private citizen normally only has the power to arrest if he has reasonable and probable grounds to suppose that the person being arrested has committed a serious crime and if, in fact, the crime has actually taken place. There are other circumstances in which the power of private citizens and other specified parties will vary, according to specific situations as set out in the *Criminal Code*. Under no circumstances, however, do the police or private citizens have the power to arrest someone if the complaint is one of simple debt.

False Imprisonment
Bahner v. Mar West Hotel Company Ltd.[10]

In this case a customer refused to pay for a bottle of wine he had ordered; the manager of the restaurant held the customer for the police, who then took him to jail. Bahner was unaware of the liquor laws, then in place in the province, requiring that all alcoholic beverages be off the table by midnight. The wine was delivered to the table and opened just 15 minutes before midnight, and Bahner was informed shortly thereafter that his party only had a few minutes to drink the wine and that they could not take it with them. When Bahner refused to drink it or to pay for it, he was held until the police arrived.

In fact, no crime had taken place. This was merely a civil dispute as to whether or not there was an obligation to pay. When he was detained and taken by the police, he was falsely imprisoned. If Bahner had not intended to pay for the wine when he ordered it, he would have committed the crime of obtaining the wine under false pretences. Therefore, it is important to distinguish between an honest disagreement and fraud.

Damages

As is the case with assault and battery, false imprisonment is a tort in which no actual injury is necessary for damages to be recovered. It is sufficient to show that the tort was committed for it to be actionable. With such intentional torts, not only is it possible to obtain general and special damages as remedies, but also the courts are willing to award punitive damages if the circumstances warrant. **Punitive damages** are an attempt by the court, not to compensate the victim for the injuries suffered, but rather to punish the wrongdoer, thus discouraging future wrongful behaviour.

Trespass

Trespass is an action in tort that can be brought when a person intentionally goes onto another's land without justification or right. Intention does not mean that the trespasser wanted to be on the land, only that she was willfully and consciously in that particular location. Trespass can take place either directly or indirectly. Trespassers may not be aware that they are on someone else's land; they may believe they were authorized to be there or that it is their own land. The trespasser can walk or drive on the other's land or throw something, such as a rock or refuse, onto it. If a person is thrown onto another person's property as the result of being struck by an automobile or is pushed onto the land by another, only then would the intruder's conduct be neither willful nor actionable. But the driver or the person doing the pushing is considered the trespasser. The trespass may be committed by making a permanent intrusion onto another's property, such as building a fence or erecting a sign, either fully or partially, on someone else's land.

A trespass may take place when the tortfeasor's authorized presence on another's property is withdrawn, or the trespasser oversteps the bounds of that authority. For example, a meter reader may have the right to come onto a property to read the gas or electric meter, but if she then goes through the backyard to get to the next street, she may have overstepped the bounds of her authority and become a trespasser. Another example of a trespasser is a pub or restaurant patron who has become intoxicated and refuses to leave when asked.

The person who can sue for trespass is the occupier, not the owner of the property, unless the occupier is also the owner. In order to bring such an action, however, the occupier must have the right to exclusive possession of the property as would a person renting a residential premises.

Overhead and Subsurface Rights

One of the problems that arises in the area of trespass law is whether or not those same rights against trespassers apply above and below the surface of the property. Can the occupier of such property complain when someone tunnels under that land or flies over it? Historically, it was thought that a person owned not only the surface of the property, but also the land below the surface and the area above it. Since modern technological advances have made these areas accessible, this has become an impossible position to maintain. Today, those rights are limited to the areas that the occupier can control, both above and below the surface. In Canada, when people acquire property, they don't get the mineral and other subsurface rights. If there are minerals in the ground, whoever has those subsurface rights can mine them, as long as any interference with the surface rights is reasonable and compensated for.

Although the area above the surface is also, in theory, the property of the owner, an airplane flying over your house will not be a trespasser. Today, the occupier only has a right to the area above the property that he can control. However, if there is any kind of permanent intrusion onto that property, such as overhead power lines or a sign hanging off an adjacent building, that would be a trespass.

Permanent Incursion

Gross v. Wright[11]

In this case the owners of adjoining buildings agreed that the defendant could build a common wall on the property line. Such a wall would intrude for half its width on the land of the plaintiff. Both property owners agreed that the wall should be tapered equally on both properties. However, as the wall tapered toward the top, the defendant tapered it only on his side so that, at the top, the wall was entirely on the plaintiff's property. Although the defendant had permission to build the wall, he violated the terms of that consent when he tapered it only on his side. Thus, he became a trespasser. When something permanently intrudes on another's land, it becomes a continuing trespass.

Duty to Trespassers

An important factor that is taken into consideration in determining whether or not someone is trespassing is establishing how careful an occupier of land must be to protect a trespasser from injury. Historically, the occupier owed no duty to trespassers except not to cause them injury intentionally or recklessly. This has been modified to some extent by statute and case law in most jurisdictions.

What steps the occupier of a property may take to eject a trespasser is another consideration in trespass cases. If a trespasser refuses to leave after being asked to do so, an occupier has the right to use "as much force as is necessary" or "reasonable force" to eject the individual. This is not a licence to use physical violence; it implies minimal force only.

Trespass to Chattels

An action in trespass is not limited to land. A tort action can also be brought when there has been a trespass to chattels. A **chattel** is a moveable possession, such as a car, boat, radio, clothing, animal, and the like. It applies in instances when the interference with the other person's property is willful and not accidental. If the damage is inadvertent, the appropriate action is a suit for negligence.

Another tort associated with chattels is conversion. **Conversion** involves a person who has so interfered with another person's goods that he has, in effect, converted that chattel to his own. As a remedy, the court can order that the tortfeasor repay the victim the full value of the chattel. In effect, this is a forced sale, because the action of the defendant is akin to theft. The key to understanding conversion is that the tortfeasor has interfered with or taken control of the chattels, making them her own. As was the case with trespass to chattels, conversion also requires that the conduct involved be intentional or willful. Obviously, there is a great overlap between trespass and conversion, in that conversion usually involves a trespass to the chattels.

Damages

Trespass is another tort that does not require any proof of damage or loss in order to be actionable. The "mere bruising of the grass" is enough to establish liability for trespass. As is the case with most intentional torts, trespassers are responsible for any damage that results from their presence on another person's land. Choosing the proper course of action when there is trespass to chattels is often confusing and involved. The remedy of *replevin* has been developed to allow recovery of goods when they are improperly in someone else's hands. Several provinces have passed legislation that makes recovery easier in these circumstances. In British Columbia, for example, the *Law and Equity Act*[12] gives a court the power to order the return of goods, other than land, to one of the parties, pending the outcome of an action for its recovery.

Nuisance

The above discussion pointed out that trespass involves direct and willful interference with another's property, without authority or permission. The tort of nuisance is intended to cover those situations in which interference with someone else's land has been indirect or inadvertent. The basic principle of such a tort is that a person can be sued for nuisance if he uses his land in such a way that it interferes with a neighbour's enjoyment of his property. This does not refer to a single act. There must be some sort of ongoing condition that interferes with someone's enjoyment of his property, such as continuous or repeated smoke from burning, water seepage or flow, a noxious smell, or sounds like machinery or loud music. Even the escape of some substance, such as noxious gas or chemicals that cause damage to the adjoining property, can be considered a nuisance.

In order to be actionable as nuisance, an activity has to involve an unusual use of the land. A person who locates in the country cannot then complain about the smell of fertilizer used on fields or the smell emanating from a dairy farm. Such activities are reasonable uses of rural property. Similarly, if a person locates in an industrial area, she cannot then complain about the noise or smells of a manufacturing plant or other such industrial activities. A person acquiring a home in a residential area, however, would not have to put up with similar inconveniences. For example, if your neighbour has a smokehouse in his back yard and the smell makes it impossible for you to use your yard, or if he has a workshop and produces loud noises late into the night, you can sue for nuisance.

Historically, the tort of nuisance was only available when the interference with the enjoyment of the plaintiff's property came from an adjoining property or one near by. In the case of *Motherwell* v. *Motherwell*,[13] the court held that a private nuisance had been committed when the plaintiff received constant, aggravating telephone calls from the defendant, to the point where the plaintiff's right to enjoy his property was seriously interfered with. The court found that a nuisance had been committed, even though this interference came from the use of a telephone across town rather than from an adjoining property. This case illustrates the direction in which the law of private nuisance is likely to develop.

The tort of public nuisance must be distinguished from private nuisance. **Public nuisance** involves an unreasonable interference with a person's rights as a citizen. In public nuisance, there is no requirement that the plaintiff's enjoyment of his land be interfered with. A brothel, a gambling den, an inn where disorderly activities are carried out, or even a crack house or other property used to sell or consume illicit drugs, to the point of disrupting others in the neighbourhood, can all constitute a public nuisance. Such public nuisances involve criminal activities and they are considerably more restricted than the private nuisances discussed above. They are, however, actionable as a tort and the injured person can seek compensation from the defendant, providing the person has suffered some sort of special damage not suffered by the general population.

Nuisance

Tock v. St. John's Metropolitan Area Board[14]

The Tocks' house was serviced by the water and sewer system operated by the St. John's Metropolitan Area Board. On a day of exceptionally heavy rainfall the storm sewer blocked and a large amount of water flooded their basement, causing substantial damage.

The issue was whether a nuisance existed and if the defence of statutory authority applied to absolve the board of liability. The Supreme Court of Canada found that the defence did not apply and the board was liable in nuisance for the damage.

The court held that if legislation imposes a duty and the nuisance is the inevitable consequence of performing that duty, the nuisance is authorized. Here the legislation created the power to operate sewers. However, the legislation did not impose a duty to operate the sewer system in the way that resulted in the nuisance. If the legislation gives discretion as to how to do the authorized activity, the board must do it in a way that does not create a nuisance.

Defamation

Another concern of tort law is the protection of a person's reputation and good name. Someone who publishes (tells others) a false statement that discredits or causes harm to a person's reputation has defamed that person. As a general rule such defamatory statements are "false statements about a person to their discredit,"[15] or, as is sometimes stated, "a statement that tends to lower a person in the estimation of right-thinking persons in society generally."[16] Such defamatory words may involve accusing someone of doing something that is shameful, of having a dishonest character, or of carrying an infectious disease. Defamation takes place whenever a statement is made that causes someone's reputation or standing to be diminished.

If a statement discredits a person in the eyes of some but enhances that person in the eyes of others, it is not defamatory. The statement, "Joe is a police informer," might be regarded by some as defamatory. To most people, however, it would indicate that Joe was a cooperative citizen. In law, that statement is no more defamatory than to say that a certain student got the highest mark in the class. It is not defamation to attribute good qualities or actions to a person.

Defamatory statements may be direct, such as "George abused children at his daycare," or they may be indirect, such as "George operates ABC Daycare." The latter statement is essentially innocent, in that there is nothing in the statement that, by itself, is defamatory. But if the audience to whom the statement is made knows that the operator of ABC Daycare has just been charged with child abuse, then the statement becomes defamatory because of their special knowledge. This is called an **innuendo** and it takes place when the audience is in possession of added facts that make the statement defamatory, or when a secondary meaning is obvious from the way in which it was said (reading between the lines).

Innuendo

Jones v. Bennett[17]

The Premier of British Columbia, while at a party gathering, made a statement about a government employee, saying, "I'm not going to talk about the Jones boy. I could say a lot, but let me just assure you of this: the position taken by the government is the right position."[18] This statement seems perfectly innocent and, had the government given Mr. Jones a bonus or a promotion for his service, the statement would not have been defamatory. However, the government had attempted to dismiss Mr. Jones for wrongdoing and, when this failed, had passed special legislation to retire him from his position. The implication of the Premier's statement was that Mr. Jones had indeed been guilty of wrongful conduct, and since most people in BC were aware of that implication, the statement became sinister and had a defamatory meaning. Mr. Jones successfully sued Premier Bennett for defamation.

Intention

Defamation must be intentional, in the sense that the words constitute a willful act. If the person thought it was true or that he was writing fiction, that would not constitute a defence if the statement later turned out to be false, or if someone turned up who fit the story's description. In the case of *E. Hulton & Co.* v. *Jones*,[19] a newspaper published a story about an A. Jones who lived a conservative life in England but a life of sin when vacationing in France. This article was entirely fictitious and was intended to poke fun at the English middle class, who were portrayed as hypocrites. Unfortunately for the paper, there really was an A. Jones who fit the description in the story and who regularly took his vacations in France. The real A. Jones sued the paper. The court held that it was no defence that the article was fictitious. The plaintiff's friends clearly took the words to refer to him, so the statement was defamatory.

Before a statement can be defamatory and actionable, it must refer to a specific person. If an instructor were to point to a class of students and say, "Half of you cheated on this exam," this statement, even if false, would not be actionable as defamation because no one student could claim that the instructor was referring to him.

Published or Broadcast

In order for a defamatory statement to be actionable, it must be published. This means that the defamatory statement must have been made to someone else other than the person defamed. If Joan met Hal in a field, with no one else in earshot, and accused him of stealing her briefcase, this would not be actionable because the statement was not overheard by any third party. On the other hand, if a third person did overhear the remark, that would be sufficient publication to make the defamation actionable even if the person making the statement didn't know the third person was there. In the case of a defamatory letter, even if no one other than a secretary sees it, that constitutes sufficient publication to satisfy the requirement. However, if the only person who overheard the statement was the spouse of the person making it, that would not constitute publication because such communications between husband and wife are privileged. On the other hand, if the spouse of the person being defamed heard the statement, this would constitute sufficient publication.

In theory, everyone who participates in the publication of a defamatory statement is liable in tort for it. In the case of a newspaper story, the reporter, the newspaper, the editor, the secretary, the typesetter, the printer and even the newsstand or delivery person would be liable. However, these secondary players are only liable if, after having been informed of the defamation or asked to remove the offending publication, they continue to sell, deliver or lend it to the public.

Libel and Slander

It is important to distinguish between libel and slander as different forms of defamation. Basically, **libel** is written or otherwise visually communicated defamation, whereas **slander** is oral. In many jurisdictions, these definitions have been somewhat modified by modern legislation. These statutes designate broadcasted slander in the form of spoken defamatory statements made on radio or TV as libel. A statement made at a public meeting, if defamatory, would be slander rather than libel. However, if that public meeting was being broadcast on television or radio, the statement would be libel. A defamatory article in the newspaper or a letter sent from one person to another would be libelous, but if one person were to yell something defamatory at another across a crowded convention hall, that would be slander.

The significance of the distinction between libel and slander is that libel is actionable *per se* and does not require proof of special damages, whereas slander is not. Special damages cover accountable losses, including out-of-pocket expenses for which receipts can be produced; general damages involve losses that cannot be quantified, such as pain and suffering or lost reputation. This means that a person suing for libel does not have to establish that specific expenses have been incurred. It is not necessary to show that he has lost a job or a consulting contract in order to gain compensation. With slander, however, as a general rule, some actual, quantifiable loss must be demonstrated. It is often extremely difficult to establish that a specific sum of money has been lost as a result of a defamatory statement, because tangible and quantifiable losses are often not present. The victim may have been harmed in a general way by loss to his reputation, but in a slander action, that is not enough to initiate proceedings.

There are some situations in which slander is involved where proof of special damages is not necessary, and the slander is treated as libel. If the slanderous statement accuses a person of being guilty of a criminal act, of being of unchaste character, or of having a communicable disease such as AIDS, there is no need to prove special damages. Also, if the statement suggests that the person is unfit for her trade or profession, that slanderous statement is treated like libel and there is no need to prove special damages.

Defamation in the Media

In the field of defamation there are two competing interests that are being protected. On the one hand, there is the tradition of freedom of expression, and on the other, an attempt to protect people from unwarranted harm to their reputations. These two interests must be delicately balanced. In the United States, the media are in a special position because the

American constitution guarantees freedom of the press. This has been interpreted to mean that the media — newspapers, radio, television and magazines — can only be successfully sued for defamation when it can be shown that the people who published the defamatory statement were malicious in what they did, and that they knew the statement was false. Historically in Canada, the media have been in no better position than a private person in relation to defamation actions. If the statement is defamatory and there is no defence, they would be liable. Because the passage of the *Charter of Rights and Freedoms* guarantees "freedom of the press and other media of communications" (paragraph 2(b)), it was thought that the Canadian courts might extend the same protections that have been given to the press in American courts. But the Supreme Court of Canada, when invited to adopt the American approach to freedom of the press at least where public officials are involved, refused to follow the American example and sustained an award of over a million dollars to a defamed public official in the process.[20]

Defences

There are a number of important defences that are available to a defamation action. A **mistake**, however, is no defence to defamation. If you thought that what you were publishing was true and it turned out to be false, even if you can show that your belief was reasonable in the circumstances, your mistake will not constitute a defence and you will be liable for defamation. In the case of *E. Hulton & Co.* v. *Jones*, discussed above, the material was clearly published under the mistaken belief that the A. Jones referred to did not exist and that the article was fictional. The publishers had no idea that there really was an A. Jones to whom his friends and acquaintances would think the article referred. That was no defence and they were liable.

Truth, on the other hand, is an effective defence to defamation. In Canada, as long as the report is accurate, even though it might be to the discredit of the person being described and of no public benefit whatsoever, it is not actionable as defamation. In several other jurisdictions (Australia and several states in the US), it is not enough that the defamatory statement be true. Legislation has been enacted requiring that the statement not only be true but also be of some public benefit, before this can be used as an effective defence. In Canada, however, truth is an absolute defence. Truth, in this sense, means that the content of the statement must be accurate and true, not that the statement is a true reporting of what someone else said.

The obligation of establishing the truth of the statement falls on the defendant, not the plaintiff. If a newspaper publishes a negative article about a prominent member of society and is sued, it is not the obligation of the public figure to show that the article contains false statements; rather, it is the obligation of the newspaper to prove that what they have published is true. In some circumstances, this may be very difficult and, if the attempt is made at trial to prove that the statement is true and the attempt is unsuccessful, the very process of trying to establish the truth of the defamatory remark will aggravate the damage done. The court will take that into consideration and increase the damage award accordingly.

Two other major defences are privilege and fair comment. **Absolute privilege** is limited to court proceedings, including the trial and all the pleadings and processes leading up to the trial, as well as to exchanges that take place on the floor of the House of Commons and Senate or the legislative assemblies of the provinces. Under no circumstances can a person sue for defamation if the defamatory remark is made by a politician speaking in Parliament. Even if a politician knows that what he is saying is false, and even if he is making it maliciously, his statement will be protected if made in Parliament. When a politician refuses to repeat his comments outside Parliament, he avoids the risk of being sued for defamation. Communications between high government officials, such as a minister to a deputy minister, are also absolutely privileged in this way, as are communications between husband and wife and between lawyer and client. The term *absolute* here means that the statement is protected no matter what the motive of the person making it.

More important to regular social interaction is the concept of **qualified privilege**. Here, *qualified* means that, although the statement is protected under the circumstances described below, that protection will be lost if the privilege is abused. The person who makes the statement must honestly believe it is true and must not be making it for any improper purpose. If it is motivated by malice, the privilege will be lost. Also, the publication of the statement must be no broader than is necessary in the circumstances. In those situations where this qualified privilege applies, the statement, even though it is defamatory, is not actionable and, thus, this is an effective defence in a defamation action.

The main situation in which qualified privilege is available occurs when the person who makes the statement has a duty to do so. This usually occurs in an employment situation. If a foreman, as part of his supervision responsibility, makes an evaluation of an employee that contains false information, and if he passes on that inaccurate evaluation to his superior, he will have a good defence against a defamation action. If making the report was part of his duty as a foreman, if he thought what he was saying was true, and if there was no ulterior motive for making such an inaccurate report, then the foreman will be protected by qualified privilege, even though the report was defamatory. Similarly, if a university professor thought someone had cheated on an exam, she would have a duty to report that to her superiors. If she was wrong and her report was defamatory, she would still be able to use qualified privilege as a defence, even though the student could suffer considerable damage in the process. Similar statements by police officers, social workers, probation officers and other public officials are also protected because of the public duty these people have to make such statements. Reporters and broadcasters, however, have no such duty. There is no general right to know, or duty to inform the public, so any defamatory statements made by them about matters of public interest are not protected by qualified privilege.

Other situations in which qualified privilege may exist occur when a person responds to an attack, protecting his interest. This is like self-defence. For example, a public figure is attacked in a newspaper or in parliament and writes a letter to the editor of a local newspaper, defending himself. If this letter is defamatory, it may be protected by qualified privilege because it is a response to an attack. Another qualified-privilege situation occurs when two parties with a similar interest get together and discuss that interest. For example, if two lawyers discuss how the law society has disbarred a member, or if two members of a club or church discuss the affairs of that organization, these conversations would be protected by qualified privilege.

It must be emphasized that the privilege extended here is qualified, in the sense that it will only be a defence if the defamatory statement was made honestly, for proper motive and without malice. Also, the statement must not be spread any further than to those who need to know. Thus, if a person has a duty to make a statement, it must be made only to those people he has a duty to inform. In the case of *Jones* v. *Bennett*, discussed above, Mr. Bennett lost any qualified privilege he may have had when he made the report about Mr. Jones to a gathering that included newspaper reporters. It was argued that, as Premier, he had a duty to make the report on Mr. Jones to the members of his party present at the gathering. The court held, however, that even if he did have such a duty, which was doubtful, he went far beyond the requirements of that duty when he knowingly made the statement in the presence of newspaper reporters, who would then make it available to the general public. Any qualified privilege he may have had was lost when he published the report too broadly.

The final defence that must be discussed under the heading of defamation is **fair comment**. When people become public figures or do things that make their work or activities the subject of public interest, they become the subject of public criticism and comment. People are entitled to have opinions about matters of public interest and to express them, even if their opinions are negative and unreasonable. When a play is put on at a theatre, when an artist has a showing at a gallery, or when a politician runs for office, the public, including reporters and other media personalities, are entitled to have opinions about those people and their activities and to express them. Even when such opinions become defamatory, the expression of them is protected by the defence of fair comment. In order to raise the defence of fair comment, however, the statement must clearly be a statement of opinion, based on some matter before the public.

The term *fair*, as it is used here, does not mean reasonable. It is only necessary that a right-thinking person could hold such an opinion. Thus, when a theatre critic reviews and savagely criticizes a play, she is entitled to that opinion even if all the other reviews are favourable. The bad review is not defamatory just because it may be unreasonable. The key to understanding fair comment is that the matter discussed must be a matter of public interest, that the statement made must be a view honestly held by the person making it, and that it be a view that it is possible to hold, given the information that is before the public.

In dealing with the defence of fair comment, it is vital to understand that there cannot be any statement of fact involved. The statement being challenged as defamatory usually contains a statement of fact, and then an opinion is made or a conclusion is drawn, based on that statement of fact. The statement of fact is not protected by fair comment, only the opinion based on it. If the factual statement forming the basis for the comment is inaccurate, an action for defamation will likely be successful. Like qualified privilege, if any improper motive or malice is involved, then an abuse of fair comment occurs and the defence of fair comment will not be available. To be fair comment, the opinion must be the honestly held belief of the person making it. Newspapers often publish letters to the editor, making it clear that the opinions stated are not those of the paper; similarly, a radio talk-show host or a television documentary will state at the outset that the opinions expressed are not those of the sponsor or station. In these situations, they cannot claim the defence of fair comment because they have made it clear that they do not have an honest belief in what has been stated.

Legislation has been introduced in many jurisdictions to modify the liability of the media for the statements they publish. British Columbia's *Libel and Slander Act*[21] is a good example. Aside from making any broadcasted defamation libel rather than slander, the Act also provides that the publication of an apology or a retraction, under certain specified conditions, will mitigate the damages. If the statement has been published in good faith and a full retraction has been made, the plaintiff can only recover compensation for actual damages suffered. It can be very difficult to prove such actual losses, so this can severely limit the effective remedies available and will usually discourage a plaintiff from proceeding.

A defamation action is involved and technical, and the costs of the process are great. It is difficult for an individual to take on a large newspaper or broadcasting company that has significant resources to bring to bear, as well as much experience in dealing with these kinds of disputes. All these factors usually discourage plaintiffs from proceeding, except in the most blatant cases.

NEGLIGENCE

> Negligence is the omission to do something which a reasonable man, guided upon those considerations which ordinarily regulate the conduct of human affairs, would do or doing something which a prudent and reasonable man would not do.[22]

Although negligence as a tort is a relatively recent creation, it has become the predominant basis of tort liability today. Negligence applies in accident situations in which the conduct has been inadvertent, rather than intentional or willful. As with other forms of tort liability, fault or blameworthy conduct on the part of the tortfeasor must be present in order to establish liability for negligence. Fault in a negligence action is based on the wrongdoer's failure to maintain a required standard of vigilance or careful conduct. An accident can take place whether or not a person is careful.

In a negligence action, the court determines the appropriate standard of care that must be applied in the circumstances, and whether or not the defendant's conduct fell below that standard. If it has been determined that the defendant's conduct did fall below that standard, she will be required to compensate the victim for any injury or harm to property that resulted from the negligence. Not in all situations, however, will the court impose such a standard of care on the defendant. One of the major functions of the court in a negligence action is to decide when there is a duty to be careful and when no such obligation exists.

Damage or injury must be present in order for liability for negligence to be imposed. It must also be established that the damage or injury was directly caused by the conduct of the defendant. If the causal connection between injury and conduct is tenuous and indirect, the right to receive compensation for such an injury can be challenged on the basis of its being too remote to be actionable. Finally, victims must not have acted in such a way as to disqualify themselves from proceeding. If the victim contributed to the loss (contributory negligence) or if the victim has assumed the risk that led to the injury (*volenti non fit injuria*), the victim's right to receive compensation for those injuries may be reduced or nonexistent.

Five elements — duty, breach, damage or injury, causation, and no prejudicial conduct — must be present in a successful negligence action. Negligence, then, is not equated with mere carelessness. Carelessness deals with the state of mind of the tortfeasor. It is, essentially, a lack of attentiveness, whereas negligence, as it is used in the field of tort law, involves the tortfeasor's relationship with the victim. This is a much more objective evaluation of the conduct. The fault and liability of the tortfeasor is established by reference to an outwardly imposed standard, in order to determine how careful the defendant should have been. If such fault is present, as well as the other elements mentioned, liability is imposed. However, such concepts as fault or blameworthiness are not always strictly adhered to by the courts. There is a great temptation to place the obligation to bear the loss on the party who is likely to have insurance coverage. Insurance is fundamentally different in its nature and approach to the problem since its purpose is to spread the loss rather than determine who is at fault. This is especially true in motor vehicle accidents. Even when this is done, however, the court will at least give lip service to the requirement of fault in such tort actions, although in some jurisdictions there is a move to a true no-fault system of automobile insurance.

Duty of Care

> The rule that you are to love your neighbour becomes in law you must not injure your neighbour; and the lawyer's question, Who is my neighbour? receives a restricted reply. You must take reasonable care to avoid acts or omissions which you can reasonably foresee would be likely to injure your neighbour.[23]

We are not required to pay compensation to all those who are injured as a result of our carelessness. It must first be established that we owe a duty to be careful to the injured party. Today, the test used to determine whether such a duty to be careful exists is the **reasonable foreseeability test**. We only owe a duty to be careful to those people whom we can reasonably anticipate might be harmed by our careless conduct.

Reasonable Foreseeability

Donoghue v. Stevenson[24]

The case of *Donoghue v. Stevenson* is important because it establishes the test of reasonable foreseeability as the basis for determining under what circumstances such a duty will be imposed. In that case, Mrs. Donoghue and her friend went to a pub where her friend bought her ginger beer and ice-cream to make a float. The ginger beer came in an opaque bottle, and, after consuming part of it, Mrs. Donoghue discovered a decomposed snail in the remainder. Mrs. Donoghue became very ill and sued for compensation. She could not sue the pub owner, who sold the drink under contract law, because she had not purchased it herself. She could not successfully sue the pub or its employees for tort, because there was no carelessness on their part. The snail had obviously gotten into the bottle at the point of manufacture, so Mrs. Donoghue sought compensation from the bottler, Mr. Stevenson.

The manufacturers claimed they owed no duty to be careful to the ultimate consumer of their product, because it had gone through several other hands. That position seemed consistent with the law as it was then. This case, however, is famous for changing that law. Mr. Justice Atkin, in rendering his decision, found that there was a duty to be careful in these circumstances. He found that a duty to be careful was owed to others who

> are so closely and directly affected by my acts that I ought reasonably to have them in contemplation as being so affected when I am directing my mind to the acts or omissions which are called into question.[25]

This test establishes that people are responsible for their inadvertent conduct when they should anticipate that their conduct may cause injury to someone else. Today, we express this simply by stating that a duty is owed when we can reasonably foresee that our conduct might cause injury to another person or damage to that person's property.

If Sam, while operating a fishing boat in the middle of Lake Superior, lashed the wheel in order to go below and prepare breakfast, and while he was thus occupied his boat hit another boat, there would be no difficulty in establishing that Sam owed a duty to be careful to the occupants of the other boat. It is reasonably foreseeable that if he is careless in the operation of his boat, he might cause damage to another boat or injury to its occupants. However, if while Sam was below, his boat struck a marathon swimmer crossing the lake, it would be arguable whether or not he owed a duty to the swimmer. Sam could argue that the presence of such a swimmer in the middle of Lake Superior was not reasonably foreseeable and, therefore, no duty was owed to her. Although he was careless, he would not be liable for any injuries caused because he owed no duty to be careful to the swimmer.

The test of reasonable foreseeability is normally applied when determining the existence of a duty. There are, however, some special situations where the courts will not impose a duty, even when injury is reasonably foreseeable; and there are other situations where they will impose a duty, even when damage is not reasonably foreseeable. For example, if a person sees someone drowning or in some other hazardous situation, there is no general duty to lend assistance, not even to inform a lifeguard or to phone the police. Even if it would take no great effort and there would be no danger involved, the law does not impose a duty on someone to render a helping hand, unless they have a special relationship, such as a guardian or parent, or have a special obligation to act, such as a police officer or lifeguard. When people drive on the highways, on the other hand, they usually owe a duty to anyone else using those highways, even if their immediate presence is not reasonably foreseeable. There are also statutorily imposed duties.

Failure to Act

If a person fails to do something, as in the examples described above, this failure to act is called **nonfeasance** and is, as a general rule, not actionable as a tort. It is only when a person does act, but acts improperly — **misfeasance** — that the conduct is actionable. Furthermore, when a person does start to render assistance in such situations, he takes upon himself an obligation to act reasonably in the circumstances and to do a good job of whatever he has started. If there is an accident at the side of the road and a doctor drives by, that doctor has no legal duty to stop and render assistance. If she does start to assist, however, she must now act carefully. If she fails to do so, she can be sued for negligence and required to pay compensation for any injuries resulting from that negligence. Because the combination of these two factors discourages people from coming to the assistance of others, many jurisdictions have passed rescue legislation making a rescuer not responsible for the damage caused in the process of rendering assistance, unless the rescuer's actions were totally unreasonable.

Standard of Care

The reasonable person is a mythical creature of the law whose conduct is the standard by which the Courts measure the conduct of all other persons and find it to be proper or improper in particular circumstances as they may exist from time to time. He is not an extraordinary or unusual creature; he is not superhuman, he is not required to display the highest skill of which anyone is capable; he is not a genius who can perform uncommon feats, nor is he possessed of unusual powers of foresight. He is a person of normal intelligence who makes prudence a guide to his conduct. He does nothing that a prudent man would not do and does not omit to do anything a prudent man would do. He acts in accord with general and approved practice. His conduct is guided by considerations which ordinarily regulate the conduct of human affairs. His conduct is the standard adopted in the community by persons of ordinary intelligence and prudence.

Mr. Justice Laidlaw in *Arland v. Taylor*[26]

Once it has been determined that a person owes a duty to another to be careful, the next question is determining just how careful that person has to be. The **reasonable person test** is used generally to set the standard required in these circumstances. A person is negligent if there is a failure to do what a reasonable person would have done in the same circumstances. This standard of a reasonable person does not mean an average person; rather, it is the standard of a prudent person, being careful. The standard required of people in order to avoid liability for negligence is quite high, certainly above what would be expected of an average person. Remember that the standard set is that of a reasonable person in the same circumstances. If we are dealing with a medical doctor, the standard demanded is that of a reasonable medical doctor. If we are dealing with other professions, the standard demanded is that of a reasonable accountant, a reasonable plumber, a reasonable teacher, and so on.

Many factors affect what constitutes reasonable conduct in the circumstances. The amount of potential damage that can be caused by the careless conduct is one such factor. For example, the standard of care imposed on a driver delivering a cart of farm produce would not be as great as the standard of care imposed on a driver delivering a load of aviation fuel. The risk of an accident might be the same but the potential harm that could result from it is much greater when the aviation fuel is involved, so the standard of care imposed is higher.

Another factor to be considered is the amount of risk of injury or damage involved. In *Bolton* v. *Stone*,[27] a person walking by a cricket pitch was struck by a wayward cricket ball. It was obvious to anyone using these facilities that such an event could happen, so a duty to be careful existed based on reasonable foreseeability. However, in the many years that the pitch had been in use, no accident had ever occurred. Therefore, the risk of injury was so slight that it was reasonable for the parties not to take any precautions.

In *Blyth* v. *Birmingham Water Works*,[28] the expense to the defendant of taking precautions to prevent injury became an important factor in determining the standard of care imposed. In that case, the plaintiff's house burned down because the fire department could not get water from the frozen fire hydrants in the district where he lived. The plaintiff sued the water works company, the body responsible for the laying and maintenance of the water lines, for negligence in not putting those lines deep enough to escape frost. However, the court held that there was no negligence. This was a rare frost, the worst in 50 years, and the better protection derived from putting the water pipes deep enough to avoid the frost did not warrant the much greater costs involved. A reasonable person would not have incurred the greater costs.

The courts may also take into consideration the social value or motivation of a defendant in determining whether the defendant's conduct was reasonable. An ambulance driving at an excessive rate of speed is much more reasonable and acceptable than a businessman speeding because he was late for an appointment.

Duty of Care — Defences

Hall v. Hebert[29]

Hebert owned a car and Hall was a passenger. The car stalled and Hebert allowed Hall to drive while they tried a rolling start. Hebert knew that Hall had drunk 11 or 12 bottles of beer. Hall lost control of the car and it crashed down a steep slope. Hall suffered head injuries. Hall sued Hebert for damages on the basis of Hebert's negligence in allowing Hall to drive knowing he was drunk. The issue on appeal was whether the defence of *ex turpi causa non oritur actio* is available to Hebert — i.e., should the court bar recovery on the ground that Hall's conduct in driving drunk was illegal.

The Supreme Court held that Hall's illegal conduct did not bar recovery in tort for damages caused by Hebert's negligent conduct. Hebert had a duty of care to prevent Hall from driving based on the foreseeable consequences of harm. The legality of Hall's conduct in driving drunk was not relevant to the foreseeability of harm. The test is foreseeability — i.e., is there a sufficiently close relationship between the parties so that, in the reasonable contemplation of a party, carelessness on its part might cause damage to another person.

Once the court determines that the harm was foreseeable, it will examine the facts of the case to determine if there is a defence to any recovery for damages based on concerns for the administration of justice. The defence will apply only in rare cases. The court held that there were not sufficient reasons to bar recovery here, although Hall's impairment is a factor in assessing his contributory negligence.

All these factors may be taken into consideration in determining just how careful a person is required to be in the circumstances. Legislation is another important source for determining just what standard should be imposed. In some cases, statutes have been enacted to set out the nature of the duty a person must comply with. When such legislation is present, failure to live up to the legislated standard will determine negligence, no matter how reasonable or unreasonable the conduct. For example, the motor vehicle legislation in many jurisdictions requires that a car be kept in proper mechanical condition. Failure to have a vehicle in the required condition, even when the defendant could not have been aware of the failure, is conduct falling below the legislated standard and constitutes negligence, without reference to the reasonable person test.

Standard of Care

Galaske v. O'Donnell[30]

An eight-year-old boy was sitting between the owner/driver and his father in the front seat of a truck. The truck had seat belts for the middle seat but the boy did not use them. The truck was hit through no fault of the driver. The father was killed and the boy was seriously injured, rendering him paraplegic. If seat belts had been worn, no serious injuries would have been suffered by either of the passengers.

The issue was whether the driver had a duty of care to the boy to require him to use the seat belt despite his father being present and not exercising his parental authority.

> The Supreme Court held that the driver owed a duty of care to the boy despite the presence of his father.
>
> All drivers owe a duty of care to passengers under 16 years of age to require them to wear seat belts. Two or more people may bear that responsibility, but one of those responsible must always be the driver of the car. In BC the *Motor Vehicle Act* requires drivers to ensure that passengers under age 16 wear their seat belts. The legislation indicates the community standard of care.

Occupier's Duty

Under common law, the nature of a duty owed by an occupier of property to people coming onto that property varies with their status. A person who comes on the property without permission or authority is a **trespasser**. The only duty owed by the occupier to such a person is simply not to cause him harm intentionally or recklessly. If the person using the property is there with permission but on sufferance, such as children playing in a vacant lot with the permission of the owner, or a guest coming for dinner, they are referred to as **licensees**. The duty of the occupier to such licensees is to warn them of any hidden dangers. The final category of visitor is the invitee. The **invitee** is a person who has been invited onto the property for some mutual advantage or business purpose, such as a client in a restaurant or a business guest in the home. The occupier owes an invitee a duty to protect him from any unusual danger. For example, an occupier would be required to warn a licensee of a hidden and dilapidated mine shaft on his property, but not of an obviously open elevator shaft. If the visitor is an invitee, however, the occupier is required not only to warn, but also to take steps to rope or fence off the mine shaft or elevator shaft, or otherwise to take active steps to protect the visitor. These are three quite different standards.

Even at common law, it is not always the reasonable person test that is used to determine the nature of the standard of care that must be adhered to. In Canada, the nature of the duty owed by occupiers to those using their land has been modified either by case law or legislation. In Manitoba, for instance, the *Occupiers' Liability Act*[31] imposes a duty on occupiers to take such care as is reasonable to protect the person or property of guests, no matter what their status. The duty here, falls on the occupier of the property, not the owner, unless they are one and the same person. The occupier is the person in actual possession of the land. The responsibility is imposed on the person in possession of the land, as a practical matter, because he is the one present on the property and more likely aware of any problems. The duty owed to trespassers in such legislation is usually considerably less.

Innkeeper's Duty

Another example of a duty modified by statute is that owed by an innkeeper (hotel keeper) to a guest. At common law, the duty of an innkeeper is unique. There is an obligation on the innkeeper to be responsible for the losses of a guest, except where the guest has actually been careless. This is an obligation similar to insurance, whereby the innkeeper is obligated to compensate the guest even if the innkeeper has not been careless in any way. This is a very high standard and most jurisdictions have modified it by the passage of innkeepers' acts, which state that the innkeeper will only be liable for the losses of the guest if the innkeeper or his servant has contributed to that loss. This protection is qualified, however, in that it is only given to the innkeeper if proper notice of this reduction of responsibility is posted in designated parts of the inn, as set out in the act. The reason for this special duty placed on innkeepers to care for their guests is historical, but in recent years the duty imposed on all commercial hosts for the alcohol-related injuries of their patrons has grown considerably.

Host Liability

Stewart v. Pettie[32]

A woman passenger was injured in a car accident. The car was driven by her brother, whose blood alcohol was well above the legal limit. The two had spent the evening having dinner and attending live theatre. The commercial host was aware of the man's condition when he left, in that the same waitress had served him all evening and had kept a running total of his tab. The issue was whether the commercial host met the standard of care required of a vendor of alcohol and whether it was negligent in failing to take any steps to ensure that the driver did not drive on leaving its premises. The commercial host was not liable in the circumstances of this case.

The Supreme Court of Canada held that a duty of care exists between alcohol-serving establishments and their patrons who are unable to look after themselves after becoming intoxicated. The establishment may be required to prevent an intoxicated patron from driving when it is apparent that he or she intends to drive. A duty is also owed to third parties who might reasonably be expected to come into contact with the intoxicated patron, and to whom that patron may pose some risk.

Here the commercial host took no steps to ensure its patron did not drive. The circumstances, however, were not such that a reasonably prudent establishment would have foreseen that the patron would drive and therefore should have taken steps to prevent this. The commercial host knew that some of the party were sober and could reasonably assume one of them would drive. It did not need to enquire as to who was driving.

Absolute Liability

In some circumstances the risk involved might be so great that the standard approaches absolute liability. In *Heimler* v. *Calvert Caterers*,[33] a woman who, unknown to all parties, was a typhoid carrier worked in the preparation of food for Calvert Caterers. Several customers contracted typhoid fever and the source was traced to food prepared by this woman. It was clearly established in evidence that typhoid is transmitted in food contaminated by the fecal matter of a carrier. The employee testified that she was very careful to wash her hands after going to the bathroom, but the judge found that she obviously wasn't careful enough. The judge said that "where the thing is in itself dangerous the care necessary approximates to and almost becomes an absolute liability."[34] No matter how careful she claimed to have been, she must not have washed her hands well enough, else the disease would not have been transmitted. Therefore, she was found negligent. This case illustrates that the standards imposed in determining the required level of care in a given situation may be a reflection of policy as much as anything else.

Defendants in these circumstances often argue that they only did what everyone else in their profession does, and that because it is an acceptable practice in the profession, it cannot be negligent. While evidence of such standard practice may be persuasive to a court, it does not necessarily establish an appropriate standard. If a judge believes that such common practice falls below what a reasonable person in the same profession would do, it is negligent conduct despite the fact that most people in the profession do it. Sloppy common practice among professionals cannot be used to justify otherwise unacceptable behaviour.

Professional Liability

In the past, for a negligence action to be successful, there had to be some sort of conduct that caused injury or damage to the other person. Mere words, even if they resulted in economic loss, were not actionable unless a contract, or some special relationship leading to a fiduciary duty between the parties, or fraud was involved. In 1964, in the case of *Hedley Byrne & Co. v. Heller & Partners*,[35] the House of Lords first recognized that a general duty to be careful in the use of mere words could also exist. In that case, an advertising company had a client who wished to acquire their services. The advertising firm asked their bank, which in turn inquired of the client's bank (the defendant in this action) as to the client's financial soundness. The client's bank sent a letter indicating that the client was in good financial shape. However, the letter included a disclaimer of responsibility for any use made of this information. In fact, the client was in poor financial shape and the defendants should have known better than to issue a positive report. They had made a mistake. The advertising company subsequently suffered a considerable loss and sued the bank for the mistaken report.

The House of Lords decided that since a disclaimer was made, there was no liability on the part of the defendant bank for their careless words. The court added, however, that had it not been for the disclaimer, the bank would have been liable, indicating, for the first time, a willingness to find a tortfeasor liable for damages caused by **negligent misstatement** or the careless use of words. This decision has been followed in Canada. It is clear now that, in negligence law, people may be held responsible for harm caused by their careless words, just as they are responsible for damage caused by their careless conduct, even in the absence of a contract, fiduciary duty or fraud.

A major problem, however, is just how far to extend this liability for negligent words. Recently the Supreme Court of Canada has clarified the standard test we have used for so many years to determine under what circumstances a duty to be careful exists. You will recall that in *Donoghue v. Stevenson* the existence of a duty of care to find negligent conduct was determined by the reasonable foreseeability test. Thus we owed a duty to anyone we could reasonably anticipate might be harmed by our conduct. In the *Hercules* case[36] the Supreme Court of Canada again confirmed their support of the 1977 English *Anns* case[37] even though it has been abandoned in England, which determined that a two-stage approach should be adopted when determining the existence of such a duty of care. The first step is to determine whether there was a degree of neighbourhood or proximity between the parties such that if the person being sued had thought about it he would have realized that his actions posed a risk of danger to the other.

This is really just a restatement of the reasonable foreseeability test developed in *Donoghue v. Stevenson*. But it is the second stage of the *Anns* test that is interesting. This second part requires the court to ask the question as to whether there was any reason that the duty should not be imposed; that the scope of the duty should be reduced; that the class to whom the duty is owed be limited or that damages be reduced. This allows the court in unique situations to apply social policy to cases where they might not want to extend such open-ended liability — as in cases where negligent words or mere economic loss is involved. In such cases the Supreme Court has stated as a matter of policy that they are not willing to extend liability "in an indeterminate amount for an indeterminate time to an indeterminate class."[38]

Product Liability

The case of *Donoghue* v. *Stevenson*, discussed above, was important for setting the test of reasonable foreseeability, used to determine the existence of a duty of care. This case also indicates the position in English and Canadian law with respect to product liability. In the United States, when a manufacturer produces a defective product that causes harm to an innocent consumer, the manufacturer is strictly liable for any injuries that occur. There is no fault or negligence required. Simple causation will determine liability. In Canada and England, however, when a product is manufactured defectively, causing injury or harm to an innocent consumer, it is not sufficient to demonstrate that the defective product caused the injury; it is also necessary to show that the care used by the manufacturer in the production of the product fell below an acceptable standard (the reasonable person test).

It is often extremely difficult for the victim to prove that the product was manufactured in a careless way in order to establish a failure to live up to the required standard of care. In some circumstances, however, the very injury or damage that takes place speaks to that negligence. For example, if a piano falling from a tall building were to crash into the street in front of a pedestrian, that incident seems to communicate in and of itself that someone was careless in handling the piano. When this sort of thing happens, it is not necessary for the plaintiff to prove that the degree of care exercised by the people handling the piano fell below the requisite standard. Rather, the obligation is on the wrongdoer to show that he was careful. This principle is referred to as *res ipsa loquitor*, which means, in essence, that the matter speaks for itself. The principle has become very important in the field of product liability, as well as in several other areas in which the conduct of the wrongdoer is not readily reviewable.

Loss

In a negligence action, it is not sufficient to show that a duty is owed and that the conduct of the defendant fell below the required standard of care; it is also necessary to demonstrate that the victim suffered some sort of loss or injury. This must be contrasted with several of the other types of torts, discussed above, in which it is not required to prove any actual loss. In negligence, however, the plaintiff must have suffered some sort of actual loss or harm. In the past, the courts were reluctant to consider mere economic loss, unaccompanied by some sort of physical injury or damage, as loss sufficient to support a negligence action. Today, however, in Canada at least, economic loss by itself, in some limited circumstances, will be sufficient harm to entitle a plaintiff to compensation in a negligence action.

Until recent times, mental distress was not enough to support a negligence action unless there was some sort of physical injury as well, or the mental distress manifested itself with physical symptoms such as vomiting or a miscarriage. Today, however, the courts are willing to recognize mental distress as sufficient in itself to support an action in negligence, providing that the mental distress is manifested in some sort of recognized mental disorder, such as depression or schizophrenia. Mere anger, anxiety, or fear resulting from the negligent conduct will not be enough.

Causation

It is also necessary to show that the conduct complained of actually caused the harm or injury. If a person were to drive his automobile on the highway at night without tail lights or brake lights, that would fall below the standard of care required of the driver of the motor vehicle and would clearly support a negligence action if he were to get into an accident. If, however, he struck a car that had come out of a side street without stopping at a stop sign, his lack of tail lights would have nothing to do with the accident. Although he was careless in not having working tail lights, that did not cause the accident, nor did it have any relationship to it. He may still have some responsibility for the accident, but not on the basis of his failure to have working tail lights or brake lights. The test that is usually used to determine whether there is a sufficiently close causal connection between the conduct complained of and the injury or damage suffered is the **but for test**. The plaintiff must show that, "but for" the defendant's careless conduct, the harm or loss suffered would not have taken place.

One of the most difficult areas of negligence law is the indirect or tenuous relationship between the conduct complained of and the resulting harm. On rare occasions, the injury is not the direct result of the defendant's conduct but is the end result of a sequence of events that the wrongdoer initiated. Alternatively, the consequences may be the immediate and direct result of the conduct, but may be so unusual or bizarre that there is some question as to whether the wrongdoer should be held responsible. It is the court's function to determine where the line is to be drawn in assessing the wrongdoer's responsibility.

In *Abbott* v. *Kasza*, Mr. Justice Clement of the Alberta Court of Appeal stated:

> The chain of cause and effect can be followed only to the point where the consequences of an act will be fairly accepted as attributable to the act in the context of social and economic conditions then prevailing and the reasonable expectations of members of society in the conduct of each other.[39]

In this case, the judge recognized that in such difficult cases the decision must be one of policy rather than the application of a hard and fast rule.

Remoteness

Still, there are some guidelines that can be applied to determine where the cause-and-effect chain discussed by Justice Clement has been broken. In Canada, it would seem that, as long as the general type of injury suffered was reasonably foreseeable, the injury or damage will not be too remote from the conduct of the defendant. In the House of Lords decision of *Hughes* v. *the Lord Advocate*,[40] postal workers left an open manhole unattended and some children came along and played in it. Beside the open manhole was a kerosene lantern, which was dropped into the manhole by one of the children while another child (the plaintiff) was climbing out. Instead of the kerosene lantern burning, as one would expect, there was an explosion and the plaintiff was injured. There was no question that, if the child had been burned in a fire, the defendant would have been liable for the injuries.

Because the child's burns were caused by the unexpected explosion, the problem was to determine whether liability could be imposed or whether the injury was too remote. The court held that the injuries suffered were burns and that burns were what was foreseeable. The fact that they were caused by explosion rather than fire would not affect the liability of the defendant, because the general type of injury was foreseeable.

This is only one of the ways in which the problem of remoteness can occur. In Canada, this same approach has been followed. If the general type of injury is reasonably foreseeable, even though the specific way it happens is unusual, liability will still be imposed. It is only when the general type of injury suffered is not reasonably foreseeable that the connection between conduct and injury will be considered too remote to support liability. It is important to distinguish between the reasonable foreseeability test, which establishes whether a duty exists, and this test, which determines if the injury is too remote. When determining whether a duty exists, the test is whether the defendant should have reasonably foreseen that any harm could be suffered by the plaintiff if he was not careful in carrying out his activities. When discussing the problem of remoteness, the test is whether or not the actual type of injury suffered or the harm done was reasonably foreseeable.

Prejudicial Conduct of the Victim

Once it has been established that injury has taken place, our attention turns to the conduct of the defendant in order to determine liability. There are, however, some situations in which the conduct of the victim may disqualify him from seeking compensation in a negligence action. The most important of these is the principle of contributory negligence. In the past, if a person contributed to his own loss, he was prevented from seeking any sort of compensation from the other party on the principle that he was the author of his own misfortune. Today, however, many accidents, especially traffic accidents, involve fault on the part of both parties. If this principle were still in place, whenever fault was determined to rest with both parties, neither could recover from the other no matter how severe their injuries.

In most jurisdictions, the regulations have been changed because of the harsh consequences. The **last clear chance doctrine** was developed. This principle sets out that, even though both parties are careless, the person who had the last opportunity to avoid the accident will bear the loss. For example, if Jones, while driving down the road, falls asleep at the wheel, and Smith drives through a stop sign and collides with Jones, Smith will be liable for all injuries because he had the last opportunity to avoid the accident by stopping at the stop sign.

However, the "last clear chance" doctrine was also considered too harsh. Most provinces have now passed legislation apportioning the loss between the parties when both are at fault. The *Contributory Negligence Act*[41] of Nova Scotia is typical of such legislation. Under this statute, when an accident takes place and one party sues the other for negligence, the defendant can raise the other party's **contributory negligence** as a defence. The court will then apportion blame between them. One driver may be determined to be 60 per cent at fault, while the other will be 40 per cent to blame. The court then reduces the award to the plaintiff according to the amount of responsibility he bears for the accident. For example, if the plaintiff, because of personal injury, suffered $200 000 damage and was 40 per cent at fault, he would be given judgment for $120 000. If the defendant counter-sued, suffering only property damage to his car in the amount of $1 000, he would be able to get judgment against the other party for $400.

Voluntarily Assuming the Risk

The victim may also be disqualified from seeking a remedy if he has voluntarily assumed the risk. The principle involved here is that the law does not assist a volunteer (*volenti non fit injuria*). The application of this principle is now rare. The courts have a tendency to disqualify a person for assuming the risk only in the most blatant cases. The risk must be obvious and there must be a clear indication on the part of the victim not only that he knowingly and voluntarily assumed the risk as he participated in the activity, but also that he gave up any claims he may have had against the other party.

This argument is often brought up when automobiles are involved and a passenger is injured on a joy-ride. His mere presence in the car does not constitute assuming the risk. Even if he gets into the car knowing that the driver has been drinking, he will not be taken to be a volunteer. Only if the passenger has actively encouraged the driver to do dangerous things and has stayed in the vehicle when he had an opportunity to leave will the courts find that he is disqualified from receiving compensation on the basis of *volenti non fit injuria*. Conduct short of this on the part of the passenger will generally be taken into consideration by the court as contributory negligence and the compensation awarded will be reduced accordingly.

This principle of *volenti non fit injuria* does not apply to a rescuer. A wrongdoer should anticipate that, if his conduct puts someone in a position of danger, it is likely that someone else may come to their aid and may suffer injuries as well. The wrongdoer is not only responsible for injury caused to the victim, but also responsible for injury caused to anyone coming to the victim's rescue.

CONCLUSION

It is clear that tort law is primarily judge-made law, and because of *stare decisis*, the following of precedent, the basic principles have remained relatively unchanged over the centuries. But with social and technological change, courts have been willing to extend or adapt tort principles to cover new situations when it seems appropriate. These are not so much fundamental changes in the law or the creation of new law that would defeat the practices that give the law consistency and stability as they are simply modification and development of tested principles. Where the need for dramatic change exists, legislators fill the gap by enacting a statute. Law does change in slow, incremental steps, and tort law is one area where this growth is manifest. We move on now to another important branch of private law that governs the commercial relations between individuals. Parties create a law unto themselves when they bargain or come to agreements. As long as those agreements are fulfilled as was anticipated by the parties, the law normally plays no part in the contract, but when difficulties arise, the law steps in to remedy the problem.

QUESTIONS FOR DISCUSSION AND REVIEW

1. Wrongful conduct can be both a crime and a tort. Should a person who has been convicted of a crime have to face civil liability as well?

2. Victims of wrongful acts usually have to prove that they have suffered injuries before they can win their case in court. This is not the case in a trespass action. Why is that so?

3. Should an athlete injured in the course of a game be able to sue the player who caused the injury?

4. Outline the defences available to a defamation action and consider whether it has become too difficult to win a defamation lawsuit.

5. Review the elements that must be proven to succeed in a negligence action.

6. Justify the imposition of a higher standard of care on innkeepers and food handlers.

7. Explain how the standard of care owed by manufacturers to the customers of their products has changed.

8. Professionals may be required by the court to act on standards that go beyond those required by their own professional bodies. Is this an appropriate demand?

9. Outline the distinctions between intentional and negligent torts.

10. Apportioning the blame for an accident is one way of distributing the costs. This also raises insurance premiums. Discuss the role of insurance companies in tort liability.

NOTES

1. *Ryland v. Fletcher* (1868), L.R. 3 H.L. 330.

2. *School Act*, S.B.C. 1989, c. 61, s. 10.

3. *Turberville v. Savage* (1699), 86 E.R. 684.

4. *Wilkinson v. Downton*, [1897] 2 Q.B. 57.

5. *Cole v. Turner* (1704), 90 E.R. 958.

6. *Lawyer's Weekly* 15:24 (Oct. 20, 1995).

7. *Norberg v. Wynrib*, [1992] 2 S.C.R. 226.

8. *Gerner v. Sparks* (1704), 1 Salk. 79.

9. *Merring v. Graham White Aviation Ltd.* (1919), 122 L.T. 44.

10. *Bahner v. Mar West Hotel* (1969), 6 D.L.R. (3d) 322 (B.C.S.C.).

11. *Gross v. Wright*, [1923] 2 D.L.R. 881.

12. *Law and Equity Act*, R.S.B.C. 1979, c. 253.

13. *Motherwell v. Motherwell*, [1976] 6 W.W.R. 550.

14. *Tock v. St. John's Metropolitan Area Board*, [1989] 2 S.C.R. 1181.

15. *Youssoupoff v. Metro-Goldwyn-Mayer Pictures Limited* (1934), 50 T.L.R. 581.

16. *Murphy v. LaMarsh* (1970), 13 D.L.R. (3d) 484.

17. *Jones v. Bennett* (1968), 66 W.W.R. 419 (S.C.C.).

18. *Ibid.*, at p. 422.

19. *E. Hulton & Co. v. Jones*, [1910] 26 T.L.R. 128.

20. *Hill v. Church of Scientology of Toronto* (1995), 126 D.L.R. (4th) 577 (S.C.C.).

21. *Libel and Slander Act*, R.S.B.C. 1979, c. 263.

22. Baron Alderson in *Blyth v. Birmingham Water Works Co.* (1856), 11 Ex. 781 at p. 784.

23. *Donoghue v. Stevenson*, [1932] All E.R. (H.L.) at p. 11.

24. *Ibid.*, pp. 1-31.

25. *Ibid.*, at p. 11.

26. *Arland v. Taylor*, [1955] O.R. 131 (C.A.) at p. 142.

27. *Bolton v. Stone*, [1951] 1 All E.R. 1078.

28. *Blyth v. Birmingham Water Works Co.* (1856), 156 E.R. 104.

29. *Hall v. Hebert*, [1993] 2 S.C.R. 159.

30. *Galaske v. O'Donnell*, [1994] 1 S.C.R. 670.

31. *Occupiers' Liability Act*, S.M. 1982-83-84, c. 3, s. 1.

32. *Stewart v. Pettie*, [1995] 1 S.C.R. 131.

33. *Heimler v. Calvert Caterers Ltd.* (1975), 56 D.L.R. (3d) 643.

34. *Ibid*, p. 644.

35. *Hedley Byrne & Co. v. Heller & Partners*, [1963] 2 All E.R. 575.

36. *Hercules Management Ltd. v. Ernst & Young* (1997), 146 D.L.R. (4th) 577 (S.C.C.).

37. *Anns v. Merton (London Borough Council)*, [1977] 2 All E.R. 492 (H.L.)

38. *Hercules,* at p. 592.

39. *Abbott v. Kasza* (1977), 71 D.L.R. (3d) 581.

40. *Hughes v. the Lord Advocate*, [1963] A.C. 837.

41. *Contributory Negligence Act*, R.S.N.S. 1989, c. 95.

FURTHER READING

Fleming, John G. *The Law of Torts*, 8th ed. Sydney: Law Book Company, 1992.

Fridman, G.H.L. *The Law of Torts in Canada* (2 vols.). Toronto: Carswell, 1989.

Linden, Allen M. *Canadian Tort Law*, 5th ed. Toronto: Butterworths, 1993.

Smyth, J.E., D.A. Soberman and A.J. Easson. *The Law and Business Administration in Canada*, 8th ed. Scarborough, Ont.: Prentice Hall Canada Inc., 1998.

Willes, J.A. *Contemporary Canadian Business Law*, 5th ed. Toronto: McGraw-Hill, 1998.

Wright, Cecil A. *Canadian Tort Law*, 9th ed. Toronto: Butterworths, 1990.

Yates, R.A. *Business Law in Canada*, 5th ed. Scarborough, Ont.: Prentice Hall Canada Inc., 1998.

FAMILY LAW AND ESTATES

The laws concerning families and estates originated in canon or church law and developed in the common law courts. They remained fairly constant until the latter half of the twentieth century, when dramatic changes in the most fundamental of social relationships prompted changes in the law. Rosalie Abella, Supreme Court Justice in Ontario, identified the relationship between the state and families. "The State has the right to demand adherence to those values it considers necessary for its survival and the family has the right to insist on implementing those values it considers necessary for survival." She follows with the important question, "Who is to say which rights within a family are most deserving of protection?"[1] We will try to respond to this and other questions as we examine family law in Canada at the beginning of a new millennium. In particular this chapter will discuss the rights and obligations of formally and informally married partners and their children, including support, custody and guardianship of children, division of property and prevention of and protection from abuse. Because the distribution of assets upon a person's death is usually a family matter, we will also consider estate law in this chapter.

DEFINITION OF A FAMILY

Family law deals with legal issues arising from creating, maintaining and dissolving marriage relationships. The most common form of marriage is created through partners entering into a legally binding contract registered with the provincial government. Our notion of family also includes informally created marriages, commonly called "common law" marriages. **Marriage** is a partnership in which the partners take on certain obligations to each other and their children.

Source of Family Law

Statutes

Family law in Canada derives from two sources: statutes of the federal and provincial governments, and precedents established in the reasons for judgment of judges deciding individual cases. *The Constitution Act, 1867* gives the power to pass legislation on matters of divorce exclusively to the federal government. This includes the divorce action itself, the division of property, the custody of children, and the support and maintenance of the spouse and the children. However, the provinces have the power to create laws relating to issues prior to divorce, including the solemnization (creation) of marriage, formalization of separation on marriage breakdown, support and maintenance of the spouse and the children, division of property, and the custody of children. Decisions made under the provincial law can be incorporated into the terms of the divorce under the federal law.

Case Law

When spouses cannot agree on how to resolve marriage-related legal issues, they can apply to the court for an interpretation of the statute law and previous case law. Case law is the set of legal principles decided in previous cases that applies to the current matter. Some provinces have lower courts, sometimes called **family courts**, which deal with such disputes, but they assign issues relating to the granting of divorces to the provincial superior trial court. Several provinces have created special unified family courts, presided over by judges of the higher court, to deal with all family disputes. We will discuss some of the legal principles that courts have decided or have yet to decide in the area of family law.

Creating a Marriage

Capacity to Marry

As in other legally binding contracts, each partner to the marriage must have the legal capacity to enter into the agreement. For example, each party must have the mental capacity to understand the nature and quality of the legal commitment. If one partner is so impaired from drugs or alcohol that he or she does not understand the commitment, the marriage is void. Similarly, if one person is coerced into marriage, in that the person lacks free will, the marriage is void. For example, a person might be threatened with physical harm if he or she does not go through with the marriage ceremony. If one party made a mistake such that he or she did not understand what he or she was doing, the marriage is void. For example, one party may reasonably believe that he or she is going through an engagement ceremony, not a marriage ceremony.

Same-Sex Partners – Partners of the same sex cannot go through a legal form of marriage, but they can acquire some of the rights and responsibilities of a marriage relationship (see "Common Law" Marriage, below). Individuals who have a close blood relationship, such as first cousins, are prohibited by provincial statute from entering into a marriage. A list of such prohibited relationships is normally available from the provincial government office where marriage licences are obtained.

Minimum Age – The minimum age at which partners can marry varies from 16 to 19 from province to province. At common law a person could not marry below the age of puberty, defined as 12 for a girl and 14 for a boy. People below the age of majority (18 in most provinces) must have their parents' permission to marry, and as a general rule, people below the age of 16 cannot marry without a court order, usually only given when the young woman is pregnant. If young people marry without permission below the age of majority and consummate the marriage, the marriage is valid.

Bigamy – A person can be married to only one partner at a time. If the person's partner has died or either partner has obtained a legal divorce or annulment, the person can remarry. A problem arises when a spouse has "gone missing" and there is no way of confirming whether that person is living or dead. If someone has been missing for seven years, the spouse is entitled to presume that the partner is dead and is free to remarry. If it later turns out that that person is alive, the new marriage is void. However, the spouse will not have committed an offence if he or she entered the new marriage in good faith. If a person has been married before and the spouse is still alive, the person must obtain a valid divorce before remarrying. For the purposes of remarriage, a foreign divorce will be valid in Canada if it was recognized and valid in the jurisdiction where the parties to it were living.

A married person who has not obtained a divorce and knows that the spouse is still alive but marries again has committed bigamy, a criminal offence punishable by up to five years in jail. If a person marries more than one spouse, and the spousal relations are going on concurrently, it is referred to as **polygamy**. Such polygamous marriages are prohibited by the *Criminal Code*.

Annulment – If the former marriage is annulled, the parties are also free to remarry. An annulment is a declaration by the court that the marriage was never valid. For example, one partner may have been married before or may have lacked the mental capacity to marry. In the absence of sexual relations, one party can apply to court to have it declared void. For example, the marriage may have been one of convenience in order to help one partner to become a permanent resident of Canada. Usually, if both parties knew in advance that it was a marriage of convenience, the courts will not annul the marriage solely on the ground of lack of sexual relations.

Marriage Contracts

An engagement is a contract to marry, and if it is broken and one party suffers damages, that person can sue for compensation. When gifts have been exchanged, the person changing his or her mind cannot insist on the return of the gifts.

Prior to a marriage, some parties enter into a marriage contract in order to modify the rights and obligations of marriage. A statute can prevent the partners from changing some legal obligations. For example, parents cannot contract out of their obligation to support their children.

Couples usually enter into a contract in order to direct how they will divide their property if their marriage breaks down. For example, an older couple with property from a first marriage may wish to ensure that the property goes to the children of the first marriage. Because of public policy, certain things cannot be included in a marriage contract, including an agreement not to have children, not to have sex, or to end the marriage at a certain time.

Formal Requirements of Marriage

In addition to the capacity to marry, provincial statutes set out the formal requirements to marry. Usually the partners must purchase a marriage **licence** from a provincial government office and wait a short period. The person who performs the marriage must be authorized to do so, and the details of the marriage must be registered with the provincial government office.

Obligations of Marriage

Support

In agreeing to marry, the partners agree to support each other "in sickness and in health." If one partner is unable to work, the other partner is obliged to supply the necessities of life to the spouse. Under *Criminal Code* section 215, one partner can be charged with an offence if he or she fails to perform that duty. Similarly, in having children together or agreeing to support the other partner's children, a spouse is responsible for supplying **necessities of life** to a child under the age of 16.

A husband or wife may make purchases or incur other obligations that he or she or that person's creditor will claim must be honoured by the other spouse. As a general rule, during the marriage one spouse is not an agent for the other unless the partner has given the impression to the creditor that the other was authorized to act on the partner's behalf. Therefore the debts of one are not automatically the debts of the other. The debt is only assumed to be the debt of both if one is purchasing necessities for the family. Often, however, creditors will require both to agree to pay, for example in applying for joint credit cards.

Children

During marriage, both parents have the right to guardianship of the person and property of the children of the marriage. They have the right to joint custody of the children and to jointly make major decisions regarding such matters as the education and religion of the children. The parents are jointly responsible for the support and care of their children during the marriage, and they are jointly responsible for the debts and other financial affairs of the children. We will discuss the rights and responsibilities of parents upon marriage breakdown a little later in the chapter.

Property

During marriage in most provinces, the partners are separate as to property during the marriage — i.e., they own and control their own property and are responsible for their own debts. If the partners decide to separate, new property rights may arise. For example in British Columbia both parties have a equal claim to half of the **family assets** only on marriage breakdown. Similarly a wife may have a claim in constructive trust to a share in property to which she contributed value during the marriage. The division of matrimonial property upon marriage breakdown will be discussed below.

Constructive Trust

Peter v. Beblow[2]

Ms. Peter lived in a common law relationship with Mr. Beblow for 12 years, doing the domestic work of the household and raising the children of their blended family without compensation. Mr. Beblow had purchased the house occupied by the couple and Ms. Peter had undertaken a number of projects, including gardening and painting, to maintain or improve it during the relationship.

The trial judge found that Mr. Beblow had been unjustly enriched by Ms. Peter's contribution and, based on the principle of constructive trust, awarded her the property. The Court of Appeal allowed an appeal. The Supreme Court of Canada reversed the Court of Appeal decision and held that Ms. Peter was entitled to the property on the basis of constructive trust.

The court can impose a constructive trust if it finds that there is a link between the contribution made and the property in which the constructive trust is claimed. The portion of the value of the property claimed and attributable to the claimant's services must be determined. Her contribution to the family enterprise was considerable for it saved Mr. Beblow large sums of money that were used to pay off the mortgage and to accumulate family assets. The house reflected a fair approximation of the value of Ms. Peter's efforts in acquiring the family assets.

Freedom from Abuse

During marriage each partner has the right to be free from physical and sexual abuse by the other partner. A partner who uses physical abuse, threatens physical abuse or forces sexual activity on the other is guilty of a crime. Similarly children have the right to be free from abuse and neglect. A parent who physically or sexually abuses a child is guilty of a crime. A child who is neglected or abused can be apprehended and taken into care by provincial child welfare authorities. The legal protections for the safety of partners and children are discussed under "Marriage Breakdown" below.

"Common Law" Marriage

Heterosexual Couples

In Canada, many couples live together for years without going through a formal marriage. The relationship is often called a "common law" marriage. However, the term is misleading because the parties have only those legal rights and obligations that are created by statutes or case law. For a common law partner to acquire the right to spousal support, the couple must live together for the period of time specified by the provincial legislation; some provinces do not give support rights to unmarried partners.

Whether or not the relationship is one of marriage, parents have an obligation to support their children. Some statutes also impose an obligation on common law partners to pay support to the dependent partner in the event of a breakup, providing the relationship has gone on for a lengthy period of time. There may also be other statutes and private arrangements that give parties to such a relationship special rights. For example, many pension plans give the surviving partner in such a relationship a right to claim death benefits usually payable to a spouse. The *Income Tax Act* gives common law spouses the same status as married couples when they have cohabited together for one year.

However, obligations and responsibilities arising from such an arrangement are not nearly as comprehensive as those imposed when a formal marriage has taken place. For example, an Ontario statute provides that if the relationship has gone on for over five years, there is a claim by the partner for support but no claim for equal division of assets, such as home, car or land, as would be the case in a marriage. If both had contributed to the acquisition of the property, then both would have a claim to it, despite who holds title. It is best for people in such relationships to enter into a contract, setting out their rights and claims with respect to any property they may acquire.

Rights of Common Law Spouse

Miron v. Trudel[3]

Mr. Miron and his common law wife lived together with their children. Although they were not married, their family functioned as an economic unit. In 1987, Mr. Miron was injured while a passenger in an uninsured motor vehicle driven by an uninsured driver. After the accident, he could no longer work and contribute to his family's support. He made a claim for accident benefits for loss of income and damages against his common law wife's insurance policy, which extended accident benefits to the "spouse" of the policy holder. The insurer denied his claim on the ground that he was not legally married to his common law spouse and hence not her "spouse."

The insurer brought a motion to determine whether the word "spouse," as used in the applicable portions of the policy, includes unmarried common law spouses. The motions court judge found that "spouse" meant a person who is legally married. The Court of Appeal dismissed their appeal but the Supreme Court of Canada held that the exclusion of unmarried partners from accident benefits available to married partners under the policy violated subsection 15(1) of the Charter. The new definition of "spouse," adopted in 1990, which included heterosexual couples who have cohabited for three years or who have lived in a permanent relationship with a child, was retroactively "read in" to the legislation.

The Supreme Court analyzed section 15 of the Charter, which provides for "equal protection" or "equal benefit" under the law. The court found that the denial of protection or benefit in this case was discriminatory because it was based on the stereotypical application of presumed group or personal characteristics. To make such a distinction would promote or perpetuate a view that people in alternative relationships were less worthy of recognition or value as human beings or as members of Canadian society. The court's decision was designed to send the message that they were equally deserving of concern, respect and consideration.

The goal of the legislation is to sustain families when one of their members is injured in an automobile accident. That goal is not rationally connected to the discriminatory distinction. Marital status is not a reasonably relevant marker of individuals who should receive benefits in the event of injury to a family member in an automobile accident.

Same-Sex Relationships

A similar problem arises in a homosexual relationship because homosexual couples cannot legally marry in Canada. Homosexual couples may acquire rights and benefits from living together for a long period. If the parties to the relationship have mutually contributed to the acquisition of property, the law of trusts may provide that both have an interest in that property, even if title is in the name of one only. The most appropriate advice is for the parties to enter into an agreement, specifying their various claims to property. Although such an agreement between homosexuals may be declared void, especially if it purports to be a marriage contract, the agreement will indicate their intent, and many of its provisions may remain enforceable and binding. Some survivors in a homosexual relationship are entitled to the same spousal benefits under pension plans as would survivors in a heterosexual relationship.

Rights of Same-Sex Partners

Egan v. Canada[4]

Mr. Egan and Mr. Nesbit had lived together since 1948 in a committed homosexual relationship. When Mr. Egan became 65 in 1986, he began to receive old-age security and guaranteed income supplements under the *Old Age Security Act*. On reaching age 60, Mr. Nesbit applied for a spousal allowance under subsection 19(1) of the Act, which is available to spouses between the ages of 60 and 65 whose combined income falls below a fixed level. His application was rejected on the basis that the relationship between the partners did not fall within the definition of "spouse" in section 2, which includes "a person of the opposite sex who is living with that person, having lived with that person for at least one year, if the two persons have publicly represented themselves as husband and wife."

Mr. Egan and Mr. Nesbit asked the Federal Court for a declaration that the definition contravenes subsection 15(1) of the Charter on the grounds that it discriminated on the basis of sexual orientation. They asked for a declaration that the definition should be extended to include "partners in same-sex relationships otherwise akin to a conjugal relationship."

The Trial Division dismissed the action. The Federal Court of Appeal and the Supreme Court of Canada dismissed the appeal. The Supreme Court held that the definition of "spouse" in section 2 of the *Old Age Security Act* is constitutional.

The Supreme Court found that Parliament had drawn a discriminatory distinction between the claimant and others. The legislation confers a benefit on legally married and common law couples but not on homosexual couples. Discrimination on the basis of sexual orientation is prohibited under section 15 of the Charter because it is analogous to enumerated grounds.

However, the court decided that the distinction based on sexual orientation was relevant to the legislative purpose and therefore not prohibited. The court found that the benefit was conferred on couples not because they mutually supported each other, but because of their ability to have children. The distinction adopted by Parliament was relevant to describe a fundamental social unit to which the legislation gives support.

Marriage Breakdown

Marriage breakdown results in the separation of the partners, the reorganizing of custody of and access to children, and the redistribution of family assets.

Mediation

Some parties to a marriage breakdown choose mediation to resolve their legal issues. The parties hire or obtain government services of a neutral mediator who is skilled in resolving these issues. Often the mediator is a lawyer or family court counsellor. However, the mediator does not represent the interests of either of the parties. Parties to mediation should also obtain independent legal advice about their proposed agreement. In relationships where there has been significant family violence, the parties may not use mediation because it is premised on both parties freely agreeing to the **negotiated agreement**. Agreements negotiated by mediators can be formalized into legally binding contracts, called separation agreements.

Separation Agreements

Separation agreements often include terms that provide for the arbitration or mediation of disputes that arise from their performance. But even in the absence of such a term, parties to a marriage separation can negotiate, either through a mediator or directly with or without legal advice, the terms of their separation. The written agreement will be a permanent record of just what the parties have agreed to do. Subsequent divorce proceedings can be much less painful if the parties have already agreed to such things as their rights and responsibilities and how their property will be divided.

As is the case with any contract, the parties are always free to renegotiate and change the terms of the contract, but it must be done voluntarily and with the agreement of both parties. One party cannot impose a change on the other unless there is a term included in the agreement providing for such a renegotiation. Such a **re-opener clause** will typically come into effect when there has been a material change in the circumstances of either party. For example, when either of the parties has become ill, lost a job, or even obtained a better job and is in a better position to bear more of the responsibility, the clause may be activated. The courts always retain the right to modify the terms of the separation agreement or depart from them entirely when the custody or support of children is involved. The primary consideration of the court in such circumstances is the welfare of the child.

For a separation agreement to be enforceable, certain formal requirements must be met. Most provinces require that the agreement be in writing and signed. Some provinces, such as Ontario, also require that it be properly witnessed. If one of the parties has not properly disclosed all of his or her assets, it brings into question the fairness and validity of the agreement. If it is determined that the marriage itself is void for some reason, any separation agreement entered into by the parties is also void. Also, if the parties reconcile and resume cohabitation, the agreement will be brought to an end; its terms will no longer apply even if the parties subsequently separate again. Terms that anticipate the permanent division of property, however, will be in force, despite such a **reconciliation**, if it is clear that the changed ownership was to stand independent of any changes to the marriage status.

Another advantage to separation agreements is that the parties can include in the agreement matters that are important to them but would not normally be included in a court order. Such items might include the division of family mementos and keepsakes, furnishings, pets, and any other matters that might be important to the parties but difficult for the courts to deal with.

Separation agreements will typically have clauses dealing with some or all of the following matters:

- ownership and division of property;
- obligations to pay support to the spouse and children;
- custody and access to children;
- matters relating to the education and upbringing of the children (including religion, dating and so on);
- who will live in the matrimonial home;
- who gets the cars, the furnishings, vacation property;
- a provision that the parties are to live separate and apart and not bother or harass each other;
- who will pay the ongoing debts and obligations of the relationship (such as credit cards, insurance payments and mortgages);
- who gets various stocks and bonds;
- a release of any claims between the parties; and usually
- a re-opener clause.

Often when a marriage breaks down, the couple will owe considerable debt. The separation agreement should provide for how those debts will be paid. Similar provisions should set out the responsibility for making insurance payments and other joint arrangements, but it must be remembered that these provisions cannot modify a person's individual obligations to honour debts made with creditors. Thus, if a creditor has a claim against both the husband and the wife, as would be the case if they co-signed or guaranteed the debt, the separation agreement cannot affect that creditor's right to seek redress from either or both parties.

Variation of Terms of Separation Agreement

Willick v. Willick[5]

Mr. and Mrs. Willick signed a separation agreement in July 1989 that was incorporated into the divorce order in November 1989. Mr. Willick was an airline pilot. He agreed to pay $450 per month child support for each of two children and $700 per month spousal support. Mr. Willick's income increased significantly. The judge agreed to vary the child support to $850 per month per child. The Court of Appeal overturned the decision and the Supreme Court of Canada allowed the appeal. The trial judge did not make an error in interpreting subsection 14(4) of the *Divorce Act*, which provides for variation of child support orders.

The court is not bound by the terms of the separation agreement in awarding support. However, the support terms are strong evidence that the parties consider the amount adequate to meet the needs of the children. To vary the support order there must be a material change of circumstances that if known at the time the agreement was signed would likely have resulted in different terms.

The court can vary child support orders under subsection 17(4) of the *Divorce Act* if there is either a change in the child's circumstances or a change in the circumstances of one or both of the former spouses. The child may benefit from any improvement in the lifestyle of one or both of the parents. The reasonable expectations of the children for future support are not frozen as of the date of the breakup.

Family Courts

Both superior and provincial courts have jurisdiction over family law matters. Most family matters are resolved in the less formal provincial family court. The family court is mainly concerned with matters of maintenance and support for the spouse and children, custody and access in relation to those children, and the right to reside in the matrimonial home. Usually the division of property must be dealt with by the superior court. Family courts are like small claims courts in that their procedures are simple and informal and the parties do not always require the services of a lawyer. Some provinces provide family court counsellors to assist the court and the parties with the proceedings.

The family court has considerable power to enforce its judgments, and the trend seems to be to extend this power rather than limit it. Steps that can be taken by the court to enforce its judgments include:

- examination in aid of execution, which is the process or requirement that the party being examined disclose under oath all assets, such as sources of income, bank accounts, property, and so on;

- garnishing (or seizing) wages and bank accounts; and

- ordering the seizure of other forms of property, such as building and lands, boats and cars.

The court can even order the person to he jailed if the court orders are not honoured. In BC even the orders of the superior courts associated with the divorce decree can be filed with the family court and enforced as if they were orders of the family court.

An order of the family court may be changed by the superior court with respect to maintenance, custody and access when the divorce decree is made. There are some things that only the superior court can do (such as order a divorce), but generally, in the areas of custody, access, and support of the children and spouse, there is considerable overlap between the powers of the family and superior courts.

Legal Separation

Many provincial statutes provide that the court can formalize the separation of the parties prior to divorce, called judicial or legal separation. Some parties do not intend to divorce due to religious beliefs. Other parties require legal separation in order to clarify property rights, for example in provinces that provide for equal division of family assets upon marriage breakdown.

Custody of Children

Legal issues relating to the custody of the children can be the most difficult to resolve on marriage breakdown. Judges rarely move children from one home to another prior to the final custody order. If one parent moves out of the family home and leaves the children in the care of the other, the court seldom changes the arrangement. Therefore many lawyers advise their clients not to move out until custody is settled, leaving the family living in conflict. If the parents cannot negotiate an arrangement, they must apply to court for an interim custody order and/or permission to move with the children or an order for exclusive residency in the family home.

If one parent has assaulted the other parent, the parent may or may not report the assault to the police and move with the children to a transition house for safety. The parent must then apply to the court for an **interim custody order**, a **restraining order** preventing the other parent from contacting the spouse and children, and an **order regarding occupancy of the family home**. If one parent flees the family home because of violence, she should immediately apply to court for an interim custody order. While courts do not look favourably on parents who take custody, they regularly grant interim emergency orders to spouses in fear of violence.

The custody of and access to children upon marriage breakdown is regulated by both the federal *Divorce Act* and by provincial statutes. If the parents cannot agree, they can apply to the court for an order either under the provincial legislation (if they are not applying for a divorce decree) or under the *Divorce Act*. There are some differences between the *Divorce Act* and provincial statutes in the factors that the court must consider in awarding custody. However, all provide that the judge must decide what is in the **best interests** of the children "...as determined by reference to the condition, means, needs and other circumstances of the child." The court cannot take into consideration the past conduct of a parent unless the conduct is relevant to the ability of that person to act as a parent. All custody orders are reviewable by the courts; they are never final, whether they are made under provincial or federal legislation.

If the parents are going to court to decide custody they must obtain a report from an expert as to the best interests of the children. They usually share the cost, but one person's share may have to be assessed at the end of litigation if that person does not control the family assets. If neither parent can afford the cost, a provincial body can conduct the

assessment in most provinces. Once the assessor submits the report, most parents agree on the custody and access terms based on the report. Unless the report is inconclusive or lacks impartiality, the judge will give the assessor's opinion a great deal of weight in deciding custody.

In all provinces, courts can appoint a lawyer or official guardian to represent the interests of the children in the custody dispute. The lawyer treats the child as any other client and acts according to the child's instructions. The child's lawyer is appointed either by a provincial authority or, where the service is not available or would cause undue delay in the trial, by the judge.

The court may make an order granting either sole custody or joint custody and access. Under a **joint custody** arrangement, both parents must agree upon and are equally responsible for all major decisions regarding the children. Joint custody is therefore not usually imposed on unwilling parents. **Sole custody** means that one parent has primary responsibility for day-to-day care and ultimate responsibility for decision-making.

Access is the right to visit and to take the child out of the home for specific periods of time. The court order may provide for specific access in which the times are set, such as every second weekend, or provide for "reasonable access," which provides the parents more flexibility in structuring their lives. A spouse who is granted access to a child has the right to information as to the health, education and welfare of the child.

If the non-custodial parent has abused the custodial parent or the child, the court may require **supervised access**, in which the parent's access to the child is supervised by a neutral third party. Supervised access is only imposed if there is a serious concern for a child's safety. Most cities have supervised access centres that may or may not charge a fee.

Most children benefit from spending as much time as possible with both parents. The *Divorce Act* requires the court to give effect to the principle that a "child of the marriage should have as much contact with each spouse as is consistent with the best interests of the child. ... and for that purpose, shall take into consideration the willingness of the person for whom custody is sought to facilitate such contact." This section puts the custodial parent at the risk of losing custody if she does not allow court-ordered access. Therefore a custodial parent who is reluctant to give access because of fear of harm to the child must apply to court to vary the court order rather than deny access, or she risks losing custody.

Mobility rights address whether one parent is entitled to move away from the other parent. Both parents must show why the move is or is not in the best interests of the children. The judge will consider the current arrangements and relationship between the parents and the children, the views of older children, whether the move is required in order for the custodial parent to support the children, and the disruption to the children. The advantages of the move are weighed against the disadvantage of less contact with the non-custodial parent. Most separation agreements provide for mobility rights, for example the right of the custodial parent to move up to 60 kilometres.

Custody orders are enforced by the courts. It is a crime to take a child from the custodial parent in contravention of the order (CCC section 282). Even if the parent fears abuse by the other parent, the parent must apply to the court to vary the custody order or face an abduction charge. Canada participates in reciprocal arrangements with over 40 countries for the return of abducted children.

Custody of Children — Custodial Parent Moving

Gordon v. Goertz[6]

The parents lived in Saskatoon and divorced in 1990. The court awarded the mother custody of their young child and the father access. The mother wished to move to Australia to study orthodontics. The father applied to restrain the mother and child from moving. The trial judge varied the access order to allow the mother to move. The Court of Appeal agreed. The Supreme Court of Canada held that the judge was correct in allowing the mother to move to Australia but that the father's access should not have been limited to Australia.

A parent with a custody order who wishes to move away from a parent with an access order must show that there is a material change in the circumstances of the child or in the ability of the parent to meet the needs of the child which could not reasonably have been contemplated by the judge who made the original access order. Then the court must decide what is in the best interests of the child, including the ability of the parents to meet the child's needs. The focus is not the interests and rights of the parents. Each case turns on its own facts.

In assessing the best interests of the child, the judge must consider:

- the existing custody arrangement and relationship between the child and the custodial parent;
- the existing access arrangement and the relationship between the child and the access parent;
- the desirability of maximizing contact between the child and both parents;
- the views of the child;
- the custodial parent's reason for moving, only in the exceptional case where it is relevant to that parent's ability to meet the needs of the child;
- disruption to the child of a change in custody; and
- disruption to the child consequent on removal from family, schools, and the community he or she has come to know.

In this case the mother needed to move to Australia to enhance her ability to support the child. However, the child benefited from contact with the father. The access need not be limited to Australia. Access in Canada had the advantage of making the father's limited time with the child more natural while allowing the child to maintain contact with friends and extended family.

Support

Either provincial statutes or *Divorce Act* sections 15.1 and 15.2 provide for support of the child and of the spouse. Both parents are required to contribute to the support of their children. Most statutes require the parties to support themselves as quickly as possible. Provincial statutes usually require the parents to support their children until they reach the age of majority. Some provinces also require the partner who has assumed the role of parent to support children from a previous marriage.

Under the *Divorce Act*, the court can order a spouse to pay for the support of children of the marriage in an amount set out in federal **child support guidelines**. The guidelines require the court to order child support in specific amounts based on the circumstances of the parents and children. If the parties consent, the court can order an amount different from the guidelines if they have made reasonable arrangements for child support. The court can also order that the parties pay the amount of an earlier court order or separation agreement if the guideline amount would be inequitable. Where the court is considering a child support order and spousal support order, the court must give priority to the child support order. The federal child support guidelines apply only to married parents.

Under the *Divorce Act* section 15.2 one spouse can also apply for a court order that the other spouse pay such amount of **spousal support** as the judge thinks reasonable. The court may impose terms, conditions or restrictions on the order as it thinks fit and just. The court must take into account

> ...the condition, means, needs and other circumstances of each spouse, including: (a) the length of time the spouses cohabited; (b) the functions performed by each spouse during cohabitation; and (c) any order, agreement or arrangement relating to support of either spouse.

The court cannot take into account any misconduct of a spouse in relation to the marriage. The following are the primary objectives of a spousal support order:

(a) to recognize any economic advantages or disadvantages to the spouses arising from the marriage or its breakdown;

(b) to apportion between the spouses any financial consequences arising from the care of any child of the marriage over and above any obligation for the support of any child of the marriage;

(c) to relieve any economic hardship of the spouses arising from the breakdown of the marriage; and

(d) to promote the economic self-sufficiency of each spouse within a reasonable period of time.

Support orders are enforced by the courts, and in several provinces the government provides a service which assists in the enforcement of support orders. The person who has not paid a support order can be required to come to court and explain. The court can order that money held in his bank account or by his employer be garnished.

Spousal Support Order

Moge v. Moge[7]

Mr. and Mrs. Moge married in Poland in the mid-1950s and moved to Canada in 1960. Mrs. Moge cared for the family home and their three children. She worked briefly cleaning offices. The Moges separated in 1973 and divorced in 1980. The court awarded Mrs. Moge custody of the children and $150 per month spousal and child support. She continued cleaning offices. Mr. Moge remarried in 1984 and continued to pay the support. Mrs. Moge was laid off in 1987. The court increased spousal and child support to $400. She worked part-time and intermittently. In 1989 Mr. Moge applied to end the spousal support.

The judge found that Mrs. Moge had had time to become financially independent and that her husband had supported her for as long as required. The Court of Appeal set aside the judgment and ordered spousal support in the amount of $150 per month for an indefinite period. The Supreme Court of Canada dismissed Mr. Moge's appeal. The Supreme Court held that the *Divorce Act* required the husband to provide ongoing support in this case.

The *Divorce Act* requires judges to take into account four principles in determining spousal support, only one of which is the objective of self-sufficiency. Women who care for their home and children rather than acquiring workplace skills experience economic disadvantage. The *Divorce Act* recognizes the economic value of work caring for the home and children and seeks to put the partners in as close a position as possible to their position before marriage breakdown.

The partners have an obligation to contribute to their own support commensurate with their abilities. However, the ultimate goal is to alleviate the disadvantaged spouse's economic losses as completely as possible. In marriages in which both partners have made economic sacrifices and share domestic responsibilities, or where one spouse has suffered economic losses in order to enable the other spouse to further a career, their roles should be considered in the spousal support order. However, an equitable sharing of the consequences of marriage does not exclude other considerations. The courts have an overriding discretion, the exercise of which will depend on the particular facts of each case, having regard to the factors and objectives set out in the Act.

Property

The guiding philosophy in division of matrimonial property is that marriage is a **partnership** and both husband and wife have an equal claim to the property acquired during the marriage. If one of the partners spends her time working in the home, this frees the other to devote full attention to business interests; the spouse at home indirectly contributes to the acquisition of assets. Provincial legislation recognizes three types of property: property that is automatically subject to sharing; property that must be shared depending upon the circumstances; and property that is excluded from sharing. In some provinces business assets are automatically shared, in some almost always shared, and in others not usually shared. Most, but not all, provinces give credit to spouses for the net worth of each at the date of marriage.

The precise property-sharing formula depends on the legislation in a specific province. In both Ontario and British Columbia the parties start from the position that each has a claim to an equal share of the assets, but in both these and other provinces, the judge retains the discretion to divide the assets in a non-equal way if it is fair to do so. This might be done if the maintenance to be paid is less or more than normal, or if one of the parties is taking a greater than normal share of the burden of the support of the children. There may be many kinds of orders involved, including specifying which asset will be taken by whom, an order for the transfer of title, or even an order that the asset be sold and the proceeds divided. The court can even order that certain of the property be placed in trust for the benefit of the children or for an incapacitated spouse.

All provinces recognize the special nature of the matrimonial home. Except in Newfoundland and New Brunswick, both partners do not automatically own the home unless both names are on the title. However, provincial legislation confers special rights regarding possession of the home and division of the property upon marriage breakdown. Exclusive possession can be granted as a part of spousal support at the discretion of the judge. A **possession order** is granted if continued cohabitation would be detrimental to the health of the spouse or children. Possession orders can be granted in conjunction with restraining orders granted in cases of fear of violence. It is an offence to breach an exclusive possession order. Provincial legislation requires that both spouses consent to the sale of the matrimonial home, even if one partner has sole title. Usually a sale is not ordered until the issues relating to the marriage breakdown are settled. If issues are still in dispute, the spouse in possession can usually have the order for sale delayed.

Canada Pension Plan credits earned by one or both partners during the marriage are automatically shared upon application to the CPP office. Spouses are not allowed to contract out of the division.

Ground for Divorce

The only ground for divorce in Canada is marriage breakdown. Under section 8 of the *Divorce Act*, the breakdown of the marriage is established if:

(a) the spouses have lived separate and apart for at least one year immediately preceding the determination of the divorce proceeding and were living separate and apart at the commencement of the proceeding; or

(b) the spouse against whom the divorce proceeding is brought has, since celebration of the marriage,
    (i) committed adultery, or
    (ii) treated the other spouse with physical or mental cruelty of such a kind as to render intolerable the continued cohabitation of the spouses.

The spouses are deemed to have lived separate and apart for any period "...during which they lived apart and either of them had the intention to live separate and apart from the other." The period is not interrupted because one spouse has become incapable of forming the intention to live separate and apart — for example, when the spouse becomes mentally incompetent. It is also not interrupted because the parties tried to reconcile and lived together for less than 90 days. The court has found that there has been separation even when the parties are living in the same house, provided they do not share cooking, cleaning, and washing duties, or otherwise live together as man and wife.

The court cannot grant a divorce if there is collusion — for example, the parties have lied about having lived separate and apart for one year. **Collusion** means an agreement or conspiracy to which an applicant for a divorce is either directly or indirectly a party for the purpose of subverting the administration of justice, and includes any agreement, understanding or arrangement to fabricate or suppress evidence or to deceive the court, but does not include a separation agreement. The court also cannot grant a divorce if it is not satisfied that "...reasonable arrangements have been made for the support of any children of the marriage...." If the grounds of divorce include adultery or cruelty the injured party cannot condone the fault — for example, forgive the adultery. It is not **condonation** to try to reconcile and cohabit for less than 90 days. And the parties cannot connive to create the ground — for example, by setting up a scheme to establish the appearance of adultery.

In the past, adultery was an important ground for divorce. Today, allegations of adultery or physical or mental cruelty as divorce grounds are rare because of the ease of bringing an application under the one-year separation provision.

Protection from Abuse

Separation can be a dangerous time for family members. Feelings run high and one partner may threaten to or actually assault the other partner or a child. If a partner has a reasonable fear of injury of herself or a child, she should call the emergency police services. The police will arrive and after ensuring that the parties are safe, investigate as to whether a crime has been committed. Many police forces also have victim services staff that will assist the family with a safety plan, including possibly a stay in a transition house, and with the criminal process.

Even if a crime has not yet been committed the victim can apply for a protection order, called a **peace bond**, if she has a reasonable fear of injury to herself, a child, or property. The police or the Crown counsel will decide whether there is enough evidence to charge the alleged assaulter with a crime. The court can order that the accused or convicted assaulter not contact the victim through a **no contact order**. The court usually orders a convicted assaulter to serve a term of probation during which he may be required to take treatment. During the criminal process, the abused partner may also have to use the services of the civil court to resolve issues such as custody and access to children, support, possession of the family home, and division of assets.

ESTATES

Whether rich or poor, most people have accumulated some property during their lifetimes and these accumulated assets are referred to as their estates. Included are real property in the form of buildings and land, personal property such as chattels, and claims they may have against others, as well as any other right or privilege they have that will survive their death. The object of this part of the chapter is to discuss how this property will be distributed upon a person's death.

What Is a Will?

A will is a document that gives instructions as to how property is to be distributed upon the death of the person making it. The author of the will is referred to as the **testator**. The instructions are directed to a specific person, the **executor**, who is charged with the responsibility of looking after the estate of the testator at death. The executor has the responsibility not only of paying the debts and obligations of the testator, but also of distributing these assets to the people, called **beneficiaries**, who are to receive them under the will. A will has no effect until the testator dies. Gifts given prior to death are not affected by the will. Before death a will can be changed or revoked at any time by the testator so long as she has mental capacity and the change is properly recorded and witnessed.

Reasons for Making a Will

People who want to have a say in who will receive the benefit of their estate should make a formal will. Parents with children who have not reached the age of majority should make a will. If a person dies **intestate** — that is, without a will — that person's estate is divided according to rules set out in the provincial intestacy legislation. If both parents die, the provincial public trustee becomes the guardian of the children and the administrator of their share of the estate. Also, parties to a common law marriage should make a will. Some provincial statutes provide for the claim of a common law spouse where the partner dies without a will. However, to ensure that they provide for their partner, the parties to a common law marriage should make wills.

Elements of a Valid Will

Provincial legislation requires that a will be in **writing**, that it be **signed** at its end, and that the signature be made in the presence of two **witnesses**, who then affix their signatures as witnesses in the presence of the testator. When a will is not prepared professionally these requirements may not be met. For example, the court has found wills to be invalid because they are not signed in the presence of the witnesses or are not signed at the end. The witnesses cannot have an interest in the estate — i.e., they or their spouses cannot be beneficiaries under the will. If this happens, the will is valid but the bequest to the witness or the spouse of the witness is void. In some provinces a holograph will is also valid.

A **holograph** will is one that is handwritten and signed by the testator, but not witnessed. In BC an unwitnessed holograph will is only valid if it is made by a military person on active duty or by a seaman in the course of a voyage because, in the face of such danger, there is pressing need and little likelihood the testator could comply with the formalities.

A will may also be invalid if the testator made it under undue influence or duress. Duress involves force, whereas undue influence involves other forms of pressure. And the will may be challenged if the testator was mentally incompetent to manage his affairs at the time he made the will.

Clauses of a Will

Wills commonly contain provisions to:
- identify the testator;
- revoke all previous wills;
- appoint an executor;
- authorize the executor to pay all debts;
- authorize the executor to distribute the remainder as prescribed;
- appoint a guardian of the children;
- indicate preferences in funeral arrangements; and
- prevent transfer of the estate to a spouse who does not survive 30 days — e.g., where they are both killed in the same accident.

The survivor clause is included to avoid probating the estate and paying fees twice. The entire estate is transferred to the remaining beneficiaries. If there is no survivorship clause, Ontario legislation provides that when one person is to inherit from another who dies at the same time, the beneficiary is deemed to survive. Other provincial legislation deems that the oldest died first. If life insurance is involved the beneficiary is deemed to die first.

The guardianship clause is included to indicate the parents' preference as to who should control the affairs of and care for the children. The court will usually honour the designation. The consent of the proposed guardian should be obtained before designating them in the will. Such a function is voluntary; no one can be forced to act as a guardian.

The acceptance of appointment as an executor is also an onerous job. The executor is responsible for winding up the testator's affairs, collecting and paying debts and other claims against the estate, collecting rents, dividing or selling the property, operating a business and otherwise preserving assets for the heirs. Assuming the role of executor is voluntary; the proposed executor should consent before they are named in the will.

The will cannot bequest assets for which the beneficiary is already designated; for example, life insurance policies have designated beneficiaries. Joint tenancy also conveys property automatically on death. When assets, e.g. a family home or a bank account, are held jointly, the property goes to the other partner by right of survivorship. The testator cannot give a bequest of his interest in the joint tenancy unless he has taken steps to legally sever the joint tenancy prior to his death.

If the testator wishes to donate organs, she should do so under provincial procedures for consent to organ donation rather than in her will. By the time the will is found and read it may be too late to give effect to her wishes.

Changing a Will

A person can change his will as often as he wishes prior to his death. He can either add a clause to the will, called creating a codicil, or he can revoke the old will and create an entirely new will, called **revocation**. A **codicil** is a supplementary note, changing one or more of the provisions of the will. The codicil must be signed and witnessed in the same way as the will itself.

A will is in force until it is revoked. However, a will is automatically revoked upon marriage. The parties to a marriage can make a will "in contemplation of marriage." Otherwise they must make new wills after they marry. In some provinces, upon divorce a will is revoked in relation to a bequest to the spouse. Separation agreements can also provide for the revocation of bequests. A will is revoked if the testator intentionally destroys the will by burning it or tearing it up, or the testator can write a new will which contains a clause revoking the previous will. Once a will is revoked, there is no longer a will until the testator makes a new will.

After Death – With a Will

When a person dies, most of his or her assets are frozen. For example, the bank manager, land titles registry or stockbroker cannot accept instructions to deal with the assets until the court appoints either an executor, where there is a will, or an administrator, where there is no will. Some assets have named beneficiaries, such as insurance policies, pension benefits or property held in joint tenancy, and can be dealt with without court-ordered probate or administration.

Probate means the person died with a will and the will has been proven valid in court. The person appointed executor under the will can then act for the estate. If the person dies with no will, someone must apply to the court to be appointed the administrator under the provincial intestacy legislation. The administrator can then act on behalf of the estate.

Where there is a will, the executor does not have the power to act under the will until he obtains probate, called **letters of probate**. The executor must make an inventory of the assets of the estate, search for all wills, and file documents with the court probate registry. Provincial legislation requires that a person who makes a will file a notice of where it will be kept. The executor must file a notice of the results of his search for wills in the provincial registry. The executor must notify potential beneficiaries and all potential creditors of the estate. The executor must make a complete inventory of the assets of the deceased. Provincial probate fees are assessed based on this inventory. The executor receives a certificate that fees have been paid in order to allow him to deal with the assets. The executor also files documents relating to the granting of probate. This process is usually completed without the executor appearing before a judge; probate is granted based on the document files in the probate court registry.

When the executor has obtained letters probate, he becomes the legal owner of the assets of the estate for the benefit of the beneficiaries. This is a trust relationship, and he must deal with the assets in the manner authorized by the will. He must obtain legal title to assets, make claims owed to the estate and settle unpaid debts of the estate. The executor is personally responsible and can be sued if he does not act according to the directions of the will and in the interests of the beneficiaries. If the estate is fairly large the executor will usually hire the services of a lawyer, accountant or professional estate administrator. The executor himself is also entitled to a fee from the estate for his services.

The testator may not have provided adequately for his dependents under the will. Under provincial legislation, his dependents can apply for a court order to vary or change the bequests under the will. Several provinces also provide for applications to vary the will by common law spouses and illegitimate children.

Variation of a Will

Tataryn v. Tataryn Estate[8]

The testator and his wife were married for 43 years. The testator did not want to leave anything to one of his two sons and feared that if he left something to his wife she would leave it to that son. Through their joint efforts they amassed an estate held in the testator's name at the time of his death consisting of the house in which they lived, a rental property next door inherited from the testator's father and money in the bank. He made a will leaving his wife a life estate in the matrimonial house and making her the beneficiary of a discretionary trust of the income from the residue of the estate.

Under the BC *Wills Variation Act*, if the testator fails to make adequate provision for the proper maintenance and support of a surviving spouse and children, the court may order the provision from the estate that it considers "adequate, just and equitable in the circumstances." The Supreme Court of Canada ordered that the testator's wife get (a) title to the matrimonial home; (b) a life interest in the rental property; and (c) the entire residue of the estate after payment of the immediate gifts to the sons. Each son got an immediate gift of $10,000.

The first consideration in determining what is "adequate, just and equitable" in the circumstances of the case is the testator's legal responsibilities during his or her lifetime. The court should next consider the testator's moral duties toward spouse and children. Where priorities among conflicting claims must be established, claims which would have been recognized during the testator's life should generally take precedence over moral claims.

In this case the testator's only legal obligations during his life were toward his wife. Since the marriage was a long one and the wife contributed much to the assets she and her husband acquired, she would have been entitled to maintenance and a share in the family assets had the parties separated. The appellant's legal claims entitle her to at least half the estate and arguably to additional maintenance. Her moral claim to the funds set aside for old age is strong and indicates that an "adequate, just and equitable" provision for her requires giving her the bulk of the estate. The remaining moral claims are those of the two grown and independent sons, which were adequately met by the immediate gift awarded by the trial judge to each of them and a residuary interest in a portion of the property upon their mother's death.

After Death — Without a Will

If a person dies without a valid will, someone, usually a potential beneficiary, must apply to the court to administer the estate. The steps that must be taken and the documents filed in the court registry are similar to those in the application for probate. The duties of the administrator are similar to those of the executor. Once **letters of administration** are granted, the administrator distributes the proceeds of the estate according to rules under the provincial intestacy legislation.

Most intestacy rules provide that the estate goes to the surviving spouse. If there are children, the rules provide for an amount to go to the spouse and the remainder to be divided between the spouse and the children. If the children are minors, their share will be held in trust by the public trustee and the parent must apply for payments out of the trust to pay for their support. If the deceased has no spouse or children, the legislation provides how the estate will be divided among relatives. If there are no relatives, a government official applies to administer the estate and the assets go to the provincial government, called **escheat**.

Under provincial legislation a surviving common law spouse may have a claim to a portion of the estate if the couple lived together for sufficient time. Any children of the deceased, whether they were born during a formal marriage or not, claim equally; there is no distinction between legitimate and illegitimate children. The administrator must therefore take special care to locate all possible heirs to the estate.

Settling an Estate

The executor or administrator must settle all obligations of the estate, including paying government fees and taxes. The estate must pay income tax and capital gains tax covering the period up to the date of the testator's death. The estate must also pay income tax and capital gains tax on any interest earned or capital gains between the date of death and the date the assets are transferred to the beneficiaries. Also the estate must pay **probate fees**, which are a provincial government fee for probating or administering the estate. These taxes and fees are payable upon the death of the testator. In order to minimize taxes, many testators obtain professional advice in planning their estates.

CONCLUSION

Family law is an area of private law although it is heavily regulated by the state. It reflects the principles established in the common law, but as social norms have changed, legislators have modified and adapted the common law principles. With the decline in the influence of the church, it has been necessary for the state to recognize other family arrangements, particularly in those areas where the state ascribes certain social benefits based on family relationships. We will now consider an area that has seen relatively little state intervention. Parties to contracts in effect create laws for themselves, and for the most part the courts will not become involved unless there has been a breach in the legal agreements that the parties have taken upon themselves. Since contract law is the basis of most commercial relationships, our discussion of contract law introduces the important area of the laws relating to business activities.

QUESTIONS FOR DISCUSSION AND REVIEW

1. Both the federal and provincial governments have responsibility for marriage and family relations. Is this sharing of jurisdiction appropriate or the most efficient way of overseeing this area of the law?

2. Why is it necessary for the state to be involved in marriage, the most private of human relationships?

3. Does the state's recognition of common law marriages or same-sex marriages contribute to the breakdown of the moral fabric of the nation?

4. Consider the usefulness of prenuptial or separation agreements and suggest whether the courts should take these agreements into consideration when a couple divorces.

5. Outline the role and value that a mediation process might have in a marriage breakdown.

6. The grounds for divorce have changed markedly in the past two decades. Has this been a positive direction in the law?

7. Changes in the rules relating to the division of property have attempted to address some social problems. Outline them and decide whether they have been effective in solving the problems.

8. Proposed changes to the legislation seek to put the needs of children first when couples divorce. What is the purpose of these changes, and will they resolve societal problems?

9. When a valid will does not adequately provide for a deceased person's dependents, should they have the right to vary the terms of the will?

10. What function is served by the complex processes that an executor of a will is required to perform?

NOTES

1. Abella, Rosalie Silberman, in *Family Law in Canada: Directions*. Ottawa: Canadian Advisory Council on the Status of Women, 1985, p. 9.

2. *Peter v. Beblow*, [1993] 1 S.C.R. 980.

3. *Miron v. Trudel*, [1995] 2 S.C.R. 418.

4. *Egan v. Canada*, [1995] 2 S.C.R. 513.

5. *Willick v. Willick*, [1994] 3 S.C.R. 670.

6. *Gordon v. Goertz*, [1996] 2 S.C.R. 27.

7. *Moge v. Moge*, [1992] 3 S.C.R. 813.

8. *Tataryn v. Tataryn Estate*, [1994] 2 S.C.R. 807.

FURTHER READING

Banfield, Jane, ed. *Readings in Law and Society*, Chapter 12.

Cochrane, Michael. *The Everyday Guide to Canadian Family Law*. Scarborough, Ont.: Prentice Hall Canada Inc., 1991.

Kronby, Malcolm C. *Canadian Family Law*, 5th ed. Toronto: Stoddart, 1991.

Minookin, Robert H. *In the Interest of Children*. New York: W. H. Freeman, 1985.

Syrtash, John. *Religion and Culture in Canadian Family Law*. Toronto: Butterworths, 1992.

Wilson, Jeffery and Mary Tomlinson. *Children and the Law*, 2nd ed. Toronto: Butterworths, 1986.

Wolfson, Lorne H. *The New Family Law*. Toronto: Random House, 1987.

Chapter

CONTRACT LAW

> The law of contract is the foundation of human
> freedom and society: stability of possession, its
> transference by consent, and the performance of
> promises. It is on the strict observance of those
> three laws that the peace, and security of human
> society depend.
>
> David Hume, *A Treatise of Human Nature*

When people enter into agreements with each other, making commitments upon which they
rely, complex social and legal relationships are established. A very important area of concern for Canadian legal institutions is enforcing those obligations and ordering compensation when they are breached. When the courts are willing to recognize and enforce such
agreements, they are referred to as contracts, and the legal rules developed to deal with
them are referred to as contract law. A thorough understanding of contract law is important not only for business people, but also for anyone participating in Canadian society.
Every time you purchase groceries, have a meal at a restaurant, buy a house or car, take a bus
or buy a newspaper, you have entered into a contract, and a web of rules setting out your rights
and responsibilities under that contract come into operation.

  When they are first exposed to the study of contract law, many people think that a contract is a written document that binds them when they sign it. While that is partially true, the
heart of the contract is the agreement or consensus reached between the parties. This consensus
may or may not be embodied in a written document. A handshake or a nod of the head may
still result in a legally binding agreement between the parties. In fact, a contract can be im-

plied from the conduct of the parties and the surrounding circumstances, and if one of the parties fails to perform as required, the victim may have the right to seek remedies in the courts.

Contracts, then, are legally enforceable agreements in which the parties have defined their legal rights and responsibilities. They have, in effect, created a world of law that is unlike other areas, such as torts or criminal law, where general rules of conduct are imposed. The modern law of contract was developed in an atmosphere where it was generally felt that people should be free to arrange their own affairs and that the economy works best when the courts interfere as little as possible. The courts are still reluctant to interfere with the content of an agreement between parties unless it is for some illegal purpose, like drug-dealing. While it is not generally their role to determine the fairness or appropriateness of the bargain struck, rather to enforce the clear intention of the parties, the courts are now showing a greater willingness to interfere when faced with unfair or unconscionable contracts. A considerable body of consumer protection law has been developed to protect people who are taken advantage of by unscrupulous merchants, but that aside, the role of the courts in contract law is to give effect to the intention of the parties, as embodied in the agreement between them.

INGREDIENTS OF A CONTRACT

Consensus

The most important qualification is that a consensus must be reached between the parties. It forms the foundation upon which the agreement is based. It is often said that there must be a meeting of the minds between the parties to a contract. That is somewhat misleading because it is clear that, in determining whether a contract exists or not, the courts are less concerned with what was actually in each party's mind or the degree of shared understanding between the parties than with what they should have understood if they had been reasonably prudent and careful in their dealings. This is the reasonable person test, which was discussed in prior chapters.

The courts will apply this test to prevent a person escaping from a contract by claiming not to have read it or not to have understood it. Failure to read the contract or misunderstanding its contents, when the meaning would be clear to others, will not provide an excuse to avoid the obligations set out in the agreement. The purpose of the law of contracts is to protect the reasonable expectations of the parties. That can only be done when the attention of the courts is directed to what the parties should have been doing, using some outside objective test such as the reasonable person test, rather than responding to the weaknesses and foibles of each individual party.

Offer

An agreement is reached when one party makes an **offer** that the other party accepts. The best way to understand the offer is to think of it as the contract prior to acceptance. It is put forward by the offeror, and sets out all the important terms of the potential agreement. If the offeree (the person to whom the offer is being made) is agreeable, he accepts, and at that point there is a contract between them with the terms as set out in the offer. The **acceptance** indicates that those terms and conditions are acceptable to the offeree, and that he is willing to be bound by them. The offer contains the terms of the agreement; the acceptance merely indicates a willingness to be bound.

The offer must contain all of the important terms of the contract. If important terms are left out, it doesn't qualify as an offer. If Sung were to say, "I will paint your house," and Henri were to say, "I accept," there would be no contract. There has been no agreement as to price, and without such an important term, there can be no contract. Similarly, if Sung were to say, "I will paint your house for $700, terms of payment to be arranged later," and Henri were to reply, "I accept," there would still be no contract because there is clearly more to be negotiated. A contract to enter into a contract is not binding.

Invitation to Treat

It must be emphasized that when an offer has been put forward by one of the parties, the relationship between them is reasonably advanced. Before that stage is reached, however, attempts are often made to attract the attention of the other party or to invite him to enter into negotiations. Advertisements in newspapers designed to attract customers, displays in store windows, even goods set out on the shelves in self-service stores are examples of such attempts. They are referred to as invitations to treat and must be distinguished from offers. Such an invitation has no legal effect. Only when direct dealings between the parties take place that result in one of them making an offer that the other accepts will binding contractual obligations result. Even when goods are set out in a self-service store, clearly priced and intended to be picked up by the customer and taken to the cashier, the display of the goods has been held by the court to be only an invitation to treat, not an offer.[1] Although the offer is usually stated orally or in writing, it may also be inferred from the conduct of the parties. In an auction, for instance, when the auctioneer says, "Do I hear fifty dollars?" he is merely inviting customers to make an offer. When the customer nods or gives some other indication of a willingness to do so, his conduct implies he is making an offer. When the auctioneer is satisfied that the highest offer has been made, he accepts it by declaring the item, "Sold!"

End of an Offer

When a person states that her offer will be open for a specific period of time, "I'll give you two days to let me know," the offeror is not bound by that promise. She can change her mind, and if she does, her action is referred to as a **revocation** of the offer. Revocation causes the offer to lapse or disappear, but the revocation is not effective until it has been communicated to the other party.[2] The offeror then must be careful to let the offeree know that she has changed her mind. The offer remains open and capable of being accepted until the other party knows of the revocation. If Jean were to offer to sell Miguel her car for $500 and to give him five days to think about it, she would be perfectly free to sell the car to Pierre the next day if she wanted to. But before doing so, she would have to let Miguel know she had changed her mind. If Jean failed to do this and Miguel were to accept within the five-day period, Jean would be in the difficult position of being bound in contract to sell her car to both Miguel and Pierre.

An offer will also come to an end when the offeree rejects it or makes a **counteroffer**. In the example above, if Miguel had replied, "I'll give you $450," and Jean said "No," it would then no longer be open for Miguel to accept the $500 offer. That offer ended with the counteroffer. If Miguel wanted to, he could then make an offer to purchase the car for $500, and Jean would be free to accept if she wanted to.

The offer also will come to an end when a specified time has elapsed. When no time limit within which the offer must be accepted is specified, it remains open for a **reasonable time**, based on the nature of the goods and other factors in the relationship between the parties. The death or insanity of the offeror also causes the offer to end.

Revocation of an Offer

Mlodinska et al. v. Malicki et al.[3]

The facts of this case arose during a trial. The parties had been negotiating a settlement when the defendant made an offer and the plaintiff responded with a higher demand. The defendant and his lawyer got together in another room and upon receiving instructions to withdraw the offer, the defendant wrote a letter to that effect and then both walked back into the courtroom. On the way to his seat the defendant walked toward the plaintiff holding up his thumb and finger in a circle and said, "Now it's zero." He then handed the plaintiff's lawyer the letter withdrawing his offer. As he did so, the plaintiff's lawyer handed him a note accepting the offer. The judge had to decide whether there was a binding contract or not.

After some deliberation about the unseemly conduct of the two parties and their haste to get their pieces of paper to each other, the judge found that the offer of the defendant had clearly been revoked before the letter of acceptance was proffered. Therefore, there was no offer to be accepted when the lawyer for the plaintiff purported to do so. This illustrates the effect that the communication of a revocation has upon an existing offer even if the revocation is communicated only a split second before the acceptance.

Acceptance

Acceptance is quite simple and involves only an indication on the part of the offeree that she is willing to be bound by the terms set out in the offer. The only requirements are that the acceptance be unqualified and that it be communicated to the person who made the offer. In the example above, if Miguel had said, "I accept your offer to sell your car to me for $500, providing you put on new tires," that is not an acceptance at all. Rather, it is a counteroffer. The acceptance must be a clear unqualified indication of a willingness to be bound by the terms set out in the offer.

Since the contract does not come into existence until the acceptance and the acceptance is not effective until the offeror knows of it, both the place of the contract and the time that it comes into existence are determined by where and when the offeror hears of the acceptance. If Jean were in Calgary and offered by telephone to sell her car for $500 to Miguel in Montreal, and he responded, "I accept," but for some reason the line went dead, preventing Jean from hearing the acceptance, there would be no contract. If she did hear the acceptance, she would hear it in Calgary, and so the place that the contract was made would be Calgary, not Montreal. The place can be of considerable importance when it has to be determined which jurisdiction applies to the contract.

Post Box Rule

There is an important exception to the general rule that an acceptance is not effective until it has been communicated. When slower means of communication are being used, such as the post, and where it is appropriate to respond by mail, the acceptance is deemed to be effective at the time and place it is posted. This principle is referred to as the **post box rule**. In the example above, if Jean in Calgary had posted the offer to sell her car to Miguel in Montreal, who then accepted by mail, the contract would have been created at the time the acceptance was posted in Montreal. The place of formation of the contract would also be Montreal, since that was where the acceptance was posted.

The same principle applies to acceptance by telegraph, but likely not to fax or other forms of electronic communication. The post box rule avoids many uncertainties that would result for business people if the general rule requiring notification of the acceptance were applied to these slower means of communication. It must always be remembered, however, that the post box rule only applies where it is reasonable to respond and send the acceptance by mail. When the subject matter of the contract indicates otherwise (e.g., when perishable goods are involved) or when the offeror directs otherwise, the post box rule will not apply, and an acceptance sent by mail will only be effective when and where received. It should also be noted that, since the post box rule is an exception to the general rule requiring notice of an acceptance, it only applies when an acceptance is involved. The post box rule does not apply to other forms of communication between the parties, such as a letter of revocation, which must be received before it will be effective.

Consideration

The second element that must be present for a contract to exist is consideration. Contract law is based on the concept of bargaining, the heart of which is the requirement that both parties to an agreement pay a price and that both parties receive a benefit. Consideration, therefore, is the price that each party agrees to pay for the promise of the other party to the agreement. Price, as it is used here, is not limited to a payment of money, but rather refers to anything of value being exchanged for the promise of the other party. This exchange of consideration involves both parties changing their legal positions pursuant to the agreement. When one person agrees to sell her car to the other for $500, a change in legal positions has taken place. Both parties are now committed to do something that they were not committed to do before they entered into the contract. Before the promise is made, there is no obligation on the owner of the vehicle to transfer the car to the other party. After the promise, there is. Similarly, after the agreement is made, there is an obligation on the purchaser to pay the $500. Both parties have paid a price, in that they have changed their legal position, and so there is consideration present.

Some rules about the requirement of consideration in contract law follow.

1. A gratuitous promise is unenforceable.

A gratuitous promise is a one-sided promise, in which only one of the parties commits to do something; for example, "I'll give you a fur coat for your birthday." Such a promise is unenforceable, since consideration flows in only one direction. Although there is no obligation to give the gift, once it has been given, title to the gift transfers and the giver cannot legally demand its return. Gratuitous promises can, however, be made enforceable by affixing a seal to the document containing the agreement. The use of the seal predates the development of contract law, and in those days it was the method of creating legally binding obligations. This principle has been incorporated into the law of contract today, and so when a seal is placed on a document by the person to be bound by it, the question of whether or not there is consideration is simply not asked.

The fact that a promise is one-sided is not always apparent. When a person is already legally obligated to do a job and demands more before finishing, there is no legal obligation to pay the extra amount even when this is agreed to by both parties. For example, if a painter agrees to paint a person's house for $300 and then demands $100 more half-way through to finish the job, even if the owner of the property agrees to pay the extra $100, the painter cannot sue to force the owner to pay. It may appear that the owner of the property has received something for his promise to pay the extra, but in fact the legal position of the painter has not changed. Before he extracted the promise to pay the extra $100, he was legally obligated to finish painting the house, and after the promise was made, his position had not changed. As a result, there is no legal obligation on the owner to pay the extra. A similar situation arises when a person is owed a debt and agrees to take less in full satisfaction for it. If Frank owed Hans $5 000 and persuaded him to take $3 000 as full payment, there would be no benefit flowing to Hans other than getting part of what he is already owed. Therefore, this agreement to take less, because of the failure of consideration, should not be binding. In fact, most jurisdictions in Canada have passed statutes declaring that where a creditor agrees to take less in full satisfaction of a debt, and in fact does take less (the money is actually paid), the creditor cannot then turn around and sue for the difference. This is inconsistent with the principle that consideration is required, but it is imposed on our legal system by legislation and so overrides this common law principle of contract law.

2. Consideration must be specific.

It is not sufficient for a person to say, "I'll pay you something for your car," or "I'll pay you some interest on the money I owe you." The amount to be paid must be specific: "I'll give you $500 for your car," or "I'll pay you 10 per cent interest on the money I owe you." It is possible, however, to tie the price to some outside measure and still have it valid. For example, when shares being sold on the open market are involved, the agreement to pay a price for those shares at some future date, based on the price of those shares as quoted on the Toronto Stock Exchange on that day, may be sufficiently definite to satisfy the requirement for specific consideration. The price is fixed, at least in the sense that it will not be the subject of further negotiations between the parties. Care must be taken to leave no uncertainty in such a case. In the example given here, there would be a problem in determining whether the parties intended the price to be based on the quoted asking price that day or on the price for which the shares were being sold, and then whether the opening price or the closing price was to be used.

3. Consideration must have some value.

If one person were to agree to pay $500 per month to another in exchange for "love and affection," that would not have a specific value. In the case of White v. Bluett[4] a father agreed to pay his son a specific sum if the son would stop bothering him. The son's promise was held by the court to have no intrinsic value, and so there was no binding contract. So long as the promise has some intrinsic value, however, the courts will not interfere in the bargaining process. If you want to sell your brand-new Rolls-Royce for $75, you are perfectly at liberty to do so. If you enter into a contract to do that, the contract will be binding. The court will not protect a fool from his folly. However, when a transaction is as obviously one-sided as this one, it may be an indication of some other problem, such as fraud, duress, feeble-mindedness or unconscionability, which would call the validity of the contract into question.

Generally when a person agrees to do something for another and no specific consideration has been agreed to, there is no obligation to pay. It is common practice, however, to request services without agreeing to any specific payment ahead of time. Much difficulty and confusion in the business world would result if these arrangements were not binding on the parties, and so the principle of *quantum meruit* has been developed. When services are requested without agreement on a specific price and those services are performed, there is a legal obligation to pay a reasonable price. When you take your car into a mechanic and say, "Fix it," even though you have not agreed to any price, you are obligated to pay a reasonable amount for the services you have requested. The *Sale Of Goods Acts* in most provinces have similar provisions, requiring a reasonable price to be paid for goods sold when no specific price has been agreed on.

4. The consideration must be both legal and possible.

An agreement in which someone agrees to perform an illegal act is not binding. For example, if Rocky agrees to break George's leg in exchange for a $500 payment from Frank, there is no contract. The act of breaking a person's leg is illegal, and illegal consideration is no consideration at all.

Not only does the promise have to be legal, it must also be possible. If a psychic were to promise to turn lead into gold for $10 000 or to bring Uncle Joe back from the dead, such an agreement would not be legally enforceable since those actions are not possible (at least in the eyes of the law).

5. Consideration may be present or future, but not past.

Since consideration involves the exchange of commitments between parties, both parties must be required to do something by the agreement. This requirement is satisfied when both parties promise to do some future act — for example, "I'll paint your house next week for $500." This is future consideration. Even when the consideration is exchanged at the time of the agreement, there is an exchange of commitments. When I hand you $500 and you give me your car, it is called present consideration. But when some act has already been done and then the benefited party agrees to do something in return out of gratitude, there is no bargain and no exchange of commitments because the benefit has already been received. For example, if a person rescued from drowning promises to pay the rescuer $500, there would be no resulting obligation to pay. At the time the promise is made the rescue has already taken place. The rescuer is promising to do nothing in exchange for getting the $500. This is past consideration, and "past consideration is no consideration."

A one-sided promise may have legal consequences even when there is no consideration to support it. If the person relying on it suffers a loss, the victim of the broken promise is not permitted to sue. There is no contract, and so there can be no obligation to honour the promise. The victim may, however, be permitted to raise that promise as a defence in an action being brought against him by the promise-breaker. This is referred to as **equitable or promissory estoppel** and it only rarely arises. Suppose James promised to give Anna a new boat for her birthday, and, in anticipation, she rented moorage from Bert. If James changed his mind, Anna could not successfully sue James for the cost of the moorage. There is no contract. But if James were the one renting the moorage to Anna, and insisted on being paid for it even though he had changed his mind about giving her the boat, Anna could refuse to pay, using James's failed promise as a defence. In Canada, James would be estopped, or prevented, from enforcing the claim for moorage because of the dishonoured promise. The expression that promissory estoppel can be used "as a shield but not as a sword" applies in Canada as well as England.

Capacity

Certain people in our society are vulnerable and are therefore in need of special protection. Thus, their freedom to bargain and enter into legally binding contracts has been limited or completely eliminated.

Infants

Infants are people under the age of majority (the specific age varies from province to province, and at common law was 21). Children's capacity to enter into contracts is restricted. The infant is free to enter into contracts, but the adult she is dealing with cannot enforce that contract against her. Thus, if an infant were to purchase a stereo from Ace Stereo Ltd., agreeing to make monthly payments, the merchant could not successfully sue her if she failed to make the payments. The infant, of course, would not be able to keep the stereo. If the infant did wish to go through with the agreement, however, the adult is bound by the contract. When the contract has been performed by both parties, the courts are reluctant to interfere even when an infant is involved. So in the example above, had the infant paid cash, the courts would not help her to get her money back. Once the contract has been performed, the courts will only get involved when there is clear evidence that the infant has been cheated.

There are some types of contracts that are binding even on infants. When an infant contracts to purchase food, clothing, and other **"necessaries,"** she is bound by the agreement and can be sued if she fails to honour the contract. The item must be a true necessary, however. The question is not just whether food or clothing is involved, but also whether the infant was in need. If she has three coats at home in the closet, the one she is buying is likely not a necessary. Infants are also bound by their contracts for **beneficial contracts of service**. These are contracts such as an agreement to act as an apprentice for a period of time. For such contracts to be binding, they must be clearly for the benefit of the infant. In British Columbia, all contracts with infants are unenforceable.[5] The courts will not force an infant to honour a contract that she has entered into, even if it deals with a necessary or a beneficial contract of service. Once the infant has performed her side of the agreement, however, the courts will not help her to get out of it. If this causes an unfair result for either the infant or the adult, the victim can apply to the court for relief. In British Columbia the court has tremendous power under this legislation to redress unfair results. Also, in BC some infants' contracts, such as student loans, are made specifically enforceable by statute.

Insanity

In contract law, insane people are also given protection in their dealings with others. For a person to escape a contract on the basis of insanity, he (or his representative) must establish two things to the court's satisfaction. He must first prove that he was so insane that he didn't understand the nature of the agreement he entered into. If a person thinks he is Napoleon and is selling his horse when in fact he is selling his car, this belief is sufficient to amount to insanity because he is not capable of understanding the nature of what he is doing.

In addition, in order to escape the contract, the insane person must show that the party he was dealing with knew or ought to have known of his insanity. When a person is obviously insane, this is not a problem, but quite often an insane person can appear normal to other people. When the person claiming insanity was insane at the time he entered into the agreement, and the other party did not know it and there was nothing in the situation to alert him to the problem, the contract will still be binding despite the insanity.

Drunkenness and other forms of intoxication are treated in the same way as insanity. The person trying to escape the contract must have been so intoxicated by drugs or alcohol that he didn't understand the nature of the agreement, and, secondly, he must show that the person he was dealing with knew or should have known he was intoxicated. In any case where insanity or intoxication is involved, there is an obligation on the person wishing to escape the contract to repudiate the agreement within a reasonable time after regaining his sanity or becoming sober. When a person in an intoxicated state purchases 5 000 shares in a company and on becoming sober realizes what he has done, he is required to repudiate right away and not to wait and see if the shares go up or down in value first.

Others

There are a number of other people and entities in our society that have limited capacity to enter into contracts. There are still remnants of the protective provisions directed at Native people in place, and so even today, Status Indians living on reserves have their capacity to deal with their property limited to some extent.[6] Enemy aliens (those who are nationals of a country with which Canada is at war) also have limited capacity to enter into contracts during the course of that war. Foreign diplomats representing their countries have certain rights that protect them against prosecution in Canada. Even in a civil action it may be difficult, if not impossible, to enforce a judgment against them or their families.

Historically, in some Canadian provinces, corporations had limited capacity to contract as well. Their power to contract was limited to whatever they were authorized to do in their incorporating documents. In most jurisdictions these limitations have been removed, and today such corporations are said to have all the power of a natural person. Crown corporations (corporations owned by government) and any other corporation that has been created by a special act of parliament may have limited capacity, depending on the statute creating them. Whenever people deal with such a body, they should check the legislation to make sure that those they are dealing with have the power to bind the corporation as agents, and that the corporation has the capacity to be involved in the activity. Bankrupts who have not yet been discharged by the courts also have their power to enter into contracts restricted, and trade unions can only contract in matters relating to their trade union activities.

Legality (Public Policy)

In order for an agreement to qualify as a contract, the subject matter must be legal. When a person agrees to break someone's leg in exchange for $5 000 and does so, he will not be able to enforce the claim for the $5 000 in court. The term legality, as it is used here, however, is somewhat misleading. At common law, agreements to perform certain types of acts have been declared to be against public policy, and while the acts involved are not illegal as such, contracts dealing with these activities are treated as if there is no contract. The selling of sexual favours for money (prostitution) is not against the law in Canada, but an agreement to do so is against public policy and so there is no legally enforceable contract.

When an activity has been made unlawful by statute, the legislation must be examined to determine the effect of its breach; otherwise, the offending provision is usually void. The whole agreement may not be void, just the part that is offensive. Illegal contracts or those that are against public policy fall into the following categories:

- contracts to commit a crime or tort;
- contracts involving immoral acts, such as prostitution;
- contracts to obstruct justice, such as bribing witnesses;
- contracts that injure the state, such as selling steel to a nation with which Canada is at war;
- contracts to promote litigation, such as paying a person to sue someone else;
- contracts injuring public service, such as bribing a politician to vote a certain way; and
- contracts related to unlicensed gambling, such as unapproved lotteries.

Illegal Contract

Boyd v. Newton[7]

This was a negligence claim that involved the Insurance Corporation of British Columbia. The plaintiff, Boyd, was trafficking in marijuana. He hung out at a pool hall in Coquitlam and had a stash of drugs on top of a nearby pinball machine. Newton approached him to purchase some of the drug. Newton told him he had his money outside in his car. Newton got in the passenger side of the car and told Boyd to go around to the driver's side to get the money from him. As Boyd began to do so Newton pushed him away and the driver drove off. Boyd grabbed Newton by the coat and held onto the door frame as the car sped away. Boyd was dragged down the street and suffered injury.

The court held that because this injury took place in the process of committing an illegal act, the insurer had no obligation to pay. "No court will lend its aid to a man who founds his action upon an immoral or illegal act." This case illustrates a principle upon which contract law is based; *ex turpi causa* means that from a base (or illegal) matter no action can arise.

Restraint of Trade

Perhaps the most significant areas against public policy today are contracts that restrict competition or that unreasonably restrain trade. When merchants get together and fix prices so one will not undersell the other, they have made an agreement to restrict competition. Such an agreement where the effect is to unduly restrain trade is not only void, but also is subject to prosecution under the federal *Competition Act*.[8] Generally, a relatively free market system in which merchants compete with each other is considered best in our society. There are, however, some situations where such competition is not desirable. When one merchant sells a business to another, a large part of the purchase price is often paid for the "good will" of the business. Good will is that part of the business that is dependent on the relationship and confidence that has been developed between the merchant and his customers. If the seller were free to open another similar business in the same area competing with the purchaser, the good will would likely be made valueless. In such circumstances, it is necessary to include a clause in the sales contract that prohibits the seller from opening a competing business, and so long as the clause is reasonable and does not go further than is necessary to protect the value of the business sold, it is valid.

Insurance

Finally, insurance agreements that bear some similarity to wagers are only valid if they will not result in a windfall. The insured must be able to demonstrate that he will lose something of value if the insured-against event takes place. Such insurance agreements are attempts to spread risk of loss, and so such risk of loss (called an insurable interest) must be demonstrated for the contract to be valid. When I insure my house against fire, I can demonstrate an insurable interest because, if the fire takes place, I will lose my house. But if I insure your house, that is just a wager, since I lose nothing from its destruction but will profit from the insurance. Such an agreement is void.

Intention

The last element that must be present for a contract to exist is that the parties must have intended legal consequences to follow from their agreement. When a woman asks a friend to dinner and later has to cancel, she would be shocked if her friend sued for breach of contract. When a parent promises an allowance to a child and fails to pay, the parent would not expect to be sued. When such domestic relationships are involved, there is a presumption that there was no intention to be legally bound, and the parties would have to show persuasive evidence to convince the court that there was such an intention. Where commercial transactions are involved, just the opposite is the case. The court presumes there is an intention to be legally bound, and the parties would have to present evidence to show a different intent. Such evidence might be a statement included in the written agreement that there was no intention to be legally bound.

In situations where exaggeration might be involved, the court applies the reasonable person test to determine whether the parties should have taken the promise seriously. If Dominic were to offer his friend Freida $1 million if she were to complete a certain billiard shot successfully, and she did it, would Dominic have to pay? A court, applying the reasonable person test, would likely say no. When sellers exaggerate the quality or features of their products, the same test is applied to determine whether they should be held to what they have said. In *Carlill* v. *Carbolic Smoke Ball Co.*[9] an English company advertised that the use of their product would prevent catching the flu. They stated that if the user became ill with the flu after the proper use of their product, they would pay £100 and that they had deposited that amount of money in a bank to indicate their sincerity. When Mrs. Carlill caught the flu after using the product, she demanded payment. The court held that a reasonable person would have thought that the company was serious, and so it had to pay.

Writing

Although, as a rule, an oral agreement is every bit as binding as a written one, in the seventeenth century the *Statute of Frauds* was passed to require that contracts dealing with certain types of subject matter be evidenced in writing before a court would enforce them. This statute caused as many problems as it solved. The *Statute of Frauds* or its equivalent, with some important variations, is in place in most Canadian provinces today. Traditionally, the Statute requires the following types of contracts to be evidenced by writing:

1. Contracts that by their nature must be performed beyond one year from when they are made; for example, if John agrees in May 1990 to build a house for Sue, but the job is not to start until July 1991.

2. Contracts dealing with interests in land; for example, where Sue agrees to sell John her house or a right of way across her land. Only interests in land are covered, such as sale, lease, easements, and so forth. Contracts to do work on the land need not be evidenced in writing.

3. Guarantees and indemnities are promises by one person to be responsible for the debts of another. When the promise is contingent on the debtor's failure to pay, it is called a guarantee. When the obligation to pay coexists with that of the debtor, the obligation is called an indemnity — for example, "I'll see that you get paid." This is often referred to as co-signing a debt. In most provinces it is only the guarantee that has to be evidenced in writing. In BC, both the guaranty and indemnity require writing.

4. Promises in consideration of marriage. This is not the engagement itself; an example of such a promise would be if a father agreed to give the couple a house if they got married.

5. If an executor (a person appointed in a will to look after the affairs of a person after that person's death) promises to pay any debts owed by the estate out of his own pocket, the promise must be evidenced in writing to be enforceable.

6. Other statutes often require matters to be in writing to be enforceable. For example, in many jurisdictions the *Sale of Goods Act* requires that the sale of goods over a certain value be evidenced in writing.

This is not necessarily a requirement that the contract itself be in writing, only that there be some written evidence indicating the important terms of the contract and signed by the defendant. If there is no evidence in writing and it falls into one of the above categories, the contract is not enforceable in the courts. The contract is valid, and if it is performed by the parties, the courts will do nothing to help them undo it, such as ordering the return of money paid. On the other hand, if it is not yet performed, the courts will not force the parties to live up to its terms or order compensation for failure to do so. Where a father orally promises to pay a creditor if his son fails to pay (a guarantee), the court will not order payment because there is no evidence in writing. But if the father does pay, the court will not assist him to get his money back.

Significant changes have been made to the *Statute of Frauds* in many jurisdictions. In Manitoba it has been repealed altogether. In BC the few remaining provisions have been incorporated into the *Law and Equity Act*.

FACTORS AFFECTING THE CONTRACTUAL RELATIONSHIP

Mistake

One of the problems that can arise when the contract is drawn up is a misunderstanding about the terms of the agreement. If this misunderstanding is serious enough, there is no consensus and no contract. Generally speaking, there are three types of mistakes that can take place. A **shared mistake** is when both parties are under the same misapprehension about some aspect of the agreement or the existence of the subject matter. If Jean enters into a contract to sell Bill the contents of a ship that is travelling from Japan to Vancouver and, unknown to both parties, the ship sank in a storm half an hour prior to the creation of the agreement, this is a shared mistake about the subject matter, and with such a serious mistake the contract would be void. Such a shared mistake would, however, have to be about some vital aspect of the subject, not some minor error.

Another example occurs when a term is written down incorrectly. If Jacques agrees to sell Sonia his house for $250 000 and the agreement is written down by a secretary as $25 000, if the court is satisfied that the higher figure represents the true agreement between the parties, it will correct the written agreement by adding the missing zero. The process of correcting the written document is referred to as **rectification**.

The second kind of mistake involves a **misunderstanding** between the parties about what the terms of an agreement mean. The courts apply a reasonable person test to determine which understanding of the agreement is most reasonable and enforce it. If Joe agrees to sell Surjeet his car for $1 000, and Joe has in mind his 1982 Ford Escort while Surjeet thinks she is purchasing Joe's other car, which is a 1986 Toyota, the courts will look at the circumstances to determine which understanding is more reasonable. If the parties were standing beside the Escort at the time the agreement was made, the court will likely choose that interpretation. When both interpretations of the contract are equally reasonable, so that no consensus has been reached between the parties, then the contract is void.

The third type of mistake that can take place is a **one-sided mistake**. It occurs when a person makes some error about the subject matter or contents of the agreement, and the other person knows he is making that error and does nothing to correct it. So long as the other person does not actively mislead and thus contribute to the error, the person making the mistake has no remedy at common law. *Caveat emptor*, or "let the buyer beware," is the operative principle in such a situation. If a person misleads himself, that is his own problem. Only where there is a special relationship of trust where one party is clearly relying on the other to disclose information, as is the case with insurance, would there be an obligation to disclose such errors.

Misrepresentation

When a person is persuaded to enter into a contract by the false or misleading statements of another, that is an actionable misrepresentation even when it does not become part of the contract. If Jones is persuaded to purchase a certain automobile because it will get high gas mileage, and it turns out after the purchase that it gets very poor gas mileage, this is an actionable misrepresentation. If the person making the misleading statement did not believe it was true, the misrepresentation is fraudulent and the victim has two options. Provided the victim has been induced to enter the agreement by the misleading statement, he can rescind the contract and/or sue for damages.

Rescission is an order requested from the court to undo the contract. Both parties are put back in their original positions; in the example above, rescission would result in the return of the car to the dealer and the return of the purchase price to the purchaser. **Damages** are a court order for a monetary payment intended to compensate the victim for any losses he has suffered. If the party making the misleading statement honestly believes what he is saying, this is innocent misrepresentation and the only remedy available is rescission. Rescission in some circumstances may be inappropriate or unavailable, and then there is no remedy for innocent misrepresentation.

If the car in the example above had been sold to some third party or destroyed, rescission would be unavailable. In these circumstances, to receive a remedy the victim must show fraud. In more recent times, Canadian courts have also been willing to award damages if the misleading statement was made negligently, even though the person making it believed it was true. If the misleading statement has been incorporated into the contract as a term, instead of merely being used to persuade someone to enter the contract, the appropriate course of action for the victim is to sue for breach of contract. All of the remedies for breach discussed below will be available. Where Frank sells his car and the agreement states that it is a 1986 Ford Thunderbird when in fact it is a 1984 Thunderbird, the purchaser can sue him for breach of contract and damages, since what he has delivered is not what he contracted to deliver. This is simple breach of contract, and there is no need to deal with the principles of misrepresentation.

Misrepresentation

Beer et al. v. Townsgate I Ltd.[10]

This case involved the sale of a number of luxury condominium units in Ontario. Before they were completed the developers promoted the units very enthusiastically and the first units were sold in an atmosphere of extreme frenzy. The trial judge described it as follows. "A picture emerges of anxious people waiting in long lines for up to seven hours in frigid cold and then up to three hours in a hot, crowded sales pavilion before seeing an agent, and of harried realtors unable to handle the crowds, affecting a demeanour sadly lacking in courtesy or candor." Under these circumstances a number of purchasers signed agreements and put deposits down on the property of up to $40 000. This was done considerably in advance (up to two years) of the date that they could take possession of their property. In the intervening time the market waned and 10 months after the grand opening a third of the suites hadn't been sold and were offered at a reduced price, making the original buyers extremely unhappy.

Several of the original purchasers challenged the sales, but two of them who were of limited education and experience are parties in this case. It was clear from the facts that these purchasers relied on the representations of the vendors, who had created a false sense of scarcity and told the purchasers that their purchases were risk-free. Because of this misrepresentation, the purchasers were able to rescind the contract regardless of the provision in the contract stating that there were "no representations, warranties, collateral agreements, or conditions affecting the agreement or the real property or supported thereby other than those expressed herein in writing." The Court of Appeal of Ontario held that the clause had not been properly brought to the purchasers' attention and therefore was not binding on them and they should have their deposits returned. The court did not deal with the problem of whether this was innocent or fraudulent misrepresentation. It wasn't necessary since the remedy being sought was rescission of the contract.

Another way the wrongful conduct of one of the parties to the contract may affect its validity is through the use of duress or undue influence. Duress involves making threats of violence, imprisonment or prosecution to force someone to enter into an agreement. If Joan threatens to reveal some dark secrets about Bob's past that could result in his imprisonment if he fails to sign an agreement to sell his brand-new Toyota to her for $50, it is duress. Undue influence deprives another of his free will to enter into a contract, through some special dominating influence resulting from a close relationship between the parties. When certain types of relationships are involved, the courts will presume undue influence. Contracts between doctors and their patients, parents and their children, a clergyman and parishioner, a husband and wife, and lawyers and their clients are presumed to be made under undue influence. A person in such a relationship can avoid the court finding undue influence by making sure that the other party gets independent legal advice before entering the agreement.

Undue Influence

Rochdale Credit Union Ltd. v. Barney[11]

This case is an example of undue influence with a twist. A solicitor found himself in financial difficulty and applied to a credit union for a loan. He persuaded his friend and client, Mr. Barney, to guarantee that loan. The solicitor also acted as the lawyer for the parties — the credit union and Mr. Barney — in this transaction. At no time in his relationship with the solicitor was Mr. Barney aware of his financial difficulties, and although the credit union was aware of the lawyer's problems, it didn't bother to tell Mr. Barney either. The solicitor then died, leaving no assets, and the credit union demanded that Mr. Barney honour the guarantee he had signed.

The court found that "where the relationship of solicitor and client exists and the solicitor stands to gain an advantage for himself at the expense of the client, a presumption of undue influence arises." The court went on to explain that because the solicitor was acting on behalf of the credit union in this case, it was responsible for the solicitor's conduct. The officer representing the credit union had a duty to warn the appellant of the financial risk involved in the guarantee and failed to do so. The officials of the credit union also failed to advise Mr. Barney to get independent legal advice. The lawyer for the credit union in this action argued that there was no evidence of the existence of undue influence. The response of the court was that there didn't have to be. Undue influence was presumed because of the relationship of solicitor/client. It was clear, however, that this presumption could have been overcome had Barney been advised to get independent legal advice.

Privity

In the case of *Donoghue v. Stevenson*[12] a woman went to a pub with a friend who bought her a ginger beer. The opaque bottle was brought to their table unopened. Mrs. Donoghue consumed a portion of the contents, and when she poured out the rest, part of a decomposed snail was discovered. She became seriously ill. Her problem was to determine who she could sue for compensation. Had she purchased the ginger beer herself, there is no doubt that she could have successfully sued the seller for breach of contract. Because it was purchased by her friend, however, there was no contract between her and the pub, and so she had to turn to the manufacturer and sue for the tort of negligence. She could not sue the manufacturer or the pub for breach of contract because she was not party to any contract with them. This case illustrates the principle of privity of contract. When two people enter into a contract, they create a world of law unto themselves. Rights and obligations cannot be bestowed on outsiders. There are, however, many important exceptions to this privity of contract rule.

Contracts dealing with interests in land are exceptions to the privity rule. The rights associated with land may be created initially by contract, but they are then said to attach to and run with the land. If Helena buys a house from Sam and there is a tenant with a two-year lease in the house, the tenant cannot be forced out. Sam can't claim that his contract is with Helena and not the tenant because the tenant's lease is tied to the land and not subject to the privity rule. Helena's right to the house is subject to the tenant's rights.

Another exception to the privity principle is the trust. A **trust** involves a person entering a contract with another to hold money or property to be eventually paid out to a third party, often a family member. Privity would normally prevent the person benefiting from the arrangement from enforcing it, since he is not a party to the agreement. But in such a case the principle would be unfair, since most of these arrangements are to be effective after the original contracting party is dead. Therefore, the Courts of Chancery developed the trust. It allows the beneficiary to enforce the agreement even though he is not a party to it, and so it is a clear exception to the privity rule. Life insurance is treated in a similar way, since the beneficiary can force the insurance company to honour the contract even after the death of the insured.

An apparent exception to the privity rule is **agency**. An agent is a go-between, entering into contracts with a third party on behalf of a principal. The restrictions of the privity rule do not apply to agency because the agent is not a party to the agreement. The contract is between the principal, the person the agent is acting for, and the third party. Thus, if I were to approach my broker to sell shares that I have in a certain company and he were to sell them to you, the contract of sale that results would be between you and me. The broker is not a party to it, and, therefore, there is no privity of contract problem.

Assignment of Contractual Rights

The most significant exception to the privity of contract principle is **assignment of contractual rights**. Just as a person can sell something she owns, such as a watch or a car, so people sell claims or benefits coming to them under a contract. The term *assignment* is used when claims rather than tangibles are being sold. Under privity one would expect that such rights could not be enforced by the purchasing party (called the assignee), because he is not a party to the contract. Over the years, however, the courts have allowed such claims to be enforced by allowing the assignee to go back through the assignor to enforce the contract.

This cumbersome way of doing things was eventually modified by statute,[13] and now an assignee can enforce claims under an assigned contract directly, without involving the assignor. These claims are referred to as statutory assignments, and in order for the claim to be directly enforceable, the assignment must meet certain qualifications: it must be in writing, there must be notice sent to the original party to the contract (against whom the contract is to be enforced), and all of the claim must be passed to the assignee. When a person purchases a commodity from a store, such as a stereo or a refrigerator, and payment is to be by monthly installments, the store will often assign the agreement to a finance company. The customer may be surprised to find he owes the money to the finance company, but this is the essence of assignment of contractual rights, and the customer must pay his new creditor.

It is vital to note, however, that the rights conveyed under an assignment are only what the assignor had to sell. If there is fraud or some other problem with the original agreement, any defence that the customer could have used against the store will be effective against the finance company as well. An assignee takes subject to the rights existing between the original contracting parties. If you purchase a car on time from a car lot and you are the victim of fraud, you will not have to make further payments, even if that contract is assigned to some innocent finance company that knows nothing of the fraud.

Negotiable Instruments

The presence of a cheque, promissory note or other form of negotiable instrument, however, can change these rights. The principle is that when a negotiable instrument gets into the hands of an innocent third party, that promissory note or cheque can be enforced, even when there has been fraud or some other wrong committed by the original contracting party. This principle goes back to the reason negotiable instruments were created in the first place. As commerce developed, it became necessary to devise a method to exchange and pass on claims for debts that had been incurred in the process of doing business. A negotiable instrument could be freely passed from one person to another, conveying with it all the rights associated with the original agreement between the parties and requiring no notice of the transaction. This principle is completely inconsistent with the doctrine of privity of contract and is a clear exception to it.

The most significant innovation of negotiable instruments was that better rights or claims than those held by the initial parties could be passed on. As was discussed under assignment, it was clear that even when it was possible to assign contractual rights, the assignee was subject to whatever equities existed between the original two parties. Thus, a defence such as fraud would be available against the assignee as well as the original party to the contract. This is not the case with negotiable instruments. Even when a defence of fraud is available against the initial party to a transaction, a third party to a negotiable instrument can enforce the obligation. When you write a bad cheque that gets into the hands of an innocent third party, you will have to pay even if you have been cheated.

Finally, only the benefits due under a contract can be assigned. A party cannot escape the obligations she has under a contract by assigning that contract to some third party. If I purchase a new car from your car lot and it doesn't work, I will be able to bring it back and demand that you satisfy your contractual obligation to deliver me a working automobile. It will be no defence for you to say that you have assigned the contract to Ace Finance Company. The obligations are still yours.

ENDING THE CONTRACT

A contractual relationship can be brought to an end in four different ways: by performance, agreement, frustration and breach.

Performance

When a contract is properly performed, the contractual relationship ends. We must be careful, however. Some contractual obligations may be ongoing, even though it seems that the performance of the contract has been completed. When a product such as a soft drink is sold to a consumer, the contract seems to be completed as soon as the money is paid and the can is taken away. But there is an ongoing obligation that the product be of good quality. If it is contaminated, for example, by acid that causes injury to the consumer, the consumer has the right to sue the seller for compensation. Many of the rights and obligations of the parties when goods are sold are determined by legislation. Parties to such a transaction don't normally put their minds to what will happen if the contract is not properly performed. The *Sale of Goods Act* in force in each province contains a number of provisions that are implied in the contract of purchase.

As long as the contract is properly performed and there is no problem, the contract is discharged. Most terms of a contract may be divided into two types: warranties and conditions. **Conditions** are important terms of the agreement, whereas **warranties** are peripheral or less significant terms. When one of these less important terms has been breached, the contract is still considered performed by the breaching party, and the victim of the breach of warranty is still required to go through with his or her part of the contract. The victim could, of course, demand compensation for the damage caused by the breach of warranty. If I were to order a new van with speakers in the back and front and one with a single set of speakers was delivered, there would be a breach of a warranty, but I would still have to go through with the deal and pay for the car. I could, however, sue for whatever it cost me to install the additional speakers. If the car were delivered without a motor, however, this would be a breach of a major term of the agreement (a condition) and entitle me to refuse delivery. For this reason, when new products are sold, such as cars, stereos, cameras and appliances, the seller calls the terms, under which they will be repaired if they do not work, warranties. By calling them warranties it tries to make the provisions into minor terms of the contract so that, if the product is defective, the customer cannot demand his money back. It remains a question of substance, however, whether a term is a major or a minor one.

Even when the breach is of a major term, if the failure to perform is only of some insignificant aspect of that term, the contract may be considered substantially performed and the other party then must live up to his obligations under it. If I were to agree to build a 1500-square-foot house for you, and the one I completed was only 1450 square feet, this would be a breach of a major term of the agreement but only in a minor way. The contract would be discharged by performance. Of course, the amount I received in payment for the house would reflect the reduced square footage.

Sometimes a person will attempt to perform a contractual obligation and the other party will refuse to let him perform. So long as the person performing was ready, willing and able and attempted performance, such tender of performance is equal to performance, and the person attempting to perform has discharged his contractual obligations. If Balwinder has a contractual obligation to deliver goods to Joe and attempts to do so at a proper time and place, and Joe refuses the goods, Balwinder has lived up to his side of the contract. He is discharged from his obligation and can sue Joe for breach of contract. Of course, Balwinder still has the goods, and this fact will be taken into consideration in assessing his damages. There are even some situations where, according to the *Sale of Goods Act*, title will have passed from seller to purchaser, and the seller will be able to sue for the price of the goods rather than just for compensation for what has been lost.

Services are treated the same way. If Hank agrees to paint Brenda's house and he comes at the appointed time, ready and willing to paint the house, but Brenda refuses to let him, Hank has discharged his obligations under the contract and can sue for compensation for what he has lost. Where money is to be paid, however, the case is treated differently. If Shawn owes Kyoko $500 and attempts to make the payment at a proper time and place, and Kyoko refuses payment, Shawn still owes the money. The debt is not discharged, although the costs of collecting it will now be borne by Kyoko.

There are some situations where performance can be refused. If performance is attempted or offered at an inappropriate time or place or when an incorrect mode of payment is used, performance can be refused. If Shawn owes Kyoko a debt of $5 000, the appropriate place and time to make payment is at Kyoko's office during office hours. If Shawn were to approach Kyoko on a downtown street and attempt to make payment, Kyoko could refuse. Similarly, if Shawn tried to pay with a cheque, which is not legal tender, unless the parties have agreed, either expressly or by implication, to payment by cheque, it could be refused. Even a certified cheque is not legal tender and can be refused. Even cash in the form of coin can be refused in some circumstances. The *Currency and Exchange Act*[14] sets out that only up to 25 pennies, $5.00 worth of nickels, and $10.00 of larger coins qualify as legal tender. There is no restriction on gold or paper money. If you are ever tempted to pay a debt by giving the creditor a wheelbarrow-full of pennies, don't do it. The creditor can refuse to accept payment in that form.

Agreement

The second major way a contract can come to an end or be modified is by agreement of the parties. This constitutes a contract to end or change a contract, so all of the elements needed to form a contract must be present. The main problems here are consensus and consideration. The changes cannot be made by just one party; both parties must benefit by the changes. The problem is usually to find consideration. When the contract has only been partially performed, both parties having something left to do under the agreement, the mutual release of these obligations satisfies the need for consideration. This is referred to as a **bilateral discharge**, and both contractual obligations are ended. If one party simply declares that he will not perform the contract, this is a breach of contract. Both parties must agree to end or alter a contract by agreement.

Problems may arise when one of the parties has performed his side of the agreement and then relieves the other party from performing her obligations. This is referred to as a **unilateral discharge**. The difficulty here is that there is no consideration, and, as a result, the one-sided discharge may not be binding. To avoid this difficulty, it is best to make sure the party being relieved agrees to do something extra, such as make some payment or do some additional work not covered in the original agreement. These principles apply whether the agreement between the parties is to end the contractual relationship or just to modify the obligations contained in the agreement. When such modifications benefit only one side, there is no obligation on the person not benefiting to honour them. When the changes are designed to substitute a new party for one of the original parties, the contract to change the agreement is referred to as a **novation**. For example, when a merchant sells a business, the purchaser will often want to take over the seller's position in a contract with a supplier. Such a substitution is valid only where there has been consent by all of the parties involved.

Finally, the contract itself might provide for its own discharge. When there is a condition set out in the agreement that must be met before any obligations are imposed on the parties, it is referred to as a **condition precedent**. This is a "subject to" clause. Quite often when a new home is purchased, the purchaser will include a clause such as "Subject to sale of my home within thirty days," or "Subject to arranging financing at twelve per cent."

This kind of clause makes the deal to purchase the new house contingent on selling the old or arranging financing. If that is not done, the purchaser has no obligation to go through with the deal. In the same way, when a contractual obligation has come into existence, it may be ended because some event specified in that agreement occurs. For example, Ingrid may agree to supply a catering service to a crew working on the construction of a bridge "until the bridge is completed." As soon as the job is done, the contract to supply the catering service will also end. This is referred to as a **condition subsequent**.

Frustration

The third major way a contract can come to an end is through frustration. Historically, a person entering into an agreement was bound to perform its terms no matter what happened. The results were often unfair, and so the doctrine of frustration was developed. When some outside event, not within the control of or anticipated by either party, takes place, making performance of the contract impossible, the contract is said to be discharged by frustration. The parties are no longer obligated to perform the terms of the agreement. For example, were Fred to agree to paint Ivan's house on a certain date for $500 and the house was destroyed by fire before then, an outside, uncontrollable event has made performance of the contract impossible, and so the contract would be frustrated. Fred would no longer be obligated to paint the house, and Ivan would no longer be obligated to pay.

In order for a contract to be frustrated, it is not enough that it has become more difficult to perform or more costly. For frustration to be present, the intervening event must go further. Initially, it was thought that performance had to be impossible for frustration to occur, but this interpretation has been expanded to include events that render performance something essentially different from what the parties have agreed to. For example, in the case of *Krell* v. *Henry*[15] a person had rented a room to view the coronation parade of King Edward VII. The parade was cancelled because of the king's illness. Although it was still possible for the person renting the flat to occupy it with no parade, to require him to do so would have been something fundamentally different from what he had agreed to, and so the contract was discharged by frustration.

If either party to an agreement had been in a position where he or she could have anticipated the frustrating event taking place when he or she entered the contract, such as having notice of it or being aware of the circumstances that would give rise to it, that party is taken to have assumed the risk and cannot claim frustration. Similarly, when the cause of the event that frustrates performance of the contract is the fault of either party, it is a breach of contract. If Hilda agrees to supply her 1927 Model T car for a parade on May 10, and on May 9 that car is destroyed by fire, the contract has been frustrated. But if, instead, on May 9 the car is destroyed in an auto accident caused by Hilda's careless driving, Hilda is in breach of contract when she fails to supply the car.

A contract can be frustrated when:

- the subject matter of the contract is destroyed or rendered unusable;
- the event that forms the basis of the contract fails to take place;
- there is an act of government such as expropriation of the property;
- the act required by the contract is made illegal; or
- a permit to complete the act required by the contract is refused.

The effect of such frustration has been modified by statute. At common law the effect of a frustrated contract was to "let the loss lie where it falls." If one of the parties has made a payment, he loses it; if another has done work for which she has not been paid, she is out of luck. This practice produced some unfair results, and today statutes are in place that change the situation.[16] In most common law provinces, if either party receives a benefit before the frustrating event, that party will be required to pay for it. If a frustrating event takes place and a deposit has been paid by one of the parties, the court can take the deposit and split it between the parties, depending on the costs they have incurred in performing the contract. In British Columbia, the courts can order the parties to pay compensation to each other based on these costs, whether or not a deposit has been paid.

Breach

The final way a contract can come to an end is through breach. If a condition or major term of the contract has been breached, the victim is entitled to treat the contract as ended. She is not required to perform any obligations she may have had under the agreement, and she can sue for breach. This breach may take place either through incomplete or incompetent performance of the contractual obligation or through refusal to perform. When refusal to perform is involved, the act is referred to as **repudiation**, and when that repudiation or refusal takes place before performance is required under the terms of the contract, it is referred to as **anticipatory breach**. If Fred promises in May to paint your house by August 30 and comes to you in June and says he will not do it, anticipatory breach has occurred.

This type of repudiation can also be implied when the person who is supposed to perform has done something that makes it impossible for him to do so, such as selling the subject matter of the agreement to someone else. In these circumstances, the victim of the repudiation has two choices: he can either ignore the refusal and insist on performance, or he can treat the contract as discharged and sue right away. In the example above, if Fred has refused to paint your house, you can ignore the refusal, insist on performance, and wait until August 30 to see if Fred performs. If he fails to, then you can sue for breach. The danger here is that if something happens to make performance impossible, such as the house burning down or Fred being injured, the contract would be discharged by frustration. Alternatively, you can treat your obligations as discharged immediately upon the repudiation, and get someone else to paint the house without waiting until August 30. If it costs more than you have agreed to pay Fred, you can sue for the additional costs. As the victim of repudiation, once you have made your choice you are bound by it. If you change your mind once the choice has been made, the contract would be discharged by frustration.

In general, when a breach of a condition or an important term of the contract has taken place, victims are entitled to treat their obligations under the contract as over and sue for breach. It takes two people to end a contract, however, and if the situation is such that the victim can still demand performance, he is entitled to do so. Similarly, the victim of the breach may accept the incomplete or improper performance as performance, and honour his side of the agreement in spite of the breached condition. For example, if you were to order a new Ford Taurus sedan from a car dealership and they were to deliver you a Taurus station wagon instead, that would normally qualify as a breach of condition and you could refuse to take delivery and not pay. But if you were happy with the station wagon, you could just as easily elect to accept the goods and perform your side of the contract.

Remedies

Where a contract has been breached there are several possible remedies, but the most common is monetary compensation, or damages. **Damages** are an order by the court to the person breaching the contract to pay monetary compensation for the breach. Such a payment is designed to put the victim as near as possible to the position she would have been in had the contract been properly performed. There are, however, some limitations on the availability of damages. Not every cost and loss that results from a breach of contract will be compensated. Any unusual or unexpected losses that could not have been reasonably foreseen by the breaching party at the time the agreement was entered into will not be included in an award of damages. If Greta owned a 1974 car and agreed to sell it to James for $500, not knowing James had an opportunity to resell it to a movie producer for $10 000 because just that year and model of car was needed for a movie, the contract would be breached if Greta had an accident in it and could not deliver. But James would not get the $9 500 ($10 000 less the $500 purchase price) he has lost if he were to sue for breach. Greta could not have anticipated this unusual loss. She would only have to pay the extra amount it would cost James to get a car that would be considered comparable (for example, a different model about the same year). Only if James had told Greta about the movie deal and the unusual profits involved would Greta be liable to pay for these losses.

Breach of Contract

Parta Industries Ltd. v. Canadian Pacific Limited et al.[17]

Parta Industries were in the process of opening a particleboard manufacturing plant in the interior of British Columbia and needed certain machinery manufactured in Europe. They entered into a contract with the defendants to ship the goods, marking the bill of lading "rush" and describing the materials being shipped as "construction material." The delivery of the goods was considerably delayed because of the derailment of three cars containing the goods. As a result the plant opened 105 days later than expected. In this action Parta Industries sought compensation for the loss of profits and other expenses incurred because of the delay.

The BC Supreme Court based its decision on the principle set out in the *Victoria Laundry* case,[18] which in effect determined that the defendants were only responsible for those damages that they could reasonably foresee and what was reasonably foreseeable was determined by the information they were given. The court decided that because the term "rush" was included on the bill of lading, CP knew that Parta was anxious to get the goods. Because they were described as construction materials, CP should have understood that their failure to arrive in a timely manner would result in a delay in construction and therefore in the opening of the plant. The court determined, however, that a delay of 105 days could not have been anticipated, but rather a 45-day delay would have been more reasonable given the information provided and reduced the claim accordingly. This illustrates the responsibility of a defendant for any damage that they could reasonably foresee given the additional information that warned them of the higher risk.

Another limitation on the breaching party's obligations to pay damages is the obligation on the victim to **mitigate** his losses; that is, to keep them as low as reasonably possible. When a person is wrongfully dismissed from her employment, she is entitled to compensation for her lost wages, but she also has an obligation to find another job as soon as possible. She will only get compensatory damages if she has sincerely attempted to find other employment and accepted it if it were offered to her.

In addition to monetary compensation, the Courts of Chancery developed some unique equitable remedies that are used in contract law. **Specific performance** is an equitable remedy where the courts order the breaching party to perform what is required under the agreement. If I agree to sell you a rare painting and then renege on the agreement, no amount of monetary payment can really compensate for the failure to perform. There is no other painting that could be purchased to replace it. In these circumstances, the courts will grant an order of specific performance and require that the painting be delivered to the purchaser. Specific performance will not be given, however, when monetary damages are appropriate or when personal services are involved. Since all land is unique, the courts will usually grant specific performance in land transactions.

A similar remedy developed by the Courts of Chancery is the equitable remedy of an **injunction**. An injunction is an order by the court for a contract-breaker to stop doing something that is inconsistent with the terms of the agreement. Here the breaching party is not ordered to perform, just to stop breaching the contract. For example, if George, a famous singer, agreed to put on a performance at Massey Hall in Toronto, and then refused and contracted with another promoter to perform at the SkyDome the same night, the courts would not order specific performance and require George to sing at Massey Hall. The courts will not grant specific performance where personal services are involved. The courts would, however, grant an injunction to stop George from singing at the SkyDome. If he does so, he will be in breach of his first agreement, and the courts will grant an injunction to prevent his wrongful conduct.

Rescission is an equitable remedy that may be available when one of the elements essential to the formation of a legal contract is missing — that is, the contract lacks consideration, legality or capacity. In such instances, the contract can be rescinded and the parties returned to the position they would have been in had they never entered into the contract. It is only available as a remedy if a substantial part of the agreement has been compromised and if it is possible to return the parties to their original positions.

To obtain these equitable remedies certain qualifications must be met. There must have been no undue delay in seeking the remedy. If the victim has waited unnecessarily for years to bring the action, she will not obtain an equitable remedy. Also, if granting the equitable remedy will cause undue hardship on others, the courts can refuse to grant it. Finally, if the person asking for the remedy has been guilty of some offensive conduct as well, the courts can refuse to grant the remedy. The person seeking an equitable remedy must come to the court with "clean hands."

Statutory Modification

It should be noted that many of the general principles set out above have been modified by statutes. Perhaps the most important is the *Sale of Goods Act*, originally enacted in England and subsequently enacted in all common law jurisdictions in Canada with only minor variations from province to province. The purpose of the *Sale of Goods Act* is to imply terms into contracts for the sale of goods that parties don't normally think about when they make purchases. The *Sale of Goods Act* will be discussed in more detail in the final chapter of this text.

Most provinces also have *Consumer Protection Acts* and *Trade Practices Acts* designed to protect consumers from unscrupulous merchants. There are many other examples of specialized acts that are important when dealing with consumer or commercial transactions or relationships. In the following chapter we will deal with the specialized contractual relationships involved in commercial relationships.

CONCLUSION

It is important to understand the principles of contract law to protect oneself in consumer and personal relationships, but it is also necessary to recognize that contract law is the basis of most business relationships. Therefore it is impossible to understand agency law, corporate law or the legal obligations between employers and employees without knowing what constitutes a valid contract. So the areas of law addressed in the last two chapters of this book rely heavily on the law of contract and share many of the same legal principles.

QUESTIONS FOR DISCUSSION AND REVIEW

1. What effect has the principle "freedom of contract" had on the development of contract law?

2. List and explain the elements that must be present for an agreement to qualify as a contract.

3. Contract law is based on the assumption that the parties are in an equal bargaining position. Describe some situations where this may not be the case and what implications this has for the contract.

4. Explain the necessity of reaching a consensus in order to have a valid contract.

5. What approach does the court usually take when interpreting the terms of a contract?

6. Explain what is meant by privity of a contract.

7. "Buyer beware" is still good advice, but what protections have been provided consumers that modify contractual agreements?

8. Explain the protections available to people who are assigned benefits under a contract.

9. Explain the purpose of the *Sale of Goods Act* in relation to the obligations of the parties in a consumer transaction.

10. Should there be a general requirement in law, independent of contract or tort law, that products be safe and capable of living up to the claims made for them?

NOTES

1. *Fisher v. Bell*, [1960] 3 All E.R. 731 (Q.B.).

2. *Henthorne v. Fraser*, [1892] 2 Ch. 27 (C.A.).

3. *Mlodinska et al. v. Malicki et al.* (1988), 60 O.R. (2d) 180 (Ont. H.C.J. (Div. Ct.)).

4. *White v. Bluett* (1853), 23 L.J. Ex. 36.

5. *Infants Act,* R.S.B.C. 1979, c. 196.

6. *Indian Act*, R.S.C. 1970, c. I–6.

7. *Boyd v. Newton* (1998), (S.C.B.C.) [unreported].

8. *Competition Act*, S.C. 1984-85-86, c. 91.

9. *Carlill v. Carbolic Smoke Ball Co.*, [1892] 2 Q.B. 484, [1893] 1 Q.B. 256 (C.A.).

10. *Beer et al. v. Townsgate I. Ltd.* (1997), 152 D.L.R. (4th) 671 (Ont. C.A.).

11. *Rochdale Credit Union Ltd. v. Barney* (1984), 14 D.L.R. (4th) 116 (Ont. C.A.).

12. *Donoghue v. Stevenson*, [1932] All E.R. 1 (H.L.).

13. For example, *Law and Equity Act*, R.S.B.C. 1979, c. 224, s. 40.

14. *Currency and Exchange Act*, R.S.C. 1985, c. C–52.

15. *Krell v. Henry*, [1903] 2 K.B. 740.

16. For example, *Frustrated Contracts Act*, R.S.O. 1980, c. 179.

17. *Parta Industries Ltd. v. Canadian Pacific Limited et al.* (1974), 48 D.L.R. (3d) 463 (B.C.S.C.).

18. *Victoria Laundry (Windsor) Ltd. v. Newman Industries, Ltd.,* [1949] 1 All E.R. 997.

FURTHER READING

Fridman, Gerald Henry Louis. *The Law of Contract in Canada*, 2nd ed. Toronto: Carswell, 1986.

Smyth, J.E., D.A. Soberman and A.J. Easson. *The Law and Business Administration in Canada*, 8th ed. Scarborough, Ont.: Prentice Hall Canada Inc., 1998.

Willes, J.A. *Contemporary Canadian Business Law*, 5th ed. Toronto: McGraw-Hill, 1998.

Yates, R.A. *Business Law in Canada*, 5th ed. Scarborough, Ont.: Prentice Hall Canada Inc., 1998.

Chapter

COMMERCIAL RELATIONSHIPS

Because our consumer-oriented society is dominated to such a great extent by commercial activities, the legal relationships created between the parties to those transactions are the basis for a significant portion of our modern law. This chapter examines the body of law that has been developed to govern the legal relationships of people when they engage in such activities. Many of these relationships rest on contracts and so the rules governing contracts apply. But when contracts involve services as in employment and agency, then the rules take on added dimensions. This chapter is concerned with employment and the legislation that has developed to facilitate employer/employee relations. Agency is another specialized contract for services that will be reviewed. There are a number of ways to carry on business, and in this chapter we will look at sole proprietorship, partnership and incorporation and discuss the advantages and disadvantages of these forms of business organization along with the legislation that controls them.

EMPLOYMENT

Employment is a contract of ongoing service, where the person working has agreed to work in the service of someone who will give him direction and assignments as required. The body of law (referred to as the law of master and servant) has been developed to govern the long-term commercial relationship of employment. Since most of us earn our living through employment, it is important to understand this complex area. Because an employment relationship entails many responsibilities and obligations on both parties that are not present when the person doing the work is an independent contractor, it is useful to begin by comparing the two forms of work. The employee has a greater obligation to act in the best interests of the employer than an independent contractor does. The employer is responsible for any wrongful conduct committed by the employee in the process of doing his job, which is not the case with independent contractors. It becomes very important, therefore, to determine where the independent contractor relationship ends and the employment relationship begins.

In the past, the courts used a **control test**, by looking at the amount of control exercised by the person having the work done over the person doing that work, to determine employment. If a relationship has been established that goes beyond merely a commitment on the part of the worker to complete a specific job, to the point where that worker could be told how and when to do that job, then the relationship created is that of employment. In more recent times this test has been shown to be somewhat limited, and the courts of Canada have added the organizational test. Simply put, the **organizational test** asks whether the worker who performs the work is an integral part of the organization of the person having the work done. Does the worker work for anyone else at the same time, and is a large portion of the sales of the firm dependent on that worker? If she is an integral and important part of the organization, an important cog in the wheel, then an employment relationship exists whether or not there is the degree of control discussed above. Using these two tests, the court is able to draw a line between the independent contractor and the situation in which the more onerous employment, or master-servant, relationship exists.

Obligations of the Parties

The employer is obligated to provide reasonably safe working conditions and not to require unlawful conduct on the part of the employee. The employer is also required to pay the agreed-upon wage for the work performed, as stipulated in the employment contract.

The employee, on the other hand, is obligated to carry out the reasonable instructions of the employer, to be honest and courteous, to be punctual, and, generally, to act in the best interests of the employer. This last obligation means, for example, that if any opportunity for financial gain comes to the employee because of his position, it must be offered to the employer first. The employee must also have the skills and ability he claimed to have when hired. Thus, if he is hired as a carpenter and it later turns out that he does not know how to do the things that a carpenter would normally do, he can be fired. The employee must not only have these skills, but also exercise them in a competent and careful way. If the employee is careless on the job, he can be fired even if he has the skills.

Wrongful Dismissal

One of the most common areas of legal conflict between an employee and the employer is wrongful dismissal. Theoretically at least, both the employer and the employee are obliged to give **reasonable notice** upon termination, unless there has been "just cause" or wrongful conduct involved. Whichever party wants to end the employment relationship must give the other reasonable notice before the termination can take place. In fact, it is extremely rare for an employee to be sued for wrongful leaving (leaving the job without giving the required notice). It is quite common, however, for an employee to sue for wrongful dismissal, and the substance of this claim in Canada is that the employee was not given sufficient notice (or pay in lieu of notice) by the employer. **Pay in lieu of notice** is a lump-sum payment by the employer equal to what the employee would have received had he been given proper notice.

In Canada the amount of notice (or pay in lieu of notice) required is "reasonable notice," which means a period of time that is reasonable, taking into account such factors as the length of service, the type of job performed, the employee's qualifications and the nature of the job market. Given these considerations, it is not unusual for the courts to find that an employee who has worked for an employer for 15 or 20 years in a managerial position is entitled to up to two years' notice or pay in lieu of notice upon termination. Where the employee has been on the job for only six months, working as a labourer, the notice required would be minimal.

If the courts find that wrongful dismissal has taken place, and the employee was not given sufficient notice or pay in lieu of notice, the **damages** awarded will be calculated on the basis of the notice he should have received and what he would have earned during that period. Of course, if he obtained another job in the meantime (as he is required to try to do), his damages would be reduced by the amount he earned in that job.

Tree Savers International Ltd. v. Savoy et al.[1]

This case involves two employees, Savoy and Derringer, who worked for Tree Savers, a company doing very specialized work in the oil industry. Darringer and Savoy gave two weeks' notice and then incorporated their own business in competition with Tree Savers. When they left their employer, they took specialized technology that was used in the industry as well as confidential information including telephone lists and contacts that belonged to Tree Savers. Tree Savers sued them and a third party, Ducharme, who had provided financing to help Savoy and Darringer set up their new business.

The court held against all three, for several reasons. The most important was that two weeks' notice was not sufficient. They were senior employees, had worked for a considerable period of time and were key employees in the organization, and therefore the court determined that 18 months' notice would have been more appropriate. Because they didn't give sufficient notice they were responsible for the lost profits caused by their leaving Tree Savers. This case illustrates that it is not only the employer that is obligated to give reasonable notice upon termination, but the employee must also give reasonable notice, and that notice might be considerable. The case also illustrates the duty of an employee to act in the best interests of the employer. They must not compete and cannot take confidential information and trade secrets when they leave.

The court applied a completely different cause of action against Ducharme, that of inducing breach of contract. Ducharme should have known that Savoy and Derringer were required to give a longer period of notice and when he encouraged them to leave by providing financial aid he induced them to breach their contract with Tree Savers. This is a tort and he was found liable and had to pay damages.

Termination

This common law requirement of reasonable notice will not apply where there has been **just cause** for termination. Simply put, just cause means that the employer can prove that the employee has failed to function as required in the employment relationship. Thus, when the employee fails to have the skills required to do the job, is careless or otherwise acts incompetently, immorally or dishonestly, or is disobedient, he can be fired without notice. If the employee cannot perform his job because of sickness or disability, even though it may not be his fault, he can also be dismissed. Failure, however, on the part of the employer to have work for the employee to do is not just cause. Where the employee is laid off because he is no longer needed, he is still entitled to reasonable notice upon termination. It should also be noted that if the employee is dismissed because of racial, religious or any other reason prohibited under human rights legislation, a complaint can be made to the appropriate tribunal even where reasonable notice has been given.

The employee is also not entitled to reasonable notice where the employment contract specifies otherwise. If the contract sets out that two months' notice is all that the employee is entitled to, that is all the notice he has to be given upon termination, even where reasonable notice would require more.

Parks v. Atlantic Provinces Special Education Authority[2]

The plaintiff, Parks, had been employed as a residence counsellor for a considerable period of time in a school catering to physically and mentally disabled children. Part of his job required him to do some heavy lifting of these children. Over the years the nature of the school changed to accommodate more severely disabled children requiring even more lifting. After several years of this Mr. Parks suffered a herniated disc in his neck, making it extremely difficult to do heavy lifting. He had other physical problems as well. He was off work for a considerable length of time but eventually came back, but could not do the heavy lifting. The employer terminated his employment in November 1989 and he brought an action for wrongful dismissal.

The court decided that because lifting was part of his job and he could no longer do it, the contract of employment was frustrated and the termination was valid. Normally, an employer has to give reasonable notice upon terminating an employee. But where there was cause, no such notice was required. This case illustrates that the cause that justifies dismissal without notice isn't always the fault of the employee. In this case he was simply unable to do the job.

Vicarious Liability

One of the most significant implications of finding that an employment relationship exists is that the employer is responsible for the wrongful conduct of employees. This is called vicarious liability, and allows a person injured by an employee to sue the employer for compensation for any injuries suffered. There is an important qualification on this liability, however: the employer's liability is limited to wrongful conduct of the employee performed in the course of employment. When the employee is on a "frolic of his own," the employer is not responsible.

For example, when Juan, who worked as a night watchman for Franco, left during working hours to visit his girlfriend across town, and in the process carelessly struck a pedestrian, Juan would be responsible for any injuries sustained. The employer, Franco, on the other hand, would not be, since Juan was on a frolic of his own. If, however, Franco had sent Juan across town to deliver a package and the pedestrian was injured, Franco would be responsible, since the wrongful conduct took place during the course of employment. The principle of vicarious liability does not remove the responsibility for the conduct from the employee. In fact the victim sues both the employee and the employer, collecting from whomever has the money to pay.

Labour Legislation

In addition to the rules developed by the courts and embodied in the common law of master and servant, many statutes have been enacted over the years that govern the employment relationship. For example, the **employment insurance** system has been introduced to deal with situations where people find themselves without income between employment. The employee is required to pay a premium while working, and claims against the fund when he loses his job. **Workers' compensation** has been put in place to provide compensation to employees who are injured on the job. This is a no-fault system where both employer and employee pay into a fund, and the injured employee is compensated for his injury out of that fund. He also gives up any right to sue the employer or fellow employees for dangerous working conditions or carelessness on the job that may have caused his injury. In conjunction with the workers' compensation system, statutes provide for safety at the workplace and fines and penalties for non-compliance.

All provinces have statutes setting out a minimum wage that must be paid, the hours of work that can be imposed without a break, including provisions for coffee and lunch breaks, and for the payment of overtime. There is also legislation prohibiting or controlling the use of children in the workforce. In more recent times all provinces, as well as the federal government, have passed legislation prohibiting discrimination on the basis of sex, religion, race or ethnic origin in the workforce and other areas of society. Many provinces have also put in place legislation setting out the minimum notice that must be given when an employee is terminated for other than just cause. Depending on the statute, this is only a minimum requirement, and when the amount of reasonable notice required under the common law is greater than this minimum, the common law reasonable notice will apply, and the employee will be able to sue for wrongful dismissal and claim the greater amount.

Collective Bargaining

One of the most significant examples of legislative involvement in the area of employment law has been in the field of collective bargaining and trade unions. To understand the present law of collective bargaining, it is important to appreciate that it was developed in an atmosphere of confrontation and violence. During the Industrial Revolution in England, workers began to band together to put pressure on employers for better wages and working conditions. The reaction of employers, and government as well, was swift and repressive. Essentially, such workers' combinations were treated as seditious and criminal in nature. Both the organizations and their members were outlawed, and steps were taken to crush them.

In the United States employers were just as violently opposed to the trade union movement, but the government took a more neutral approach. As violence increased, the public demanded that steps be taken to stop it. In 1935 Congress passed the *Wagner Act*.[3] This act is of particular significance, for it forms the foundation of our modern labour legislation in Canada.

The *Wagner Act* drastically reduced the confrontation involved in collective bargaining, by introducing the government as a third party and removing the employer from the volatile organization process. Most assaults, riots and other violent acts took place when unions tried to force employers to recognize them as the representatives of the workers. The *Wagner Act* structured the organizational process by holding a government-supervised certification vote to determine whether the workers wanted to be represented by the union. If they did, then the union was certified, and the employer was required to recognize and negotiate with that union exclusively. The employer was excluded from the organization process completely, not even being allowed to comment on what the consequences of having to deal with a union would be for the business. Although the result of the changes may not have been altogether fair, they were effective in significantly reducing the violence and confrontation associated with the beginnings of the trade union movement.

Union Certification

Today, although the percentages and procedures vary somewhat, this same government certification procedure is in place in all jurisdictions in Canada. Although there are some employee groups and some types of jobs (mostly management) that are excluded from this process, the majority of the workforce in Canada comes under the collective bargaining legislation and has the option of being represented by **trade unions**.

If a group of employees wants to be represented by a union, it can, either independently or with the assistance of one of the large union organizations, such as the Teamsters or Canadian Union of Public Employees, approach other employees. After a given percentage (usually 50%) of the workforce has signed up, they make application to the government for a certification vote. The department of labour in the particular jurisdiction then holds a vote by secret ballot, to determine whether the workforce generally wants to be represented by the union. If the majority of those voting (the percentage needed may vary from jurisdiction to jurisdiction) vote for the union, the union is certified as the exclusive bargaining agent for that group of employees. From then on, the employer's dealings with the employees in such matters as wages, conditions of work, benefits and the like must be through the **bargaining agent**.

These union organizations must meet certain qualifications in order to be recognized by the government as bargaining agents. They have to be democratic in nature, with their leadership in place as a result of a proper election process. There also must not be any discrimination on the basis of race, religion, ethnic origin and so forth.

Unfair Labour Practices

An essential part of this government-supervised certification process is to prohibit certain types of behaviour by both employer and employee. These prohibited practices are called **unfair labour practices**, and provisions defining them are set out in the legislation. For example, an employer is prohibited from firing an employee who is trying to form a union, and he cannot require new employees to promise not to join a union. Once the organization process has started, any attempt by the employer to forestall it by increasing wages or otherwise changing conditions of work is also considered an unfair labour practice and is prohibited. Similarly, the union is prohibited from threatening or otherwise coercing the workers to join the union.

Although the legislation requires the employer to submit to the certification process, it does not give the union representatives the right to carry out their organization activities on his property or during working hours. Employers, however, often voluntarily allow such activities so that they can keep an eye on what is happening. Today, most jurisdictions also permit the creation of employer organizations, where a group of employers band together to bargain collectively with the unions to offset this growing power. Finally, the government-established labour relations boards have the power and status of a court in some circumstances to enforce their decisions.

Bargaining

Once the union is certified, the law requires that the employer recognize the union as the exclusive bargaining agent, and commence the bargaining process with the object of reaching a **collective agreement**. The parties are required to bargain fairly, but often, at least when certification first takes place, because of inexperience or animosity it is impossible for the parties to agree. In many jurisdictions, the legislation allows the government labour board to impose a first contract. This power, however, is seldom used. If the parties have difficulties in reaching an agreement, there are many mechanisms in place to assist them. In Canada, one of the most significant developments has been the growth of the **conciliation** (sometimes called mediation) process. When talks break down, either one of the parties or the government has the power to ask for outside help, and a conciliator (mediator) is appointed. This person acts as a go-between, trying to assist the parties to reach an agreement, persuading first one and then the other to change their positions. Many techniques are used, including going public to embarrass the parties if they have taken an unreasonable position. The services of a talented mediator are invaluable in the collective bargaining process. Still, if the parties cannot reach an agreement there is the option of strike or lockout.

Strike and Lockout

It is only during the bargaining process that a strike or lockout can lawfully take place. A **strike** takes place when the employees withdraw their services and walk off the job. A **lockout** occurs when the employer orders the workers to leave the job. Before this form of drastic **job action** can take place, certain legal steps have to be complied with: the parties must have tried to negotiate in good faith; when a mediator is involved, the mediator must have given up or completed his efforts; and a notice (as set out in the statute) must be served on the other party.

During the strike or lockout, the employees usually **picket** the job site. Some jurisdictions allow picketing not only of the job site, but also of other areas where the employer carries on business, but most restrict the right to picket to the actual site or plant where the workers are employed. When they are picketing, workers place themselves outside the employer's premises and try to persuade those attempting to enter not to do business with the employer. So long as they act in a peaceful and informational way, pickets are permitted. When the persuasion becomes intimidation or violence takes place, however, there is a breach of law. In this case, legal steps can be taken to stop the picketing, including obtaining an injunction with the full weight of the court system behind it, or the laying of criminal or civil charges against those who physically abuse people crossing the picket line. This may seem to weaken the picketing weapon, but there is an important and profound ethic among trade unionists never to cross a properly constituted picket line, and it usually makes the picket line effective in severely hampering the continued operation of the struck business.

The Contract

Once an agreement has been completed and approved by the parties, strikes and lockouts cannot take place. There must be a provision to provide for resolution of disputes arising out of the interpretation of the agreement by arbitration. Arbitration is quite different from mediation; an arbitrator acts like a judge. The arbitrator does not merely facilitate the decision-making process, but actually makes a decision and imposes it on the parties. When a strike arises out of such a dispute, it is often referred to as an illegal strike. A wildcat strike is one that takes place against the instructions of the union leadership (when the workers walk off the job on their own, defying their leaders).

AGENCY

When one person does work for another on a job-by-job basis, with an agreed price to be paid when the job (or service) as set out in the agreement is completed, an **independent contractor** relationship is created. This relationship is created and governed by the terms of the contract entered into between the parties, as well as any government legislation controlling that specific profession.

When one person acts on behalf of another, either as an employee or as an independent contractor, and creates new legal obligations for that person, an agency relationship is involved. For example, when Jane employs Robert to act on her behalf in the purchase of a new computer, and Robert makes the purchase, the resulting contract for the purchase of the computer is between Jane and the seller. Robert has merely acted as a go-between, and legally he is referred to as Jane's agent in the transaction. The law of agency is vitally important because almost all commercial transactions, including normal consumer purchases, involve an agent, at least on the side of the seller. Agents represent their principals in dealings with other people, called third parties. The agent is the go-between, and although there are many examples of agents representing their principals in other types of legal relationships, by far the most common is where an agent enters into a contract on behalf of a principal. When people sell houses, for example, they usually use the services of real estate agents. When someone buys something from a store, the sales clerk is acting as an agent for the store owner. The agent may be an independent supplier of services, such as an insurance broker, real estate agent travel agent, or stockbroker, but more likely the agent will be an employee of the principal, as in the case of a sales clerk in a department store or a purchasing agent for a business.

Creation

Although it is possible for an agent to represent a principal gratuitously, the agency relationship is usually created by a contract between the agent and the principal. This contract, of course, will set out the obligations and benefits of both parties, such as the payment and nature of service, but one of its most important aspects is that it sets out the extent of the authority that the agent has to bind the principal in the contracts he enters into.

Authority

The actual authority the agent has is often set out specifically in the contract, but frequently it must be implied from other terms, such as the position to which the agent has been appointed. In an employment contract in which a person is appointed sales manager for a used car lot, there is the implication that he has the authority to enter into contracts for the sale of cars on behalf of the business. The authority that the agent is given in the contract (either expressly or by implication) is referred to as the agent's **actual authority**, and it is important when it becomes necessary to determine whether the agent has lived up to his contractual obligations with the principal. The principal's responsibilities to third parties for the conduct of his agent, however, are a little broader than this. The principal will be responsible not only for transactions entered into by an agent that fall within the actual authority that he has been given, but also for conduct that has led the third party to believe the agent is authorized, even if he is not. This is referred to as **apparent authority**, and from the point of view of people dealing with agents, the principal is bound by the contracts if the agent has acted within his actual or apparent authority.

Here is an example of **estoppel**. When one person leads another to believe that something is true (i.e., that the agent has authority from the principal to do what he has done), the person doing the misleading is not later permitted to deny in court that the facts were as he stated. For example, Mike hired Susan as a purchasing agent in a steel-fabricating business. He informed the suppliers of the new appointment, but he did not inform them that he had qualified Susan's authority by stating that she could make no purchases over $200 without his express approval. Were Susan to enter into contracts with the suppliers for amounts in excess of the $200 limit, even though she has exceeded her actual authority, those contracts would still be binding on Mike. By appointing Susan as his purchasing agent, Mike has led the suppliers to believe that she has all the authority that a purchasing agent in that business would normally have. Since such authority would not normally have such a limitation, the suppliers are entitled to assume, on the basis of apparent authority, that Susan has the power to bind Mike to the contracts that have been made. Mike is estopped from denying that his agent has the authority that he has indicated to the suppliers she has. It is this apparent authority of agents that extends the liability of principals for their actions.

When the agent exceeds both his actual and apparent authority in entering into a contract with a third party on behalf of the principal, that contract is not binding on the principal. In the example above, so long as the purchase falls into the normal activity of a purchasing agent in that business, it would be binding on the employer on the basis of apparent authority, although Mike would likely have the right to discipline Susan for disobedience. If, however, she were to purchase a new office tower, it would not be regarded as the kind of purchase one would expect a purchasing agent for a steel-fabrication business to make. Such a contract would not be binding on Mike, because Susan has no actual or apparent authority to make it. If Mike liked the deal, however, and wanted to go through with the purchase of the office tower, he could **ratify** the agreement (give the agent authority after the fact), but in the absence of such ratification, he would not be bound. This situation does not leave the third party without a remedy. When the agent has exceeded both her actual and apparent authority, the agent herself is responsible for any damages caused, and the third party has the right to turn to the agent for redress.

Duty

An agent owes a **fiduciary duty** to his principal. This means that the agent must act in the best interests of the principal at all times, and put the principal's interests ahead of his own. The agent is not permitted to profit personally from the transactions he is entering into on behalf of the principal, other than by receiving the agreed-on wage or salary for his services. If he takes a commission from both the principal and the third party, he is violating his fiduciary duty. If a real estate agent finds that his principal is selling his home for a particularly attractive price and wants to purchase it himself, he can only do so after making full disclosure to the principal that he is the purchaser and that the value of the property exceeds what it is being sold for. If some sort of business opportunity comes to him because of his position as agent, he must give that business opportunity first to the principal and not privately profit from it. Similarly, the agent must not enter into competition with the principal. The principal, on the other hand, is obligated to pay the agent as set out in the contract, and also to reimburse him for any reasonable expenses incurred in carrying out his function.

Ocean City Realty Ltd. v. A & M Holdings Ltd. et al.[4]

Mrs. Forbes was a licensed real estate salesperson working for Ocean City Realty Ltd. She was approached by Mr. Halbower to find a commercial building in downtown Victoria. After some investigation, Mrs. Forbes approached the owners of the Weiler building to determine whether it might be for sale. Through the owner, A & M entered into an arrangement with her whereby they agreed to pay a commission if she acted as their agent in selling that building.

Negotiations followed and a sale was concluded between A & M and Mr. Halbower. This agreement included the payment of a commission of 1 3/4 per cent of the sale price which was $5.2 million. Unknown to the seller, A & M, Mr. Halbower insisted that Mrs. Forbes pay back to him $46 000, which was half of her commission. Mrs. Forbes went to her principal, Ocean City Realty, to discuss the appropriateness of the deal, and Mr. Fife told her that she should go ahead with it providing she owed Mr. Halbower the money. She informed Mr. Fife that in fact she didn't owe Mr. Halbower anything except for this tentative deal. Mr. Fife gave her a letter for Mr. Halbower in which he authorized Mr. Halbower to withhold $46 000 from the commissions being paid, on the understanding that the money was owed to him by Mrs. Forbes. There was some delay in completing the transaction and when A & M discovered the secret deal between Mrs. Forbes and Mr. Halbower, they refused to pay any commission.

The problem in this case was that Mrs. Forbes had a fiduciary obligation to act in the best interests of her principal, A & M. She argued that A & M ended up paying exactly what they expected to. She was the one who gave up part of her commission so the deal could go through. That didn't hurt A & M but helped them. The court held, however, that one of the key elements in the duty of the fiduciary is to disclose all pertinent information with respect to the transaction that would be considered important by the principal. In this case, the knowledge that she was paying part of her commission back to Halbower was important to A & M and it may have determined whether they would go through with the deal or not. In effect, they thought that Halbower was paying one price when in fact he was paying less for the property. They were entitled to this information and it may have influenced their decision. Therefore, the fiduciary obligation of the agent had been breached and the agent was entitled to no commission at all.

This case strongly illustrates the nature of fiduciary duty, where a person owing that duty must submerge personal interests in favour of the interests of the principal he or she represents.

Liability

Because the agent is merely acting as a go-between, the third party must look to the principal for compensation or redress if any disagreements arise. The principal can then sue the agent. When the agent has exceeded both his actual and his apparent authority, the third party can sue the agent for compensation, as if he were the principal. In rare circumstances, an **undisclosed principal** relationship is created, where the agent will not disclose to the third party that he is functioning as an agent or, even if he does so, will not disclose the identity of the principal. For example, it is sometimes necessary in large land development projects to acquire many separate properties. An agent will be employed to buy the properties, with specific instructions not to disclose the nature of the project or who he is acting for, to avoid driving up the purchase price. To the seller, the agent appears to be the purchaser. In other cases the agent simply refuses to say who he is acting for. When such an undisclosed principal relationship is created, the third party may seek redress from the agent as if he were the principal or, when he finds out who the principal is, sue him directly. Once the choice has been made, however, the third party is bound by it and can't change his mind.

Under very limited circumstances, the principal is responsible for the wrongful (tortious) conduct of the agent. When an agent is an employee of a principal, there is no question that the employer is responsible for torts committed by an employee during the course of the job, whether or not that employee is acting in an agency capacity. This is the principle of **vicarious liability**. When the agent is acting independently, however, vicarious liability does not apply. It is only when an agent makes a misrepresentation in his dealings with the third party that the principal will be held responsible for that misrepresentation, even in the absence of an employment. Thus, when a real estate agent, selling a house for her principal, misrepresents the zoning so that the purchaser is led to believe that a suite can be built in the basement, the purchaser can seek redress from the principal for any injuries suffered if the intended suite cannot be completed.

SOLE PROPRIETORSHIP

Some people in our society are not employed by others, but work for themselves. When a person carries on a business by himself, is solely responsible for the decisions made and the obligations undertaken, he is said to be a sole proprietor. He may employ others or use agents to act on his behalf, but so long as he has not created a corporation, is the only one in charge, and is solely responsible, he is a sole proprietor. Such a person is unusual in the business world. More commonly, entrepreneurs will band together in partnerships or create corporations to carry on their commercial activities.

In a sole proprietorship the business does not become a separate person; it is merely a possession of the person who owns and operates it, much as a car or house is owned. The proprietor makes all of the business decisions and is personally entitled to all of the benefits that accrue. The sole proprietor may employ others, but he is the one responsible. While the owner of a business must acquire the appropriate licences and keep sufficient records to satisfy government agencies, such as the tax department, the sole proprietorship is the most independent and is generally free from government interference and regulation.

Liability

One of the most significant drawbacks to carrying on business as a sole proprietorship is the unlimited liability involved. If a sole proprietor incurs debts because of bad decisions or as a result of liability for injuries suffered through the operation of the business, he is personally responsible for those debts. If the debts are in excess of the assets of the business, the sole proprietor stands to lose all that he has, including his home, car and other investments. **Unlimited liability** means that a person must use all of his assets, including future assets, to satisfy business debts. His entire personal fortune is at risk, and he is responsible not only for his own wrongful conduct but also, vicariously, for any wrongful conduct committed by employees in the course of their jobs. Carrying on business as a sole proprietor is therefore a risky proposition, and most people turn to incorporation as a more attractive alternative. It should be mentioned, however, that in most jurisdictions professionals such as doctors, lawyers, and engineers are not permitted to incorporate by law, and so if they are going to carry on a private practice, they must do it as a sole proprietor or in a partnership.

PARTNERSHIP

In a partnership, several sole proprietors pool their talents and resources to carry on business in common. Like the sole proprietorship, the business does not take on a personality separate from the partners who make it up, and therefore each of the partners is individually responsible for the business obligations.

Liability

The primary characteristic of a partnership is that when a person deals with one of the partners, she is dealing with all of them; each partner is an agent of all the other partners, binding them to any agreement that he or she enters into on behalf of the partnership. Partners, therefore, are responsible for any contractual arrangements entered into by other partners. Partners are also liable for their partners' wrongful conduct, just as an employer is vicariously liable for wrongful acts of employees. If any injury is caused by carelessness or other tort committed by one of the partners in the course of carrying on partnership business, all of the partners are responsible for compensating the victim.

The Partnership Agreement

When people decide to become partners, they usually enter into a partnership agreement, which sets out their rights and obligations. Outsiders to such an agreement are not affected by it. If the agreement were to state that each of five partners will be responsible for no more than 20 per cent of any liabilities incurred by the partnership, it will not affect the position of a person dealing with the partnership who is unaware of this arrangement. If that person has a claim against the partnership and the partnership assets are not enough to cover it, she can collect the amount owed from whichever partner has the assets to pay. Similarly, if the authority of one of the partners to bind the partnership in contract is limited in some way in the agreement, a person dealing with that partner will not be affected by the limitation unless he has been made aware of it.

A partnership can be created inadvertently without such a contract. The simple definition of a partnership is two or more people carrying on business in common with a view toward making a profit. There is no requirement that there be a specific intention to create a partnership. Two college students promoting dances together to earn money for tuition would likely be a partnership, even though neither of them intended that result. The significance of finding that a partnership exists is that it determines the liability of the parties. Since a partner is responsible not only for the contracts entered into by his partners but also for any injuries or other damage caused by them while carrying out business activities, it is important that people working together recognize the risks they undertake. If the victim can show that the person who injured him was in partnership with someone, he can turn to the other partner for compensation if the first partner has no resources to pay. The risk for partners is extreme, since this liability for a partner's actions is unlimited. If the assets of the business are not enough to cover the claim, each partner stands to lose not only what he has invested, but also any other assets he has. This unlimited liability aspect of partnership, combined with responsibility for every partner's conduct, discourages most business people from using the partnership method. There are, however, some professions that are prohibited from incorporating, and, therefore, if they wish to carry on their profession with others, they have no choice but to create a partnership.

Legislation

Partnership, traditionally, was the most common method of carrying on business. It is only in this century that it has been eclipsed by incorporation. Much case law developed in the field of partnership, and in 1890 English case law was summarized in the *Partnership Act*, which in turn was adopted by most common law countries, including all of the common law provinces of Canada. There have been only a few changes in the Act over the years. One of its most important aspects is that it defines just what kinds of activities will establish the existence of a partnership. The Act sets out that, when people carry on business in common with a view toward profits, a partnership is created, but it goes on to indicate activities that will not, by themselves, constitute a partnership. A profit-sharing scheme in which employees receive a bonus based on the profits of the business, or a debt being repaid out of profits made by a business will not by itself establish a partnership. Similarly, jointly holding real estate and sharing the profits derived from it will not by itself constitute a partnership arrangement.

Duties

The *Partnership Act* also sets out the obligations of the partners to each other in the absence of an agreement to the contrary. Each partner has a fiduciary duty to act in the best interests of the partnership and his partners. A **fiduciary duty** requires that one partner not personally profit or benefit at the expense of the others. If a business opportunity comes to a person because of his position as partner, he must share it with his partners. Also, a partner can't act in competition with the partnership. If a partner is a principal shareholder in a company that is supplying materials to the partnership, she must pay over any profits she makes from the company as a result of the sales to the partnership. A lawyer who is a partner in a law firm cannot do extra work on the side, for that is part of his partnership activity. He must pay over all profits made in this way to the partnership. Similarly, if a partner uses any of the partnership assets, such as a photocopier, computer, or printing press, for personal purposes and makes a profit, she must account to the partnership for those profits.

The *Partnership Act* also sets out other rights and responsibilities of the partners.

- Any profits and losses are to be shared between the partners equally or according to the scale set out in their agreement.
- No salaries are to be paid to partners.
- Any expenses incurred by a partner are to be reimbursed from the partnership income.
- Each partner has an equal right to share in the management of the partnership. Any important decisions must be made by the unanimous agreement of all partners.

The rights and obligations set out in the statute can be modified by the partnership agreement. A common change is to create various levels of partners (junior and senior) who have different shares of profits, different degrees of responsibility for losses, and different ways of participating in the management of the business. It is important to emphasize again that it is only rights between the partners that are affected by such an agreement, and outsiders will still be able to look to any partner for redress no matter what the agreement says.

Advantages and Disadvantages

A partnership is generally a less costly method of carrying on business than incorporation. There is less government interference in the operation and fewer accounting, procedural and reporting requirements. The requirement of unanimous consent to make business decisions protects the position of the minority, and the prohibition against a partner selling his partnership interest without the approval of the other partners eliminates the risk of having strangers imposed upon the business. These characteristics may be seen as advantages or disadvantages, depending on one's point of view. The major disadvantage is the unlimited liability aspect discussed above.

Public Trustee v. Mortimer et al.[5]

Mortimer was a lawyer whose long-time client, Mrs. Cooper, approached him to make a will. She named Mortimer and his partner Andrews as executors and trustees of that will in 1965. In 1966 Mrs. Cooper died and Mortimer took on the responsibility of executing the will. There were a number of bequests, some of which involved the remaining assets of Mrs. Cooper being invested and the income from the estate being distributed to the heirs. In fact, Mortimer stole $197 000 from the estate while the partnership existed and a further $10 000 after the dissolution of the partnership. The question that the court had to decide was whether or not Andrews was also responsible for the loss. Mortimer was charged, convicted and disbarred. The evidence produced showed that Andrews had left the matter entirely in the hands of Mortimer and didn't even remember having met Mrs. Cooper. There was no negligence or wrongdoing on Andrews' part. The Public Trustee stepped in and pursued remedies against Mortimer. Was Andrews responsible for the wrongful acts of his partner?

The court held that so long as those wrongful acts had taken place in the course of the partnership business, then Andrews was vicariously liable for the wrongful acts of his partner. Because Mortimer was allowed to use the staff and facilities of the firm and the correspondence was on the firm's letterhead, then his actions were in the ordinary course of the business of the firm and therefore Andrews was liable as well.

This case illustrates how one partner can be responsible for the conduct of another partner even when completely innocent and that such liability is unlimited in the sense that Andrews was personally responsible for the debts.

Dissolution

The *Partnership Act* sets out that, when one of the partners dies, becomes bankrupt or simply notifies the others that he wants to leave the partnership, the whole partnership comes to an end. When this happens, the partnership must cease operation, sell its assets and distribute the money to the partners. Because dissolution can be very inconvenient, partnership agreements usually contain clauses that allow the rest of the partnership to continue when one of these events takes place. In British Columbia the approach is different. The *Partnership Act* states that, when a partner dies or becomes bankrupt, the partnership will only be dissolved in relation to that partner.[6] He or his estate is entitled to a share of assets, but if there are more than two partners, the partnership remains intact as far as the other partners are concerned. The court, however, retains the power to dissolve a partnership on the request of one of the partners, no matter what the partnership agreement says.

When the partnership is dissolved, the assets of the partnership go first to pay off its debts. Any remainder is used to pay off any expenses incurred by the partners and to return any monies invested. If there is any excess, it is then distributed equally among the partners, unless the partnership agreement provides otherwise. If the assets of the partnership are not sufficient to pay off the debts, then the debtors can claim against the partners.

The Limited Partner

A recent development in the field of partnership law has been the recognition of the limited partner. Most provinces today allow for a partner who has merely invested money in the partnership to have **limited liability**. Where such an investor properly registers as a limited partner, does not participate in the management of the business and does not allow his name to be associated with the partnership, as a partner his liability will be limited to the amount he has invested. If a limited partner has invested $50 000 and the assets of the partnership are not enough to pay off a creditor, that creditor can seek redress from the partners personally. But once the $50 000 invested in the partnership, or what is left of it, has been taken to satisfy the debt, the creditor cannot look to the limited partner for any more. If the partner fails to register, participates in the management of the business or allows his name to be used, he will lose his limited partner status and will have the same unlimited liability as any other partner.

INCORPORATION

The corporation is by far the most common and most important method of carrying on business today. In fact, the complex commercial world that dominates the modern western economy is based on the corporate entity. The most important single feature of the corporation is that in law it is a person separate and apart from those who deal with it and have interests in it, such as the shareholders, managers and employees. When a person decides to incorporate a company by himself, at law another person is created, separate and apart from the person who incorporates the company even if that person is now its shareholder, director and manager. That second person is the company itself. This imaginary person is often referred to as the **corporate myth**, a legal fiction created for the convenience of the business world. The corporation does not exist any more than Santa Claus does, but the business and legal community conventionally treats the incorporated business as a separate legal person, and as long as all of the parties continue to do so, the effect is profound. It is important to understand that we are not discussing the assets of the corporation here, but the corporation itself. Sears, Petrocan, IBM, and Bell all exist, in the sense that they have office towers, drilling rigs, computer terminals and transmitter stations, but just as you own your car, those are assets owned by the company. It is the company, which at law owns those assets, that is the fiction. The real people involved, the shareholders, managers, directors and employees, are separate persons, and while they have certain rights and claims in relation to the company, in law they are clearly treated as separate persons from that fictional legal person.

Historically, when many investors were needed to carry out some large business venture, they had to band together in partnerships that were unwieldy and not very attractive. The investors had to take part in the management, and they were liable beyond their investment if things went wrong. The idea was developed of a **joint stock company**, where the business venture itself was treated as a person for legal purposes, much as a town or university is. The shareholder could then invest without becoming involved in the operation of the business and without being responsible for its success or failure. This corporate myth was so successful that it has become the predominant method of carrying on business today.

Implications

Many consequences flow from the incorporated company being a separate legal entity. First and foremost, the shareholders of the corporation have limited liability — that is, if debts or other liabilities are incurred by the company, it is only the corporation that is responsible. The debts are those of the corporation, not the shareholder, and so the shareholders can lose only what they have invested. They cannot be sued for the debts of the corporation if the assets of the company are not enough to cover the claims. Thus, the shareholders have limited liability. Similarly, the managers are not responsible, since they are merely employees of the corporation. To illustrate, Fernandez owned a small manufacturing business and decided to incorporate. Once the new company was incorporated, he sold his manufacturing business to the corporation, lending it the money to make the purchase and taking a mortgage on the assets of the business as security for the loan. As a result, the corporation, of which Fernandez was the sole shareholder, owed Fernandez a significant amount of money secured on the assets of the business. Later, when the business ran into difficulties and the other creditors came to Fernandez for payment, they found not only that he was not responsible for the debt, but also that, as a secured creditor, he had first claim on the assets of the insolvent corporation. This case illustrates the significance of the corporation being a separate legal entity, and the importance of limited liability.

Also, because the incorporated company is a separate legal entity, the shareholders have no fiduciary obligation to it or each other. They are not participating in the business; they are merely investors, and so they don't have any obligation to act in the best interests of the other shareholders or even the company itself. They are free to compete with the company and to take advantage of knowledge they acquire from their membership in it. However, there are laws preventing them from profiting from insider knowledge in trading their shares. If they have learned something from people working in the company that will affect the value of its shares and that is not generally available to the public, they cannot use that knowledge to cheat other investors. Some of the advantages for shareholders have been lost in modern business practice. Moneylenders are fully aware of the protections afforded shareholders because of limited liability, and generally refuse to lend a corporation money unless the loan is guaranteed by a real person, such as a shareholder. As soon as she signs such a guarantee, the shareholder becomes personally liable for the debt and loses the advantage of limited liability. Such guarantees are not usually used with suppliers, and where liability for accidents resulting from the business activities is involved, there will be no such guarantee and limited liability will still have an important effect.

This lack of responsibility does not extend to corporate officers. The directors of the company, the president, vice-president, and other managers all have a fiduciary duty to the company and must act in its best interests. It is only the shareholders who enjoy such freedom from responsibility. Several statutes have recently been passed that hold directors personally liable for decisions they make on behalf of the company that cause injury to outsiders or to employees. This is particularly true when the company causes environmental damage that can be traced back to a company policy or practice or the negligence of one of its officers. This liability has been placed on the person who should have been responsible, preventing him or her from hiding behind the corporate veil. Directors are also personally liable for unpaid wages or corporate taxes. These offences are called **strict liability** offences, and the only way that a director can escape liability is if he can show **due diligence,** which means essentially that he took reasonable steps to avoid the problem.

Another effect of the corporation being a separate legal person is that it does not die. There are many corporations that have existed for hundreds of years. The Hudson's Bay Company, for example, has been around for more than 300 years and shows no sign of dying yet. When a shareholder dies, the shares pass on to the estate of the shareholder as would any other form of property, and the corporation is not affected.

Rich v. Enns[7]

In this case a contract was entered through solicitors between Sargent Properties Limited (the vendor) and Enns (the defendant). Enns, the purchaser, repudiated the contract and refused to go through with it before performance was due. This action was brought by Rich, the sole shareholder of Sargent Properties, for damages for breach of the contract. The reason the action was brought by Rich instead of the corporation is that the corporation had been dissolved for failure to file the annual reports that were necessary under Manitoba legislation. The question therefore was whether Rich, the sole shareholder of the now defunct company, could bring this action. The position taken by Enns was that while he had a contract it was with Sargent Properties and not with Rich. The court agreed.

The corporation was a separate legal entity distinct from the shareholder, Rich, and in none of the dealings between Enns and Sargent Properties had there been any indication that Rich was a party to the contract. Rich therefore, had no rights under the contract and could not enforce it. This case is interesting in that these questions quite often arise when a contract is created purporting to be on behalf of a corporation that is not yet incorporated. The pre-incorporation contracts are invalid for the same reason, although some jurisidictions have modified this by legislation. In this case, however, the same problem arises but after the corporation has been dissolved. In both situations the company doesn't exist and is not in a position to bring an action.

Methods of Incorporation

Because the creation of the corporation is an artificial process accomplished under legislation, several different approaches have been developed. Corporations were originally created by royal proclamation and later by special acts of government. These were specially tailored corporations, usually created for important public undertakings. Today, the vast majority of corporations are created for the private purposes of the shareholders and have to be incorporated through the standard procedures established in each jurisdiction. Quebec and Prince Edward Island use the **letters patent** means of incorporation, which was derived from the process of incorporating through **royal proclamation**. British Columbia and Nova Scotia still use the **registration method**. In more recent times another approach, referred to as the **certificate of incorporation** approach, has been introduced, and is used by the federal government, Ontario, Alberta, Saskatchewan, Manitoba, New Brunswick and Newfoundland. Although the methods vary, the effect is the same. A separate legal entity is created, with a group of members, referred to as shareholders, who invest in the corporation by purchasing shares. The shareholders have the right to elect directors of the company, and those directors are the ultimate decision-makers. Because the directors are elected, the majority rules, which can be a real hardship to minority shareholders, who can be effectively frozen out of the decision-making process.

Funding

In addition to the sale of shares, the company can also obtain funds by borrowing through the issue of **bonds** or **debentures**. This debt may be secured or unsecured, and the company must live up to its obligations like any real person. Investments by shareholders, on the other hand, are not debts, and there is no obligation to repay the investment. This is true even where special shares such as preferred shares are involved. The shareholder obtains income from dividends paid by the company out of the profits of the business. The stock market is an institution where these shares are purchased and sold. There is a similar market for the purchase and sale of bonds and debentures.

Large and Small Companies

In all jurisdictions these companies are divided into broadly held and closely held categories. A broadly held company, sometimes referred to as a **public company**, is usually a large corporation that has its shares purchased and sold on the stock market. It is closely regulated by government agencies and has many involved obligations to the shareholders in the form of voting rights, shareholders' meetings, providing audited financial statements and the like. The closely held corporation, however, is usually much smaller and can be viewed essentially as an **incorporated partnership**, where the personalities of the shareholders and their ability to get along are often important to its operation. Such a company is not as closely regulated as a broadly held corporation, and it is not permitted to sell shares on the stock market. In fact, there is usually a requirement that there be a restriction on the free transferability of shares, such as a provision in the incorporating documents that when one shareholder wants to sell shares, he must offer them to the other shareholders first. To avoid being frozen out of the decision-making process, a minority shareholder in a closely held company will often insist on a **shareholders' agreement**. This is a contract with the other shareholders setting out that certain things will not be tampered with, such as the shareholder having a specific position with the company or other shareholders having an obligation to purchase his shares at a set rate when certain events take place.

CONCLUSION

Of all the business relations discussed in this chapter, the corporation is unique because it involves a fictional creation. Each of the other legal relationships described, however, play important roles in our commercial activities. There is also a considerable overlap between them because corporations and partnerships employ workers and use agents to conduct their business affairs. In the final chapter of this text we will look at the rights people have to the property that is frequently being transferred as part of business relationships.

QUESTIONS FOR DISCUSSION AND REVIEW

1. An employer can be held liable for the tort of an employee during the course of employment. Is this a reasonable responsibility to put on an employer?

2. Is legislative intervention setting out standards for employment justifiable in times of high unemployment?

3. Outline the effect of trade unions on labour relations.

4. What principles of agency law protect consumers when they have been taken advantage of by agents?

5. What role does contract law play in the principal/agent relationship?

6. Partners participate equally in the management of a partnership. Consider the advantages and disadvantages of such a requirement.

7. Discuss the extent of liability in a partnership.

8. Why is it not possible to understand what a company is without understanding what a person is in the eyes of the law?

9. Because a corporation is a separate legal entity, shareholders who are also directors are protected from liability. Is it reasonable to give them this protection when their actions have resulted in injury?

10. Should directors and officers be held legally and morally responsible for the decisions they make on behalf of the company?

NOTES

1. *Tree Savers international Ltd. v. Savoy et al.* (1992), 87 D.L.R. (4th) 202 (Alta. C.A.).

2. *Parks v. Atlantic Provinces Special Education Authority* (1992), 87 D.L.R. (4th) 369 (N.S.S.C. (A.D.)).

3. *National Labor Relations Act*, ch. 372, 49 Stat. 449 (1935).

4. *Ocean City Realty Ltd. v. A & M Holdings Ltd. et al.* (1984), 36 D.L.R. (4th) 94 (B.C.C.A.).

5. *Public Trustee v. Mortimer et al.* (1985), 16 D.L.R. (4th) 404 (Ont. H.C.J.).

6. *Partnership Act*, R.S.B.C. 1979, c. 312, s. 36.

7. *Rich v. Enns* (May 25, 1995), (Man. C.A.) [unreported].

FURTHER READING

Bell, Stacey and Reginald J. Braithwaite. *Canadian Employment Law*. Aurora, Ont.: Canada Law Book, 1996.

Smyth, J.E., D.A. Soberman and A.J. Easson. *The Law and Business Administration in Canada*, 8th ed. Scarborough, Ont.: Prentice Hall Canada Inc., 1998.

Yates, R.A. *Business Law in Canada*, 5th ed. Scarborough, Ont.: Prentice Hall Canada Inc., 1998.

C h a p t e r

PROPERTY RIGHTS

The term *property* describes the legal relationship between a person and a thing. Used accurately, the term does not refer to the item itself but to the rights that a person has in relation to it. Because the term property is commonly applied to the actual thing, it is important in this discussion to keep in mind the technical meaning. When we talk about some item of property, then, we are not just referring to the thing itself, but also to all of those rights and obligations people have in relation to it.

Ownership is the highest property interest that a person can have in a thing, and it gives that person exclusive right to do with the property as he or she wishes, including the right to sell or otherwise dispose of it. Even when ownership is involved, however, there may be legal restrictions on what the owner can do. In our legal system, ownership can be separated from possession of the property, and so it is common to have an item owned by one person in the possession of another. In addition, there are many property interests that people can have in an item that are less than ownership.

The two major forms of property are personal property and real property. **Real property** refers to land and buildings attached to it. **Personal property** is moveable property of two types. Things that are tangible, that can be hefted and felt, thus having form and substance, are called **chattels** (the term being derived from cattle, the most important form of personal property in the Middle Ages). Non-tangible personal property in the form of rights or claims one person may have against another, such as the right to collect debts, cheques, and other forms of negotiable instruments, as well as stocks and bonds, is referred to as *choses in action.* A third division, known as intellectual property, is in common usage today, but this category is separate only for convenience. In fact, intellectual property rights are a special form of *choses in action.*

269

PERSONAL PROPERTY

Although personal property can be divided into tangible items called chattels and intangible rights called *choses in action*, the discussion below is confined primarily to a summary of rights in relation to chattels. Intangible claims were described in the chapters on contract law and commercial relationships. Other topics that involve *choses in action*, such as banking law and negotiable instruments, are much too technical to deal with in a general text.

Fixtures

Tangible, moveable items of property, such as baggage, appliances, animals and even large boats, are chattels, and the laws governing them are quite different from the law of real property. Chattels can become affixed to real property. When a furnace, stove or some other appliance is built into a house, it is a chattel until installed, but afterward it becomes part of the real property and is known as a fixture. The process of affixing a chattel to real property can have important implications for a person claiming a property interest in the chattel. When a person purchases a new furnace on credit, the seller may retain a property interest in it in the form of a lien so long as it remains separate from the house, but as soon as it is installed in the building, it becomes part of the real property. If the house is sold, the furnace goes with it, independent of any claim that the original seller may have had. He can still sue the original purchaser for debt, but he no longer has any claim against the furnace itself.

There are, in fact, different classes of fixtures. When a person rents a building to carry on business and installs heavy-duty machinery, display cases or other items requiring installation to be effective, they are known as **trade fixtures**. When the tenancy arrangement ends, the tenant has the right to detach and remove trade fixtures. As a general rule, when people attach things to their home, such as pictures, mirrors or cabinets, they have a right to take those items with them when they go, providing, of course, that the property will not be damaged in the process of removal.

Some chattels are not meant to be removed once installed, and these must stay with the property in the absence of any agreement to the contrary. For example, throw rugs over a hardwood floor are not permanently affixed and can be removed, but wall-to-wall carpet is usually installed over a rough, unfinished floor and becomes part of the finished structure. If a tenant replaces such a carpet, the new one becomes part of the building and cannot be removed without permission.

Disputes over whether such a chattel must stay arise not only at the end of a tenancy arrangement, but also when creditors of the tenant claim an interest in the item against the landlord and when there is a dispute about what was included in the sale of a house. When a tenant installs something that he or she does not own, title to that item remains with the rightful owner, and it can be reclaimed even if the building changes hands.

As a general rule, the person in possession of a chattel has a right to it against anyone, except someone with a prior right or claim. An item found in a public place belongs to the finder, unless the original owner claims it. But when an item is found in a part of an establishment that is not open to the public, or by an employee in a public area of an establishment, the owner of the establishment is entitled to the item.

Sale of Goods

There are several ways that the title to a chattel can be transferred. Sale and gift are the most important of these. The sale of a chattel is governed by the law of contract and *Sale of Goods Acts* in the various jurisdictions. One of the main purposes of the Act is to establish the rights and obligations of the parties to the sale. Because sellers and purchasers often don't consider what will happen if something goes wrong with the deal, the *Sale of Goods Act* supplies the missing terms. It must be emphasized that these terms are implied only when the parties have not agreed otherwise, and therefore specific terms in the contract of purchase that are inconsistent with the terms of the Act override the provisions of the Act.

One of the questions that comes up often when goods are sold is who bears the risk once a contract has been made and the goods remain with the seller or are in the process of transport. The *Sale of Goods Act* says in essence that **risk follows title** and then sets out a number of rules that determine when title transfers. These rules apply unless the parties agree otherwise.

The most important terms embodied in the *Sale of Goods Act* relate to **title**, **fitness** and **quality**. There is a requirement that the seller of the goods have the right to sell them and be able to deliver clear title. When goods are purchased by description, from a catalogue, for example, there is a provision that the goods must match the description. When bought by sample the goods must match the sample. But most importantly, there is a provision requiring all mass-produced goods sold by description to be of **merchantable quality**, which means they must be free from any inherent defect which would, if known by the purchaser, make him avoid the transaction. Thus when a person purchases a car that is so defective it doesn't run, the purchaser can demand that the seller fix the car or that the money be returned. Also, where it is in the seller's normal course of business to sell a particular product, and a buyer makes it known to the seller that she is relying on the seller's skill and assurance that the product will do a specific job, then that product must be suitable for the purpose for which it was purchased.

These two provisions relating to fitness and quality have become extremely important and are the main reason that the **exemption clauses** that manufacturers and sellers try to impose, referred to as **manufacturers' warranties**, attempt to limit liability. These typically reduce the purchasers' protections, rather than give added benefits. In most provinces such exemption clauses are valid, but some jurisdictions include a provision making any attempt to limit, qualify or reduce the requirement of merchantability and durability void when it is applied to consumer-type transactions.

Most jurisdictions have passed separate consumer protection legislation designed to protect the purchaser and to ensure that there will be some recourse against the seller when shoddy or defective merchandise is sold. Such legislation also provides protection for the consumer from misleading or otherwise unfair or inappropriate sales tactics and merchandising practices.

Sale of Goods

Gee v. White Spot Ltd.[1]

In July 1985 Mr. Gee consumed a meal at the White Spot, a restaurant in Vancouver, and he contracted botulism as result of that meal. In a separate action being heard at the same time, Mr. and Mrs. Pam suffered botulism from a meal they ate in September of the same year at the same restaurant. To determine liability, the first problem the court had to deal with was whether this was a contract of goods under the Sale of Goods Act or a contract for services which that Act would not cover. The court looked at the nature of the transaction and decided that although there were some elements of service involved, the primary purpose was the purchase and consumption of the food, which was a good and therefore covered by the Act. The court then applied section 18 of the BC Act to the transaction. That section states that where a purchaser relies on the skill and ability of the seller and makes known to the seller the purpose for which the goods are being purchased, those goods must be fit for the purpose.

In this case it was clear that the seller was in the business of selling food, that the purchaser was relying on the seller's skill and judgment and that the food was to be consumed; therefore, it had to be fit for that purpose. It wasn't; therefore, the implied term that the goods had to be fit for the purpose was breached. The judge pointed out that the second part of the section is also satisfied in that the goods were purchased by description from a menu and therefore had to be of merchantable quality, which they weren't. The plaintiffs were successful in their action against White Spot for the damages suffered.

Gifts

The title to goods and chattels can also be transferred by gift. A gift involves the voluntary transfer of ownership of an item without any consideration or benefit flowing back to the person giving the gift. Such a gratuitous transfer of ownership can apply when chattels, real property or even *choses in action* are involved. As soon as the delivery of the chattel to the person receiving it takes place, the transfer is complete and ownership passes irrevocably. Of course, a person cannot be forced to honour a gratuitous promise, so if the transfer is to take place some time in the future, the person promising to give the gift can change his mind any time before delivery. Gifts that are given in contemplation of death are a special case, and usually they are controlled by legislation dealing with wills and estates.

Usually the transfer of ownership takes place with the actual delivery of the goods from the person giving the gift to the person receiving it. When dealing with some unwieldy, large or valuable gift or one in the keeping of a third party, some sort of symbolic or constructive delivery of the gift may be sufficient. For example, if Joanne owned a yacht and was giving it to Sam, merely handing him the key with intention of delivering the yacht would be sufficient. Similarly, the delivery of a key to a safety deposit box in which valuables are kept may have the same effect, if that is the intention of the parties.

Transfer by Deed

It is also possible for the title or possession of the goods being given to be transferred by deed, a written instrument under seal purporting to transfer the property. The seal is the essential element of such a transfer. Once a gift is completed through the delivery of possession, constructive delivery or a deed, the transfer of title is completed, and the donor cannot later change his mind and demand the gift's return.

A *chose in action*, such as claims of debt, bank accounts, negotiable instruments, bonds and shares of stocks, can also be transferred. When such a transfer takes place and there is consideration on both sides, it is referred to as an assignment. A similar arrangement when tangible property such as a chattel is involved is referred to as a sale. When the transfer of such a *chose in action* is gratuitous, however, it is usually accomplished by notifying the person against whom the claim exists that it is now to be paid to the person receiving the gift.

Where negotiable instruments such as cheques, bills of exchange, promissory notes and even bonds are involved, however, the transfer is complete simply with endorsement where required and the delivery of the instrument — for example, the cheque — to the person receiving the gift. These instruments have the characteristic that their possession determines the right to collect, and therefore delivery and endorsement where required is sufficient to convey the gift. Other *choses in action*, such as bank accounts, insurance policies or corporate share certificates, require notification of transfer before the gift can be effective. Many of these transfers are controlled by provisions of the original agreement creating the obligation, or by legislation specifying how, if at all, such transfers can take place. When a *chose in action* is involved, how the transfer of the rights is to be accomplished depends on the nature of the interest being given.

Bailment

Often people have goods in their possession without actually owning them. When the owner of a chattel allows another to possess it, a bailment exists. The obligations on the **bailee** (the person in possession of the chattel) and the **bailor** (the person who owns the chattel) are determined by the nature of the relationship between them and the purpose for which the transfer has taken place. The transfer must be voluntary and temporary. A car parked in a mall parking lot is not normally a bailment. Rather, the mall's owner has simply given permission or a licence to the driver to use that space to park. The car remains in the control and, therefore, the possession of the driver. If the car is given to an employee of a hotel or restaurant to park or if the keys are given to a parking lot attendant, control of the vehicle has been given over to someone else and a bailment has taken place.

In general, a bailee is responsible for any willful, negligent or fraudulent act that damages or interferes with the bailor's goods. The standard of care the bailee must exercise when looking after the chattels varies with the nature of the bailment. Examples of such bailments would be an appliance left with a repairperson or clothing left at a dry-cleaners or with a coat-check person at a restaurant.

Exculpatory Clauses

Quite often, contracts for bailment contain exculpatory clauses in which the bailee attempts to limit or restrict liability as much as possible. Such terms must be brought to the attention of customers before they are binding on them. Even then, exculpatory clauses are strictly interpreted by the courts, which means any ambiguity will be interpreted in favour of the customer. If a restaurant has a designated area for customers to place coats while dining and posts a sign stating that they would not be liable for any lost or stolen goods, the customer is not bound by the sign unless it is brought to her attention or located where she is bound to see it. If the coat is damaged in a fire, the exculpatory clause would not protect the restaurant even if it was properly displayed, because it did not cover damage to the coat, but just loss and theft.

Goods in Transport

Historically, common carriers and innkeepers have had a particularly high duty to take care of the goods of their customers. Common carriers are public truck lines, bus lines, railways and airlines that provide a regular service transporting goods and people from one location to another. A common carrier offers its services to the public generally, whereas a private carrier enters into specific contracts to transport goods for selected customers. A common carrier has a higher duty to care for goods and can be required to compensate the customer for loss or damage to them, even in the absence of any fault or negligence on its part. The obligations of common carriers are usually modified by legislation in the various jurisdictions.

Innkeepers

A hotel or innkeeper has similar responsibilities toward the property of guests left at the hotel. An innkeeper is liable for any damage or loss to a guest's property while it is on their premises, unless that loss was caused by the carelessness or recklessness of the guest. Thus, the innkeeper must compensate the guest even though he or his employee was not to blame for the loss. Even when some third party comes into the hotel and steals those goods, the innkeeper is still responsible. Note that this responsibility is broader than bailment, because the innkeeper is responsible even for goods left in a guest's room.

This regulation was considered particularly harsh, and it has been modified in most jurisdictions by statute. Although there are some minor variations, in most provinces the *Innkeepers' Act*[2] provides that the innkeeper is liable for the loss of the guest's property only when it can be shown that the innkeeper or an employee was at fault by their willful or negligent conduct. The effect of this legislation, then, is to significantly reduce the liability of the innkeeper, but in order for those provisions to apply, appropriate notices of the reduction of liability must be properly posted throughout the inn.

Borrowing

A bailment relationship can be created gratuitously. A neighbour borrowing a lawnmower creates a gratuitous bailment for the benefit of the bailee. A request that a neighbour look after a dog is a gratuitous bailment for the benefit of the bailor. When the bailee is receiving the benefit of having the goods in his possession, the obligation on that person to look after them is high. But when the bailee is looking after the goods as a favour to the bailor, the obligation to take care of them is much lower. Of course, when both parties are benefiting from the arrangement — for example, when someone looks after someone else's car with the privilege of using it — the obligation to care for the goods would be similar to the care a reasonable person would be expected to use in the care of his own goods. What is reasonable in all of these circumstances will vary with the value and vulnerability of those goods. If the car involved is a brand-new Ferrari worth $150 000, one would expect the bailee to be much more careful with it than would be the case if it was an old, well-used pickup truck. In an action to recover compensation from a bailee for damage done to goods in his care, once the plaintiff has proved the existence of the bailment, it is up to the bailee to prove that he was not negligent. In other cases, in contrast, it is usually the person claiming negligence who is obligated to prove that the person being claimed against failed to live up to the standard of care required.

Found Property

When a person acquires goods from another involuntarily, as would be the case with a watch found on the beach or a hat or coat left on a chair in a restaurant or other public building, the obligations on the person acquiring the goods are similar to those imposed when a gratuitous bailment for the benefit of the bailor is involved. Of course, a person put in this position has no obligation to accept the responsibility, but as soon as she exercises any control over the item, such as picking up the watch or even moving the coat or hat to another location, she has assumed responsibility as a bailee with the associated obligations. One very important and basic obligation that a finder of property, as well as any bailee, has is to make sure that the property is returned to the rightful owner.

INTELLECTUAL PROPERTY

Creative people who produce ideas, manuscripts and inventions need to have their efforts protected in the same way that chattels need protection from theft. Although intellectual property is a form of personal property, there are some characteristics of it that are unique. When a chattel is stolen or destroyed, it is no longer available to the rightful owner, whereas when intellectual property such as an invention is taken and used by someone else, it is still available to the creator of the original work. The problem is that the value of the work to the creator may have been considerably reduced. Moreover, free flow of ideas and information has been vitally important for human development and progress. So, while it is important to protect the results of our creative efforts, the free flow of information must also be encouraged. Intellectual property laws attempt to maintain the fine balance necessary between these two competing interests.

Copyright

The federal *Copyright Act*[3] is designed to protect people who record their ideas in some permanent form, such as writing. It covers literary works such as books, articles and even computer programs; dramatic works such as movies, theatre scripts, musical productions and manuscripts; and artistic works such as paintings, photographs and sculptures. In Canada a copyright is automatically created when the work is produced. Registration or publication is not required. However, in the United States and several other countries, the material must be registered at a designated government office to receive copyright protection. Because there is such an interchange of information between countries, it is advisable that anyone creating original works in Canada comply with the registration requirements in other countries. Even within Canada registration is a good idea, since it establishes when the work was created and by whom. This evidence can be invaluable in disputes that may arise later. To avoid confusion and simplify the process, there are two international agreements in place to deal with copyright protection (the Berne Convention and the Universal Copyright Convention). These international treaties establish a common approach to providing copyright protection in the various countries that are signatories to them.

Rights

When an original work is created, the copyright in that work rests, as a rule, with the author or creator of it. However, if that person was working as an employee and acting under the direction of an employer, the copyright will be the property of the employer unless the parties have agreed otherwise. A copyright is a form of intangible personal property, and like any other kind of possession, it can be sold. The holder of the copyright has the right to assign (sell) that copyright to someone else, but he still retains some rights (called moral rights) in relation to the work. One such right is that the new owner may not modify the work in a way that degrades it, causing harm to the reputation of the author, without his or her express approval.

The protection provided under the copyright legislation means that the work cannot be reproduced, performed, published, copied or otherwise used by anyone without the approval of the copyright holder. Thus, the holder of the copyright will receive any benefits that are to be derived from it. There are some exceptions; for example, materials can be reproduced for such purposes as private study and research without any infringement of copyright. When the copyright is infringed in any way, the statute provides that the holder of the copyright can bring an action and seek redress. This copyright protection lasts for the life of the author plus 50 years. It must be emphasized, however, that it is only the expression of the idea in the form of the written or otherwise produced work that is protected, not the idea itself. If someone else has the same ideas and expresses them in different forms, there is no complaint. The words used in this text are copyrighted. They cannot be reproduced without permission, but if another author wishes to express these ideas in his or her own words, there is no copyright protection to prevent it.

Copyright

British Columbia Jockey Club et al. v. Standon[4]

The British Columbia Jockey Club published a circular entitled "Overnight Entries Exhibition Park." This circular contained information about each day of racing including the date of the race, the order of races, the length of each race, the purses, assigned weights for each entry, and track conditions. There is no question that a considerable amount of work and skill went into the preparation of this publication. The defendant published another newsletter, "The Vancouver Sporting Special News." In that publication much of the information set out in the Jockey Club publication was taken and included in this newsletter although the form or structure of the special news publication was quite different than the Jockey Club's "Overnight" publication. When the Jockey Club sued claiming copyright infringement, the defence was that the information contained in the "Special News" was embodied in a completely different form and as it is only the expression of the idea that can be copyrighted, there was no copyright violation.

This case illustrates that since the information produced by the Jockey Club and published in the "Overnight" was unique and novel, that information itself was protected by copyright. Although the "Special News" expressed the information in a different format, it still copied that information, and this was a violation of copyright. It is true that ideas can't be copyrighted, but a person can't simply reword unique information, expressing it in a different way, and claim that he is not breaching copyright.

The appeal judge supported the trial judge's decision when he said,

In my opinion the facts here show that the defendant has made a substantial use of all the essential facts compiled by the club. Although he adopted the information to his own style and added information of his own, the defendant nevertheless appropriated a substantial amount of the work, skill, judgment and knowledge of the club. The copyright of the club does not reside solely in the order of the information which it has compiled. Although the defendant has rearranged and republished that information in a different style, he nevertheless continued to appropriate a substantial part of the club's original work.

Mr. Justice Hutcheon of the Appeal Court found that the error that was made by the publishers of the "Special News" was that they assumed that the copyright was in the form and not the information and that assumption was incorrect. The important point here is that although we think of copyright in the expression of the idea and not the idea itself, this shows that copyright protection is somewhat broader.

Remedies

A very important remedy that is available when a copyright has been infringed is the **injunction**. This is a court order to the offending party to stop wrongfully using the work. An injunction may be obtained before trial (an interlocutory injunction), or in the form of a permanent injunction granted as a remedy in the trial itself. Damages are another important remedy, but the person who holds the copyright may also have the right to an **accounting of the profits**. This is a court order that any profits that have been wrongfully obtained through the infringement of copyright be paid over to the rightful owner. Some significant amendments to the *Copyright Act* were published in 1988 that provided, among other things, for the creation of a copyright board, which has the power to handle disputes arising under copyright law and also to regulate the industries involved.

Patents

Patents are governed by the federal *Patent Act*,[5] and the protection it gives is quite different from that provided under copyright law. When a patent is granted on an invention, the person receiving it gains a monopoly on the use of the idea represented by that invention. With a patent it is the idea that is being protected, whereas with a copyright it is the expression of the idea that is protected. Only the person with the patent has the right to produce, sell or otherwise profit from the use of that invention. As is the case with any other form of property, this patent can be assigned or sold to others. In order to be patentable in the first place, the idea must be original and the product of the inventor, not others. If an invention is already known to the public but has not been patented, no one can come along and obtain the patent. It must also be unique, having properties that separate it from other products, and not simply an obvious improvement on an already existing product or process. It also must have some practical value, and so it cannot be a theory or concept, such as Einstein's theory of relativity or Newton's laws of thermodynamics.

Process

A patent is obtained by filing an application along with accompanying documentation at the appropriate government office, and the priority, if there is more than one application, is based on the time of application. It is important, therefore, for the inventor to apply for the patent as soon as possible. An inventor who fails to patent an invention immediately runs the risk that someone else will independently come up with the same invention and patent it first. If this happens, the inventor not only will be denied a patent, but will be prohibited from profiting from or even producing his or her invention. Because procedures for obtaining a patent are involved and require a great deal of expertise, specialized professionals are available to act as agents for inventors. While under copyright law the protection granted lasts until 50 years after the death of the author, patent protection is only given for a period of 20 years.

Purpose

At first it may appear that patent legislation is designed to keep information protected and unavailable to the public, but in fact the purpose of patent law is to ensure disclosure of the idea so that advancements can be stimulated. When a person develops an invention, there is a tendency to keep the idea and process secret so that only she can profit. The patent legislation requires full disclosure of all of the pertinent information, to the extent that the invention or process could be produced from it. This information is then made available to the public through the patent office in exchange for the patent, which grants the patent holder exclusive rights to profit from the invention for 20 years. Other scientific advancements and inventions are encouraged, based on the information disclosed. If someone does infringe the patent protection and makes use of the invention without the permission of the patent holder, she can seek redress in court. The remedies available are like those discussed for copyright, usually an injunction, damages and/or an accounting of profits.

Trademarks

Businesses often use a logo or other identifying mark to help the public quickly identify their business. The mark may be a word such as Xerox, a symbol such as the golden arches placed in front of McDonald's restaurants, or a combination of words and symbols such as the distinctive Coca-Cola logo found on that company's soft drinks and advertisements. Trademarks represent an investment of money and effort, and when someone else uses them or something similar, it both threatens the investment and deceives the public into thinking that they are dealing with the business identified with the logo. The federal *Trademarks Act*[6] is designed to prevent others from wrongfully using these symbols. The protection is acquired by registering the trademark with the appropriate government office. Registration provides protection in the countries that are participants in the International Trademark Agreement. This protection is available for a period of 15 years, and it is renewable.

Process and Remedies

As in the case of patents, the process of obtaining a trademark is complicated, and the services of an expert ought to be employed. When someone infringes on a trademark right, it is not sufficient to show that the owner actually holds the registered trademark; he must also demonstrate that the public is likely to be confused by its wrongful use. It is, therefore, important to establish for the court that the trademark has become associated with the business of the plaintiff in the minds of the public. As in the case of patents and copyrights, the usual remedies are injunctions and damages. It is also possible, however, for the court to order that the goods that infringe the copyright be surrendered to the plaintiff, to be disposed of as the plaintiff sees fit. Thus, when fake Seiko and Rolex watches were manufactured and the fraud was detected, the courts ordered them to be surrendered to the offended companies, and they then had the copies destroyed.

Passing-off

Even when there is no trademark protection involved, when someone tries to mislead the public into believing that they are doing business with one company when they are really dealing with another, an actionable wrong has been committed under common law, and the injured party can seek redress through a **passing-off action**. Were an independent hamburger stand to use the same colour scheme as McDonald's in order to make people think they were actually eating at McDonald's, McDonald's could bring a passing-off action. This tort action is available when someone uses the trademark, name or some other feature of a business that will encourage the public to think they are dealing with that business when they are not.

Confidential Information

Trade secrets and other forms of confidential business information, such as customer lists, suppliers of products, and profits, can be very valuable, and it can be extremely damaging if this information gets into the hands of a competitor. At common law a duty has been developed, requiring people in privileged and trusting relationships (including fiduciary relationships) not to disclose this confidential information to others. If they do so, they could be sued by the party whose confidence has been violated.

It must be emphasized that it is the disclosure of the confidential information that constitutes the wrongful conduct, not the fact that the competitor has that information. In this sense, the person harmed by the disclosure does not usually have a proprietary interest in the information. If a trade secret is involved, such as a unique recipe for fried chicken, and a competitor discovers the same recipe independently, there could be no complaint. If, however, an employee of the fried chicken company disclosed that confidential information to the competitor, that would be an actionable wrong.

If an employee acquires skills and abilities while in the employ of one company, he can use those skills and abilities when he works for a competitor. But if there is a secret formula involved or some specialized process, the details of which are known only to the original employer, and these are disclosed to a competitor, that would be a violation of confidentiality.

REAL PROPERTY

Shelter is a basic need, and acquiring it usually requires a significant part of one's personal wealth. As a result, the law in relation to real property is extremely important, and it has been a driving force in the development of the common law. Real property consists of land and the buildings attached to it.

Although, theoretically, a person owns the area above and below the surface of his land, in practical terms this ownership is limited by several factors. In most situations the owner of the surface rights does not own the mineral rights under the property; the government does. Mineral rights are retained by the Crown, but they can be assigned to others, who then acquire the right to come onto the property and take the minerals. In addition, a person owns the area below his property only to the extent that he can make use of it. Similarly, the area above the land is only his insofar as he can make use of and occupy it. An airplane passing overhead, or some other kind of intrusion, would not constitute a trespass. Some permanent intrusions, however, such as a sign hanging off an adjoining building, or a balloon used for advertising purposes, affixed to nearby property by a rope but which strays over your property because of the prevailing winds, would be trespass. In theory, at least in Canada, all land is ultimately owned by the Crown and has merely been granted for the use of those holding it. This concept is a holdover from the feudal system and has little relevance today, since the highest interest that a person can have in land today (the fee simple estate) is analogous to ownership and conveys with it the same rights.

Interests in Land

There are several different interests that a person can have in land. The holder of a **fee simple estate** has the right to use the property as she wants and the right to dispose of it. In Canada the estate of fee tail has been all but abolished. The person holding a **fee tail estate** has all the rights of ownership except the right to dispose of the property, which must be passed down through the family line. Even when a person has a fee simple estate, there may be some restrictions on his free use of his land, such as zoning laws and other land use restrictions in the form of government regulations. The property owner may even face the prospect of it being expropriated for some greater community good. These restrictions are generally considered necessary to have an ordered society, and they are part of the cost of living in this country. They are not a limitation on a person's ownership of property as such.

When someone owns property in the form of a fee simple interest, he or she can sell the entire interest or confer only part of that interest on another party. A **life estate** is such a partial conveyance of the fee simple. The person who receives the life estate in the property has the right to use that property during her lifetime, but she cannot pass that property on to her heirs. When she dies (if it is her lifetime the estate is based on), the estate reverts to the person who originally conveyed the life estate. Thus, while the life estate is in place, the original grantor of it is said to have a reversionary interest. If, however, the original grantor conveys that reversionary interest to someone else, the person who has the right to recover the property upon the death of the life tenant is said to be a **remainderman**.

These three types of estates — the fee simple, the fee tail and the life estate — are known as **freehold estates** because there is no specified time involved. It is also possible to create a **leasehold estate** (a lease). In modern times this has become a very common and very important interest in property. Rented property, commercial or residential, is a leasehold estate. One of the most important features of a lease is that it has a specific time period. The duration of such leases may be for some considerable length of time, such as 99 years, but more commonly they are for only a year or two.

Tenancy

It is also possible and common to have a periodic tenancy. This is a leasehold estate that has no time limit. The period is simply the agreed rental period, usually one month, renewable each month. People who rent apartments or houses by the month without a lease have a **periodic tenancy** arrangement. As a rule, to end a periodic tenancy one of the parties gives the other notice. The appropriate length of time for such notice is one clear rental period. For example, when a person who is paying his rent on the first of the month decides he wants to leave at the end of November, he must give notice to terminate by the end of October, at least the day before that last month's rent is paid.

During the period of the tenancy the tenant has exclusive rights to the possession of the premises, and even the landlord cannot come onto the premises without permission. Of course, since a lease is a special kind of contract, the parties can modify these rights and obligations by agreement. In most provinces a leasehold interest that runs for over three years must be registered and in writing, in order to be enforceable against third parties purchasing or otherwise acquiring an interest in the property. Another important feature of leasehold interests is that they run with the land. A normal contract only binds the parties to it. With leasehold interests, however, the interest conveyed is in the land itself. It is binding against subsequent owners, even though they were not parties to the agreement. So when someone purchases a house with tenants, the purchaser takes possession subject to the terms of the lease.

Landlord and Tenant Obligations

The lease entered into by the tenant and landlord will typically set out the obligations of the parties. In the absence of such specified provisions, the tenant must pay rent on a regular basis and repair any damage that he causes, but is not, as a rule, required to repair normal wear and tear. The landlord must not interfere with the tenant's use of the property, since it is exclusively his for the duration of the lease. Both parties, of course, are required to give each other proper notice in the event of termination.

Tenancy Legislation

An important development in recent times has been the proliferation of specialized legislation designed to control residential tenancies. Most provinces have enacted legislation making minimal changes to the law relating to commercial tenancies, but the law in relation to residential tenancies in all jurisdictions has been significantly modified. Some jurisdictions have imposed rent controls that set a maximum percentage that the landlord can raise the rent in a given year, and have taken disputes between landlord and tenant out of the hands of the courts with the creation of an **ombudsperson's office**. This is a government agency that mediates and adjudicates disputes between landlord and tenant. Because they are not courts but take on many of the functions of the court, they are examples of the administrative tribunals that were discussed in earlier chapters.

Another significant change enacted has often been a lengthening of the notice period that must be given to the tenant in the event of termination or a rent increase. The notice that must be given by the tenant to the landlord in the event of a termination has also often been lengthened, but usually not in such an onerous way. Typically, the *Residential Tenancy Acts*[7] in the various jurisdictions impose certain obligations on the landlord to keep the property in good repair and in a sanitary and healthy condition. The practice has also developed for the landlord to take a security deposit from the tenant to ensure that the last month's rent is paid upon termination and to cover any damage done to the premises. Generally there is legislation in place that restricts the amount that can be required as a security deposit.

Other Interests in Land

Although freehold interests and life estates are the most common kinds of interests in land, there are several other lesser interests that can be important. An **easement** gives the holder the right to use a portion of the land owned by another. An easement can be in the form of a permanent incursion, such as when one landowner grants his neighbour an easement for a roof that hangs over his property, or it may be in the form of a right of way. A right of way gives someone the right to travel across the property but not to stay there permanently. Easements require a dominant tenement, which is the property that derives the benefit of the easement, and a serviant tenement, which is the property against which the easement is taken.

When a person allows another to use her land but no easement is actually conveyed, this is merely a licence. A **licence** is permission to use the property, and no interest in land is conveyed. Something similar is a ***profit à prendre***. This gives the holder the right to go on the property and take something from it, such as trees, gravel, sand or some similar material. Unlike a licence, a *profit à prendre* is an interest in land.

It is also possible for the person selling the land to restrict the use of it in the hands of the new owner. When a person subdivides his property and sells off a portion of it, he may wish to restrict what can be built. If he states in the documents of sale that no building higher than three stories can be erected, he has made a **restrictive covenant**. If the covenant is made correctly, it creates an interest in land that runs with it, binding subsequent owners, and that is not merely a contractual term of the sale. Extended to large developments like subdivisions, it can be quite effective in controlling the kinds of construction that take place. For example, it will often be required in a particular housing development that all of the houses be of a minimum size, built with the same construction material, such as brick, and have slate roofs. This is referred to as a building scheme, and it has many of the attributes of zoning legislation with the advantage of being much more flexible.

Joint and Common Tenancy

Often people want to share the ownership they have in real property. There are two ways that this can be accomplished. A **tenancy in common** is an arrangement where each party has a half interest in the property. This tenancy is an undivided half interest; neither party can point to any one portion of it and say, "That is my part." In fact, both share all of the property. When one of the parties dies, his half interest goes to his estate and then to his heirs. This feature makes a tenancy in common quite different from the other way of sharing an interest in property, the joint tenancy. The main difference between the two is that with a **joint tenancy** there is a right of survivorship. That means that when a person dies, the remaining person is automatically entitled to the whole property. If a person owns a house in joint tenancy with his wife, he cannot will his half interest to his child. Upon his death, his wife automatically acquires his portion as the survivor, and so there is no interest to pass on. Of course, if he decides that he doesn't want this to happen, he can sever the joint tenancy. This simply changes the joint tenancy to a tenancy in common.

Kish v. Tompkins[8]

Mr. and Mrs. Tompkins owned property together as joint tenants. Their marriage broke down. The husband made a new will naming Kish as the executrix of the will and as the beneficiary. The husband died. The question for the court was whether or not the joint tenancy had been severed prior to the death so that Mrs. Kish would be entitled to half interest in the house. Mrs. Kish argued that Mrs. Tompkins had made an application under the *Family Relations Act* and in the process made a declaration that there was no reasonable prospect of reconciliation and asking for a determination of family assets as well as a declaration of the ownership and division of those assets. In addition to that, Mr. and Mrs. Tompkins had entered into negotiations to effect a settlement with respect to their claims against each other including the sale of the house and a division of the proceeds between them. Mrs. Kish argued that, taking all this together it effectively severed the joint tenancy and eliminated Mrs. Tompkins' right of survivorship.

The court disagreed. This was a joint tenancy and although there may have been an indication of an intent to sever, that severance had not taken place. Certainly the action under the *Family Relations Act* had not yet happened. For a joint tenancy interest to be severed, this can be accomplished by the sale of the property, by an agreement between the parties changing the joint tenancy to a tenancy in common, or evidence of a course of dealings between them which shows they have mutually treated their interests as being in common as opposed to joint tenancy. In this case none of those events had taken place. Therefore Mrs. Tompkins was entitled to her deceased's interests by right of survivorship.

This case not only shows the importance of distinguishing between owning property jointly and in common — that is, the right of survivorship — but also shows how important it is that if any of the parties want to change that relationship, they must do so overtly.

Conveyancing

One of the great difficulties that has arisen over the years is the problem of assuring that the person selling the property has the right to give good title to it to the purchaser. In the past, the only way that a purchaser could be absolutely sure of who the rightful owner was, was to trace the ownership back through every transaction, establishing the validity of each sale right back to the original grant from the Crown. That could require going back through scores of owners and claims, and then you could still never be sure that a sale had not taken place that you were unaware of. To avoid this difficulty, all provinces have introduced a system of registering land transactions. There are two major approaches used in Canada.

Land Titles

In the western provinces and portions of Ontario, the Torrens System of land registry is used, and it is often referred to as a **land titles system**. In other parts of Canada, a normal system of registration is in place. The difference is that with the normal system of land registry, the only assurance a purchaser has is that all documents that can affect the title to the property are registered at the registry office. If there has been a sale of the property that has not been recorded, that document will not affect the position of parties unaware of it. But it is still up to the parties to examine the transactions to see which are valid and to determine the state of the title from the registered documents.

Under the land titles system, a certificate of title is issued by the government land titles office, and that certificate of title determines the title and the rights of the parties. In fact, the certificate of title is conclusive evidence of who is entitled to the property. Any mortgages, judgments, easements and so forth that affect the title are listed in order of registration on the back of the certificate. The effect of these provisions is that in a land titles jurisdiction the government has guaranteed that the rights as set out in the certificate of title are accurate. The purchaser is not only freed from worry about any unregistered documents, but also doesn't have to be concerned about the legal effect of past transactions that have been recorded.

Property as Security

Another important interest in land is conveyed when real property is used as security for a loan, either in the form of an agreement for sale or a mortgage. When money is borrowed with a simple contractual commitment to repay the debt, the creditor is referred to as **general creditor**. In these circumstances, if there is a default, the creditor must sue and obtain judgment for the amount owed. When other creditors are involved and the assets of the debtor are not enough to satisfy them all, each gets a portion and an individual creditor's share may be little or nothing.

The purpose of a security is to protect the moneylender's interest, by giving him priority or first claim against some specific asset of the debtor. The creditor is thus assured of repayment no matter how insolvent the debtor becomes, at least so long as the value of the security taken is sufficient to cover the loan. It is possible to give such assurance of repayment to the creditor in other ways, such as by involving some other reliable person to guarantee repayment. The more common approach to creating a security, however, is to bestow on the creditor a prior claim against some property that is worth more than the debt. Both personal and real property can be used as security. When this is done, the creditor is referred to as a secured creditor, as opposed to a general creditor, who has no such priority.

Mortgages

The most common form of real property security is the mortgage. On some occasions, however, an agreement for sale is used. In both cases, the key element is that the title to the property is vested in the creditor until the debt is paid. When an **agreement for sale** is involved, the property is sold and the seller provides the financing to the purchaser. In effect, this sale takes place in two stages. Initially, the possession of the property is transferred to the purchaser, who then makes regular payments back to the seller. When sufficient payments have been made to pay off the debt, the seller then conveys the title to the purchaser as well. The first stage is to transfer the possession of the property to the purchaser, and the second stage, which usually takes place many years later, is the conveyance of the title after the debt has been paid.

The reason the agreement for sale is not common is that its use is restricted to those situations where the creditor is the seller of the property. A mortgage, on the other hand, can be used as a method for securing a loan any time the owner of real property needs to borrow money. A **mortgage** involves a person borrowing money, called the **mortgagor**, conveying her title or interest in real property as security for the loan to the creditor, who is referred to as the **mortgagee**. The creditor then has the title to the property during the period of the loan, and upon the repayment of the debt, the title is reconveyed to the debtor, signifying the end of the relationship. When someone says that the bank owns his house, he may be joking, but if a mortgage is involved, the concept is accurate. The bank as mortgagee does, in fact, hold the title to the house as security for the loan. That basic concept is not difficult, but as with other aspects of real property, over the years people have managed to make real property mortgages much more complex.

At common law, when such a mortgage relationship is entered into, the contractual relationship that formed the basis of it required the repayment of the loan. Transferring or conveying the title of the property as security was merely incidental to the transaction. If a person failed to make the appropriate payments to repay the loan, he lost the title to his property but was still obligated to repay the loan. One of the greatest contributions of the Courts of Chancery was to overturn this inequity. Since the main thrust of the contractual relationship between the parties is one of debt, not the transferring of property, it was thought unfair and inappropriate that the mortgagee could hold the title and still insist on repayment of the debt.

Equity of Redemption

The Courts of Chancery recognized a right vested in the mortgagor debtor to reclaim the property through payment of the debt. In effect, although the mortgagor conveyed title to the mortgagee, the mortgagor retained an interest in the property that gave him the right to redeem the property through payment of the debt, even after default. This is known as the equity of redemption.

The effect of the creation of the equity of redemption was to give the mortgagor an interest in his property, even after he conveyed title to it to the mortgagee. This interest had a value equal to the difference between the value of the property and the amount of the debt owing. If the property was worth $100 000 and $25 000 was owing on a mortgage, the value of the equity of redemption was $75 000. The use of the term **equity** in the business world today is derived from shortening the proper name of this legal concept, and equity as it is commonly used refers to the value of a person's interest in an asset after any money owing on it is deducted.

Because the mortgagor still has an interest that is of considerable value, it can also be used as security for another loan. This time, however, instead of the title being conveyed, it's the equity of redemption, or the right to reclaim the property, that is conveyed to the new creditor. This right is referred to as a second mortgage. The Courts of Chancery will also recognize a right to redeem an equity of redemption conveyed to the second creditor, and so there can be a third or fourth mortgage as well. Theoretically, there is no limit to the number of such mortgages that can be created, but as a practical matter, even third and fourth mortgages are rare. Since the first mortgage is the conveyance of the title at common law and the other mortgages are merely interests recognized in equity, second, third, and fourth mortgages are referred to as equitable mortgages.

Equitable Mortgages

Because of the nature of these interests, a person who has taken a second or third mortgage must be prepared to buy out the interests above him in order to protect his investment. If Carmen borrowed $25 000 from Sandhu, giving him a first mortgage as security, and then borrowed a further $15 000 from Brady, giving Brady a second mortgage, what Brady has obtained is only the right to reclaim the property by paying off the debt owed to Sandhu. If there is a default, in order to collect on the security, Brady must pay Sandhu the $25 000 he is owed, as well as any charges and costs that may have been incurred. The value of the property must be enough to allow for this expenditure and still cover Brady's $15 000 investment. There is thus much more risk attached to the position of a second mortgagee than there is to having a first mortgage against the property. Similarly, a third or fourth mortgage is that much more risky, because those creditors must be prepared to buy out all interests above them.

One of the major difficulties associated with this type of arrangement is that the right to reclaim the property embodied in the equity of redemption could be exercised at any time in the future. This may seem fair, except that the right to redeem could be exercised, at least in theory, many years after the default, making the position of the mortgagee who has taken possession of the property hopelessly uncertain. To prevent this, the Courts of Chancery recognized a further right on the part of the mortgagee to go to court after a default has taken place, and ask the court to set a time limit within which that equity of redemption must be exercised. If it is not exercised within that time, the right to redeem will be forever lost. This process is known as foreclosure, and it takes place, even today, in a two-stage process.

Foreclosure

The first stage in a foreclosure is for the creditor, faced with a default, to go to court and seek an order giving judgment against the debtor and setting a time limit within which the equity of redemption must be exercised. This order is called an order *nisi*, and the time limit, called the redemption period, is usually only a few months. If the debtor does not pay off what is owing within that period, the mortgagee makes a second application to the court. This time an order absolute is made, which declares that the mortgagor is forever barred from reclaiming the property.

When a first mortgagee goes through the foreclosure process, it is not only the mortgagor who will be forever barred from reclaiming the property, but also any other holder of an equitable mortgage. This is the reason those creditors must be prepared to pay out all money owed to anyone with a higher interest in the property. It also imposes considerably more risk on such subsequent mortgagees. In most jurisdictions, however, there is an alternative provided, in the form of the judicial sale. Under this procedure, a court order is granted to have the property sold and the creditors paid, according to their priority, out of the proceeds. When such an order is granted, the property must be sold before the expiration of the redemption period, to avoid the effect of foreclosure. The order is sought by the other creditors, usually at the same time as the order *nisi* is granted to the first mortgagee. When the parties go to court and the order *nisi* and order for sale are granted, the mortgagor usually thinks that he has six months (or whatever redemption period has been set) to get his affairs in order and recover the property. The order of sale has a very different effect, however, and the property may be sold immediately, pursuant to this order. As a result, the mortgagor may find all rights and claims to the property extinguished in a very short time. But this limitation on the mortgagor's rights is necessary to protect the position of the other equitable mortgagees, who stand to lose all their security in the property if the redemption period is allowed to expire.

Some provinces have modified this procedure to some extent, but in all provinces the positions of such multiple creditors are protected through the availability of the process of a judicially supervised sale. A judicial sale, when combined with the process of foreclosure, is the most significant remedy available when mortgages are involved in real estate transactions.

Like all such interests in land, these security interests must be registered at the appropriate government office to have any effect on subsequent purchasers and others who acquire interest in the property.

Personal Property as Security

Chattels and other forms of personal property can also be used to provide security. Just as the title is transferred to a creditor to provide security in a real property mortgage, the title of a chattel such as a car or a boat can also be transferred in a chattel mortgage arrangement. If the debtor defaults on the loan, the creditor has the right to take possession of the property, thus having a prior claim over and above other creditors. The document used to create such a chattel mortgage is a bill of sale, the borrower simply giving the creditor a bill of sale conditionally transferring title to the chattel to the creditor. By this arrangement, if the payments are properly made and the loan repaid, the title reverts to the debtor.

Conditional sales also involve the creditor having title to the goods as security for debt, but they differ from chattel mortgages, in that the creditor is also the seller of the goods. As in the case of an agreement for sale of real property, such a conditional sale of a chattel is essentially a sale taking place in two stages. The first stage is the transfer of possession to the purchaser, and the second stage, coming some time later, involves the transfer of title to the purchaser after all the payments have been made. In the meantime, title remains with the seller, giving her security for the amount owed; hence the term conditional sale.

When chattels are used to provide security in this way, possession stays with or is passed to the debtor, and limitations on his right to the chattel are not readily apparent to an innocent third party who may be prepared to purchase the goods from him. It is thus very easy for a debtor to defraud an innocent person by selling him goods such as a car or boat without informing him of the chattel mortgage or conditional sale, and then simply defaulting on the payments. If the innocent purchaser were allowed to keep the goods in such a situation, unaffected by the chattel mortgage or conditional sale, it would defeat the whole purpose of such security arrangements. On the other hand, if the creditor having such a security interest in the chattels is allowed to simply retake the goods from the innocent purchaser, that innocent purchaser is also unfairly dealt with.

Registration

To avoid these difficulties, an additional step has been created that requires the creditor to register the conditional sale or chattel mortgage at an appropriate government office. If he fails to do so, he loses many of the claims that he may have, including the right to retake the goods once they get into the hands of an innocent third party. If the transaction has been properly registered, however, he retains those rights. This does not place a great hardship on the innocent purchaser, since he need only make inquiries at the appropriate government office to find out if such a security has been registered against the goods he wishes to purchase. If the purchaser fails to make such a search, the fault is his, and the creditor will have the right to retake the goods from him in the event of default by the debtor.

These requirements, as well as provisions setting out under what circumstances the goods can be repossessed, and the procedure required for resale, are contained in special legislation in place in the various jurisdictions. These acts are typically called the *Personal Property Security Act*, though in a few provinces separate acts still exist, such as the *Conditional Sale Act* and the *Bills of Sale Act*.

Registration of Chattel Mortgage

Re Purschke et al. and Avco Financial Services Canada Ltd.[9]

Sandra Harris entered into a chattel mortgage with a bank in 1985. The bank registered this chattel mortgage, but the vehicle serial number was recorded incorrectly. Ms. Harris then granted another chattel mortgage to Avco in 1986 that was properly registered. Before Avco registered the mortgage they contacted the bank for a credit check on Ms. Harris and were told that the bank had a chattel mortgage already on the vehicle. After Avco registered their chattel mortgage, they contacted the bank telling them that they had done a search, found the incorrect number and had registered their mortgage ahead of the bank. Avco seized the motor vehicle and after correcting the serial number the bank challenged Avco's right to the car.

The court in this case found that because Avco was aware of the prior interest of the bank, the bank's incorrectly registered chattel mortgage took priority. It's clear that had Avco or any other party obtained an interest with respect to these goods before the bank corrected their registration number, not knowing of the bank's interest they would have gained priority over the bank. But in this case Avco had notice of the bank's interest, and notice is the main purpose of the registration process. This case not only illustrates the importance of properly registering a chattel mortgage or a personal property security, but also shows the consequence of not doing that properly. Although registration is an artificial step, it protects both the creditors and innocent third parties in these circumstances.

Assignment of Accounts Receivable

Choses in action can also be used to secure a loan. Businesses will often make an assignment of their accounts receivable to a creditor to secure such a loan. **Accounts receivable** are the funds owed to the merchant from his customers as part of his ongoing business. This is a debt or claim, and although it does not have substance like a chattel, it still has value, and the transfer of this right to collect the account receivable to the creditor does provide effective security for the repayment of debt. If the merchant defaults on his payments, the creditor has the right to collect on those debts.

Farmers and manufacturers have a different problem. Their assets are usually tied up in crops being grown or goods being manufactured, and these change in their nature as time goes by. The crops, for example, are only seeds when they are planted, but they are a fully ripe field of corn just before harvest. Because of their changing nature, these items don't fit easily into the kinds of things normally used as security. A special provision of the *Bank Act*[10] permits banks to take goods in the process of manufacture and crops being grown as security.

Personal Property Security Acts

The methods discussed above are only the most common methods of providing security. Because there are so many different ways that debt can be secured, each with different legislation and procedures, many provinces have taken steps to simplify the process. Saskatchewan, Manitoba, Ontario, Alberta, Yukon and, most recently, British Columbia have passed *Personal Property Security Acts* in order to create one cohesive set of regulations and one procedure for using personal property as security, with the exception of security under the *Bank Act*, which is federal jurisdiction. Chattel mortgages, conditional sales and the assignment of accounts receivable, as well as most other methods of using personal property as security have been included in this Act.

Under the *Personal Property Security Acts* the existence of the security is not determined by the conveyance of the title, and so the situations in which security can be obtained are even broader than those discussed above. Even rented property and leasing arrangements can create a security under the legislation. Under these acts, the creation of the security takes place in three steps. The first is to create a contractual relationship between the parties. This stage comes into existence as soon as a binding contract is entered into through offer and acceptance. The second stage, which is referred to as the attachment of the security to the item of personal property to be used as security, takes place when the contract is executed and the debtor receives the money or other benefit that is the subject matter of the contract. Of course, the terms of the contract must provide that the creditor will obtain a priority against other creditors. But once that is done and the benefit provided to the debtor has been advanced, the secured interest attaches to the item of property, and the creditor has the right to retake that property upon default from the debtor. However, this stage still only affects the rights between the creditor and debtor. An innocent third party unaware of such an arrangement cannot be affected by it until the third stage has taken place.

The final stage involves the perfection of the security. This perfection can take place in one of two ways. The first is to take possession of the property used as security. If you borrow money from a creditor and she retains possession of the item used as security — for example, when an item is pawned at a pawnshop — the security is perfected by the retention of the chattel by the creditor, and she thus has good claim against third parties claiming an interest. Even if a normal chattel mortgage or conditional sale is involved and the debtor has defaulted, once the creditor has repossessed those goods from the debtor, she has perfected her security and can maintain her claims against innocent third parties. But if she does not have possession and those goods get into the hands of an innocent third party, she cannot retake them.

Registration

To protect herself in such circumstances, the creditor must make use of the second method of **perfecting the security** — that is, by registering the secured transaction contract at the appropriate government office. Registration has the effect of providing notice to any outside party of the secured interest in the goods. Possession stays with the debtor, but there now is a place where any third party can find out if there is any charge or lien against the goods. Once registration is completed, the security is perfected and, in the event of default, the creditor can reclaim the goods even from the possession of an innocent third party. If you borrow money and use your camera as security, once you hand the camera over to the creditor, the security is perfected because he has possession. But if you want to continue to use the camera and possession is left with the debtor, the creditor must register the contract at the government office to perfect the security and protect himself against any third parties acquiring an interest.

When a *Personal Property Security Act* is involved, there is only one place of registration. Also, there is only one procedure to follow for all situations when personal property is used as a security, rather than the many different approaches that can be involved when there are several different statutes in place. Personal property security statutes also impose significant obligations on creditors when they retake and dispose of the property used as security. Essentially, the obligation is to take reasonable steps to protect the interests of the defaulting debtor in relation to that property. The creditor must follow the normally accepted business procedures involved in selling those assets, so that as much as possible can be realized from the sale. The creditor must also keep the goods in his possession and take reasonable steps to care for them, making sure they are not damaged or otherwise devalued, for a specified period of time. This gives the debtor an opportunity to get his affairs in order and reclaim the goods by paying what is owed.

Bankruptcy

Another important concern involving the creditor-debtor relationship arises when the debtor becomes insolvent and several classes of creditors are involved. It is not very constructive to have anyone so encumbered by debt that he or she can never recover and become a productive member of society. Bankruptcy law has been developed to deal with such an eventuality. Under federal bankruptcy legislation an orderly process has been created whereby the interests of the creditors are protected to the extent that as much as possible is extracted from the assets of the debtor for their benefit. But once this has taken place, the debtor may be completely discharged from any remaining debt and encouraged to get on with his life. It should be noted that secured creditors retain their priority, even when a bankruptcy is involved.

When the debtor is insolvent and unable to pay her debts, bankruptcy is accomplished either by the debtor assigning her assets voluntarily to a trustee or by the creditors obtaining the assets through a receiving order from the court. In either case, all of the assets of the debtor are conveyed to an individual called the **trustee in bankruptcy**, whose job is to sell the assets or otherwise deal with them to the benefit of the creditors. Although there are some exceptions, such as some furniture and tools, the trustee's disposition of these assets ensures that the creditors get as much as is reasonably possible on the debt owed. In the process, the trustee in bankruptcy will have to examine carefully all of the affairs of the bankrupt to determine that all of the assets have been conveyed. He will also make sure there have been no fraudulent preferences or transfers made, when one creditor is paid to the disadvantage of the others or goods are hidden or sold to friends or relatives to protect them from the creditors.

During the period of time between the assignment in bankruptcy and the ultimate discharge, the bankrupt is referred to as an **undischarged bankrupt**, and his ability to carry on business is restricted in several ways, including quite strict limitations on the amount of money he can borrow. After a period of months, an application is made to the court, and if it is satisfied that there has been no wrongdoing involved, such as making fraudulent preferences or transfers, the court will discharge the bankrupt from any further obligations. Once this is done, the creditors have no more claim on the discharged bankrupt.

Even if they have only been paid 50 per cent of what they are owed, the creditors have no further claim, and even if the debtor wins a lottery or otherwise comes into a large sum of money, they cannot insist on receiving the unpaid portion of their claims. The discharged bankrupt has no further obligation to them. Some obligations, however, such as a family court order to pay maintenance to children, remain. The two objectives of bankruptcy legislation are, first, to ensure that the creditors get as much as possible from the remaining assets of the debtor, and second, to rehabilitate the debtor.

Arrangements with Creditors

An alternative to this bankruptcy process provided for in the *Bankruptcy and Insolvency Act*[11] is for the debtor to make a proposal to the creditors to pay back a certain portion of the debt, in return for being discharged from the rest. If the offer is agreed to, the ultimate aim is accomplished without the intrusion of the trustee, but if the proposal is not accepted, the creditors are free to obtain a receiving order and force the debtor into bankruptcy. There are also provisions when small debts are involved, usually in the form of consumer debt, to provide for the orderly payment of those debts. Often a person will find that it is impossible to meet all of the payments due each month, because of the many different creditors involved. Here, assistance is provided to help the debtor arrange with the creditors for one lower monthly payment to be made, making it possible to pay off the debt eventually. Creditors will usually agree to these arrangements, if they are realistic, because they would generally prefer to be repaid their whole debt, even if more slowly than anticipated, rather than trip the debtor into bankruptcy and recover only a small fraction of the amount owed to them. Debtors are likely to prefer these arrangements if they, in good conscience, want to pay their debts but at present cannot, or if they want to avoid the social and commercial stigma of bankruptcy. When a corporation becomes bankrupt the result is different. It is not discharged at the end of the process; rather it is dissolved, ceasing to exist. It should be noted, however, that corporations can seek protection under the Act to give them the opportunity to rearrange their affairs to avoid bankruptcy.

QUESTIONS FOR DISCUSSION AND REVIEW

1. List the different categories of personal property and the legislation that has affected them.

2. Explain the main objectives of *Sale of Goods Acts*.

3. When people "hold" property for others, they assume the risk if it is damaged or stolen. Why shouldn't bailees be simply subjected to the reasonable person test rather than this higher standard of care?

4. Outline the goals of copyright law and comment on their practicality when they are so difficult to enforce.

5. It is possible to trademark a colour, a sound or a shape. Is this appropriate, and what purpose does it serve?

6. How far should the law go to prohibit employees from using information they have gained from one job in another employment situation?

7. Contrast a tenancy in common with a joint tenancy and indicate how one can be changed to another. Why is the distinction important?

8. What is meant by the terms mortgage, equity of redemption, and foreclosure?

9. Explain the importance of registering a chattel or real property.

10. What is the purpose of bankruptcy legislation?

NOTES

1. *Gee v. White Spot Ltd.* (1986), 32 D.L.R. (4th) 238 (B.S.S.C.).

2. For example, *Innkeepers' Act*, R.S.O. 1980, c. 217.

3. *Copyright Act*, R.S.C. 1985, c. C-42 (as amended by R.S.C. 1985 [4th Supp.], c. 10).

4. *British Columbia Jockey Club et al. v. Standon* (1985), 22 D.L.R. (4th) 467.

5. *Patent Act*, R.S.C. 1985, c. P-4, and Patent Act Amendments, R.S.C. 1985 (3rd Supp), c. 33.

6. *Trademarks Act*, R.S.C. 1985, c. T-13.

7. For example, *Residential Tenancies Act*, R.S.O. 1980, c. 452, s. 57.2.

8. *Kish v. Tompkins* [indexed as *Tompkins Estate v. Tompkins*] (1993), 99 D.L.R. (4th) 193 (B.C.C.A.).

9. *Re Purschke et al. and Avco Financial Services Canada Ltd.* (1987), 43 D.L.R. 464 (Alta. Q.B.).

10. *Bank Act*, R.S.C. 1985, c. B-1, s. 178.

11. *Bankruptcy Act*, R.S.C. 1985, c. B-3.

FURTHER READING

Sinclair, A.M. *Introduction to Real Property Law*, 3rd ed. Toronto: Butterworths, 1981.

Smyth, J.E., D.A. Soberman and A.J. Easson. *The Law and Business Administration in Canada*, 8th ed. Scarborough, Ont.: Prentice Hall Canada Inc., 1998.

Yates, R.A. *Business Law in Canada*, 5th ed. Scarborough, Ont.: Prentice Hall Canada Inc., 1998.

Appendix

CONSTITUTION ACT, 1867

(THE BRITISH NORTH AMERICA ACT, 1867)

[Note: The present short title was substituted for the original short title (in italics) by the *Constitution Act, 1982* (No. 44 *infra*).]

30 & 31 Victoria, c. 3 (U.K.)

An Act for the Union of Canada, Nova Scotia, and New Brunswick, and the Government thereof; and for Purposes connected therewith

[29th March 1867]

Whereas the Provinces of Canada, Nova Scotia, and New Brunswick have expressed their Desire to be federally united into One Dominion under the Crown of the United Kingdom of Great Britain and Ireland, with a Constitution similar in Principle to that of the United Kingdom:

And whereas such a Union would conduce to the Welfare of the Provinces and promote the Interests of the British Empire:

And whereas on the Establishment of the Union by Authority of Parliament it is expedient, not only that the Constitution of the Legislative Authority in the Dominion be provided for, but also that the Nature of the Executive Government therein be declared:

And whereas it is expedient that Provision be made for the eventual Admission into the Union of other Parts of British North America:

Be it therefore enacted and declared by the Queen's most Excellent Majesty, by and with the Advice and Consent of the Lords Spiritual and Temporal, and Commons, in this present Parliament assembled, and by the Authority of the same, as follows:

[Note: The enacting clause was repealed by the *Statute Law Revision Act, 1893* (No. 17 *infra*).]

I. Preliminary

1. *This Act may be cited as The British North America Act, 1867.*   *Short Title*

1. This Act may be cited as the *Constitution Act, 1867*.   Short title

[Note: Section 1 (in italics) was repealed and the new section substituted by the *Constitution Act, 1982* (No. 44 *infra*).]

293

Application of Provisions referring to the Queen

2. *The Provisions of this Act referring to Her Majesty the Queen extend also to the Heirs and Successors of Her Majesty, Kings and Queens of the United Kingdom of Great Britain and Ireland.*
[Note: Repealed by the *Statute Law Revision Act, 1893* (No. 17 *infra*).]

II. Union

DECLARATION OF UNION

Declaration of Union

3. It shall be lawful for the Queen, by and with the Advice of Her Majesty's Most Honourable Privy Council, to declare by Proclamation that, on and after a Day therein appointed, not being more than Six Months after the passing of this Act, the Provinces of Canada, Nova Scotia, and New Brunswick shall form and be One Dominion under the Name of Canada; and on and after that Day those Three Provinces shall form and be One Dominion under that Name accordingly.
[Note: The first day of July, 1867 was fixed by proclamation dated May 22, 1867.]

Construction of subsequent Provisions of Act

4. *The subsequent Provisions of this Act shall, unless it is otherwise expressed or implied, commence and have effect on and after the Union, that is to say, on and after the Day appointed for the Union taking effect in the Queen's Proclamation; and in the same Provisions,* unless it is otherwise expressed or implied, the Name Canada shall be taken to mean Canada as constituted under this Act.
[Note: The words in italics were repealed by the *Statute Law Revision Act, 1893* (No. 17 *infra*).]

Four Provinces

5. Canada shall be divided into Four Provinces, named Ontario, Quebec, Nova Scotia, and New Brunswick.
[Note: Canada now consists of ten provinces (Ontario, Quebec, Nova Scotia, New Brunswick, Manitoba, British Columbia, Prince Edward Island, Alberta, Saskatchewan and Newfoundland) and two territories (the Yukon Territory and the Northwest Territories). See the note to section 146.]

Provinces of Ontario and Quebec

6. The Parts of the Province of Canada (as it exists at the passing of this Act) which formerly constituted respectively the Provinces of Upper Canada and Lower Canada shall be deemed to be severed, and shall form Two separate Provinces. The Part which formerly constituted the Province of Upper Canada shall constitute the Province of Ontario; and the Part which formerly constituted the Province of Lower Canada shall constitute the Province of Quebec.

Provinces of Nova Scotia and New Brunswick

7. The Provinces of Nova Scotia and New Brunswick shall have the same Limits as at the passing of this Act.

Decennial Census

8. In the general Census of the Population of Canada which is hereby required to be taken in the Year One thousand eight hundred and seventy-one, and in every Tenth Year thereafter, the respective Populations of the Four Provinces shall be distinguished.

III. Executive Power

9. The Executive Government and Authority of and over Canada is hereby declared to continue and be vested in the Queen.

Declaration of Executive Power in the Queen

10. The Provisions of this Act referring to the Governor General extend and apply to the Governor General for the Time being of Canada, or other the Chief Executive Officer or Administrator for the Time being carrying on the Government of Canada on behalf and in the Name of the Queen, by whatever Title he is designated.

Application of Provisions referring to Governor General

11. There shall be a Council to aid and advise in the Government of Canada, to be styled the Queen's Privy Council for Canada; and the Persons who are to be Members of that Council shall be from Time to Time chosen and summoned by the Governor General and sworn in as Privy Councillors, and Members thereof may be from Time to Time removed by the Governor General.

Constitution of Privy Council for Canada

12. All Powers, Authorities, and Functions which under any Act of the Parliament of Great Britain, or of the Parliament of the United Kingdom of Great Britain and Ireland, or of the Legislature of Upper Canada, Lower Canada, Canada, Nova Scotia, or New Brunswick, are at the Union vested in or exerciseable by the respective Governors or Lieutenant Governors of those Provinces, with the Advice, or with the Advice of Consent, of the respective Executive Councils thereof, or in conjunction with those Councils, or with any Number of Members thereof, or by those Governors or Lieutenant Governors individually, shall, as far as the same continue in existence and capable of being exercised after the Union in relation to the Government of Canada, be vested in and exerciseable by the Governor General, with the Advice or with the Advice and Consent of or in conjunction with the Queen's Privy Council for Canada, or any Members thereof, or by the Governor General individually, as the Case requires, subject nevertheless (except with respect to such as Exist under Acts of the Parliament of Great Britain or of the Parliament of the United Kingdom of Great Britain and Ireland) to be abolished or altered by the Parliament of Canada.

All Powers under Acts to be exercised by Governor General with Advice of Privy Council, or alone

[Note: See the note to section 129.]

13. The Provisions of this Act referring to the Governor General in Council shall be construed as referring to the Governor General acting by and with the Advice of the Queen's Privy Council for Canada.

Application of Provisions referring to Governor General in Council

14. It shall be lawful for the Queen, if Her Majesty thinks fit, to authorize the Governor General from Time to Time to appoint any Person or any Persons jointly or severally to be his Deputy or Deputies within any Part or Parts of Canada, and in that Capacity to exercise during the Pleasure of the Governor General such of the Powers, Authorities, and Functions of the Governor General as the Governor General deems it necessary or expedient to assign to him or them,

Power to Her Majesty to authorize Governor General to appoint Deputies subject to any Limitations or Directions expressed or given by the Queen; but the Appointment of such a Deputy or Deputies shall not affect the Exercise by the Governor General himself of any Power, Authority, or Function.

Command of
Armed Forces to
continue to be
vested in the Queen

15. The Command-in-Chief of the Land and Naval Militia, and of all Naval and Military Forces, of and in Canada, is hereby declared to continue and be vested in the Queen.

Seat of
Government of
Canada

16. Until the Queen otherwise directs, the Seat of Government of Canada shall be Ottawa.

IV. LEGISLATIVE POWER

Constitution of
Parliament of
Canada

17. There shall be One Parliament for Canada, consisting of the Queen, an Upper House styled the Senate, and the House of Commons.

*Privileges, etc., of
Houses*

18. *The Privileges, Immunities, and Powers to be held, enjoyed, and exercised by the Senate and by the House of Commons and by the Members thereof respectively shall be such as are from Time to Time defined by Act of the Parliament of Canada, but so that the same shall never exceed those at the passing of this Act held, enjoyed, and exercised by the Commons House of Parliament of the United Kingdom of Great Britain and Ireland and by the Members thereof.*

18. The privileges, immunities and powers to be held, enjoyed, and exercised by the Senate and by the House of Commons, and by the members thereof respectively, shall be such as are from time to time defined by Act of the Parliament of Canada, but so that any Act of the Parliament of Canada defining such privileges, immunities, and power shall not confer any privileges, immunities, or powers exceeding those at the passing of such Act held, enjoyed, and exercised by the Commons House of Parliament of the United Kingdom of Great Britain and Ireland, and by the members thereof.

[Note: Section 18 (in italics) was repealed and the new section substituted by the *Parliament of Canada Act, 1875* (No. 13 *infra*).]

First Session of the
Parliament of
Canada

19. The Parliament of Canada shall be called together not later than Six Months after the Union.

[Note: The first session of the first Parliament began on November 6, 1867.]

*Yearly Session of
the Parliament of
Canada*

20. *There shall be a Session of the Parliament of Canada once at least in every Year, so that Twelve Months shall not intervene between the last Sitting of the Parliament in one Session and its first sitting in the next Session.*

[Note: Repealed by the *Constitution Act, 1982* (No. 44 *infra*). See also section 5 of that Act, which provides that there shall be a sitting of the Parliament at least once every twelve months.]

The Senate

21. The Senate shall, subject to the Provisions of this Act, consist of *Seventy-two* Members, who shall be styled Senators.

Number of Senators

[Note: The Senate now consists of 104 Members, as amended by the *Constitution Act, 1915* (No. 23 *infra*) and modified by the *Newfoundland Act* (No. 32 *infra*) and as again amended by the *Constitution Act (No. 2), 1975*, (No. 42 *infra*).]

22. In relation to the Constitution of the Senate Canada shall be deemed to consist of *Three* Divisions:

Representation of Provinces in Senate

1. Ontario;
2. Quebec;
3. *The Maritime Provinces, Nova Scotia and New Brunswick*;

which *Three* Divisions shall (subject to the Provisions of this Act) be equally represented in the Senate as follows: Ontario by Twenty-four Senators; Quebec by Twenty-four Senators; and the Maritime Provinces by Twenty-four Senators, *Twelve* thereof representing Nova Scotia, and *Twelve* thereof representing New Brunswick.

In the case of Quebec each of the Twenty-four Senators representing that Province shall be appointed for One of the Twenty-four Electoral Divisions of Lower Canada specified in Schedule A. to Chapter One of the Consolidated Statutes of Canada.

[Note: Prince Edward Island, on admission into the Union in 1873, became part of the third division with a representation in the Senate of four members, the representation of Nova Scotia and New Brunswick being reduced from twelve to ten members each. See section 147.

A fourth division represented in the Senate by twenty-four senators and comprising the Western Provinces of Manitoba, British Columbia, Alberta and Saskatchewan, each represented by six senators, was added by the *Constitution Act, 1915* (No. 23 *infra*).

Newfoundland is represented in the Senate by six members. See the *Constitution Act, 1915* (No. 23 *infra*) and the *Newfoundland Act* No. 32 *infra*).

The Yukon Territory and the Northwest Territories are represented in the Senate by one member each. See the *Constitution Act (No. 2), 1975* (No. 42 *infra*).]

23. The Qualifications of a Senator shall be as follows:

Qualifications of Senator

1. He shall be of the full age of Thirty Years:
2. He shall be either a natural-born Subject of the Queen, or a Subject of the Queen naturalized by an Act of the Parliament of Great Britain, or of the Parliament of the United Kingdom of Great Britain and Ireland, or of the Legislature of One of the Provinces of Upper Canada, Lower Canada, Canada, Nova Scotia, or New Brunswick, before the Union, or of the Parliament of Canada after the Union:

3. He shall be legally or equitably seised as of Freehold for his own Use and Benefit of Lands or Tenements held in Free and Common Socage, or seised or possessed for his own Use and Benefit of Lands or Tenements held in Franc-alleu or in Roture, within the Province for which he is appointed, of the Value of Four thousand Dollars, over and above all Rents, Dues, Debts, Charges, Mortgages, and Incumbrances due or payable out of or charged on or affecting the same:

4. His Real and Personal Property shall be together worth Four thousand Dollars over and above his Debts and Liabilities:

5. He shall be resident in the Province for which he is appointed:

6. In the Case of Quebec he shall have his Real Property Qualification in the Electoral Division for which he is appointed, or shall be resident in that Division.

[Note: For the purposes of the *Constitution Act (No. 2), 1975* (No. 42 *infra*), the term "Province" in section 23 has the same meaning as is assigned to the "province" by section 35 of the *Interpretation Act* (Canada).]

Summons of Senator

24. The Governor General shall from Time to Time, in the Queen's Name, by Instrument under the Great Seal of Canada, summon qualified Persons to the Senate; and, subject to the Provisions of this Act, every Person so summoned shall become and be a Member of the Senate and a Senator.

Summons of First Body of Senators

25. *Such Persons shall be first summoned to the Senate as the Queen by Warrant under Her Majesty's Royal Sign Manual thinks fit to approve, and their Names shall be inserted in the Queen's Proclamation of Union.*

[Note: Repealed by the *Statute Law Revision Act, 1893* (No. 17 *infra*).]

Addition of Senators in certain Cases

26. If at any Time on the Recommendation of the Governor General the Queen thinks fit to direct that *Three or Six* Members be added to the Senate, the Governor General may by Summons to *Three or Six* qualified Persons (as the Case may be), representing equally the *Three* Divisions of Canada, add to the Senate accordingly.

[Note: The number of members who may be added to the Senate was increased from three or six to four or eight, representing equally the four divisions of Canada. See the *Constitution Act, 1915* (No. 23 *infra*).]

Reduction of Senate to normal number

27. In case of such Addition being at any Time made, the Governor General shall not summon any Person to the Senate, except on a further like Direction by the Queen on the like Recommendation, until each of the *Three* Divisions of Canada is represented by Twenty-four Senators and no more.

[Note: Superseded by the *Constitution Act, 1915*, paragraph 1(1)(iv), No. 23 *infra*). This paragraph reads as follows:

"In case of such addition being at any time made the Governor General of Canada shall not summon any person to the Senate except upon a further like direction by His Majesty the King on the like recommendation to represent one of the four Divisions until such Division is represented by twenty-four senators and no more:"]

28. The Number of Senators shall not at any Time exceed *Seventy-eight.*

Maximum Number of Senator

[Note: The maximum number of senators is now 112, as amended by the *Constitution Act, 1915 (No. 23* infra) and the *Constitution Act (No. 2), 1975* (No. 42 *infra*).]

29. *A Senator shall, subject to the Provisions of this Act, hold his Place in the Senate for Life.*

Tenure of Place in Senate

29. (1) Subject to subsection (2), a Senator shall, subject to the provisions of this Act, hold his place in the Senate for life.

Tenure of place in Senate

(2) A senator who is summoned to the Senate after the coming into force of this subsection shall, subject to this act, hold his place in the Senate until he attains the age of seventy-five years.

Retirement upon attaining age of seventy-five years

[Note: Section 29 (in italics) was repealed and the new section substituted by the *Constitution Act, 1965* (No. 39 *infra*).]

30. A Senator may by Writing under his Hand addressed to the Governor General resign his Place in the Senate, and thereupon the same shall be vacant.

Resignation of Place in Senate

31. The Place of a Senator shall become vacant in any of the following Cases:

Disqualification of Senators

1. If for Two consecutive Sessions of the Parliament he fails to give his Attendance in the Senate:

2. If he takes an Oath or makes a Declaration or Acknowledgement of Allegiance, Obedience, or Adherence to a Foreign Power, or does an Act whereby he becomes a Subject or Citizen, or entitled to the Rights or Privileges of a Subject or Citizen, of a Foreign Power:

3. If he is adjudged Bankrupt or Insolvent, or applies for the Benefit of any Law relating to Insolvent Debtors, or becomes a public Defaulter:

4. If he is attainted of Treason or convicted of Felony or of any infamous Crime:

5. If he ceases to be qualified in respect of Property or of Residence; provided, that a Senator shall not be deemed to have ceased to be qualified in respect of Residence by reason only of his residing at the Seat of the Government of Canada while holding an Office under that Government requiring his Presence there.

32. When a Vacancy happens in the Senate by Resignation, Death, or otherwise, the Governor General shall by Summons to a fit and qualified Person fill the Vacancy.

Summons on Vacancy in Senate

Questions as to
Qualifications and
Vacancies in
Senate

33. If any Question arises respecting the Qualification of a Senator or a Vacancy in the Senate the same shall be heard and determined by the Senate.

Appointment of
Speaker of Senate

34. The Governor General may from Time to Time, by Instrument under the Great Seal of Canada, appoint a Senator to be Speaker of the Senate, and may remove him and appoint another in his Stead.

[Note: See also the *Canadian Speaker (Appointment of Deputy) Act, 1895* (No. 18 *infra*) and the provisions concerning the Speaker of the Senate in the *Parliament of Canada Act* (Canada).]

Quorum of Senate

35. Until the Parliament of Canada otherwise provides, the Presence of at least Fifteen Senators, including the Speaker, shall be necessary to constitute a Meeting of the Senate for the Exercise of its Powers.

Voting in Senate

36. Questions arising in the Senate shall be decided by a Majority of Voices, and the Speaker shall in all Cases have a Vote, and when the Voices are equal the Decision shall be deemed to be in the Negative.

The House of Commons

Constitution of
House of Commons
in Canada

37. The House of Commons shall, subject to the Provisions of this Act, consist of *One hundred and eighty-one* Members, of whom *Eighty-two* shall be elected for Ontario, *Sixty-five* for Quebec, *Nineteen* for Nova Scotia, and *Fifteen* for New Brunswick.

[Note: On October 31, 1987, the House of Commons consisted of 282 members: 95 for Ontario, 75 for Quebec, 11 for Nova Scotia, 10 for New Brunswick, 14 for Manitoba, 28 for British Columbia, 4 for Prince Edward Island, 21 for Alberta, 14 for Saskatchewan, 7 for Newfoundland, 1 for the Yukon Territory and 2 for the Northwest Territories.

These figures result from the application of section 51 as re-enacted by the *Constitution Act, 1974* (No. 40 *infra*) and amended by the *Constitution Act (No. 1), 1975* (No. 41 *infra*), and of the *Electoral Boundaries Readjustment Act* (Canada).]

Summoning of
House of Commons

38. The Governor General shall from Time to Time, in the Queen's Name, by Instrument under the Great Seal of Canada, summon and call together the House of Commons.

Senators not to sit
in House of
Commons

39. A Senator shall not be capable of being elected or of sitting or voting as a Member of the House of Commons.

Electoral Districts
of the Four
Provinces

40. Until the Parliament of Canada otherwise provides, Ontario, Quebec, Nova Scotia, and New Brunswick shall, for the Purposes of the Election of Members to serve in the House of Commons, be divided into Electoral Districts as follows:

1. ONTARIO

Ontario shall be divided into the Counties, Ridings of Counties, Cities, Parts of Cities, and Towns enumerated in the First Schedule to this Act, each whereof shall be an Electoral District, each such District as numbered in that Schedule being entitled to return One Member.

2. QUEBEC

Quebec shall be divided into Sixty-five Electoral Districts, composed of the Sixty-five Electoral Divisions into which Lower Canada is at the passing of this Act divided under Chapter Two of the Consolidated Statutes of Canada, Chapter Seventy-five of the Consolidated Statutes for Lower Canada, and the Act of the Province of Canada of the Twenty-third Year of the Queen, Chapter One, or any other Act amending the same in force at the Union, so that each such Electoral Division shall be for the Purposes of this Act an Electoral District entitled to return One Member.

3. NOVA SCOTIA

Each of the Eighteen Counties of Nova Scotia shall be an Electoral District. The County of Halifax shall be entitled to return Two Members, and each of the other Counties One Member.

4. NEW BRUNSWICK

Each of the Fourteen Counties into which New Brunswick is divided, including the City and County of St. John, shall be an Electoral District. The City of St. John shall also be a separate Electoral District. Each of those Fifteen Electoral Districts shall be entitled to return One Member.

[Note: The federal electoral districts of the 10 provinces and the Northwest Territories are now set out in the schedule to Proclamations issued from time to time pursuant to the *Electoral Boundaries Readjustment Act* (Canada), as amended for particular districts by other Acts of Parliament.

The electoral district of the Yukon Territory is set out in section 30 of the *Electoral Boundaries Readjustment Act* (Canada).]

41. Until the Parliament of Canada otherwise provides, all Laws in force in the several Provinces at the Union relative to the following Matters or any of them, namely,—the Qualifications and Disqualifications of Persons to be elected or to sit or vote as Members of the House of Assembly or Legislative Assembly in the several Provinces, the Voters at Elections of such Members, the Oaths to be taken by Voters, the Returning Officers, their Powers and Duties, the Proceedings at Elections, the Periods during which Elections may be continued, the Trial of controverted Elections, and Proceedings incident thereto, the vacating of Seats of Members, and the Execution of new Writs in case of Seats vacated otherwise than by Dissolution,— shall respectively apply to Elections of Members to serve in the House of Commons for the same several Provinces.

Continuance of existing Election Laws until Parliament of Canada otherwise provides

Provided that, until the Parliament of Canada otherwise provides, at any Election for a Member of the House of Commons for the District of Algoma, in addition to Persons qualified by the Law of the Province of Canada to vote, every Male British Subject, aged Twenty-one Years or upwards, being a Householder, shall have a Vote.

[Note: The principal provisions concerning elections are now found in the *Parliament of Canada Act, Canada Elections Act* and *Dominion Controverted Elections Act* (all three enacted by Canada). The right to vote and hold office is provided for in section 3 of the *Constitution Act, 1982* (No. 44 *infra*).]

Writs for first Election

42. *For the First Election of Members to serve in the House of Commons the Governor General shall cause Writs to be issued by such Person, in such Form, and addressed to such Returning Officers as he thinks fit.*

The Person issuing Writs under this Section shall have the like Powers as are possessed at the Union by the Officers charged with the issuing of Writs for the Election of Members to serve in the respective House of Assembly or Legislative Assembly of the Province of Canada, Nova Scotia, or New Brunswick; and the Returning Officers to whom Writs are directed under this Section shall have the like Powers as are possessed at the Union by the Officers charged with the returning of Writs for the Election of Members to serve in the same respective House of Assembly or Legislative Assembly.

[Note: Repealed by the *Statute Law Revision Act, 1893* (No. 17 *infra*).]

As to Casual Vacancies

43. *In case a Vacancy in the Representation in the House of Commons of any Electoral District happens before the Meeting of the Parliament, or after the Meeting of the Parliament before Provision is made by the Parliament in this Behalf, the Provisions of the last foregoing Section of this Act shall extend and apply to the issuing and returning of a Writ in respect of such Vacant District.*

[Note: Repealed by the *Statute Law Revision Act, 1893* (No. 17 *infra*).]

As to Election of Speaker of House of Commons

44. The House of Commons on its first assembling after a General Election shall proceed with all practicable Speed to elect One of its Members to be Speaker.

As to filling up Vacancy in Office of Speaker

45. In case of a Vacancy happening in the Office of Speaker by Death, Resignation, or otherwise, the House of Commons shall with all practicable Speed proceed to elect another of its Members to be Speaker.

Speaker to preside

46. The Speaker shall preside at all Meetings of the House of Commons.

Provision in case of Absence of Speaker

47. Until the Parliament of Canada otherwise provides, in case of the Absence for any Reason of the Speaker from the Chair of the House of Commons for a Period of Forty-eight consecutive Hours, the House may elect another of its Members to act as Speaker, and the

Member so elected shall during the Continuance of such Absence of the Speaker have and execute all the Powers, Privileges, and Duties of Speaker.

[Note: See also the provisions concerning the Speaker of the House of Commons in the *Parliament of Canada Act* (Canada).]

48. The Presence of at least Twenty Members of the House of Commons shall be necessary to constitute a Meeting of the House for the Exercise of its Powers, and for that Purpose the Speaker shall be reckoned as a Member.

Quorum of House of Commons

49. Questions arising in the House of Commons shall be decided by a Majority of Voices other than that of the Speaker, and when the Voices are equal, but not otherwise, the Speaker shall have a Vote.

Voting in House of Commons

50. Every House of Commons shall continue for Five Years from the Day of the Return of the Writs for choosing the House (subject to be sooner dissolved by the Governor General), and no longer.

Duration of House of Commons

[Note: See for an extension of this term the *British North America Act, 1916* (No. 24 *infra*). See also section 4 of the *Constitution Act, 1982* (No. 44 *infra*).]

51. *On the Completion of the Census in the Year One thousand eight hundred and seventy-one, and of each subsequent decennial Census, the Representation of the Four Provinces shall be readjusted by such Authority, in such Manner, and from such Time, as the Parliament of Canada from Time to Time provides, subject and according to the following Rules:*

Decennial Readjustment of Representation

1. Quebec shall have the fixed Number of Sixty-five Members:

2. There shall be assigned to each of the other Provinces such a Number of Members as will bear the same Proportion to the Number of its Population (ascertained at such Census) as the Number Sixty-five bears to the Number of the Population of Quebec (so ascertained):

3. In the Computation of the Number of Members for a Province a fractional Part not exceeding One Half of the whole Number requisite for entitling the Province to a Member shall be disregarded; but a fractional Part exceeding One Half of that Number shall be equivalent to the whole Number:

4. On any such Re-adjustment the Number of Members for a Province shall not be reduced unless the Proportion which the Number of the Population of the Province bore to the Number of the aggregate Population of Canada at the then last preceding Re-adjustment of the Number of Members for the Province is ascertained at the then latest Census to be diminished by One Twentieth Part or upwards:

5. Such Re-adjustment shall not take effect until the Termination of the then existing Parliament.

Readjustment of representation in Commons

51. (1) The number of members of the House of Commons and the representation of the provinces therein shall, on the coming into force of this subsection and thereafter on the completion of each decennial census, be readjusted by such authority, in such manner, and from such time as the Parliament of Canada from time to time provides, subject and according to the following rules:

Rules

1. There shall be assigned to each of the provinces a number of members equal to the number obtained by dividing the total population of the provinces by two hundred and seventy-nine and by dividing the population of each province by the quotient so obtained, counting any remainder in excess of 0.50 as one after the said process of division.

2. If the total number of members that would be assigned to a province by the application of rule 1 is less than the total number assigned to that province on the date of coming into force of this subsection, there shall be added to the number of members so assigned such number of members as will result in the province having the same number of members as were assigned on that date.

Yukon Territory and Northwest Territories

(2) The Yukon Territory as bounded and described in the schedule to chapter Y-2 of the Revised Statutes of Canada, 1970, shall be entitled to one member, and the Northwest Territories as bounded and described in section 2 of chapter N-22 of the Revised Statutes of Canada, 1970, shall be entitled to two members.

[Note: The original section 51 (in italics) was repealed and a new section 51 substituted by the *British North America Act, 1946* (No. 30 *infra*).

The section enacted in 1946 was repealed and a new section 51 substituted by the *British North America Act, 1952* (No. 36 *infra*).

Subsection (1) of the section 51 enacted in 1952 was repealed and a new subsection 51(1) substituted by the *Constitution Act, 1974* (No. 40 *infra*). The subsection 51(1) enacted in 1974 was repealed and the present subsection 51(1) substituted by the *Constitution Act, 1985 (Representation)* (No. 47 *infra*).

Subsection (2) of the section 51 enacted in 1952 was repealed and the present subsection 51(2) substituted by the *Constitution Act (No. 1), 1975* (No. 41 *infra*).

The words from "of the census" to "seventy-one and" and the word "subsequent" of the original section had previously been repealed by the *Statute Law Revision Act, 1893* (No. 17 *infra*).]

Constitution of House of Commons

51A. Notwithstanding anything in this Act a province shall always be entitled to a number of members in the House of Commons not less than the number of senators representing such province.

[Note: Added by the *Constitution Act, 1915* (No. 23 *infra*).]

Increase of Number of House of Commons

52. The Number of Members of the House of Commons may be from Time to Time increased by the Parliament of Canada, provided the proportionate Representation of the Provinces prescribed by this Act is not thereby disturbed.

Money Votes; Royal Assent

53. Bills for appropriating any Part of the Public Revenue, or for imposing any Tax or Impost, shall originate in the House of Commons.

Appropriation and Tax Bills

54. It shall not be lawful for the House of Commons to adopt or pass any Vote, Resolution, Address, or Bill for the Appropriation of any Part of the Public Revenue, or of any Tax or Impost, to any Purpose that has not been first recommended to that House by Message of the Governor General in the Session in which such Vote, Resolution, Address, or Bill is proposed.

Recommendation of Money Votes

55. Where a Bill passed by the Houses of the Parliament is presented to the Governor General for the Queen's Assent, he shall declare, according to his Discretion, but subject to the Provisions of this Act and to Her Majesty's Instructions, either that he assents thereto in the Queen's Name, or that he withholds the Queen's Assent, or that he reserves the Bill for the Signification of the Queen's Pleasure.

Royal Assent to Bills, etc.

56. Where the Governor General assents to a Bill in the Queen's Name, he shall by the first convenient Opportunity send an authentic Copy of the Act to One of Her Majesty's Principal Secretaries of State, and if the Queen in Council within Two Years after Receipt thereof by the Secretary of State thinks fit to disallow the Act, such Disallowance (with a Certificate of the Secretary of State of the Day on which the Act was received by him) being signified by the Governor General, by Speech or Message to each of the Houses of the Parliament or by Proclamation, shall annul the Act from and after the Day of such Signification.

Disallowance by Order in Council of Act assented to by Governor General

57. A Bill reserved for the Signification of the Queen's Pleasure shall not have any Force unless and until, within Two Years from the Day on which it was presented to the Governor General for the Queen's Assent, the Governor General signifies, by Speech or Message to each of the Houses of the Parliament or by Proclamation, that it has received the Assent of the Queen in Council.

Signification of Queen's Pleasure on Bill reserved

An Entry of every such Speech, Message, or Proclamation shall be made in the Journal of each House, and a Duplicate thereof duly attested shall be delivered to the proper Officer to be kept among the Records of Canada.

V. PROVINCIAL CONSTITUTIONS

Executive Power

58. For each Province there shall be an Officer, styled the Lieutenant Governor, appointed by the Governor General in Council by Instrument under the Great Seal of Canada.

Appointment of Lieutenant Governors of Provinces

Tenure of office of
Lieutenant
Governor

59. A Lieutenant Governor shall hold Office during the Pleasure of the Governor General; but any Lieutenant Governor appointed after the Commencement of the First Session of the Parliament of Canada shall not be removeable within Five Years from his Appointment, except for Cause assigned, which shall be communicated to him in Writing within One Month after the Order for his Removal is made, and shall be communicated by Message to the Senate and to the House of Commons within One Week thereafter if the Parliament is then sitting, and if not then within One Week after the Commencement of the next Session of the Parliament.

Salaries of
Lieutenant
Governors

60. The Salaries of the Lieutenant Governors shall be fixed and provided by the Parliament of Canada.
[Note: See the *Salaries Act* (Canada).]

Oaths, etc., of
Lieutenant
Governor

61. Every Lieutenant Governor shall, before assuming the Duties of his Office, make and subscribe before the Governor General or some Person authorized by him Oaths of Allegiance and Office similar to those taken by the Governor General.

Application of
Provisions refer-
ring to Lieutenant
Governor

62. The Provisions of this Act referring to the Lieutenant Governor extend and apply to the Lieutenant Governor for the Time being of each Province, or other the Chief Executive Officer or Administrator for the Time being carrying on the Government of the Province, by whatever Title he is designated.

Appointment of
Executive Officers
for Ontario and
Quebec

63. The Executive Council of Ontario and of Quebec shall be composed of such Persons as the Lieutenant Governor from Time to Time thinks fit, and in the first instance of the following Officers, namely,— the Attorney General, the Secretary and Registrar of the Province, the Treasurer of the Province, the Commissioner of Crown Lands, and the Commissioner of Agriculture and Public Works, within Quebec the Speaker of the Legislative Council and the Solicitor General.
[Note: See the *Executive Council Act* (Ontario) and the *Executive Power Act* (Quebec).]

Executive
Government of
Nova Scotia and
New Brunswick

64. The Constitution of the Executive Authority in each of the Provinces of Nova Scotia and New Brunswick shall, subject to the Provisions of this Act, continue as it exists at the Union until altered under the Authority of this Act.
[Note: The instruments admitting British Columbia, Prince Edward Island and Newfoundland contain similar provisions and the *Manitoba Act, 1897, Alberta Act* and *Saskatchewan Act* establish the executive authorities in the three provinces concerned. See the note to section 146.]

Powers to be exer-
cised by Lieutenant
Governor of
Ontario or Quebec
with Advice, or
alone

65. All Powers, Authorities, and Functions which under any Act of the Parliament of Great Britain, or of the Parliament of the United Kingdom of Great Britain and Ireland, or of the Legislature of Upper Canada, Lower Canada, or Canada, were or are before or at the Union vested in or exerciseable by the respective Governors or Lieutenant

Governors of those Provinces, with the Advice or with the Advice and Consent of the respective Executive Councils thereof, or in conjunction with those Councils, or with any Number of Members thereof, or by those Governors or Lieutenant Governors individually, shall, as far as the same are capable of being exercised after the Union in relation to the Government of Ontario and Quebec respectively, be vested in and shall or may be exercised by the Lieutenant Governor of Ontario and Quebec respectively, with the Advice or with the Advice and Consent of or in conjunction with the respective Executive Councils, or any Members thereof, or by the Lieutenant Governor individually, as the Case requires, subject nevertheless (except with respect to such as exist under Acts of the Parliament of Great Britain, or of the Parliament of the United Kingdom of Great Britain and Ireland,) to be abolished or altered by the respective Legislatures of Ontario and Quebec.

[Note: See the note to section 129.]

66. The Provisions of this Act referring to the Lieutenant Governor in Council shall be construed as referring to the Lieutenant Governor of the Province acting by and with the Advice of the Executive Council thereof.

Application of provisions referring to Lieutenant Governor in Council

67. The Governor General in Council may from Time to Time appoint an Administrator to execute the Office and Functions of Lieutenant Governor during his Absence, Illness, or other Inability.

Administration in Absence, etc., of Lieutenant Governor

68. Unless and until the Executive Government of any Province otherwise directs with respect to that Province, the Seats of Government of the Provinces shall be as follows, namely,—of Ontario, the City of Toronto; of Quebec, the City of Quebec; of Nova Scotia, the City of Halifax; and of New Brunswick, the City of Fredericton.

Seats of Provincial Governments

Legislative Power

1. ONTARIO

69. There shall be a Legislature for Ontario consisting of the Lieutenant Governor and of One House, styled the Legislative Assembly of Ontario.

Legislature for Ontario

70. The Legislative Assembly of Ontario shall be composed of Eighty-two Members, to be elected to represent the Eighty-two Electoral Districts set forth in the First Schedule to this Act.

[Note: See the *Representation Act* (Ontario).]

Electoral districts

2. QUEBEC

71. There shall be a Legislature for Quebec consisting of the Lieutenant Governor and of Two Houses, styled the Legislative Council of Quebec and the Legislative Assembly of Quebec.

Legislature for Quebec

[Note: The Legislative Council was abolished by the *Act respecting the Legislative Council of Quebec*, Statutes of Quebec, 1968, c. 9. Sections 72 to 79 following are therefore spent.]

Constitution of
Legislative Council

72. The Legislative Council of Quebec shall be composed of Twenty-four Members, to be appointed by the Lieutenant Governor, in the Queen's Name, by Instrument under the Great Seal of Quebec, one being appointed to represent each of the Twenty-four Electoral Divisions of Lower Canada in this Act referred to, and each holding Office for the Term of his Life, unless the Legislature of Quebec otherwise provides under the Provisions of this Act.

Qualification of
Legislative
Councillors

73. The Qualifications of the Legislative Councillors of Quebec shall be the same as those of the Senators for Quebec.

Resignation,
Disqualification,
etc.

74. The Place of a Legislative Councillor of Quebec shall become vacant in the Cases, *mutatis mutandis*, in which the Place of Senator becomes vacant.

Vacancies

75. When a Vacancy happens in the Legislative Council of Quebec by Resignation, Death, or otherwise, the Lieutenant Governor, in the Queen's Name, by Instrument under the Great Seal of Quebec, shall appoint a fit and qualified Person to fill the Vacancy.

Questions as to
Vacancies, etc.

76. If any Question arises respecting the Qualification of a Legislative Councillor of Quebec, or a Vacancy in the Legislative Council of Quebec, the same shall be heard and determined by the Legislative Council.

Speaker of
Legislative Council

77. The Lieutenant Governor may from Time to Time, by Instrument under the Great Seal of Quebec, appoint a Member of the Legislative Council of Quebec to be Speaker thereof, and may remove him and appoint another in his Stead.

Quorum of
Legislative Council

78. Until the Legislature of Quebec otherwise provides, the Presence of at least Ten Members of the Legislative Council, including the Speaker, shall be necessary to constitute a Meeting for the Exercise of its Powers.

Voting in
Legislative Council

79. Questions arising in the Legislative Council of Quebec shall be decided by a Majority of Voices, and the Speaker shall in all Cases have a Vote, and when the Voices are equal the Decision shall be deemed to be in the Negative.

Constitution of
Legislative
Assembly of
Quebec

80. The Legislative Assembly of Quebec shall be composed of Sixty-five Members, to be elected to represent the Sixty-five Electoral Divisions or Districts of Lower Canada in this Act referred to, subject to Alteration thereof by the Legislature of Quebec: Provided that it shall not be lawful to present to the Lieutenant Governor of Quebec for Assent any Bill for altering the Limits of any of the Electoral

Divisions or Districts mentioned in the Second Schedule to this Act, unless the Second and Third Readings of such Bill have been passed in the Legislative Assembly with the Concurrence of the Majority of the Members representing all those Electoral Divisions or Districts, and the Assent shall not be given to such Bill unless an Address has been presented by the Legislative Assembly to the Lieutenant Governor stating that it has been so passed.

[Note: Declared to be of no effect by the *Act respecting electoral districts*, Statutes of Quebec, 1970, c. 7.]

3. ONTARIO AND QUEBEC

81. *The Legislatures of Ontario and Quebec respectively shall be called together not later than Six Months after the Union.*

First Session of Legislatures

[Note: Repealed by the *Statute Law Revision Act, 1893* (No. 17 *infra*).]

82. The Lieutenant Governor of Ontario and of Quebec shall from Time to Time, in the Queen's Name, by Instrument under the Great Seal of the Province, summon and call together the Legislative Assembly of the Province.

Summoning of Legislative Assemblies

83. Until the Legislature of Ontario or of Quebec otherwise provides, a Person accepting or holding in Ontario or in Quebec any Office, Commission, or Employment, permanent or temporary, at the Nomination of the Lieutenant Governor, to which an annual Salary, or any Fee, Allowance, Emolument, or Profit of any Kind or Amount whatever from the Province is attached, shall not be eligible as a Member of the Legislative Assembly of the respective Province, nor shall he sit or vote as such; but nothing in this Section shall make ineligible any Person being a Member of the Executive Council of the respective Province, or holding any of the following Offices, that is to say, the Offices of Attorney General, Secretary and Registrar of the Province, Treasurer of the Province, Commissioner of Crown Lands, and Commissioner of Agriculture and Public Works, and in Quebec Solicitor General, or shall disqualify him to sit or vote in the House for which he is elected, provided he is elected while holding such Office.

Restriction on election of Holders of offices

[Note: See also the *Legislative Assembly Act* (Ontario) and the *National Assembly Act* (Quebec).]

84. Until the Legislatures of Ontario and Quebec respectively otherwise provide, all Laws which at the Union are in force in those Provinces respectively, relative to the following Matters, or any of them, namely,—the Qualifications and Disqualifications of Persons to be elected or to sit or vote as Members of the Assembly of Canada, the Qualifications or Disqualifications of Voters, the Oaths to be taken by Voters, the Returning Officers, their Powers and Duties, the Proceedings at Elections, the Periods during which such Elections

Continuance of existing Election Laws

may be continued, and the Trial of controverted Elections and the Proceedings incident thereto, the vacating of the Seats of Members and the issuing and execution of new Writs in case of Seats vacated otherwise than by Dissolution,—shall respectively apply to Elections of Members to serve in the respective Legislative Assemblies of Ontario and Quebec.

Provided that, until the Legislature of Ontario otherwise provides, at any Election for a Member of the Legislative Assembly of Ontario for the District of Algoma, in addition to Persons qualified by the Law of the Province of Canada to vote, every Male British Subject, aged Twenty-one Years or upwards, being a Householder, shall have a Vote.

[Note: See also the *Election Act* and *Legislative Assembly Act* (Ontario) and the *Elections Act* and *National Assembly Act* (Quebec).]

Duration of Legislative Assemblies

85. Every Legislative Assembly of Ontario and every Legislative Assembly of Quebec shall continue for Four Years from the Day of the Return of the Writs for choosing the same (subject nevertheless to either the Legislative Assembly of Ontario or the Legislative Assembly of Quebec being sooner dissolved by the Lieutenant Governor of the Province), and no longer.

[Note: Now five years in both provinces: see the *Legislative Assembly Act* (Ontario) and the *National Assembly Act* (Quebec). See also section 4 of the *Constitution Act, 1982* (No. 44 *infra*).]

Yearly Session of Legislature

86. There shall be a Session of the Legislature of Ontario and of that of Quebec once at least in every Year, so that Twelve Months shall not intervene between the last sitting of the Legislature in each Province in one Session and its first Sitting in the next Session.

[Note: See section 5 of the *Constitution Act, 1982* (No. 44 *infra*).]

Speaker, Quorum, etc.

87. The following Provisions of this Act respecting the House of Commons of Canada shall extend and apply to the Legislative Assemblies of Ontario and Quebec, that is to say,—the Provisions relating to the Election of a Speaker originally and on Vacancies, the Duties of the Speaker, the Absence of the Speaker, the Quorum, and the Mode of voting, as if those Provisions were here re-enacted and made applicable in Terms to each such Legislative Assembly.

4. Nova Scotia and New Brunswick

Constitutions of Legislatures of Nova Scotia *and* New Brunswick

88. The Constitution of the Legislature of each of the Provinces of Nova Scotia and New Brunswick shall, subject to the Provisions of this Act, continue as it exists at the Union until altered under the Authority of this Act; *and the House of Assembly of New Brunswick existing at the passing of this Act shall, unless sooner dissolved, continue for the Period for which it was elected.*

[Note: The words in italics were repealed by the *Statute Law Revision Act, 1893* (No. 17 *infra*). The note to section 64 also applies to the Legislatures of the provinces mentioned therein. See also sections 3 to 5 of the *Constitution Act, 1982* (No. 44 *infra*) and sub-item 2(2) of the Schedule to that Act.]

First Elections

5. ONTARIO, QUEBEC, AND NOVA SCOTIA

89. *Each of the Lieutenant Governors of Ontario, Quebec and Nova Scotia shall cause Writs to be issued for the First Election of Members of the Legislative Assembly thereof in such Form and by such Person as he thinks fit, and at such Time and addressed to such Returning Officer as the Governor General directs, and so that the First Election of Member of Assembly for any Electoral District or any Subdivision thereof shall be held at the same Time and at the same Places as the Election for a Member to serve in the House of Commons of Canada for that Electoral District.*

[Note: Repealed by the *Statute Law Revision Act, 1893* (No. 17 *infra*).]

Application to Legislatures of Provisions respecting Money Votes, etc.

6. THE FOUR PROVINCES

90. The following Provisions of this Act respecting the Parliament of Canada, namely,—the Provisions relating to Appropriation and Tax Bills, the Recommendation of Money Votes, the Assent to Bills, the Disallowance of Acts, and the Signification of Pleasure on Bills reserved,—shall extend and apply to the Legislatures of the several Provinces as if those Provisions were here re-enacted and made applicable in Terms to the respective Provinces and the Legislatures thereof, with the Substitution of the Lieutenant Governor of the Province for the Governor General, of the Governor General for the Queen and for a Secretary of State, of One Year for Two Years, and of the Province for Canada.

VI. DISTRIBUTION OF LEGISLATIVE POWERS

Powers of the Parliament

Legislative Authority of Parliament of Canada

91. It shall be lawful for the Queen, by and with the Advice and Consent of the Senate and House of Commons, to make Laws for the Peace, Order, and good Government of Canada, in relation to all Matters not coming within the Classes of Subjects by this Act assigned exclusively to the Legislatures of the Provinces; and for greater Certainty, but not so as to restrict the Generality of the foregoing Terms of this Section, it is hereby declared that (notwithstanding anything in this Act) the exclusive Legislative Authority of the Parliament of Canada extends to all Matters coming within the Classes of Subjects next hereinafter enumerated; that is to say,—

Amendment as to legislative authority of Parliament of Canada

1. *The amendment from time to time of the Constitution of Canada, except as regards matters coming within the classes of subjects by this Act assigned exclusively to the Legislatures of the provinces, or as regards rights or privileges by this or any other Constitutional Act granted or secured to the Legislature or the Government of a*

*province, or to any class of persons with respect to schools or as re-
gards the use of the English or the French language or as regards the
requirements that there shall be a session of the Parliament of
Canada at least once each year, and that no House of Commons
shall continue for more than five years from the day of the return of
the Writs for choosing the House: Provided, however, that a House
of Commons may in time of real or apprehended war, invasion or insurrection be continued by the Parliament of Canada if such continuation is not opposed by the votes of more than one-third of the
members of such House.*

[Note: Class 1 was added by the *British North America Act (No. 2), 1949* (No.
33 *infra*) and repealed by the *Constitution Act, 1982* (No. 44 *infra*).]

1A.   The Public Debt and Property.

[Note: Re-numbered 1A by the *British North America Act (No. 2), 1949* No.
33 *infra*).]

2. The Regulation of Trade and Commerce.

2A.   Unemployment insurance.

[Note: Added by the *Constitution Act, 1940* (No. 28 *infra*).]

3. The raising of Money by any Mode or System of Taxation.

4. The borrowing of Money on the Public Credit.

5. Postal Service.

6. The Census and Statistics.

7. Militia, Military and Naval Service, and Defence.

8. The fixing of and providing for the Salaries and Allowances of
Civil and other Officers of the Government of Canada.

9. Beacons, Buoys, Lighthouses, and Sable Island.

10. Navigation and Shipping.

11. Quarantine and the Establishment and Maintenance of Marine
Hospitals.

12. Sea Coast and Inland Fisheries.

13. Ferries between a Province and any British or Foreign Country
or between Two Provinces.

14. Currency and Coinage.

15. Banking, Incorporation of Banks, and the Issue of Paper
Money.

16. Savings Banks.

17. Weights and Measures.

18. Bills of Exchange and Promissory Notes.

19. Interest.

20. Legal Tender.

21. Bankruptcy and Insolvency.

22. Patents of Invention and Discovery.

23. Copyrights.

24. Indians, and Lands reserved for the Indians.

25. Naturalization and Aliens.

26. Marriage and Divorce.

27. The Criminal Law, except the Constitution of Courts of Criminal Jurisdiction, but including the Procedure in Criminal Matters.

28. The Establishment, Maintenance, and Management of Penitentiaries.

29. Such Classes of Subjects as are expressly excepted in the Enumeration of the Classes of Subjects by this Act assigned exclusively to the Legislatures of the Provinces.

And any Matter coming within any of the Classes of Subjects enumerated in this Section shall not be deemed to come within the Class of Matters of a local or private Nature comprised in the Enumeration of the Classes of Subjects by this Act assigned exclusively to the Legislatures of the Provinces.

[Note: Legislative authority has also been conferred by the *Rupert's Land Act, 1868* (No. 6 *infra*), *Constitution Act, 1871* (No. 11 *infra*), *Constitution Act, 1886* (No. 15 *infra*), *Statute of Westminster, 1931* (No. 27 *infra*) and section 44 of the *Constitution Act, 1982* (No. 44 *infra*), and see also sections 38 and 41 to 43 of the latter Act.]

Exclusive Powers of Provincial Legislatures

Subjects of exclusive Provincial Legislation

92. In each Province the Legislature may exclusively make Laws in relation to Matters coming within the Classes of Subjects next hereinafter enumerated; that is to say,—

1. The Amendment from Time to Time, notwithstanding anything in this Act, of the Constitution of the Province, except as regards the Office of Lieutenant Governor.

[Note: Class 1 was repealed by the *Constitution Act, 1982* (No. 44 *infra*). The subject is now provided for in section 45 of that Act, and see also sections 38 and 41 to 43 of the same Act.]

2. Direct Taxation with-in the Province in order to the raising of a Revenue for Provincial Purposes.

3. The borrowing of Money on the sole Credit of the Province.

4. The Establishment and Tenure of Provincial Offices and the Appointment and Payment of Provincial Officers.

5. The Management and Sale of the Public Lands belonging to the Province and of the Timber and Wood thereon.

6. The Establishment, Maintenance, and Management of Public and Reformatory Prisons in and for the Province.

7. The Establishment, Maintenance, and Management of Hospitals, Asylums, Charities, and Eleemosynary Institutions in and for the Province, other than Marine Hospitals.

8. Municipal Institutions in the Province.

9. Shop, Saloon, Tavern, Auctioneer, and other Licences in order to the raising of a Revenue for Provincial, Local, or Municipal Purposes.

10. Local Works and Undertakings other than such as are of the following Classes:—

a. Lines of Steam or other Ships, Railways, Canals, Telegraphs, and other Works and Undertakings connecting the Province with any other or others of the Provinces, or extending beyond the Limits of the Province:

b. Lines of Steam Ships between the Province and any British or Foreign Country:

c. Such Works as, although wholly situate within the Province, are before or after their Execution declared by the Parliament of Canada to be for the general Advantage of Canada or for the Advantage of Two or more of the Provinces.

11. The Incorporation of Companies with Provincial Objects.

12. The Solemnization of Marriage in the Province.

13. Property and Civil Rights in the Province.

14. The Administration of Justice in the Province, including the Constitution, Maintenance, and Organization of Provincial Courts, both of Civil and of Criminal Jurisdiction, and including Procedure in Civil Matters in those Courts.

15. The Imposition of Punishment by Fine, Penalty, or Imprisonment for enforcing any Law of the Province made in relation to any Matter coming within any of the Classes of Subjects enumerated in this Section.

16. Generally all Matters of a merely local or private Nature in the Province.

Non-Renewable Natural Resources, Forestry Resources and Electrical Energy

Laws respecting non-renewable natural resources, forestry resources and electrical energy

92A. (1) In each pro-vince, the legislature may exclusively make laws in relation to

(a) exploration for non-renewable natural resources in the province;

(b) development, conservation and management of non-renewable natural resources and forestry resources in the province, including laws in relation to the rate of primary production therefrom; and

(c) development, conservation and management of sites and facilities in the province for the generation and production of electrical energy.

Export from provinces of resources

(2) In each province, the legislature may make laws in relation to the export from the province to another part of Canada of the primary production from non-renewable natural resources and forestry resources in the province and the production from facilities in the province for the generation of electrical energy, but such laws may not authorize or provide for discrimination in prices or in supplies exported to another part of Canada.

Authority of Parliament

(3) Nothing in subsection (2) derogates from the authority of Parliament to enact laws in relation to the matters referred to in that subsection and, where such a law of Parliament and a law of a province conflict, the law of Parliament prevails to the extent of the conflict.

Taxation of resources

(4) In each province, the legislature may make laws in relation to the raising of money by any mode or system of taxation in respect of
  (a) Non-renewable natural resources and forestry resources in the province and the primary production therefrom, and
  (b) sites and facilities in the province for the generation of electrical energy and the production therefrom,
whether or not such production is exported in whole or in part from the province, but such laws may not authorize or provide for taxation that differentiates between production exported to another part of Canada and production not exported from the province.

"Primary production"

(5) The expression "primary production" has the meaning assigned by the Sixth Schedule.

Existing powers or rights

(6) Nothing in subsections (1) to (5) derogates from any powers or rights that a legislature or government of a province had immediately before the coming into force of this section.

[Note: Added by section 50 of the *Constitution Act, 1982* (No. 44 *infra*).]

Legislation respecting Education

Education

93. In and for each Province the Legislature may exclusively make Laws in relation to Education, subject and according to the following Provisions:—

(1) Nothing in any such Law shall prejudicially affect any Right or Privilege with respect to Denominational Schools which any Class of Persons have by Law in the Province at the Union:

(2) All the Powers, Privileges, and Duties at the Union by Law conferred and imposed in Upper Canada on the Separate Schools and School Trustees of the Queen's Roman Catholic Subjects shall be and the same are hereby extended to the Dissentient Schools of the Queen's Protestant and Roman Catholic Subjects in Quebec:

(3) Where in any Province a System of Separate or Dissentient Schools exists by Law at the Union or is thereafter established by the Legislature of the Province, an Appeal shall lie to the Governor General in Council from any Act or Decision of any Provincial Authority affecting any Right or Privilege of the Protestant or Roman Catholic Minority of the Queen's Subjects in relation to Education:

(4) In case any such Provincial Law as from Time to Time seems to the Governor General in Council requisite for the due Execution of the Provisions of this Section is not made, or in case any Decision of

the Governor General in Council on any Appeal under this Section is not duly executed by the proper Provincial Authority in that Behalf, then and in every such Case, and as far only as the Circumstances of each Case require, the Parliament of Canada may make remedial Laws for the due Execution of the Provisions of this Section and of any Decision of the Governor General in Council under this Section.

[Note: Altered for Manitoba by section 22 of the *Manitoba Act, 1870* (No. 8 *infra*) confirmed by the *Constitution Act, 1871* No. 11 *infra*); for Alberta, by section 17 of the *Alberta Act* (No. 20 *infra*); for Saskatchewan, by section 17 of the *Saskatchewan Act* (No. 21 *infra*); and for Newfoundland, by Term 17 of the Terms of Union of Newfoundland with Canada, confirmed by the *Newfoundland Act* (No. 32 *infra*). See also sections 23, 29 and 59 of the *Constitution Act, 1982* (No. 44 *infra*).]

Legislation for Uniformity of Laws in Three Provinces

Uniformity of Laws in Ontario, Nova Scotia, and New Brunswick

94. Notwithstanding anything in this Act, the Parliament of Canada may make Provision for the Uniformity of all or any of the Laws relative to Property and Civil Rights in Ontario, Nova Scotia, and New Brunswick, and of the Procedure of all or any of the Courts in those Three Provinces, and from and after the passing of any Act in that Behalf the Power of the Parliament of Canada to make Laws in relation to any Matter comprised in any such Act shall, notwithstanding anything in this Act, be unrestricted; but any Act of the Parliament of Canada making Provision for such Uniformity shall not have effect in any Province unless and until it is adopted and enacted as Law by the Legislature thereof.

Legislation respecting old age pensions and supplementary benefits

94A. The Parliament of Canada may make laws in relation to old age pensions and supplementary benefits, including survivors' and disability benefits irrespective of age, but no such law shall affect the operation of any law present or future of a provincial legislature in relation to any such matter.

[Note: Substituted by the *Constitution Act, 1964* (No. 38 *infra*) for the section 94A that was originally added by the *British North America Act, 1951* (No. 35 *infra*).]

Concurrent Powers of Legislation respecting Agriculture, etc.

Agriculture and Immigration

95. In each Province the Legislature may make Laws in relation to Agriculture in the Province, and to Immigration into the Province; and it is hereby declared that the Parliament of Canada may from Time to Time make Laws in relation to Agriculture in all or any of the Provinces, and to Immigration into all or any of the Provinces; and any Law of the Legislature of a Province relative to Agriculture or to Immigration shall have effect in and for the Province as long and as far only as it is not repugnant to any Act of the Parliament of Canada.

Appointment of Judges

VII. Judicature

Selections of
Judges in Ontario,
etc.

96. The Governor General shall appoint the Judges of the Superior, District, and County Courts in each Province, except those of the Courts of Probate in Nova Scotia and New Brunswick.

Selection of Judges
in Quebec

97. Until the Laws relative to Property and Civil Rights in Ontario, Nova Scotia, and New Brunswick, and the Procedure of the Courts in those Provinces, are made uniform, the Judges of the Courts of those Provinces appointed by the Governor General shall be selected from the respective Bars of those Provinces.

*Tenure of Office of
Judges of Superior
Courts*

98. The Judges of the Courts of Quebec shall be selected from the Bar of that Province.

Tenure of office of
judges

99. *The Judges of the Superior Courts shall hold Office during good Behaviour, but shall be removable by the Governor General on Address of the Senate and House of Commons.*

99 (1) Subject to subsection (2) of this section, the judges of the superior courts shall hold office during good behaviour, but shall be removable by the Governor General on address of the Senate and House of Commons.

(2) A judge of a superior court, whether appointed before or after the coming into force of this section, shall cease to hold office upon attaining the age of seventy-five years, or upon the coming into force of this section if at that time he has already attained that age.

[Note: Section 99 (in italics) was repealed and the new section substituted by the *Constitution Act, 1960* (No. 37 *infra*).]

Salaries, etc., of
Judges

100. The Salaries, Allowances, and Pensions of the Judges of the Superior, District, and County Courts (except the Courts of Probate in Nova Scotia and New Brunswick), and of the Admiralty Courts in Cases where the Judges thereof are for the Time being paid by Salary, shall be fixed and provided by the Parliament of Canada.

[Note: See the *Judges Act* (Canada).]

General Court of
Appeal, etc.

101. The Parliament of Canada may, notwithstanding anything in this Act, from Time to Time provide for the Constitution, Maintenance, and Organization of a General Court of Appeal for Canada, and for the Establishment of any additional Courts for the better Administration of the Laws of Canada.

[Note: See the *Supreme Court Act, Federal Court Act* and *Tax Court of Canada Act* (Canada).]

Creation of
Consolidated
Revenue Fund

VIII. Revenues; Debts; Assets; Taxation

102. All Duties and Revenues over which the respective Legislatures of Canada, Nova Scotia, and New Brunswick before and at the Union had and have Power of Appropriation, except such

Expenses of
Collection, etc.

Portions thereof as are by this Act reserved to the respective Legislatures of the Provinces, or are raised by them in accordance with the special Powers conferred on them by this Act, shall form One Consolidated Revenue Fund, to be appropriated for the Public Service of Canada in the Manner and subject to the Charges in this Act provided.

Interest of
Provincial Public
Debts

103. The Consolidated Revenue Fund of Canada shall be permanently charged with the Costs, Charges, and Expenses incident to the Collection, Management, and Receipt thereof, and the same shall form the First Charge thereon, subject to be reviewed and audited in such Manner as shall be ordered by the Governor General in Council until the Parliament otherwise provides.

Salary of Governor
General

104. The annual Interest of the Public Debts of the several Provinces of Canada, Nova Scotia, and New Brunswick at the Union shall form the Second Charge on the Consolidated Revenue Fund of Canada.

Appropriation from
Time to Time

105. Unless altered by the Parliament of Canada, the Salary of the Governor General shall be Ten thousand Pounds Sterling Money of the United Kingdom of Great Britain and Ireland, payable out of the Consolidated Revenue Fund of Canada, and the same shall form the Third Charge thereon.

Transfer of Stocks,
etc.

[Note: See the *Governor General's Act* (Canada).]

106. Subject to the several Payments by this Act charged on the Consolidated Revenue Fund of Canada, the same shall be appropriated by the Parliament of Canada for the Public Service.

Transfer of
Property in
Schedule

107. All Stocks, Cash, Banker's Balances, and Securities for Money belonging to each Province at the Time of the Union, except as in this Act mentioned, shall be the Property of Canada, and shall be taken in Reduction of the Amount of the respective Debts of the Provinces at the Union.

Property in Lands,
Mines, etc.

108. The Public Works and Property of each Province, enumerated in the Third Schedule to this Act, shall be the Property of Canada.

109. All Lands, Mines, Minerals, and Royalties belonging to the several Provinces of Canada, Nova Scotia, and New Brunswick at the Union, and all Sums then due or payable for such Lands, Mines, Minerals, or Royalties, shall belong to the several Provinces of Ontario, Quebec, Nova Scotia, and New Brunswick in which the same are situate or arise, subject to any Trusts existing in respect thereof, and to any Interest other than that of the Province in the same.

Assets connected
with Provincial
Debts

[Note: The Provinces of Manitoba, British Columbia, Alberta and Saskatchewan were placed in the same position as the original provinces by the *Constitution Act, 1930* (No. 26 *infra*).

Newfoundland was also placed in the same position by the *Newfoundland Act* (No. 32 *infra*).

With respect to Prince Edward Island, see the Schedule to the *Prince Edward Island Terms of Union* (No. 12 *infra*).]

110. All Assets connected with such Portions of the Public Debt of each Province as are assumed by that Province shall belong to that Province.

111. Canada shall be liable for the Debts and Liabilities of each province existing at the Union.

112. Ontario and Quebec conjointly shall be liable to Canada for the Amount (if any) by which the Debt of the Province of Canada exceeds at the Union Sixty-two million five hundred thousand Dollars, and shall be charged with Interest at the Rate of Five per Centum per Annum thereon.

113. The Assets enumerated in the Fourth Schedule to this Act belonging at the Union to the Province of Canada shall be the Property of Ontario and Quebec conjointly.

114. Nova Scotia shall be liable to Canada for the Amount (if any) by which its Public Debt exceeds at the Union Eight million Dollars, and shall be charged with Interest at the Rate of Five per Centum per Annum thereon.

[Note: As to sections 114, 115 and 116, see the *Provincial Subsidies Act* (Canada).]

115. New Brunswick shall be liable to Canada for the Amount (if any) by which its Public Debt exceeds at the Union Seven million Dollars, and shall be charged with Interest at the Rate of Five per Centum per Annum thereon.

116. In case the Public Debts of Nova Scotia and New Brunswick do not at the Union amount to Eight million and Seven million Dollars respectively, they shall respectively receive by half-yearly Payments in advance from the Government of Canada Interest at Five per Centum per Annum on the Difference between the actual Amounts of their respective Debts and such stipulated Amounts.

117. The several Provinces shall retain all their respective Public Property not otherwise disposed of in this Act, subject to the Right of Canada to assume any Lands or Public Property required for Fortifications or for the Defence of the Country.

118. *The following Sums shall be paid yearly by Canada to the several Provinces for the Support of their Governments and Legislatures:*

	Dollars
Ontario	*Eighty thousand.*
Quebec	*Seventy thousand.*

Marginal notes:

Canada to be liable for Provincial Debts

Debts of Ontario and Quebec

Assets of Ontario and Quebec

Debt of Nova Scotia

Debt of New Brunswick

Payment of interest to Nova Scotia and New Brunswick

Provincial Public Property

Grants to Provinces

Nova Scotia ....*Sixty thousand.*

New Brunswick...*Fifty thousand*

Two hundred and sixty thousand;

and an annual Grant in aid of each Province shall be made, equal to Eighty Cents per Head of the Population as ascertained by the Census of One thousand eight hundred and sixty-one, and in the Case of Nova Scotia and New Brunswick, by each subsequent Decennial Census until the Population of each of those two Provinces amounts to Four hundred thousand Souls, at which Rate such Grant shall thereafter remain. Such Grants shall be in full Settlement of all future Demands on Canada, and shall be paid half-yearly in advance to each Province; but the Government of Canada shall deduct from such Grants, as against any Province, all Sums chargeable as Interest on the Public Debt of that Province in excess of the several Amounts stipulated in this Act.

Further Grant to New Brunswick

[Note: Repealed by the *Statute Law Revision Act, 1950* (No. 34 *infra*). The section had been previously superseded by the *Constitution Act, 1907* (No. 22 *infra*). See the *Provincial Subsidies Act* and the *Federal-Provincial Fiscal Arrangements and Federal Post-Secondary Education and Health Contributions Act* (Canada).]

Form of Payments

119. New Brunswick shall receive by half-yearly Payments in advance from Canada for the Period of Ten Years from the Union an additional Allowance of Sixty-three thousand Dollars per Annum; but as long as the Public Debt of that Province remains under Seven million Dollars, a Deduction equal to the Interest at Five per Centum per Annum on such Deficiency shall be made from that Allowance of Sixty-three thousand Dollars.

Canadian manufactures, etc.

120. All Payments to be made under this Act, or in discharge of Liabilities created under any Act of the Provinces of Canada, Nova Scotia, and New Brunswick respectively, and assumed by Canada, shall, until the Parliament of Canada otherwise directs, be made in such Form and Manner as may from Time to Time be ordered by the Governor General in Council.

Continuance of Customs and Excise Laws

121. All Articles of the Growth, Produce, or Manufacture of any one of the Provinces shall, from and after the Union, be admitted free into each of the other Provinces.

Exportation and Importation as between Two Provinces

122. The Customs and Excise Laws of each Province shall, subject to the Provisions of this Act, continue in force until altered by the Parliament of Canada.

[Note: See the current federal customs and excise legislation.]

Lumber Dues in New Brunswick

123. Where Customs Duties are, at the Union, leviable on any Goods, Wares, or Merchandises in any Two Provinces, those Goods, Wares, and Merchandises may, from and after the Union, be imported from one of those Provinces into the other of them on Proof of Payment of the Customs Duty leviable thereon in the Province of Exportation, and on Payment of such further Amount (if any) of Customs Duty as is leviable thereon in the Province of Importation.

124. Nothing in this Act shall affect the Right of New Brunswick to levy the Lumber Dues provided in Chapter Fifteen of Title Three of the Revised Statutes of New Brunswick, or in any Act amending that Act before or after the Union, and not increasing the Amount of such Dues; but the Lumber of any of the Provinces other than New Brunswick shall not be subject to such Dues.

Exemption of Public Lands, etc.

Provincial Consolidated Revenue Fund

125. No Lands or Property belonging to Canada or any Province shall be liable to Taxation.

126. Such Portions of the Duties and Revenues over which the respective Legislatures of Canada, Nova Scotia, and New Brunswick had before the Union Power of Appropriation as are by this Act reserved to the respective Governments or Legislatures of the Provinces, and all Duties and Revenues raised by them in accordance with the special Powers conferred upon them by this Act, shall in each Province form One Consolidated Revenue Fund to be appropriated for the Public Service of the Province.

As to Legislative Councillors of Provinces becoming senators

IX. Miscellaneous Provisions

General

127. *If any Person being at the passing of this Act a Member of the Legislative Council of Canada, Nova Scotia, or New Brunswick, to whom a Place in the Senate is offered, does not within Thirty Days thereafter, by Writing under his Hand addressed to the Governor General of the Province of Canada or to the Lieutenant Governor of Nova Scotia or New Brunswick (as the Case may be), accept the same, he shall be deemed to have declined the same; and any Person who, being at the passing of this Act a Member of the Legislative Council of Nova Scotia or New Brunswick, accepts a Place in the Senate, shall thereby vacate his Seat in such Legislative Council.*
[Note: Repealed by the *Statute Law Revision Act, 1893* (No. 17 *infra*).]

Oath of Allegiance, etc.

128. Every Member of the Senate or House of Commons of Canada shall before taking his Seat therein take and subscribe before the Governor General or some Person authorized by him, and every Member of a Legislative Council or Legislative Assembly of any Province shall before taking his Seat therein take and subscribe before the Lieutenant Governor of the Province or some Person authorized by him, the Oath of Allegiance contained in the Fifth Schedule to this Act; and every Member of the Senate of Canada and every Member of the Legislative Council of Quebec shall also, before taking his Seat therein, take and subscribe before the Governor General,

Continuance of existing Laws, Courts, Officers, etc.

or some Person authorized by him, the Declaration of Qualification contained in the same Schedule.

129. Except as otherwise provided by this Act, all Laws in force in Canada, Nova Scotia, or New Brunswick at the Union, and all Courts of Civil and Criminal Jurisdiction, and all legal Commissions, Powers, and Authorities, and all Officers, Judicial, Administrative, and Ministerial, existing therein at the Union, shall continue in Ontario, Quebec, Nova Scotia, and New Brunswick respectively, as if the Union had not been made; subject nevertheless (except with respect to such as are enacted by or exist under Acts of the Parliament of Great Britain or of the Parliament of the United Kingdom of Great Britain and Ireland,) to be repealed, abolished, or altered by the Parliament of Canada, or by the Legislature of the respective Province, according to the Authority of the Parliament or of that Legislature under this Act.

Transfer of Officers to Canada

[Note: The restriction against altering or repealing laws enacted by or existing under statutes of the United Kingdom was removed by the *Statute of Westminster, 1931* (No. 27 *infra*), except in respect of certain constitutional documents. See also Part V of the *Constitution Act, 1982* (No. 44 *infra*).]

Appointment of new Officers

130. Until the Parliament of Canada otherwise provides, all Officers of the several Provinces having Duties to discharge in relation to Matters other than those coming within the Classes of Subjects by this Act assigned exclusively to the Legislatures of the Provinces shall be Officers of Canada, and shall continue to discharge the Duties of their respective Offices under the same Liabilities, Responsibilities, and Penalties as if the Union had not been made.

Treaty Obligations

131. Until the Parliament of Canada otherwise provides, the Governor General in Council may from Time to Time appoint such Officers as the Governor General in Council deems necessary or proper for the effectual Execution of this Act.

Use of English and French Languages

132. The Parliament and Government of Canada shall have all Powers necessary or proper for performing the Obligations of Canada or of any Province thereof, as Part of the British Empire, towards Foreign Countries, arising under Treaties between the Empire and such Foreign Countries.

133. Either the English or the French Language may be used by any Person in the Debates of the Houses of the Parliament of Canada and of the Houses of the Legislature of Quebec; and both those Languages shall be used in the respective Records and Journals of those Houses; and either of those Languages may be used by any Person or in any Pleading or Process in or issuing from any Court of Canada established under this Act, and in or from all or any of the Courts of Quebec.

The Acts of the Parliament of Canada and of the Legislature of Quebec shall be printed and published in both those Languages.

[Note: See also section 23 of the *Manitoba Act, 1870* (No. 8 *infra*) and sections 17 to 23 of the *Constitution Act, 1982* (No. 44 *infra*).]

Appointment of Executive Officers for Ontario and Quebec

Ontario and Quebec

134. Until the Legislature of Ontario or of Quebec otherwise provides, the Lieutenant Governors of Ontario and Quebec may each appoint under the Great Seal of the Province the following Officers, to hold Office during Pleasure, that is to say,—the Attorney General, the Secretary and Registrar of the Province, the Treasurer of the Province, the Commissioner of Crown Lands, and the Commissioner of Agriculture and Public Works, and in the Case of Quebec the Solicitor General, and may, by Order of the Lieutenant Governor in Council, from Time to Time prescribe the Duties of those Officers, and of the several Departments over which they shall preside or to which they shall belong, and of the Officers and Clerks thereof, and may also appoint other and additional Officers to hold Office during Pleasure, and may from Time to Time prescribe the Duties of those Officers, and of the several Departments over which they shall preside or to which they shall belong, and of the Officers and Clerks thereof.

Powers, Duties, etc. of Executive Officers

[Note: See the *Executive Council Act* (Ontario) and the *Executive Power Act* (Quebec).]

135. Until the Legislature of Ontario or Quebec otherwise provides, all Rights, Powers, Duties, Functions, Responsibilities, or authorities at the passing of this Act vested in or imposed on the Attorney General, Solicitor General, Secretary and Registrar of the Province of Canada, Minister of Finance, Commissioner of Crown Lands, Commissioner of Public Works, and Minister of Agriculture and Receiver General, by any Law, Statute, or Ordinance of Upper Canada, Lower Canada, or Canada, and not repugnant to this Act, shall be vested in or imposed on any Officer to be appointed by the Lieutenant Governor for the Discharge of the same or any of them; and the Commissioner of Agriculture and Public Works shall perform the Duties and Functions of the Office of Minister of Agriculture at the passing of this Act imposed by the Law of the Province of Canada, as well as those of the Commissioner of Public Works.

Great Seals

136. Until altered by the Lieutenant Governor in Council, the Great Seals of Ontario and Quebec respectively shall be the same, or of the same Design, as those used in the Provinces of Upper Canada and Lower Canada respectively before their Union as the Province of Canada.

Construction of temporary Acts

137. The Words "and from thence to the End of the then next ensuing Session of the Legislature," or Words to the same Effect, used in any temporary Act of the Province of Canada not expired before the Union, shall be construed to extend and apply to the next Session of the Parliament of Canada if the Subject Matter of the Act is within the Powers of the same as defined by this Act, or to the next Sessions of the Legislatures of Ontario and Quebec respectively if the Subject Matter of the Act is within the Powers of the same as defined by this Act.

As to Errors in Names

138. From and after the Union the Use of the Words "Upper Canada" instead of "Ontario," or "Lower Canada" instead of "Quebec," in any Deed, Writ, Process, Pleading, Document, Matter, or Thing, shall not invalidate the same.

As to Issue of Proclamations after Union

139. Any Proclamation under the Great Seal of the Province of Canada issued before the Union to take effect at a Time which is subsequent to the Union, whether relating to that Province, or to Upper Canada, or to Lower Canada, and the several Matters and Things therein proclaimed, shall be and continue of like Force and Effect as if the Union had not been made.

As to issue of Proclamations before Union, to commence after Union

140. Any Proclamation which is authorized by any Act of the Legislature of the Province of Canada to be issued under the Great Seal of the Province of Canada, whether relating to that Province, or to Upper Canada, or to Lower Canada, and which is not issued before the Union, may be issued by the Lieutenant Governor of Ontario or of Quebec, as its Subject Matter requires, under the Great Seal thereof; and from and after the Issue of such Proclamation the same and the several Matters and Things therein proclaimed shall be and continue of the like force and Effect in Ontario or Quebec as if the Union had not been made.

Penitentiary

141. The Penitentiary of the Province of Canada shall, until the Parliament of Canada otherwise provides, be and continue the Penitentiary of Ontario and of Quebec.
[Note: See the *Penitentiary Act* (Canada).]

Arbitration respecting Debts, etc.

142. The Division and Adjustment of the Debts, Credits, Liabilities, Properties, and Assets of Upper Canada and Lower Canada shall be referred to the Arbitrament of Three Arbitrators, One chosen by the government of Ontario, One by the Government of Quebec, and One by the Government of Canada; and the Selection of the Arbitrators shall not be made until the Parliament of Canada and the Legislatures of Ontario and Quebec have met; and the Arbitrator chosen by the Government of Canada shall not be a Resident either in Ontario or in Quebec.

Division of Records

143. The Governor General in Council may from Time to Time order that such and so many of the Records, Books, and Documents of the Province of Canada as he thinks fit shall be appropriated and delivered either to Ontario or to Quebec, and the same shall thenceforth be the Property of that Province; and any Copy thereof or Extract therefrom, duly certified by the Officer having charge of the Original thereof, shall be admitted as Evidence.

Constitution of Townships in Quebec

144. The Lieutenant Governor of Quebec may from Time to Time, by Proclamation under the Great Seal of the Province, to take effect from a Day to be appointed therein, constitute Townships in those Parts of the Province of Quebec in which Townships are not then already constituted, and fix the Metes and Bounds thereof.

X. Intercolonial Railway

145. *Inasmuch as the Provinces of Canada, Nova Scotia, and New Brunswick have joined in a Declaration that the Construction of the Intercolonial Railway is essential to the Consolidation of the Union of British North America, and to the Assent thereto of Nova Scotia and New Brunswick, and have consequently agreed that Provision should be made for its immediate Construction by the Government of Canada: Therefore, in order to give effect to that Agreement, it shall be the Duty of the Government and Parliament of Canada to provide for the Commencement, within Six Months after the Union, of a Railway connecting the River St. Lawrence with the City of Halifax in Nova Scotia, and for the Construction thereof without Intermission, and the Completion thereof with all practicable speed.*

[Note: Repealed by the *Statute Law Revision Act, 1893* (No. 17 *infra*).

Power to admit Newfoundland, etc., into the Union

XI. Admission of Other Colonies

146. It shall be lawful for the Queen, by and with the Advice of Her Majesty's Most Honourable Privy Council, on Addresses from the Houses of the Parliament of Canada, and from the Houses of the respective Legislatures of the Colonies or Provinces of Newfoundland, Prince Edward Island, and British Columbia, to admit those Colonies or Provinces, or any of them, into the Union, and on Address from the Houses of the Parliament of Canada to admit Rupert's Land and the North-western Territory, or either of them, into the Union, on such Terms and Conditions in each Case as are in the Addresses expressed and as the Queen thinks fit to approve, subject to the Provisions of this Act; and the Provisions of any Order in Council in that Behalf shall have effect as if they had been enacted by the Parliament of the United Kingdom of Great Britain and Ireland.

[Note: Rupert's Land and the North-Western Territory (subsequently designated the Northwest Territories) became part of Canada, pursuant to this section and the *Rupert's Land Act, 1868* (No. 6 *infra*), by the *Rupert's Land and North-Western Territory Order* (June 23, 1870) (No. 9 *infra*).

The Province of Manitoba was established by the *Manitoba Act, 1870* (No. 8 *infra*). This Act was confirmed by the *Constitution Act, 1871* (No. 11 *infra*).

British Columbia was admitted into the Union pursuant to this section by the *British Columbia Terms of Union* (May 16, 1871) (No. 10 *infra*).

Prince Edward Island was admitted into the Union pursuant to this section by the *Prince Edward Island Terms of Union* (June 26, 1873 (No. 12 *infra*).

The Provinces of Alberta and Saskatchewan were established, pursuant to the *Constitution Act, 1871* (No. 11 *infra*), by the *Alberta Act* (July 20, 1905) (No. 20 *infra*) and the *Saskatchewan Act* (July 20, 1905) (No. 21 *infra*) respectively.

Newfoundland was admitted as a province by the *Newfoundland Act* (March 23, 1949) (No. 32 *infra*), which confirmed the Agreement containing the Terms of Union between Canada and Newfoundland.

The Yukon Territory was created out of the Northwest Territories in 1898 by *The Yukon Territory Act* (No. 19 *infra*).

As to
Representation of
Newfoundland and
Prince Edward
Island in Senate

147. In case of the Admission of Newfoundland and Prince Edward Island, or either of them, each shall be entitled to a Representation in the Senate of Canada of Four Members, and (notwithstanding anything in this Act) in case of the Admission of Newfoundland the normal Number of Senators shall be Seventy-six and their maximum Number shall be Eighty-two; but Prince Edward Island when admitted shall be deemed to be comprised in the third of the Three Divisions into which Canada is, in relation to the Constitution of the Senate, divided by this Act, and accordingly, after the Admission of Prince Edward Island, whether Newfoundland is admitted or not, the Representation of Nova Scotia and New Brunswick in the Senate shall, as Vacancies occur, be reduced from Twelve and Ten Members respectively, and the Representation of each of those Provinces shall not be increased at any Time beyond Ten, except under the Provisions of this Act for the Appointment of Three or Six additional Senators under the Direction of the Queen.

[Note: See the notes to sections 21, 22, 26, 27 and 28.]

CANADA ACT 1982

including the

CONSTITUTION ACT, 1982

1982, c. 11 (U.K.)
[29th March 1982]

[Note: The English version of the *Canada Act 1982* is contained in the body of the Act; its French version is found in Schedule A. Schedule B contains the English and French versions of the *Constitution Act, 1982*.]

An Act to give effect to a request by the Senate and House of Commons of Canada

Whereas Canada has requested and consented to the enactment of an Act of the Parliament of the United Kingdom to give effect to the provisions hereinafter set forth and the Senate and the House of Commons of Canada in Parliament assembled have submitted an address to Her Majesty requesting that Her Majesty may graciously be pleased to cause a Bill to be laid before the Parliament of the United Kingdom for that purpose.

Be it therefore enacted by the Queen's Most Excellent Majesty, by and with the advice and consent of the Lords Spiritual and Temporal, and Commons, in this present Parliament assembled, and by the authority of the same, as follows:

1. The *Constitution Act, 1982* set out in Schedule B to this Act is hereby enacted for and shall have the force of law in Canada and shall come into force as provided in that Act.

Constitution Act, 1982 enacted

2. No Act of the Parliament of the United Kingdom passed after the *Constitution Act, 1982* comes into force shall extend to Canada as part of its law.

Termination of power to legislate for Canada

3. So far as it is not contained in Schedule B, the French version of this Act is set out in Schedule A to this Act and has the same authority in Canada as the English version thereof.

French version

4. This Act may be cited as the *Canada Act, 1982*.

Short title

SCHEDULE B

CONSTITUTION ACT, 1982

PART I

CANADIAN CHARTER OF RIGHTS AND FREEDOMS

Whereas Canada is founded upon principles that recognize the supremacy of God and the rule of law:

Guarantee of Rights and Freedoms

Rights and freedoms in Canada

1. The *Canadian Charter of Rights and Freedoms* guarantees the rights and freedoms set out in it subject only to such reasonable limits prescribed by law as can be demonstrably justified in a free and democratic society.

Fundamental Freedoms

Fundamental freedoms

2. Everyone has the following fundamental freedoms:

(a) freedom of conscience and religion;
(b) freedom of thought, belief, opinion and expression, including freedom of the press and other media of communication;
(c) freedom of peaceful assembly; and
(d) freedom of association.

Democratic Rights

Democratic rights of citizens

3. Every citizen of Canada has the right to vote in an election of members of the House of Commons or of a legislative assembly and to be qualified for membership therein.

Maximum duration of legislative bodies

4. (1) No House of Commons and no legislative assembly shall continue for longer than five years from the date fixed for the return of the writs at a general election of its members.

Continuation in special circumstances

(2) In time of real or apprehended war, invasion or insurrection, a House of Commons may be continued by Parliament and a legislative assembly may be continued by the legislature beyond five years if such continuation is not opposed by the votes of more than one-third of the members of the House of Commons or the legislative assembly, as the case may be.

Annual sitting of legislative bodies

5. There shall be a sitting of Parliament and of each legislature at least once every twelve months.

Mobility Rights

Mobility of citizens

6. (1) Every citizen of Canada has the right to enter, remain in and leave Canada.

(2) Every citizen of Canada and every person who has the status of a permanent resident of Canada has the right

Rights to move and gain livelihood

(a) to move to and take up residence in any province; and

(b) to pursue the gaining of a livelihood in any province.

(3) The rights specified in subsection (2) are subject to

Limitation

(a) any laws or practices of general application in force in a province other than those that discriminate among persons primarily on the basis of province of present or previous residence; and

(b) any laws providing for reasonable residency requirements as a qualification for the receipt of publicly provided social services.

(4) Subsections (2) and (3) do not preclude any law, program or activity that has as its object the amelioration in a province of conditions of individuals in that province who are socially or economically disadvantaged if the rate of employment in that provide is below the rate of employment in Canada.

Affirmative action programs

Legal Rights

7. Everyone has the right to life, liberty and security of the person and the right not to be deprived thereof except in accordance with the principles of fundamental justice.

Life, liberty and security of person

8. Everyone has the right to be secure against unreasonable search or seizure.

Search or seizure

9. Everyone has the right not to be arbitrarily detained or imprisoned.

Detention or imprisonment

10. Everyone has the right on arrest or detention

Arrest or detention

(a) to be informed promptly of the reasons therefor;

(b) to retain and instruct counsel without delay and to be informed of that right; and

(c) to have the validity of the detention determined by way of *habeas corpus* and to be released if the detention is not lawful.

11. Any person charged with an offence has the right

Proceedings in criminal and penal matters

(a) to be informed without unreasonable delay of the specific offence;

(b) to be tried within a reasonable time;

(c) not to be compelled to be a witness in proceedings against that person in respect of the offence;

(d) to be presumed innocent until proven guilty according to law in a fair and public hearing by an independent and impartial tribunal;

(e) not to be denied reasonable bail without just cause;

(f) except in the case of an offence under military law tried before a military tribunal, to the benefit of trial by jury where the maximum punishment for the offence is imprisonment for five years or a more severe punishment;

(g) not to be found guilty on account of any act or omission unless, at the time of the act or omission, it constituted an offence under Canadian or international law or was criminal according to the general principles of law recognized by the community of nations;

(h) if finally acquitted of the offence, not to be tried for it again and, if finally found guilty and punished for the offence, not to be tried or punished for it again; and

(i) if found guilty of the offence and if the punishment for the offence has been varied between the time of commission and the time of sentencing, to the benefit of the lesser punishment.

Treatment or punishment

12. Everyone has the right not to be subjected to any cruel and unusual treatment or punishment.

Self-crimination

13. A witness who testifies in any proceedings has the right not to have any incriminating evidence so given used to incriminate that witness in any other proceedings, except in a prosecution for perjury or for the giving of contradictory evidence.

Interpreter

14. A party or witness in any proceedings who does not understand or speak the language in which the proceedings are conducted or who is deaf has the right to the assistance of an interpreter.

Equality Rights

Equality before and under law and equal protection and benefit of law

15. (1) Every individual is equal before and under the law and has the right to the equal protection and equal benefit of the law without discrimination and, in particular, without discrimination based on race, national or ethnic origin, colour, religion, sex, age or mental or physical disability.

Affirmative action programs

(2) Subsection (1) does not preclude any law, program or activity that has as its object the amelioration of conditions of disadvantaged individuals or groups including those that are disadvantaged because of race, national or ethnic origin, colour, religion, sex, age or mental or physical disability.

[Note: This section became effective on April 17, 1985. See subsection 32(2) and the note thereto.]

Official Languages of Canada

Official languages of Canada

16. (1) English and French are the official languages of Canada and have equality of status and equal rights and privileges as to their use in all institutions of the Parliament and government of Canada.

(2) English and French are the official languages of New Brunswick and have equality of status and equal rights and privileges as to their use in all institutions of the legislature and government of New Brunswick.

Official languages of New Brunswick

(3) Nothing in this Charter limits the authority of Parliament or a legislature to advance the equality of status or use of English and French.

Advancement of status and use

17. (1) Everyone has the right to use English or French in any debates and other proceedings of Parliament.

Proceedings of Parliament

(2) Everyone has the right to use English or French in any debates and other proceedings of the legislature of New Brunswick.

Proceedings of New Brunswick legislature

18. (1) The statutes, records and journals of Parliament shall be printed and published in English and French and both language versions are equally authoritative.

Parliamentary statutes and records

(2) The statutes, records and journals of the legislature of New Brunswick shall be printed and published in English and French and both language versions are equally authoritative.

New Brunswick statutes and records

19. (1) Either English or French may be used by any person in, or in any pleading in or process issuing from, any court established by Parliament.

Proceedings in courts established by Parliament

(2) Either English or French may be used by any person in, or in any pleading in or process issuing from, any court of New Brunswick.

Proceedings in New Brunswick courts

20. (1) Any member of the public in Canada has the right to communicate with, and to receive available services from, any head or central office of an institution of the Parliament or government of Canada in English or French, and has the same right with respect to any other office of any such institution where
(*a*) there is a significant demand for communications with and services from that office in such language; or
(*b*) due to the nature of the office, it is reasonable that communications with and services from that office be available in both English and French.

Communications by public with federal institutions

(2) Any member of the public in New Brunswick has the right to communicate with, and to receive available services from, any office of an institution of the legislature or government of New Brunswick in English or French.

Communications by public with New Brunswick institutions

21. Nothing in sections 16 to 20 abrogates or derogates from any right, privilege or obligation with respect to the English and French languages, or either of them, that exists or is continued by virtue of any other provision of the Constitution of Canada.

Continuation of existing constitutional provisions

Rights and privileges preserved

22. Nothing in sections 16 to 20 abrogates or derogates from any legal or customary right or privilege acquired or enjoyed either before or after the coming into force of this Charter with respect to any language that is not English or French.

Minority Language Educational Rights

Language of instruction

23. (1) Citizens of Canada

(a) whose first language learned and still understood is that of the English or French linguistic minority population of the province in which they reside, or

(b) who have received their primary school instruction in Canada in English or French and reside in a province where the language in which they received that instruction is the language of the English or French linguistic minority population of the province,

have the right to have their children receive primary and secondary school instruction in that language in that province.

[Note: See also section 59 and the note thereto.]

Continuity of language instruction

(2) Citizens of Canada of whom any child has received or is receiving primary or secondary school instruction in English or French in Canada, have the right to have all their children receive primary and secondary school instruction in the same language.

Application where numbers warrant

(3) The right of citizens of Canada under subsections (1) and (2) to have their children receive primary and secondary school instruction in the language of the English or French linguistic minority population of a province.

(a) applies wherever in the province the number of children of citizens who have such a right is sufficient to warrant the provision to them out of public funds of minority language instruction; and

(b) includes, where the number of those children so warrants, the right to have them receive that instruction in minority language educational facilities provided out of public funds.

Enforcement

Enforcement of guaranteed rights and freedoms

24. (1) Anyone whose rights or freedoms, as guaranteed by this Charter, have been infringed or denied may apply to a court of competent jurisdiction to obtain such remedy as the court considers appropriate and just in the circumstances.

Exclusion of evidence bringing administration of justice into disrepute

(2) Where, in proceedings under subsection (1), a court concludes that evidence was obtained in a manner that infringed or denied any rights or freedoms guaranteed by this Charter, the evidence shall be excluded if it is established that, having regard to all the circumstances, the admission of it in the proceedings would bring the administration of justice into disrepute.

General

25. The guarantee in this Charter of certain rights and freedoms shall not be construed so as to abrogate or derogate from any aboriginal, treaty or other rights or freedoms that pertain to the aboriginal peoples of Canada including

(a) any rights or freedoms that have been recognized by the Royal Proclamation of October 7, 1763; and

(b) any rights or freedoms that may be acquired by the aboriginal peoples of Canada by way of land claims settlement.

(b) any rights or freedoms that now exist by way of land claims agreements or may be so acquired.

[Note: Paragraph 25*(b)* (in italics) was repealed and the new paragraph substituted by the *Constitution Amendment Proclamation, 1983* (No. 46 *infra*).]

26. The guarantee in this Charter of certain rights and freedoms shall not be construed as denying the existence of any other rights or freedoms that exist in Canada.

27. This Charter shall be interpreted in a manner consistent with the preservation and enhancement of the multicultural heritage of Canadians.

28. Notwithstanding anything in this Charter, the rights and freedoms referred to in it are guaranteed equally to male and female persons.

29. Nothing in this Charter abrogates or derogates from any rights or privileges guaranteed by or under the Constitution of Canada in respect of denominational, separate or dissentient schools.

30. A reference in this Charter to a province or to the legislative assembly or legislature of a province shall be deemed to include a reference to the Yukon Territory and the Northwest Territories, or to the appropriate legislative authority thereof, as the case may be.

31. Nothing in this Charter extends the legislative powers of any body or authority.

Application of Charter

32. (1) This Charter applies

(a) to the Parliament and government of Canada in respect of all matters within the authority of Parliament including all matters relating to the Yukon Territory and Northwest Territories; and

(b) to the legislature and government of each province in respect of all matters within the authority of the legislature of each province.

Exception

(2) Notwithstanding subsection (1), section 15 shall not have effect until three years after this section comes into force.

[Note: This section came into force on April 17, 1982. See the proclamation of that date (No. 45 *infra*).]

Exception where express declaration

33. (1) Parliament or the legislature of a province may expressly declare in an Act of Parliament or of the legislature, as the case may be, that the Act or a provision thereof shall operate notwithstanding a provision included in section 2 or sections 7 to 15 of this Charter.

Operation of exception

(2) An Act or a provision of an Act in respect of which a declaration made under this section is in effect shall have such operation as it would have but for the provision of this Charter referred to in the declaration.

Five year limitation

(3) A declaration made under subsection (1) shall cease to have effect five years after it comes into force or on such earlier date as may be specified in the declaration.

Re-enactment

(4) Parliament or the legislature of a province may re-enact a declaration made under subsection (1).

Five year limitation

(5) Subsection (3) applies in respect of a re-enactment made under subsection (4).

Citation

Citation

34. This Part may be cited as the *Canadian Charter of Rights and Freedoms*.

PART II

RIGHTS OF THE ABORIGINAL PEOPLES OF CANADA

Recognition of existing aboriginal and treaty rights

35. (1) The existing aboriginal and treaty rights of the aboriginal peoples of Canada are hereby recognized and affirmed.

Definition of "aboriginal peoples of Canada"

(2) In this Act, "aboriginal peoples of Canada" includes the Indian, Inuit and Métis peoples of Canada.

Land claims agreements

(3) For greater certainty, in subsection (1) "treaty rights" includes rights that now exist by way of land claims agreement or may be so acquired.

Aboriginal and treaty rights are guaranteed equally to both sexes

(4) Notwithstanding any other provision of this Act, the aboriginal and treaty rights referred to in subsection (1) are guaranteed equally to male and female persons.

[Note: Subsections 35(3) and (4) were added by the *Constitution Amendment Proclamation, 1983* (No. 46 *infra*).]

Commitment to participation in constitutional conference

35.1 The government of Canada and the provincial governments are committed to the principle that, before any amendment is made to Class 24 of section 91 of the "*Constitution Act, 1867*", to section 25 of this Act or to this Part, *(a)* a constitutional conference that includes in its agenda an item relating to the proposed amendment, composed of the Prime Minister of Canada and the first ministers of the provinces, will be convened by the Prime Minister of Canada; and

(b) the Prime Minister of Canada will invite representative of the aboriginal peoples of Canada to participate in the discussions on that item.

[Note: Added by the *Constitution Amendment Proclamation, 1983* (No. 46 *infra*).]

PART III

EQUALIZATION AND REGIONAL DISPARITIES

36. (1) Without altering the legislative authority of Parliament or of the provincial legislatures, or the rights of any of them with respect to the exercise of their legislative authority, Parliament and the legislatures, together with the government of Canada and the provincial governments, are committed to

Commitment to promote equal opportunities

(a) promoting equal opportunities for the well-being of Canadians;

(b) furthering economic development to reduce disparity in opportunities; and

(c) providing essential public services of reasonable quality to all Canadians.

(2) Parliament and the government of Canada are committed to the principle of making equalization payments to ensure that provincial governments have sufficient revenues to provide reasonably comparable levels of public services at reasonably comparable levels of taxation.

Commitment respecting public services

PART IV

CONSTITUTIONAL CONFERENCE

37. (*1*) *A constitutional conference composed of the Prime Minister of Canada and the first ministers of the provinces shall be convened by the Prime Minister of Canada within one year after this Part comes into force.*

Constitutional conference

(*2*) *The conference convened under subsection (1) shall have included in its agenda an item respecting constitutional matters that directly affect the aboriginal peoples of Canada, including the identification and definition of the rights of those peoples to be included in the Constitution of Canada, and the Prime Minister of Canada shall invite representatives of those peoples to participate in the discussions on that item.*

Participation of aboriginal peoples

(*3*) *The Prime Minister of Canada shall invite elected representatives of the governments of the Yukon Territory and the Northwest*

Participation of territories

Territories to participate in the discussions on any item on the agenda of the conference convened under subsection (1) that, in the opinion of the Prime Minister, directly affects the Yukon Territory and the Northwest Territories.

[Note: Part IV was repealed effective April 17, 1983 by section 54 of this Act.]

PART IV.1

CONSTITUTIONAL CONFERENCES

37.1 *(1) In addition to the conference convened in March 1983, at least two constitutional conferences composed of the Prime Minister of Canada and the first ministers of the provinces shall be convened by the Prime Minister of Canada, the first within three years after April 17, 1982 and the second within five years after that date.*

Constitutional conferences

(2) Each conference convened under subsection (1) shall have included in its agenda constitutional matters that directly affect the aboriginal peoples of Canada, and the Prime Minister of Canada shall invite representatives of those peoples to participate in the discussion on those matters.

Participation of aboriginal peoples

(3) The Prime Minister of Canada shall invite elected representatives of the governments of the Yukon Territory and the Northwest Territories to participate in the discussions on any item on the agenda of a conference convened under subsection (1) that, in the opinion of the Prime Minister, directly affects the Yukon Territory and the Northwest Territories.

Participation of territories

(4) Nothing in this section shall be construed so as to derogate from subsection 35(1).

[Note: Part IV.1 was added by the *Constitution Amendment Proclamation, 1983* (No. 46 *infra*). By the same proclamation, it was repealed effective April 18, 1987. See section 54.1 of this Act.]

Subsection 35(1) not affected

PART V

PROCEDURE FOR AMENDING CONSTITUTION OF CANADA

38. (1) An amendment to the Constitution of Canada may be made by proclamation issued by the Governor General under the Great Seal of Canada where so authorized by

(a) resolutions of the Senate and House of Commons; and

General procedure for amending Constitution of Canada

(b) resolutions of the legislative assemblies of at least two-thirds of the provinces that have, in the aggregate, according to the then latest general census, at least fifty per cent of the population of all the provinces.

(2) An amendment made under subsection (1) that derogates from the legislative power, the proprietary rights or any other rights or privileges of the legislature or government of a province shall require

a resolution supported by a majority of the members of each of the Senate, the House of Commons and the legislative assemblies required under subsection (1).

(3) An amendment referred to in subsection (2) shall not have effect in a province the legislative assembly of which has expressed its dissent thereto by resolution supported by a majority of its members prior to the issue of the proclamation to which the amendment relates unless that legislative assembly, subsequently, by resolution supported by a majority of its members, revokes its dissent and authorizes the amendment.

(4) A resolution of dissent made for the purposes of subsection (3) may be revoked at any time before or after the issue of the proclamation to which it relates.

39. (1) A proclamation shall not be issued under subsection 38(1) before the expiration of one year from the adoption of the resolution initiating the amendment procedure thereunder, unless the legislative assembly of each province has previously adopted a resolution of assent or dissent.

(2) A proclamation shall not be issued under subsection 38(1) after the expiration of three years from the adoption of the resolution initiating the amendment procedure thereunder.

40. Where an amendment is made under subsection 38(1) that transfers provincial legislative powers relating to education or other cultural matters from provincial legislatures to Parliament, Canada shall provide reasonable compensation to any province to which the amendment does not apply.

41. An amendment to the Constitution of Canada in relation to the following matters may be made by proclamation issued by the Governor General under the Great Seal of Canada only where authorized by resolutions of the Senate and House of Commons and of the legislative assembly of each province:

(a) the office of the Queen, the Governor General and the Lieutenant Governor of a province;

(b) the right of a province to a number of members in the House of Commons not less than the number of Senators by which the province is entitled to be represented at the time this Part comes into force;

(c) subject to section 43, the use of the English or the French language;

(d) the composition of the Supreme Court of Canada; and

(e) an amendment to this Part.

42. (1) An amendment to the Constitution of Canada in relation to the following matters may be made only in accordance with subsection 38(1):

(a) the principle of proportionate representation of the provinces in the House of Commons prescribed by the Constitution of Canada;

(b) the powers of the Senate and the method of selecting Senators;

(c) the number of members by which a province is entitled to be represented in the Senate and the residence qualifications of Senators;

(d) subject to paragraph 41(*d*), the Supreme Court of Canada;

(e) the extension of existing provinces into the territories; and

(f) notwithstanding any other law or practice, the establishment of new provinces.

(2) Subsections 38(2) to (4) do not apply in respect of amendments in relation to matters referred to in subsection (1).

43. An amendment to the Constitution of Canada in relation to any provision that applies to one or more, but not all, provinces, including

(a) any alteration to boundaries between provinces, and

(b) any amendment to any provision that relates to the use of the English or the French language within a province,

may be made by proclamation issued by the Governor General under the Great Seal of Canada only where so authorized by resolutions of the Senate and House of Commons and of the legislative assembly of each province to which the amendment applies.

44. Subject to sections 41 and 42, Parliament may exclusively make laws amending the Constitution of Canada in relation to the executive government of Canada or the Senate and House of Commons.

45. Subject to section 41, the legislature of each province may exclusively make laws amending the constitution of the province.

46. (1) The procedures for amendment under sections 38, 41, 42 and 43 may be initiated either by the Senate or the House of Commons or by the legislative assembly of a province.

(2) A resolution of assent made for the purposes of this Part may be revoked at any time before the issue of a proclamation authorized by it.

47. (1) An amendment to the Constitution of Canada made by proclamation under section 38, 41, 42 or 43 may be made without a resolution of the Senate authorizing the issue of the proclamation if, within one hundred and eighty days after the adoption by the House of Commons of a resolution authorizing its issue, the Senate has not adopted such a resolution and if, at any time after the expiration of that period, the House of Commons again adopts the resolution.

Margin notes:

Amendment by general procedure

Exception

Amendment of provisions relating to some but not all provinces

Amendments by Parliament

Amendments by provincial legislatures

Initiation of amendment procedures

Revocation of authorization

(2) Any period when Parliament is prorogued or dissolved shall not be counted in computing the one hundred and eighty day period referred to in subsection (1).

48. The Queen's Privy Council for Canada shall advise the Governor General to issue a proclamation under this Part forthwith on the adoption of the resolutions required for an amendment made by proclamation under this Part.

49. A constitutional conference composed of the Prime Minister of Canada and the first ministers of the provinces shall be convened by the Prime Minister of Canada within fifteen years after this Part comes into force to review the provisions of this Part.

PART VI

AMENDMENT TO THE CONSTITUTION ACT, 1867

50. The *Constitution Act, 1867* (formerly named the *British North America Act, 1867*) is amended by adding thereto, immediately after section 92 thereof, the following heading and section:

"Non-Renewable Natural Resources, Forestry Resources and Electrical Energy

92A. (1) In each province, the legislature may exclusively make laws in relation to

(a) exploration for non-renewable natural resources in the province;

(b) development, conservation and management of non-renewable natural resources and forestry resources in the province, including laws in relation to the rate of primary production therefrom; and

(c) development, conservation and management of sites and facilities in the province for the generation and production of electrical energy.

(2) In each province, the legislature may make laws in relation to the export from the province to another part of Canada of the primary production from non-renewable natural resources and forestry resources in the province and the production from facilities in the province for the generation of electrical energy, but such laws may not authorize or provide for discrimination in prices or in supplies exported to another part of Canada.

(3) Nothing in subsection (2) derogates from the authority of Parliament to enact laws in relation to the matters referred to in that subsection and, where such a law of Parliament and a law of a province conflict, the law of Parliament prevails to the extent of the conflict.

Marginalia: Amendments without Senate resolution; Computation of period; Advice to issue proclamation; Constitutional conference; Amendment to Constitution Act, 1867; Laws respecting non-renewable natural resources, forestry resources and electrical energy; Export from provinces of resources

(4) In each province, the legislature may make laws in relation to the raising of money by any mode or system of taxation in respect of

(a) non-renewable natural resources and forestry resources in the province and the primary production therefrom, and

(b) sites and facilities in the province for the generation of electrical energy and the production therefrom,

whether or not such production is exported in whole or in part from

the province, but such laws may not authorize or provide for taxation that differentiates between production exported to another part of Canada and production not exported from the province.

(5) The expression "primary production" has the meaning assigned by the Sixth Schedule.

(6) Nothing in subsections (1) to (5) derogates from any powers or rights that a legislature or government of a province had immediately before the coming into force of this section."

51. The said Act is further amended by adding thereto the following Schedule:

"THE SIXTH SCHEDULE

Primary Production from Non-Renewable Natural Resources and Forestry Resources

1. For the purposes of Section 92A of this Act,

(a) production from a non-renewable natural resource is primary production therefrom if

(i) it is in the form in which it exists upon its recovery or severance from its natural state, or

(ii) it is a product resulting from processing or refining the resource, and is not a manufactured product or a product resulting from refining crude oil, refining upgraded heavy crude oil, refining gases or liquids derived from coal or refining a synthetic equivalent of crude oil; and

(b) production from a forestry resource is primary production therefrom if it consists of sawlogs, poles, lumber, wood chips, sawdust or any other primary wood product, or wood pulp, and is not a product manufactured from wood."

PART VII

GENERAL

52. (1) The Constitution of Canada is the supreme law of Canada, and any law that is inconsistent with the provisions of the Constitution is, to the extent of the inconsistency, of no force or effect.

(2) The Constitution of Canada includes

(a) the *Canada Act 1982*, including this Act;

(b) the Acts and orders referred to in the schedule; and

(c) any amendment to any Act or order referred to in paragraph *(a)* or *(b)*.

(3) Amendments to the Constitution of Canada shall be made only in accordance with the authority contained in the Constitution of Canada.

53. (1) The enactments referred to in Column I of the schedule are hereby repealed or amended to the extent indicated in Column II thereof and, unless repealed, shall continue as law in Canada under the names set out in Column III thereof.

(2) Every enactment, except the *Canada Act 1982*, that refers to an enactment referred to in the schedule by the name in Column I thereof is hereby amended by substituting for that name the corresponding name in Column III thereof, and any British North America Act not referred to in the schedule may be cited as the *Constitution Act* followed by the year and number, if any, of its enactment.

54. Part IV is repealed on the day that is one year after this Part comes into force and this section may be repealed and this Act renumbered, consequentially upon the repeal of Part IV and this section, by proclamation issued by the Governor General under the Great Seal of Canada.

[Note: On October 31, 1987, no proclamation had been issued under this section.]

54.1 *Part iv.1 and this section are repealed on April 18, 1987.*

[Note: Added by the *Constitution Amendment Proclamation, 1983* (No. 46 *infra*).]

55. A French version of the portions of the Constitution of Canada referred to in the schedule shall be prepared by the Minister of Justice of Canada as expeditiously as possible and, when any portion thereof sufficient to warrant action being taken has been so prepared, it shall be put forward for enactment by proclamation issued by the Governor General under the Great Seal of Canada pursuant to the procedure then applicable to an amendment of the same provisions of the Constitution of Canada.

[Note: On October 31, 1987, no proclamation had been issued under this section.]

56. Where any portion of the Constitution of Canada has been or is enacted in English and French or where a French version of any portion of the Constitution is enacted pursuant to section 55, the English and French versions of that portion of the Constitution are equally authoritative.

Primacy of Constitution of Canada

Constitution of Canada

Amendments to Constitution of Canada

Repeals and new names

Consequential amendments

Repeal and consequential amendments

Repeal of Part iv.1 and this section

French version of Constitution of Canada

57. The English and French versions of this Act are equally authoritative.

58. Subject to section 59, this Act shall come into force on a day to be fixed by proclamation issued by the Queen or the Governor General under the Great Seal of Canada.

[Note: The *Constitution Act, 1982* was, subject to section 59 thereof, proclaimed in force on April 17, 1982 (No. 45 *infra*).]

59. (1) Paragraph 23(1) (a) shall come into force in respect of Quebec on a day to be fixed by proclamation issued by the Queen or the Governor General under the Great Seal of Canada.

(2) A proclamation under subsection (1) shall be issued only where authorized by the legislative assembly or government of Quebec.

(3) This section may be repealed on the day paragraph 23(1)(a) comes into force in respect of Quebec and this Act amended and renumbered, consequentially upon the repeal of this section, by proclamation issued by the Queen or the Governor General under the Great Seal of Canada.

[Note: On October 31, 1987, no proclamation had been issued under this section.]

60. This Act may be cited as the *Constitution Act, 1982*, and the Constitution Acts 1867 to 1975 (No. 2) and this Act may be cited together as the *Constitution Acts, 1867 to 1982*.

61. A reference to the "*Constitution Acts, 1867 to 1982*" shall be deemed to include a reference to the "*Constitution Amendment Proclamation, 1983.*"

[Note: Added by the *Constitution Amendment Proclamation, 1983* (No. 46 *infra*). See also section 3 of the *Constitution Act, 1985 (Representation)* (No. 47 *infra*).]

Glossary

Absolute liability—*see* **Liability**.

Acceleration clause—when a borrower is in default of payment, an acceleration clause makes the entire outstanding debt due and payable immediately; in contracts—the time allowed for payment of a debt is shortened because of the breach of a condition of the contract, such as failure to make payment on interest due, insolvency of the debtor, or failure to maintain insurance coverage on mortgaged premises.

Access—order of the court determining rights of parent to visit children in the custody of other parent.

Accident—a defence in a tort action that the incident causing an injury was unintentional and unavoidable.

Accounting of profits—an order requiring a person to reveal profits and pay them to plaintiff.

Accounts receivable—debt owed to a person.

Actus reus—(Lat.) a person can only be found guilty of a criminal act if the act complained of was committed.

Administrative tribunal—(as distinguished from a judicial court) part of the executive branch of government rather than the judicial branch; deals with disputes arising out of implementation of government policy, e.g., Workers' Compensation Board.

Admissible evidence—evidence that the court determines has been legally acquired.

Adverse possession—a method of acquiring title to property by having possession for a statutory period, where a person claims ownership of a piece of property which he has held possession of for many years, with full knowledge (and tolerance) of the actual owner, such that the owner loses the right to reclaim possession of the land.

Affirm—to ratify, confirm, reassert; in appellate courts—to affirm a judgment is to declare it is valid and must stand as rendered, and to concur in its correctness and confirm it; in contracts — to ratify and accept a voidable contract; in practice—to make affirmation is to make a solemn and formal declaration that an affidavit is true.

Agent/Agency—one who enters legal arrangements with third parties on behalf of a principal; an agent may be an employee or an independent contractor.

Alien—a foreigner; a person who owes allegiance to a foreign government.

Alternative dispute resolution (ADR)—a variety of mechanisms or strategies for resolving disputes outside the courts (*see also* **Arbitration**, **Mediation**).

Ambiguity—(ambiguities, ambiguous) to have more than one possible meaning; to be unclear, indistinct, or uncertain as to meaning because there is more than one possible interpretation of wording which is otherwise plain and intelligible.

Apportionment—spreading the loss/profit proportionately among the parties involved in the agreement.

Arbitration—the submission for determination of a disputed matter to persons selected in a manner provided by law or agreement.

Articles of association—used in provinces where a registration method of incorporation is used (e.g., BC). In this case the incorporating document (analogous to a constitution) is the memorandum of association and the operating rules are contained in the articles of incorporation. Both documents must be filed to incorporate a company.

Articles of incorporation—used federally and in several provinces (e.g., Ontario) where an articles of incorporation method of incorporating is in place (sometimes referred to as a certificate of incorporation). This is the incorporating document (analogous to a constitution) and corresponds to the memorandum of association in a jurisdiction which uses the registration method. Care must be taken not to confuse the articles of association used in the registration system with the articles of incorporation discussed here.

Assault—a threat of force directed toward a person such that there is fear of danger or injury.

Assessment—a court's determination of the fitness of a custodial parent.

Assignee—the person to whom the rights/benefits are assigned by the original contracting party (the assignor).

Assignor—the original contracting party who transfers his benefits under the contract to a third party.

Assignment—the transfer of one's rights, obligations or properties to another person; where a debtor voluntarily assigns property to a "trustee in bankruptcy" for distribution to creditors. **Statutory assignment**—under certain qualifications an assignee has the right to enforce a claim directly against a debtor and does not need to join the assignor in the action.

Attachment of a debt—*see* **Garnishment**.

Authority—jurisdiction, power, control. **Actual authority**—the real power granted to an agent either expressly or by implication. **Apparent authority**—where the principal knowingly or carelessly allows an agent to exercise powers or privileges which have not been actually granted. **Express authority**—powers granted explicitly, either in written or oral form. **Implied authority**—powers that the agent actually possesses as proven by the implications of the principal's conduct. **Of agent**—power given by a principal to an agent to act on the principal's behalf to create legal relations in accordance with specific instructions.

Automatism—involuntary behaviour that results in a criminal act.

Bailment—contract of bailment—goods are cared for by someone else; delivery of goods, upon contract that (after the purpose of delivery has been accomplished) the goods shall be returned to the possession of the bailor.

Balance of probabilities—test used in civil case; judgment made in favour of side which holds the more probable position.

Bankrupt/Bankruptcy—process by which a debtor voluntarily or involuntarily conveys assets to a trustee in bankruptcy or receiver for distribution to creditors; not the same as receivership (*see also* **Assignment, Insolvency, Receiving order**).

Bargaining agent—the person or persons designated to negotiate for the members of a certified trade union in a labour action.

Battery—a beating, wrongful physical violence, or constraint, inflicted upon another human being without his/her consent; to merely threaten a person with the use of force or bodily injury is **assault**, whereas the *use* of that force constitutes **battery**; the slightest touching is enough to qualify as battery, if done in anger or any other manner which would convey a threat of injury or uninvited interference.

Beneficiary—person designated to inherit property in an estate or a person for whom a trust is created.

Beneficial contract of service—an arrangement whereby an infant receives long-term benefits from a contract, e.g. education or training.

Beyond a reasonable doubt—test in criminal prosecutions—guilt of the accused must be more than just probable or likely; there must be no reasonable doubt.

Bill of exchange—the written instruction (order, note) from a drawer, directing a drawee to pay a specified amount to the third party named (may be to the bearer); must be unconditional, dated, signed by the drawer, e.g. drafts, cheques.

Bona fide—in good faith; honestly, without deceit or fraud; in trust and confidence.

Breach—(of contract) failure of one party to perform his/her contractual obligations. **Anticipatory breach**—when one party repudiates the contract before performance is due. **Fundamental breach**—failure to perform an aspect of the contract so basic to the nature of the agreement that any semblance of a contract is destroyed.

Canon law—church law; law used in ecclesiastical courts; decrees on the rights of ecclesiastical persons, and the manner of their election, ordination, etc. Historically, much broader; included areas where ecclesiastical courts had jurisdiction in temporal affairs such as wills and estates, and family law.

Capacity—ability; e.g., "capacity to sue"—the right to bring court action; capacity to contract.

Causation—the event or action that results in an injury or loss.

Caveat emptor—(Lat.) "let the buyer beware"; the seller is not required to disabuse the purchaser of any incorrect assumptions so long as the seller did not mislead the purchaser.

Certiorari—(Lat.) "to be informed of"; writ of review or inquiry applied to determine whether a tribunal or lower court acted within its jurisdiction, after a case has concluded (*see also* **Prerogative writ**).

Chancellor—chief judge in the court of chancery; a title used variously in different parts of the world and in different professions to refer to an officer given some special duties or responsibilities.

Charter—a document issued by a governing power, granting rights, liberties, or other powers appropriate to be held by the population it affects. **Charter of incorporation**—a certificate granted to create a corporation which outlines the structure and constitution of the corporation.

Chose—(Fr.) an item of personal property; a chattel personal. **Chose in action**—a right to a personal thing which the owner does not possess but has a "right of action," i.e., a right to bring suit at law for its possession (this includes all personal chattels which are not in the owner's possession); the right of the creditor of a dishonoured debt to initiate an action to recover the money; e.g., cheque, promissory note. **Chose in possession**—a personal belonging of which the owner has possession; e.g., taxes, if paid, are a chose in possession, but if unpaid are a chose in action.

Church law—*see* **Canon law**.

Civil law—a codified list of rules stating principles of law to be applied to any legal question (includes French civil law or Roman civil law). Civil law action also refers to matters of private action or suits between individuals as opposed to criminal actions involving government prosecution.

Codicil—an addition or change to a will.

Collective agreement—an agreement between an employer and a labour union which regulates terms and conditions of employment.

Collusion—an agreement between two or more people to defraud a person of his/her rights under the law.

Common law—that body of law which originated in England, distinguished from law created solely by acts or statutes of Parliament; a system where law is "discovered," rather than created, by judges interpreting and applying the accepted customs and standards of society and looking to concepts provided in such sources as civil law, canon law or the Law Merchant in determining "justice" in any particular case—subsequent to that, future judgments are required to follow that same application of the law in similar cases (*see also* **Precedent**, *Stare decisis*).

Compensation—payment of damages; making whole that which has been damaged, by giving an equivalent or substitute of equal value; recompense or reward for a loss or injury; as compared with consideration and damages—"consideration," amends for something given by consent or by the owner's choice, "damages," amends for a wrongdoing in an action for a tort, "compensation," amends for something which was taken without the owner's choice but without the commission of a tort.

Conciliation—a form of negotiation used in labour disputes.

Condition—term essential to the substance of a contract. **Condition precedent**—a requirement that must be satisfied before either party is obligated to perform their part of the agreement—also called a "subject to" clause. **Condition subsequent**—an event which prematurely ends the agreement.

Conditional privilege—*see* **Privilege**.

Consensus—unanimous agreement; a meeting of the minds; where all parties involved in an agreement share a common understanding and intentions on the subject-matter of the agreement.

Consent—a defence against an action in tort in which the tortfeasor claims the victim agreed to the battery

Consideration—inducement, cause, price or motive influencing a party to enter into a contract; something which is of value in the eyes of the law, which passes from one party to another, in exchange for the other party's promise or action; may be a right, interest, advantage or profit to the promisor, or a detriment, prejudice, disadvantage, service given or act of forbearance by the promisee.

Consignee—person named on a bill of lading as having the right to receive the goods at the point of destination.

Constitution—a written document setting out the laws which will govern a group of people, e.g., a nation, or a corporation; a constitution is issued by the members of that body, setting out the rules by which it will conduct itself.

Consumer bill—a bill of exchange or cheque given for the advancement of credit in a consumer transaction.

Consumer note—a promissory note signed by anyone purchasing goods or services for a non-commercial purpose (i.e., not for resale or use in any business).

Consumer transaction—where goods or services are acquired by the ultimate consumer, not for resale or other business activities.

Contract—a promissory agreement between two or more parties which creates a legal relationship, based upon an offer by one party and an acceptance of that offer by the other, establishing a consensus between the parties as to the terms of the agreement and involving the transfer of some consideration.

Contributory negligence—a claim that a victim of a tort was partially responsible for the injuries suffered.

Cooling-off period—a specified period of time given to the purchaser after signing a contract in a sales transaction, within which time she/he can rescind the contract.

Copyright—a right of literary property, granted to an author of literature or other artistic productions, where the author holds, for a limited period of time, the sole and exclusive right to publish and sell the materials created.

Corporation—a group of individuals united for a common purpose (to make money) acting collectively as an artificial person created by the law, as a personality separate and apart from the individuals which comprise it. **Broadly-held corporation**—a public corporation; also referred to as a "reporting" corporation in some provinces. **Closely-held corporation**—a private, rather than public, corporation; also referred to as a "non-reporting" corporation in some provinces.

Courts—a segment of the government, under the judicial branch, that applies the law to the causes of action brought before it and that is responsible for the public administration of justice; "court" and "judge" are often used synonymously; term may also be applied to various administrative tribunals which are not strictly judicial in nature. (The trial court is a court of first instance; the forum provided for the presentation of all evidence and witness testimony, concluding with the judge's decision on the matter, whereas an appeal court involves a panel of judges reviewing the evidence previously presented in the trial court and is limited to settling conflicts over questions of law rather than fact.)

Common law courts—the Court of Common Pleas, Court of King's Bench and Exchequer Court were originally referred to as the common law courts. **Court of Chancery**—*see* **Court of Equity**, below. **Court of Common Pleas**—also called the Common Bench; the common law court with jurisdiction of all real actions and common pleas, "common pleas" being causes of action between one subject and another rather than pleas by the Crown; in early times, unsatisfied disputes were appealed to the King's Bench, later to the Exchequer Chamber. **Court of Equity**—more properly called Court of Chancery, the chief judge being referred to as Chancellor; as distinct from a court applying the rules of the common law, under the jurisdiction of the king's Chancellor judges were free to administer justice in accordance with principles of equity, i.e., according to the merits of the individual case and in keeping with fairness and good conscience, rather than being restricted by the rules and precedents of the common law courts. Such restrictive practices were introduced in later years. **Court of King's Bench**—the supreme court of the common law courts in early English law, which heard cases appealed from the Court of Common Pleas; later called the High Court of Justice under the *Judicature Acts* of 1873-75; this court received its name because originally the king sat in it in person; during the reign of a queen it is called the Queen's Bench; during Cromwell's Protectorate it was called the Upper Bench. **Exchequer Chamber**—former English court of appeal, originally heard appeals from the superior courts of the common law, but was inferior

to the House of Lords; after the *Judicature Acts* (1873-75) was called the Court of Appeal. **Exchequer Court**—the common law court charged with keeping the king's accounts and collecting royal revenues; inferior to the Court of Common Pleas and the Court of King's Bench, it heard cases involving the non-payment of taxes.

Canadian Federal Courts—affect all Canadians; (a) the **Supreme Court of Canada**—appellate function, hearing cases both criminal and civil, as well as passing direct rulings on federal/provincial constitutional disputes, and (b) the **Federal Court of Canada**—comparable to Provincial Superior Court; contains both trial and appellate divisions—the trial division rules on cases involving matters which fall under federal jurisdiction (as determined by the constitutional division of powers), while the appellate division hears appeal cases from the trial division, and from cases which have been dealt with by federal administrative tribunals or regulatory bodies; appeals from the above matters are directed to the Supreme Court of Canada.

Provincial Courts of Canada—see chart p. 99. *Lowest level*: (a) **Criminal Division** (sometimes referred to as Magistrates' Court)—trial court for minor criminal charges, i.e., summary, and mixed offences (which are indictable but have an option open to the accused to be heard in Provincial Court); (b) **Small Claims Court**—deals with civil matters involving small sums of money (specific limit varies between provinces); (c) **Family Court**—enforcement of family relations matters, e.g., custody and maintenance, and often enforces the *Young Offenders Act* as a youth court. *Highest level*: (d) Provincial **Court of Appeal**—the highest court of the province; may be one division of the provincial Supreme Court or an entirely separate body; exercises only an appellate function, hearing cases from any court in the province and being a required preliminary before any case can go before the Supreme Court of Canada; (e) Provincial

Supreme Court—the superior court of the province, being the highest trial court at the provincial level; also referred to in some provinces as High Court or Court of Queen's Bench; holds jurisdiction over un-limited amount of money in civil matters.

Court orders—in family courts—custody of children can be granted to either parent or to both; **interim custody**—a temporary court order; **restraining order**—prohibits one of the parents from being in contact with the other or the children.

Damages—remedy of monetary compensation recovered in court by any person who has suffered loss, detriment or injury to his/her person, property or rights through the unlaw-ful act, omission or negligence of another. **Special damages**—awarded for specific cal-culable losses. **General damages**—awarded for pain and suffering. **Punitive damages**—also referred to as "exemplary" or "presump-tive" damages—awarded to a victim above and beyond what is required to reimburse for any losses, in order to serve as a punishment of the defendant (e.g., where the situation in-cluded evidence of violence).

Debenture—a document acknowledging a debt.

Declaratory judgment—the court declares the rights of the parties or expresses the opin-ion of the court on the question of law.

Defamation—the offence of injuring a per-son's character, fame or reputation by false statements; includes both libel and slander.

Defendant—the party summoned to court to answer to a complaint in most legal actions. The accused in a criminal action.

Deposit—(distinguished from **down-payment**) a prepayment made at the outset of an agreement (in order to secure some condition or goods of value) meant to be forfeited in the event of a breach of con-tract.

Detinue—(Fr.) a form of action which allows for the recovery of personal chattels from someone who has acquired possession of them lawfully but retains them without right.

Discharge—to release from the obligations of a contract. **Discharge by agreement**—an agreement to end or modify the previous contract. **Bilateral discharge**—where both parties are relieved of obligations under the contract by striking a new agreement to ei-ther discharge or modify the original con-tract. **Discharge by frustration**—a change in circumstances that makes it impossible to carry out the terms of the contract. **Discharge by performance**—the conclu-sion of a contract by the fulfillment or ac-complishment of the obligations promised in the terms of the agreement. **Unilateral discharge**—where only one of the contract-ing parties is relieved of the obligations re-quired by the original contract, when a new agreement is struck to either end or modify the previous contract; additional considera-tion is required in order for the discharge to be legally binding. In criminal law the court may grant an **absolute discharge**, which is an unconditional dismissal of a charge, or a **conditional discharge**, which requires the accused to perform some obligation set by the court.

Disclaimer—the repudiation of a claim which was previously alleged; denial of a right, in-terest or property imputed to a person.

Dissolution—termination; in contracts—the ending or cancellation of the agreement, restoring all parties to their original rights and position.

Dower—the right of a wife to claim one third of the estate of her husband if she becomes widowed.

Down-payment—(distinguished from **deposit**) a prepayment made as a first in-stallment to a series of payments, with no intention that the amount be forfeited in the event of a breach of contract.

Drawee—the party (or institution) being asked to pay the sum of money on a bill of ex-change, e.g. a bank.

Drawer—the maker of a bill of exchange, i.e., the party signing the bill of exchange to au-thorize payment of the monies.

Dry judgment—where a creditor has successfully sued against a defaulted debt but the debtor is unable to pay.

Due diligence—acting with the care, prudence and vigilance that would be expected of a careful person looking after his/her own important affairs.

Due process—requires an adjudicative body to adhere to the fundamental rules of justice, which include the right to notice, a fair hearing and an unbiased decision-maker making a decision based on the evidence presented.

Duress—force or threat brought to bear upon someone in order to induce him/her to enter a contract against their will (*see also* **Undue influence**).

Easement—accommodation; convenience; a privilege, without profit, that may exist by right of the owner of one piece of land to use some portion of the land adjacent to his own which is possessed by another, for some particular purpose, e.g., waterway, road access. **Easement by prescription**—a right-of-way over property, acquired by using the property over a period of time. **Public easement**—requirement of an owner to submit some portion of land for the use and benefit of the general public, e.g., for such purposes as the installation of power lines or sewers.

Employee—a person working for another who is told not only what to do but how to do it.

Encumber—to make something subject to a charge or liability, e.g., a mortgage. **Encumbrance**—a claim, lien, or charge attached to and binding real property.

Endorsement—a signature on the back of a document such as a cheque.

Equitable estoppel—*see* **Promissory estoppel**.

Equitable remedy—e.g., specific performance, remedies developed by the courts of chancery to deal with situations where damages would not be adequate compensation for the injuries suffered (*see* **Specific performance**, **Injunction**).

Equity—the body of law created by the Courts of Chancery; giving each man his due; principles of fairness and justice applied in legal disputes where there is no fair remedy in positive law (*see also* **Law of equity**, **Court of equity** [under **Common law courts**]).

Equity of redemption—the right of the mortgagor of an estate to redeem the property after default.

Escheat—in the absence of anyone with the right to inherit, the property reverts to the government.

Estate—an interest in lands, or any other kind of property, whether real or personal; in conveyances, "estate" is often used synonymously with "right," "title" and "interest." **Estate in fee simple**—owner holds complete title and control of the property, without any conditions limiting the power to use or dispose of the property, except for the requirements of local law. **Fee-tail estate**—where a condition has been imposed upon the property which requires that the estate pass to particular heirs upon death of the current owner. **Freehold estate**—an estate for life (non-specified duration of time) e.g., estate in fee simple, fee tails, life estates. **Joint estate**—an estate where there is more than one tenant; includes "tenancies in common" and "joint tenancies"; implies a unity of interest, title, time, and possession; joint tenants must have the same interest accruing under the same conveyance, commencing at the same time, held under the same undivided possession. **Leasehold estate**—an estate held under lease for a fixed duration of time. **Life estate**—an estate which is limited in duration to the life of the party owning it, or the life of another designated person, e.g., his/her children.

Estoppel—deals with a statement of fact or claim made by the principal in an agency relationship; law prevents anyone from holding/establishing an inconsistent legal position in order to take advantage of a situation, i.e., once facts have been established by a person's own evidence or statements, that person cannot later allege a contradictory set of facts in order to obtain some advantage or cause another person some harm or disadvantage (*see also* **Promissory estoppel**).

Ex parte—where a legal proceeding is conducted with only one party present.

Examination in aid of execution—a hearing held after a judgment has been rendered, to determine which of the debtor's assets are available to satisfy the debt.

Excessive force—when the physical force used is greater than is absolutely necessary or "called for" in the particular circumstances; undue force.

Exclusion clause—*see* **Exemption clause**.

Exculpatory clause—*see* **Exemption clause**.

Executor of an estate—person appointed to look after distribution of assets of deceased person.

Exemption clause—a contractual term significantly limiting the liability of the seller; also referred to as "exclusion clause" or "exculpatory clause."

Fair comment—a defence to defamation; statements must be based on facts truly stated, but must not contain inferences of corrupt or dishonourable motives, except those which are warranted by the facts and which are the actual beliefs of the author; statements made regarding acts performed by any public official, so long as the writer holds an honest belief that they are true.

False imprisonment—unlawful arrest; detention of a person either without warrant, by an illegal warrant or a warrant illegally executed; unlawful detention may be for any length of time, under any circumstances where a person is deprived of his/her personal liberty.

Fee simple—*see* **Estate**.

Fiduciary—a person holding the character of a trustee. **Fiduciary duty**—an obligation to act in a trustworthy and honest manner.

Fitness—the requirement that manufactured goods be fit for the use intended.

Force—a measure of the method or might used to repel an attack; **reasonable** or **excessive.**

Foreclosure—a process by which all further right of a mortgagor to redeem the estate is lost and the estate becomes the absolute property of the mortgagee; a method of enforcing payment of a debt secured by a mortgage, by taking and selling the mortgaged estate.

Fraud—an intentional misrepresentation of facts for the purpose of deceiving someone in order to cheat or take advantage of them. **Fraudulent preference**—where an insolvent debtor chooses to pay only specific creditors, leaving other creditors unpaid. **Fraudulent transfer**—where a person attempts to keep property out of the hands of creditors by transferring it to friends or relatives, as a gift or for a nominal amount.

Frustration—when an unforeseen event makes it impossible for a contract to be performed or causes performance to be something essentially different than what the parties anticipated when entering into the agreement. **Self-induced frustration**—frustration caused by one of the parties; it is treated as a breach rather than frustration.

Garnishment—where judgment against a debt is executed by seizure of a bank account, wages or other outstanding claim; also referred to as "attachment of a debt."

Goods—tangible items of personal property, e.g., watches, televisions; does not include real estate.

Government branches—(a) **executive**—the branch of the government that is responsible for the administration of the government, i.e., for seeing that the laws of the country are carried out; (b) **judicial**—the branch of the government that interprets and applies the law; offices which are responsible for the administration of justice; the body of judges that comprise the court system of a country; (c) **legislative**—the branch of government which has the responsibility of making the laws of a country.

Guarantee—method of securing repayment of debt where a third party assumes responsibility for ensuring that a debt will be repaid, such that if the borrower defaults on the debt the third party will be liable for the remainder of the contractual obligation (*see also* **Indemnity**).

Habeas corpus—(Lat.) "you have the body"; a prerogative writ used to settle whether a person is being detained in custody unlawfully, such that the court issues an order to the custodial institution to bring before the court a person who is being detained (*see also* **Prerogative writ**).

Holder—a person legally in possession of a cheque, promissory note or bill of exchange. **Holder in due course**—a party who, though not the original payee of an instrument, has subsequently come into possession of a bill of exchange through legal negotiation with a previous holder; to qualify as a holder in due course a party must meet the following conditions: (a) the party became the holder of the instrument before it was overdue, without notice of it being previously dishonoured, the instrument being complete and regular on its face, and (b) the bill was taken in good faith, for value, and there was no notice of a defect in title of the person who negotiated it. **Remote holder**—a party who subsequently holds a bill of exchange but has failed to qualify as a holder in due course.

Immunity—freedom or exemption from some obligation or duty, e.g., taxation.

Imprisonment—incarceration; to be confined; the restraint of personal liberty; may take place without actual physical restraint—verbal compulsion, or the display of the possibility of physical force, if they cause a submission of the person's will to that of the one who is attempting to confine, are sufficient to constitute imprisonment.

In camera—(Lat.) hearings which are closed to the public; "camera" refers to a chamber or room, such as a judge's chamber.

In loco parentis—(Lat.) in the place of a parent; instead of a parent; charged with a parent's rights, duties, and responsibilities, e.g., teachers.

In toto—(Lat.) totally, completely.

Inadvertent—(misleading statement) unintentional, heedless; careless; excusable neglect.

Indemnity—security against potential losses; a relationship in which a third party assumes a primary obligation for the repayment of the debt along with the debtor.

Independent contractor—a person who works for him/herself, rather than being employed by someone else, and who makes his own decisions and uses his own methods, rather than being instructed by the person with whom he/she contracts.

Inducement—motive; in contracts—the benefit or advantage to be received by the promisor from the contract is the inducement for entering into it.

Infant—anyone under the age of majority; age of majority varies among provinces—under common law it is 21 years of age.

Injunction—a remedy used to prevent some undesirable action; where the court orders a defaulting party to stop an offending action. **Interlocutory injunction**—court order issued before the final determination of a case which stands in effect until the closing of the case, or until another order is issued. **Mandatory injunction**—issued by the court where a person violating a contractual term has thereby created an ongoing problem and he/she is ordered to correct the problem. **Permanent injunction**—once ordered by the court, this injunction remains in effect until all legal actions are concluded for that case.

Injurious reliance—*see* **Promissory estoppel**.

Innuendo—("meaning"); an oblique hint; remote intimation; insinuation; a construction of meaning placed upon words that is not the usual meaning of the words but is inferred from the special way they are communicated in the particular circumstances.

Insanity—the state of being incapable of understanding the nature of what you are doing.

Insolvency—the state of being unable to pay debts (not the same as bankruptcy).

Insurable interest—a real and substantial interest in specific property.

Intangible property—*see* **Property**.

Intention—will; purpose; design; meaning; decision to act in a certain way; the sense and meaning of a document, as logically follows from the words used.

Intra vires—(Lat.) opposite of *ultra vires*; within the power (authority) of the body that passes it.

Intrinsic—inherent; nature; the very essence of the thing itself.

Invitation to treat—to "invite" the public to enter into a business transaction.

Invitee—an individual who has business on the property of the owner or occupier.

Ipso facto—(Lat.) by the fact itself; by the mere effect of a fact or an act.

Job action—union or employees reduce service to an employer through strikes, pickets or work-to-rule.

Joint and several—a legal position of standing both alone in an obligation and being bound to others in the consequences resulting from the obligation; i.e., liability is joint and several when the creditor may sue one or more of the parties separately, or all of them together, at the option of the person suing.

Judicial review—an action taken under the supervisory capacity of a superior court over the judicial system, as distinct from judicial appeal, which is the legal process whereby the decisions of a lower court/tribunal are reviewed at a higher court level.

Jurisdiction—the authority, power or right to act.

Jurisprudence—the philosophy of law; the science which deals with the principles of positive law and legal relations.

Just cause—an employer acting on a legal right to fire or dismiss an employee.

Last clear chance doctrine—the party who has the last clear chance to avoid damage or injury to another is liable.

Law of equity—developed as individuals sought redress from the king when they felt they were not justly dealt with in the common law courts. Courts of chancery were established to deal with these cases and more flexible remedies were allowed in order to find a fair solution to each case.

Law Merchant—originally developed by merchant guilds in order to deal with disputes between their members as they conducted trading business; adopted into common law system to provide law relating to negotiable instruments.

Legal positivism—a philosophy which holds that rules qualify as law only if the person/body enacting it had the proper authority to do so.

Liability—responsibility which exists presently or has some likelihood of becoming a duty in the future; an obligation, actual or potential—particularly a financial debt. **Absolute liability**—complete responsibility for loss even when there has been no fault or negligence. **Limited liability**—a person can only lose what he/she has invested in a company. **Strict liability**—liability that cannot be excused or modified by extraneous factors, such as ignorance of the law, good/bad faith. **Unlimited liability**—the owner or partner of a business has responsibility for all losses.

Libel—written defamation; defamatory, slanderous statement put in writing; publication of false statements which damage someone's reputation.

Lien—a charge or encumbrance against goods used as security for a loan, which gives a creditor the right to seize and sell the goods if the debt is not honoured.

Life estate—*see* **Estate**.

Lockout—a type of job action in which the

employer prevents employees from doing their jobs.

Malfeasance—to commit an act which should not be done at all (neither lawfully nor unlawfully). *See also* **Misfeasance, Nonfeasance**.

Malice—to commit a wrongful act in such circumstances which imply an evil intent toward another; includes hatred, anger and revenge, with a disregard of the law and the rights of other persons; to injure others intentionally, without just cause and for personal gratification.

Mandamus—(Lat.) "we command"; a writ issued by the court directing an officer of a corporate, administrative, or judicial body to perform a specific act which he/she is under a duty to perform—thus relieving an undue delay in the delivery of justice (see also **Prerogative writ**).

Marriage—a civil status condition, or relation of one man and one woman united in law for life, or the ceremony which creates the relationship.

Mediation—a form of alternative dispute resolution in which the parties agree on a neutral third party to assist them in resolving their dispute. The mediator does not impose an decision but rather helps the disputants to come to an agreement.

Mini-trial—a form of resolving disputes within an organization that simulates what would happen in the courts if the parties were to proceed with legal action.

Misfeasance—a trespass or wrongdoing; to commit unlawfully an action which a person can do lawfully—in contrast with **Nonfeasance**, which is omitting/failing to do an act which a person should have done, or **Malfeasance**, which is to commit an act which should not be done at all.

Misrepresentation—false statement of fact that persuades someone to enter into a contract; distinguished from **Mistake**—in misrepresentation the mistake was a direct result of being misled by the other party. **Fraudulent**

misrepresentation—an intentional misrepresentation of fact meant to induce someone to enter into a contract. **Innocent misrepresentation**—a false statement that the speaking person believes to be true.

Mistake—must change the very basis of the agreement such that the element of consensus never truly existed; must be factual, as to identity of parties or as to subject matter of the contract; must pertain to the nature of the agreement rather than the effect or consequences of the agreement. **Common mistake**—the two parties are in complete agreement but they have both made the same mistake regarding a fundamental aspect of the subject matter of the contract. **Mutual mistake**—a misunderstanding; when there is a misunderstanding between the two parties as to the nature of the agreement itself; both parties make a mistake but neither is aware of the other's error; consensus is questionable. **Shared mistake**—same as **Common mistake**. **Unilateral mistake**—a one-sided mistake; one of the parties makes a mistake in relation to the contract and the other party is aware that this mistake is being made.

Mitigate—to lessen, moderate or alleviate the severity of a penalty or punishment; "to mitigate the losses" is the obligation of a victim to keep the losses (from a breach of contract) as low as possible.

Mortgage—security against property where title to the land transfers temporarily to the lender but the borrower retains possession of the property. **Chattel mortgage**—a mortgage against personal property other than land.

Motive—cause or reason that moves the will and induces action. An inducement, or that which lead or tempts the mind to indulge in a criminal act.

Natural justice—a requirement of a minimal standard of conduct which must be adhered to by public servants when they act in a judicial capacity, involving such principles as: fair hearing, decisions made impartially and in good faith, and that evidence be heard by a decision-maker.

Natural law—a concept of law that holds that law flows naturally from a basic moral code that can be found in the natural qualities of all humankind, and that these morals should be accepted as law, and in fact override any orders established by rulers which conflict with humans' "natural" morals, regardless of whether or not they are codified in written law.

Necessaries—essential goods required for an individual to function in society, e.g., food, clothing (or "necessities of life").

Negligence—lack of care in the quality of actions, the standard for which is "reasonable conduct/care"; the omission to do something which a person has a duty to do; inadvertence, thoughtlessness or inattention to the quality of action; a failure to use ordinary, prudent care, which can be reasonably expected of every person in similar circumstances. **Contributory negligence**—when someone's carelessness is a factor in his/her own injury, that person must bear a portion of the loss.

Negligent misstatement—an incorrect statement made carelessly that induces another to enter into a contract or make a decision to act that causes loss.

Negotiable instrument—written commitment to pay a specific amount which may be transferred from one person to another, by endorsement or delivery, e.g., bill, cheque, promissory note; must be in writing, signed, contain unconditional promise to pay a specific sum of money on demand (or at a specified time), be made payable to order of specified party or to bearer, drawee must be named if the instrument is addressed.

Non est factum—(Lat.) "it is not my act"; where one of the parties was not aware of the nature of the contract, "non est factum" may be claimed as a defence and the courts may declare the contract void; a form of unilateral mistake.

Non-disclosure—failure to disclose pertinent facts when there is a special duty to provide the information requested.

Nonfeasance—omitting/failing to do an act that a person has a duty to perform—in contrast to **Malfeasance**, which is to commit an act which should not be done at all (neither lawfully nor unlawfully), or **Misfeasance**, which is to commit unlawfully an action which a person can do lawfully.

Notice—the amount of time set out in legislation that is required when an employee is fired from or is leaving his/her position. **Reasonable notice** is determined by the standards set in tort law.

Nuisance—something which interferes with a person in the possession or ordinary use of his/her property; annoyance; any act or condition which interferes with another person's enjoyment of life or property. **Common nuisance**—*see* **Public nuisance**, below. **Private nuisance**—any annoyance or injury being suffered by an individual, whether involving condition of life or property. **Public nuisance**—a nuisance which affects an indefinite number of people in a community, thereby involving the public in general rather than merely a few particular individuals; also called a **Common nuisance**.

Obiter dicta/Obiter dictum—(Lat.) opinions expressed or referenced used in setting out the reasons for the judgment of a court case which have no direct bearing on the case now being decided; comments or "asides" which are "incidental" to the legal issues at stake in the case at bar, which are simply expressed for the purpose of discussion or to illustrate an example or parallel point of view.

Offence—an act set out in the *Criminal Code* for which the state can extract a penalty. **Summary offence**—a minor or lesser offence to which the accused admits and is summarily convicted and sentenced. **Indictable offence**—a more serious charge involving more complex hearing and trial procedures. **Hybrid or dual procedure offence**—one in which the Crown can choose to process as either a summary or indictable offence.

Offer—a tentative promise by one party to do something if the other person is willing to meet an expressed request; contains all terms of the contract.

Offeree—the party to whom an offer is made.

Offeror—a party who makes an offer to another.

Ombudsperson—an agent of the government appointed to mediate disputes and hear complaints.

Omission—the failure to do what the law requires.

Onus—weight of responsibility; burden of proof; the party that holds the responsibility to provide proof/evidence to substantiate their claims at law. **Reverse onus**—when the court requires the accused to prove that he/she did not commit the offence he/she has been charged with.

Paramountcy—the doctrine settling any conflict where valid legislation has been passed by both federal and provincial governments on identical subject matter; federal legislation will take precedence, the provincial legislation will go into abeyance.

Parol—(Fr.) (parol evidence rule) where a written term of a contact is clear and unambiguous, the parties will not be permitted to introduce evidence outside of the contract to contradict that meaning.

Partnership—two or more people working together to make a profit.

Passing-off action—the means of redress when someone tries to mislead others into thinking that they are dealing with one business when in fact they are dealing with another.

Patent—the granting of a privilege, property or authority by the government to one or more individuals. **Letters patent**—documentation issued by the government conveying a right or authority; used in some provinces to incorporate companies.

Pawn—also called pledge; where personal property is used as security for a debt; pawnbroker has possession of the goods to hold until repayment but the debtor retains title and ownership of the goods.

Payee—the person to whom a negotiable instrument is made payable.

Performance—to perform obligations agreed to in a contract; one way to discharge a contract. **Part performance**—some portion of the contract has been performed, but not sufficient to fulfill the purpose and substance of the agreement. **Specific performance**—where the awarding of damages would be inadequate compensation for the breach of a contract, the breaching party is ordered to fulfill the obligations specifically as set out in the terms of the agreement. **Substantial performance**—a party has performed most of the obligations under the agreement, but has left out some element which is of only trivial consequence to the contract. **Tender of performance**—a person is ready, willing and able to perform a contractual obligation and attempts to do so, but is refused.

Picketing—a form of job action in which striking employees walk in front of the employer's place of business and hand out information to passersby relative to the strike and discourage customers from doing business with the employer.

Plaintiff—the person who brings a legal action.

Pledge—*see* **Pawn**.

Precedent—a decision of a judge which is binding on other judges, i.e., where a judge has interpreted and applied a statute, thereby establishing how a law will be applied from that time on, in that specific set of circumstances (also called *Stare decisis*).

Prerogative writ—where there is evidence presented that a citizen may have been denied his/her rights at the hands of some administrative tribunal, a prerogative writ provides a remedy used by the courts to exercise their supervisory capacity, ensuring the legal rights of citizens who are under the care and control of administrative bodies (*see also* *Certiorari*, *Habeas corpus*, *Mandamus*, **Prohibition**).

Prima facie—(Lat.) "at first sight"; on the face of it; a fact accepted as true until disproved by evidence to the contrary.

Principal—the source of authority or right, i.e., the employer of an agent or lawyer; the primary sum of money in a debt—as distinguished from the interest or other charges.

Privative clause—a provision of many statutes designed to remind the courts that they are not to interfere with the decisions of tribunals, and thus supporting the power of tribunals over areas of their own jurisdiction.

Privilege—(in law of libel and slander)—an exemption from liability for the speaking or publishing of defamatory words based on the fact that the statement was made in the performance of a duty that is political, judicial, social or personal. **Qualified privilege**—the speaker or publisher may be protected from liability where the substance of the statement related to a matter of public interest, where it was necessary to protect the speaker's private interests and was made to a person also having an interest in that matter, or where the person had a duty to make the statement; also referred to as "conditional privilege."

Privity—(of contract) parties to a contract create a private agreement (a world of law unto themselves), and outsiders cannot enforce, be affected by or be bound to perform its terms.

Probate—a judicial act or determination of a court having competent jurisdiction establishing the validity of a will. **Probate fees**—an assessment by the court when filing probate documents.

Probation—a requirement that may be imposed by the court in lieu of imprisonment after conviction of a criminal offence or sentence has been partially completed.

Profit à prendre—(Fr.) an interest in property acquired by grant or prescription, in order that some aspect of the estate may be accessed for personal profit, such as the taking of mineral or other resources from the land itself.

Prohibited—prevented or forbidden under the law.

Prohibition—a prerogative writ issued by a superior court ordering an inferior court or tribunal to cease its prosecution of a case due to a lack of proper jurisdiction (see also **Prerogative writ**).

Promissory estoppel—also referred to as equitable estoppel or, in the United States, injurious reliance; deals with a gratuitous promise to do something in the future; if a promise has been made and the promisee incurs debts or other liabilities because of relying upon that promise, the promisor may be held liable for compensation of the losses incurred; the principle applies despite the lack of consideration required to establish the promise as a contractual relationship; in Canada this principle can only be used as a defence, not as a cause of action—hence the phrase "as a shield, not as a sword."

Property—a relationship of ownership which establishes a right or interest between some person and some item of value. **Intangible property**—a right or interest in relation to another person, e.g., a **Chose in action**. **Intellectual property**—rights over materials produced by one's talent and/or intellect; a chose in action; includes copyright, patents, trademarks and trade secrets. **Tangible property**—proprietory owner relationship involving physical items, e.g., chattels.

Qualified privilege—*see* **Privilege**.

Quid pro quo—(Lat.) the consideration necessary between parties in order to make a contract valid.

Ratification—when an agent has acted beyond his/her authority, principal may "ratify" the contract entered into by the agent by confirming his commitment to the agreement either in writing, by spoken word or by action; to give approval of, or confirm, an agreement made by an agent which was outside the agent's authority, thereby creating a valid contract from one which would otherwise not have been binding on the principal. **Inadvertent ratification**—ratification occurring due to a principal's unintentional action, from which can be inferred an intention to ratify an agreement; occurs when the principal accepts some benefit under the contract before attempting to avoid the contract.

Ratio decidendi—(Lat.) the point in a case which determines the judgment.

Reasonable—behaviour which is ordinarily to be expected of a reasonable person under the particular circumstances; not excessive. **Reasonable force**—such physical power as would be reasonably expected to be necessary to protect oneself in the given circumstances. **Reasonable time**—the length of time which may reasonably be required in face of the nature of the act or duty which is being done and under the prevailing circumstances.

Receivership—when an agreement provides for a creditor taking over the operation of the business when certain important terms of the agreement have not been met. The effect is similar to obtaining a receiving order in a bankruptcy but is based on the terms provided in the contract, thus avoiding the bankruptcy process.

Receiving order—may be granted when creditors petition the court to force a debtor into bankruptcy against his/her will.

Rectification—remedy for breach of contract through correction, by the courts, of a "shared" mistake on a written document.

Remoteness—refers to the fact that the breaching party is only responsible for the damages which would seem to be likely if the contract were breached (note similar principle in tort law).

Re-opener clause—a term in an agreement which provides for renegotiation when some material change has taken place in the circumstances of the parties.

Replevin—(Fr.) a personal action brought to recover possession of goods unlawfully in the possession of another.

Repudiation—when one party in a contract indicates an intention to abandon the contract, refusing to perform the obligations agreed to (*see also* **Anticipatory breach** [under **Breach**]).

Rescission—returns both parties to their original positions, i.e., subject matter of the contract returns to original owner and any monies paid are returned; one remedy for breach of contract or where the contract is void.

Res ipsa loquitor—(Lat.) the thing or action speaks for itself.

Res judicata— (Lat.) "a thing decided"; something judged legally, i.e., by a court of valid jurisdiction.

Restitution—an alternative means of punishing an offender by requiring that he/she compensate the victim for his/her injury.

Restrictive covenant—restrictions on the use of land, specified by the party who grants an estate in land, that are binding upon all subsequent holders of the property.

Reversionary interest—interest held in an estate that will revert to the original owner at some future time but is currently possessed by another, such as in the case of a life estate holding.

Revocation/Revoke—to annul, make void, rescind or cancel a previously granted authority or power, e.g., a power of attorney or an offer to enter into a contract.

Right of way—a right of passage through the property of another (*see also* **Easement**).

Risk—any potential loss due to destruction or damage of goods or property.

Royalties—payments made to the originator of a product for use or application of that product by a second party, e.g., book sales; the payments are made as a set proportion of the revenues garnered from use of the product.

Rule of law—the constitutional principle that,

although parliament is supreme in its powers, it cannot act in an arbitrary manner, but rather must conduct all of its actions within the bounds of the law.

Rules of evidence—rules governing the kinds of evidence that can be presented at trial and how that evidence can be obtained.

Sale—a transaction in which title and goods are transferred immediately — as distinct from an agreement to sell, where goods or title will be transferred at some future time. **Conditional sale**—the seller of the goods provides credit for the sale; purchaser obtains possession of the goods, title remains with the seller until final payment is made.

Self-defence—to protect oneself or one's property against potential injury by another; the right to use a reasonable degree of force against another person in order to preserve one's own life and safety.

Self-help—where a person avails him/herself of remedies available without recourse to court or any other institution, e.g., to seize goods (repossess).

Shareholder—member of a corporation holding some portion of the capital interests of the company.

Slander—spoken defamation; untrue statements, communicated orally to another person, which damage either the personal or business reputation of a third party (*see also* **Libel**).

Stare decisis—(Lat.) a process in which judges follow each others' decisions in interpreting and applying the law, so long as the facts are substantially the same in each case (also referred to as "following precedent").

Statute—law enacted by Parliament or provincial legislative assemblies (also called legislation, acts, bills).

Strict liability—*see* **Liability**.

Suing on the covenant—a mortgage contains (within the terms of the contract) a "covenant" or promise to repay the amount of the loan, so that in the event of default of payment the creditor may decline to seize the property (which is named as security) and instead sue the mortgagor directly on his/her promise to repay.

Support—amount ordered by the court that the non-custodial parent must pay to the spouse and children of the marriage.

Supremacy of parliament—superior authority over all other government bodies; power of federal Parliament to overrule any previously established law by enactment of parliamentary statute.

Tenancy at sufferance—a tenant, having been served proper notice of termination of tenancy, has no further right to remain in the premises, but continues simply to remain in possession of the property and refuses to vacate. **At will**—the landlord permits a purchaser to move into a property before the date specified for the exchange of title. **In common**—property owned and occupied by two or more persons, each owning a proportional interest such that one party's interest can be sold to a third party and when one of the tenants dies his/her interest falls to that party's heir(s). **Joint tenancy**—property owned and occupied by two or more parties, each owning the entire property outright, such that upon the death of one of the parties the interests in the property fall to the remaining parties. **Periodic tenancy**—a rental arrangement with no specific period for the lease agreement. **Term lease**—a rental agreement established for a specific, set duration of time.

Tenement—**Dominant tenement**—a property whose owner is deriving some benefit of easement from a neighbouring property. **Servient tenement**—a property upon which a right of easement has been imposed.

Testator—one who has made a will or one who dies leaving a will.

Torrens Title System—a system of land registry which creates a "certificate of title" (binding on all parties and guaranteed by the government as proof of title or owner-

Glossary   359

ship) once the property has been entered into the central registry.

Tort— (Lat.) "to twist"; any private or civil wrong causing injury to a person or property.

Tortfeasor—a person who commits a tort.

Trade fixtures—items installed in a rented building to facilitate business are the property of the business and can be removed by the owner.

Trademark—a mark or emblem that has been adopted by, and henceforth identified with, a specific manufacturer, and that has been attached to any goods or properties belonging to that manufacturer, in order to identify the origin/ownership of goods in the marketplace.

Trespass—to unlawfully enter land belonging to another; to intrude or encroach upon the property of another. **Continuing trespass**—to invade someone's property, or his/her right to enjoy the property, on an ongoing basis.

Trust—one party holds property for another. **Constructive trust**—creation of a trust can be implied from surrounding circumstances and conduct of the parties. **In bankruptcy**—

property of bankrupt conveyed to trustee to eventually be dispersed to the creditors.

Ultra vires—(Lat.) beyond, or in excess of, the power that passed it.

Unconscionable transactions—one of the parties to a contract has been taken advantage of because of factors such as intellectual impairment.

Undue influence—similar to duress, but more subtle; an unacceptable level of social pressure affecting the ability to bargain freely.

Vicarious—delegated to another; done by a deputy or substitute.

Voir dire—(Lat.) to speak the truth. Trial within a trial.

Volenti non fit injuria—(Lat.) "he who consents cannot receive an injury"; voluntarily assuming the risk, i.e., if a person voluntarily puts him/herself into a position where there is obvious risk of injury, he/she cannot later hold another person responsible for that injury suffered.

Warranties—terms insignificant or peripheral to the substance of a contract, as contrasted with "conditions" (which are the essential terms).

Index